THE WIZARD
OF MENLO PARK

THE WIZARD
OF
MENLO PARK

How Thomas Alva Edison
Invented the Modern World

RANDALL STROSS

CROWN PUBLISHERS / NEW YORK

ISBN 978-1-4000-4762-8

Printed in the United States of America

Design by Leonard W. Henderson

To Ellen

CONTENTS

INTRODUCTION

THOMAS ALVA EDISON is the patron saint of electric light, electric power, and music-on-demand, the grandfather of the Wired World, great-grandfather of iPod Nation. He was the person who flipped the switch. Before Edison, darkness. After Edison, media-saturated modernity.

Well, not exactly. The heroic biography we were fed as schoolchildren does have its limitations, beginning with the omission of other inventors who played critical roles—not just Edison's gifted assistants, but also his accomplished competitors. What's most interesting about the standard Edison biography that we grew up with is not that it is heroic but that it is outsized, a projected image quite distinct from the man who stood five foot nine. Once brought into being, Edison's image inhabited its own life and acted autonomously in ways that its namesake could not control. Edison is famously associated with the beginnings of movies, which is where the modern business of celebrity begins. But he deserves to be credited with another, no less important, discovery related to celebrity that he made early in his own public life, accidentally: the application of celebrity to business.

The celebrity is distinguished from the merely well known by the public's bottomless desire for closeness, for learning anything and everything about the person. The first celebrities in American history were political and military figures, the Founders and Lincoln. Treating them as objects of fascination, the public experienced a feeling of personal, and wholly spurious, closeness. In the 1870s, Edison joined the ranks of larger-than-life demigods, making way for the civilian celebrity. Other nineteenth-century figures, like Mark Twain and P. T. Barnum, also gained fame on a scale impossible to imagine in an earlier time for those who worked outside of politics, but Edison's celebrity exceeded everyone else's. He achieved it well before he and others had created the technology to mass produce visual intimacy on a larger-than-life scale. When Edison initially became famous, the public could see him only with images conjured by newspaper text, supplemented with the occasional line drawing. During his lifetime, however, the technology for depicting images advanced rapidly. His face became so well known that an envelope mailed on a lark from North Carolina with nothing but his picture on it to serve as both name and address arrived in his hands in New Jersey a few weeks later.

No one of the time would have predicted that it would be an inventor, of all occupations, who would become the cynosure of the age. In retrospect, fame may appear to be a justly earned reward for the inventor of practical electric light—yet Edison's fame came before light. It was conferred for an earlier invention: the phonograph. Who would have guessed that the announcement of the phonograph's invention would be sufficient to propel him in a matter of a few days from obscurity into the firmament above? Any one of dozens of technical breakthroughs that had come before had much greater impact on the U.S. economy. Their creators were more likely candidates for the top rank of fame. Eli Whitney's cotton gin, or his muskets made with interchangeable parts, Robert Fulton's steamboat, John Jethro Wood's iron-tipped plough, Cyrus McCormick's reaper, Charles Goodyear's rubber-manufacturing process, Samuel Morse's telegraph, Elisha Graves Otis's elevator, Lucien Smith's barbed wire, and Alexander Graham Bell's telephone, which appeared one year before the phonograph—these were prior inventions that fundamentally changed the U.S. economy. Why would the phonograph, of all things, have made its inventor famous beyond imagining? More mysterious is that it was not the phonograph itself—it would take two decades before the machine was ready to be actually commercialized on a mass scale—but the mere idea of the phonograph that instantly seized the imagination of everyone who heard of it, inspiring essayists to expect machines capable of thinking as well as speaking.

Edison's admirers endowed him with fantastical powers that would permit him to invent anything he wished (one humorist suggested that he invent "a pocketbook that will always contain a dollar or two"). Edison did not himself lack for self-confidence and held fast to the conviction that he could remove any technical obstacle that impeded his progress, no matter what field of invention he explored. This conviction would lead him into blind alleys, but it also led to astonishing successes, planned and unplanned. More than anything else, the utterly fearless range of his experimental activities draws our attention today.

Fearlessness was needed when he elected to become a full-time inventor at the tender age of twenty-two, a bold step for a young man without family money. Both of the two previous generations of Edisons had been politically active and cursed with unfortunate luck, having to move permanently and far away to avoid the consequences that followed from backing a losing cause. Edison's grandfather had been a Loyalist in New Jersey during the War for Independence and had moved the family to Canada at the end of the war. Two years before Edison was born, his Canadian father, Samuel, an innkeeper by trade and Thomas Paine–like firebrand by temperament, backed an insurrection against the Canadian provincial government. When the uprising failed, Samuel had to flee for his life without his wife and four children and headed south to the United States. He landed in a canal town, Milan, Ohio, eight miles south of Lake Erie, where his family rejoined him. He dabbled in shingle manufacturing, land speculation, and truck farming, prospering by small-town standards as regional trade grew, then losing his gains when railroads took canal traffic away.

Thomas Alva Edison—known as "Al" as a child—would be the last of the seven children born to his mother, Nancy. High infant and childhood mortality in the mid-nineteenth century is encapsulated in the family history: only three of his six siblings survived beyond the age of six. All three were in their teens when he arrived on 11 February 1847—his oldest sister was eighteen—so he was soon the only child left living at his parents' house. When he was seven, the family moved to Port Huron, Michigan, a frontier town offering opportunities in lumbering and real estate speculation. His mother, a former schoolteacher, provided the homeschooling that constituted the entirety of his education, other than two brief stints at local schools. These circumstances, along with his progressive loss of hearing, nurtured the autodidact in Edison's makeup.

His father introduced his son to the highly esteemed writings of Paine, but young Edison did not inherit his father's interest in politics. He did, however, show an entrepreneurial bent that resembled his father's. Before Edison, the inventor, made a precocious appearance, Edison, the boy tycoon, had emerged. The opportunities he discovered as a twelve-year-old wheeler-dealer were opened when he persuaded his mother to let his home studies end so that he could take a position as newsboy on a train that ran from Port Huron to Detroit. Once on board, he saw that he could buy goods cheaply in the big city and retail them in little Port Huron at a nice markup. He opened two stores—a newsstand and a fresh-produce stand—and hired two other boys to staff them and share in the profits. Loading a U.S. mail car with his baskets of vegetables, without charge, would likely have brought the disapproving attention of some authority figure on the railroad. But here, too, young Edison showed a gift for knowing how to enlist the cooperation of everyone: He offered to the wives of the engineers and trainmen the fresh blackberries, butter, and other delectables at the same low wholesale prices that he had paid.

At the age of fifteen, Edison expanded into newspaper publishing, using a galley-proof press and worn type he bought secondhand and set up in the baggage car of the train. When a British passenger happened to catch a glimpse of the adolescent publisher at work, he bought the entire run of Edison's *Weekly Herald* as souvenirs, and Edison later heard he planted mention in the London *Times* that it was the first newspaper in the world to be printed on a train in motion.

In his spare time, Edison spent time with a small chemistry laboratory that he set up in the baggage car. Flammable chemicals did not travel as well as the printing press. When a bottle of phosphorus fell and set the car on fire, the conductor ejected Edison, his chemical laboratory, and his printing press. The other diversion that occupied Edison every spare moment was telegraphy's Morse code, which he tried to absorb on his own by osmosis, sitting close by the telegraph instruments in railroad offices, listening and watching. Edison fell into the good graces of James MacKenzie, a station agent, when he rescued MacKenzie's young son, who was playing obliviously on the tracks when an uncoupled freight car rolled toward the tyke. Edison happened to be looking out the window just in time to dash out and swoop the child out of harm's way—but not in time to prevent the child's mother from catching sight of the near fatal miss and fainting. This was the tale that was told, and it invites being treated as apocryphal were it not for corroborating facts and MacKenzie's palpable gratitude. He became Edison's personal Morse code tutor, and Edison soon became proficient.

Edison's own account of the rescue of the MacKenzie boy is matter-of-fact and free of heroic embellishment ("I luckily came out just in time"). It was told as the preamble to the main event, which was MacKenzie's taking "considerable pains to teach me" and his own willingness to practice Morse code "about 18 hours a day." (Edison's capacity for extended bursts of work would be his principal vanity his entire life.) This intensive tutelage soon enabled him to become a professional telegraph operator.

At the same time he told the rescue story, he also told one in which his own role was anything but heroic. He had secured his first paid position as a telegraph operator in the local Western Union office, then, at the age of sixteen, gained a position with the Grand Trunk Railroad, which assigned him to the night shift in a station at Stratford Junction, Ontario. One night, he received instructions to hold a freight train that would soon arrive—on the other side, another train had already left the last station and was approaching from the opposite direction on the single track. When Edison headed out into the yard to find the signalman, the train that he was supposed to halt flew past, unaware. He ran back into the office and reported, "I couldn't hold her." The telegraphed

reply was succinct: "Hell." At this point, there was one remaining chance
for Edison to reprise his role as the hero who averted catastrophe: If he
could get to the place along the route where the daytime operator was
presently sleeping, a signal could still be set to prevent the impending
collision. The only way to reach it would be by racing in the darkness
on foot. Edison set off but never made it in time: "I fell in a culvert and
was knocked senseless."

Carnage was avoided that night because the track was straight and
the two engineers saw each other in time to avoid the collision. Afterward, Edison and his immediate supervisor were summoned to the
main office in Toronto. The general superintendent was interested in
knowing why the supervisor had given a sixteen-year-old a position of
such grave life-and-death responsibility. As for Edison, the superintendent threatened to send him off to prison for his criminal negligence
while on duty. Edison did not wish to test the seriousness of the superintendent's threat, and when, in the midst of this dressing-down, three
self-important visitors happened to arrive at the office ("English swells,"
in Edison's description) and created a momentary diversion, he made a
hasty exit. He caught the first freight train that would take him to sanc-
tuary, the United States.

The incident did not keep him from landing his next telegraph operator job, in Adrian, Michigan. For the next five years, he hopped from
one post to the next—Fort Wayne; Indianapolis; Cincinnati; Memphis;
Louisville; Cincinnati again—as a member of the fraternity of "tramp"
operators. They were young, single men who were a peripatetic, but
close-knit, fraternity. They came to know one another if not by meeting
in person, then by their distinctive patterns of tapping when sending
messages. They did not stay in one place long. One or the other would
move to a new post, then, when their movements later brought them
back together, they renewed acquaintance. In a rare surviving letter
that Edison wrote home as a nineteen-year-old, he was conscious that
he had matured since his parents had last seen him: "I have growed
Considerably—I don't look much like a Boy Now."

Within the club, two talents were prized most highly: technical skill when operating the apparatus and creativity when devising practical jokes for the unaware. Edison was highly regarded by his peers on both counts. He had great prowess as a telegraph receiver (but not as a sender). He had diligently investigated how to write as fast as possible (by writing each letter extremely small, and separately, without wasting time with cursive connectors). When receiving, he could always stay ahead of transmissions from the speediest sender. He also came to be known for inventiveness in the good cause of fun. Batteries used for the telegraph apparatus were plentiful, and many of his pranks involved electric shock—these stunts gain interest in retrospect, knowing as we do of Edison's future work on the ultimate instrument of shock, the electric chair. In Cincinnati in 1867, Edison purchased an induction coil that was sufficiently powerful to "twist the arms & clinch the hands of a man so he couldn't let go of the electrodes." He and a colleague connected one electrode to a washstand in the roundhouse and grounded the other, then climbed onto the roof and peered down through a hole they had drilled for the purpose. The first person came in, stepped on the wet floor while washing, closed the circuit—and up went his hands, without volition. A succession of unwary victims were similarly shocked, and all were confounded; no one guessed the cause. Edison commented about observing the events from his perch above: "We enjoyed the sport immensely."

Reaching the top rank of skilled operators did not give Edison much satisfaction. He was increasingly devoting time to tinkering with telegraphic apparatus, looking for ways to gain speed, in sending and mechanically printing messages. He secured permission from office managers to use idle equipment and scavenge discards, and he used his wages to purchase the tools and equipment he could not beg or borrow.

When he landed in Boston in 1868 to work as a night-shift operator at the main Western Union office, he arrived hungry and penniless, and when he presented himself at the office upon arrival, he was, in the words of an operator who witnessed the scene, "the worst-looking specimen of humanity I ever saw." He wore jeans that were six inches too short, a jacket that he had bought off the back of a railroad laborer on his trip across country, and a wide-brimmed hat with a tear on the side, through which his ear poked out. When he finished his trial test—easily—and reached the boardinghouse where he would stay with fellow operators he knew from earlier, the first question he had for them was this: Would their boss permit him to tinker during his free time? The answer was yes. Edison soon sought investors who would provide funds in exchange for half-interest in resulting patents. Three individuals quickly stepped forward to help him work on various projects, such as improved telegraph transmitters, a stock-price printer, a fire alarm that used telegraph technology, and an electric vote recorder for Congress and state legislatures.

All of this work was carried on by a twenty-one-year-old experimenting part-time. Edison filed patent applications as fast as the ideas arrived. The first application that was successful—the first of 1,093 U.S. patents he would accumulate—was for the legislative chambers's vote recorder, which could shorten tabulation by hours. With buttons provided at each member's desk, the chamber's speaker could see twin dials displaying running totals for "aye" and "nay." The deficiencies of the manual voting system seemed obvious to Edison, but not to his prospective customers. When Edison and his investor angel met with a politically savvy operator whose recommendation would be needed to secure a sale in the Capitol, the insider's reaction to Edison's invention was undisguised horror. The minority faction would not embrace an expedited voting process because it eliminated the opportunity to lobby for votes, nor would the majority want a change, either. The vote recorder was a bust, and the lesson Edison drew from the experience was that invention should not be pursued as an exercise in technical cleverness, but should be shaped by commercial needs.

The vote recorder had temporarily pulled Edison away from his core expertise, telegraphy, which was that day's preeminent high-tech field. Traders in stocks and gold were keenly interested in whatever means provided them with faster communications that gave them a competitive edge. Anyone who helped them gain an edge was paid a premium, and a bright telegraphy expert like twenty-two-year-old Edison could make a nice living inventing and manufacturing improved equipment. Or so at least it seemed to him. After a year in Boston, Edison took the big step and quit his day job, which happened to be a night job, resigning his position at Western Union to try to make his living as a full-time inventor and manufacturer in the field of telegraphic equipment.

Judging by the accounts of his contemporaries, at the time he set off on his own in 1869 he was not just respected but also well liked, so much so that he could work harder than everyone else without antagonizing his peers. He was open to participating in long bull sessions at his boardinghouse and had opinions he did not keep to himself. A fellow boarder, a student at the Massachusetts Institute of Technology, later described the clear division of labor in their long conversations. Edison did the talking, and he, the listening. Still, Edison remained wholly unpretentious and clubbable. He was also trusted, the person who on one occasion could collect contributions from more than fifty coworkers and friends to get a gift for a departing employee without anyone worrying that the funds would end up in his pocket. Trust was not unrelated to Edison's temperance, a characteristic rare in that circle.

Edison was disinclined to drink with his fellows because it would pull him off track, interfering with the greater pleasures: tinkering, learning, problem solving. His outlook was secular and matter-of-fact. He once got in trouble when sacrilegiously transcribing "J.C." whenever "Jesus Christ" came across the wire; he could not understand the fuss over his "J.C." when "B.C." for designating historical time was regarded as perfectly acceptable. His early career was fueled by something other than resentments, which he lacked. Whatever advantages in education or financial resources that other inventors enjoyed were of no interest to him. Nor did he regard his partial deafness as an impediment. He claimed that the deafness was actually an advantage, freeing him from time-wasting small talk and giving him undisturbed time to "think out my problems." Late in life he would say that he was fortunate to have been spared "all the foolish conversation and other meaningless sounds that normal people hear."

Immune to the clanging sounds of the city, Edison's ears provided him with a soothing insulation, better suited to "the conditions of modern city life" than those of the average person's. The insulation would also prove helpful when he became famous, partially protecting him from the unceasing demands from strangers for conversation and speeches.

Edison's fame came suddenly, while he was still young. Between the ages of thirty and thirty-five, he became the first hybrid celebrity-inventor. This book examines how he became one of the most famous people in the world, and once fame arrived, how he sought to use it for his own ends, with uneven success. He could act as master of his own image only sometimes. He did not understand the power of the press to shape the life story of the celebrity, to create (and destroy, should it wish to do so).

When he stood on the threshold of fame, he could not have predicted what would follow—and he did not shy away. He directed assistants to maintain newspaper clippings about him, a practice that he would maintain his entire life. The existence of those scrapbooks suggests that Edison gave up an appealing attribute of his young adulthood: his utter indifference to the expectations of others. After "Edison" became a household name, he would pretend that nothing had changed, that he was as indifferent as ever. But this stance is unconvincing. He did care, at least most of the time. When he tried to burnish his public image with exaggerated claims of progress in his laboratory, for example, he demonstrated a hunger for credit unknown in his earliest tinkering. The mature Edison, post-fame, is most appealing whenever he returned to acting spontaneously, without weighing what action would serve to enhance his public image.

One occasion when Edison cast off the expectations of others in his middle age was when he met Henry Stanley, of "Dr. Livingstone, I presume" fame, and Stanley's wife, who had come to visit him at his laboratory. Edison provided a demonstration of the phonograph, which Stanley had never heard before. Stanley asked, in a low voice and slow cadence, "Mr. Edison, if it were possible for you to hear the voice of any man whose name is known in the history of the world, whose voice would you prefer to hear?"

"Napoléon's," replied Edison without hesitation.

"No, no," Stanley said piously, "I should like to hear the voice of our Savior."

"Well," explained Edison, "you know, I like a hustler."

PART I

Success

1869–1882

CHAPTER ONE

ALMOST FAMOUS

1869–1877

HAVING ONE'S OWN shop, working on projects of one's own choosing, making enough money today so one could do the same tomorrow: These were the modest goals of Thomas Edison when he struck out on his own as full-time inventor and manufacturer. The grand goal was nothing other than enjoying the autonomy of entrepreneur and forestalling a return to the servitude of employee.

Edison's need for autonomy was primal and unvarying; it would determine the course of his career from beginning to end. Having no financial assets of his own, he was dependent upon partners who were willing to contribute capital. He had the good fortune to live within the American business ecosystem that valued technical talent and permitted him to attain equal-partner status with wealthy financiers solely on the basis of his wits. For a few restless years, until he would have the wherewithal to shake free of partners, at least active ones who impinged upon his day-to-day activities, Edison hopped from one business venture and short-lived partnership to another, moving from Boston to New York City, then to a succession of cities in New Jersey, ending up in Newark.

Sometimes, the partners remained anonymous (Newark Telegraph Works; American Telegraph Works; News Reporting Telegraph Company; Domestic Telegraph Company). Other times, Edison shared the marquee. The order of names suggests that Edison's importance was progressively recognized, as he moved from the back (Pope, Edison & Company) to the front (Edison and Unger; Edison and Murray). But it would be wrong to infer a hunger on his part for wide public recognition. Edison's reputation grew within the insular circle of telegraph equipment customers, but neither they nor he thought anyone who dwelled within this tiny world would be a subject of interest to a wider one.

All of Edison's first ventures were dependent upon securing contracts that funded product development and procured small lots of completed telegraph instruments. Financial prospects for Edison's partnerships brightened and darkened and brightened again month to month, wholly typical of small firms with a highly specialized product and re-stricted customer base. On the eve of founding the American Telegraph Works in 1870, Edison wrote his parents in Port Huron in ebullient spirits. He reported that his shop had 18 employees and a new shop that he was starting (no mention of his partner) would employ 150. He joked he had become a "Bloated Eastern Manufacturer." The next year, however, meeting the weekly payroll of $578 was so difficult that Edison wrote one of his backers in a foul state of mind, hinting that he was on the verge of being "completely broken down in health & mind." He underlined the following for emphasis: "You Cannot expect a man to invent & work night and day, and then be worried to a point of exasperation about how to obtain money to pay bills."

Notwithstanding such occasional moments of terror—and the fact that his hair turned white, which he attributed to stress—Edison was succeeding, building several businesses whose balance sheets reflected modest, but real, gains. When he and partner William Unger took stock of their shop at the beginning of 1872, three years after Edison decided to try his luck as an entrepreneur, his half share in the business was val-ued at about $11,438. When R. G. Dun & Company prepared a credit report about the firm, whose business was categorized as "Telegraph Fixtures," Unger was the principal who handled the finances and Edi-son was "an ingenious Mechanic & inventor." Not enough was known about the firm to warrant a positive credit recommendation, but the available evidence suggested to the outside investigators that the firm's "transactions indicate a large business."

The News Reporting Telegraph Company, another Edison coventure with Unger, was brilliant in its conception, but 1871 may have been about a hundred years ahead of the most propitious time for launch. The company was conceived with the same insight that would give birth to Bloomberg News: businesspeople, unlike general readers, are able to convert news into immediate financial gain for themselves, and for that reason can be persuaded to pay for access to a news pipeline dedicated to their interests. The News Reporting Telegraph Company offered subscribers a private telegraph line and alphabetic printer that delivered news "hours before such news is published in the papers."

When twenty-four-year-old Edison and his partner opened for business in the fall of 1871, they hired sixteen-year-old Mary Stilwell, the daughter of a lawyer and sometime inventor, as one of several female employees. The surviving records do not make clear whether the company ever secured even a single client, but before it closed, Miss Stillwell and her employer had an encounter that was described in a biographical sketch, *Edison and His Inventions,* published a few years later.

Among the young women whom he employed to manipulate these machines, with a view to testing their capacity for speed, was a rather demure young person who attended to her work and never raised her eyes to the incipient genius. One day Edison stood observing her as she drove down one key after another with her plump fingers, until, growing nervous under his prolonged stare, she dropped her hands idly in her lap, and looked up helplessly into his face. A genial smile overspread Edison's face, and he presently inquired rather abruptly:

"What do you think of me, little girl? Do you like me?"

"Why, Mr. Edison, you frighten me. I—that is—I———"

"Don't be in any hurry about telling me. It doesn't matter much, unless you would like to marry me."

The young woman was disposed to laugh, but Edison went on: "Oh, I mean it. Don't be in a rush, though. Think it over; talk to

your mother about it, and let me know soon as convenient—
Tuesday say. How will Tuesday suit you, next week Tuesday,
I mean?"

The language may strike modern ears as sinister—*What do you think
of me, little girl?*—but its veracity is bolstered by a strikingly similar account in the *Christian Herald & Signs of Our Times*. Even the author of
the chronicle in the *Christian Herald* felt compelled to comment on Edison's "off-hand business-like" manner of courtship.

Another story was told of how a telegrapher friend happened by Edison's laboratory late one night and upon seeing a light on, climbed the
stairs and found his friend half-dozing at his desk.

"Halloo Tom?" cried the visitor cheerily, "what are you doing
here this late? Aren't you going home?"

"What time is it?" inquired Edison, sleepily rubbing his eyes
and stretching like a lion suddenly aroused.

"Midnight easy enough. Come along."

"Is that so?" returned Edison in a dreamy sort of a way. "By
George. I must go home, then. I was *married* to day."

After the wedding and a weeklong honeymoon in Boston in December
1871, the newlyweds moved into a new home in Newark, which Edison
outfitted with servants and $2,000 worth of furnishings, including a
piano. The domestic sphere became the new Mrs. Edison's bailiwick.
According to one source, she "did not appreciate a genius for a husband" and attempted to make Edison into a well-dressed, sociable companion. The couple's first child, Marion, born in 1873 (Edison gave
her the telegraphic nickname of "Dot") recalled a less critical, but not
incompatible, impression. She remembered her mother giving parties
that her father never attended, but supposedly was never pressed to
do so.

When Edison was married, he was financially comfortable, able not
only to purchase his first house but also sufficiently flush to make in-

vestments in his father's and older brother's businesses in Port Huron at the same time he had stakes in five separate shops scattered around Newark. Edison's own businesses were dependent, however, on client firms in the telegraph business, whose fortunes were in turn dependent upon Wall Street firms. When the Panic of 1873 hit, the financial sector was hit hard, and so, too, were the businesses that served it. By 1874, Edison was in serious financial straits and had to sell his house at a loss and move his family into an apartment.

Edison did not close his laboratory, however. He could still grapple with the big problem of his professional field: how to push more messages simultaneously down a single telegraph line. The modern history of communications can be divided into two separate epochs: In the first, the race was to find a means to beat the speed of a horse, and this telegraphy achieved (technically speaking, this came even before telegraphy was electrified: "visual" telegraphy using manned signal towers were built in the 1790s in France). As Marshall McLuhan observed, the telegram was the first message to outrun the messenger. In the second epoch, from the time of early telegraphy to the present-day Internet, the race has involved sending as many messages as possible from point A to point B down a single conduit.

In the first decades of telegraphy, the very idea that more than one message could be sent at a time was incomprehensible to most. Edison had already devised a way to send two messages simultaneously in opposite directions—what would be called duplex telegraphy—but he was both too late (someone else had nabbed the first patent and placed the first working system in the field) and too early (a supervisor had lost patience with Edison and fired him because "any damned fool ought to know that a wire can't be worked both ways at the same time"). Edison set to work on a quadruplex system—two messages sent simultaneously from one direction, and two more from the other. Succeeding, a feat involving complex electromechanical devices, he solidified his reputation in the field of telegraph equipment and pushed the limits of that particular line of multiplexing technology about as far as possible. (He later tried, but failed, to design a similar sextuplex system.)

Edison only had experience selling telegraph equipment, batteries, supplies, and related equipment in the business-to-business trade. A mass market for consumer goods, with the potential of far greater sales, also existed, if he could only come up with a suitable product. In May 1874, he and his partner, Joseph Murray, introduced the Inductorium, battery-powered induction coils for inducing electric shocks. Advertisements claimed that the device "should be in every family as a specific cure for rheumatism, and as an inexhaustible fount of amusement." It sold well enough that the price was raised 33 percent after its introduction and it would eventually be advertised in more than three hundred newspapers. It was sufficiently successful to provide its inventor with the feeling that marketing to the masses was not particularly difficult. Invent it, and they will come.

Edison had not started out with grand ambition, but his appetite for business success was whetted. The quadruplex seemed destined for great success, though who would reap the profits would be complicated by protracted legal disputes that bogged down in the courts and would spill into Congress. The quadruplex greatly increased the carrying capacity of the existing telegraph network, but it did not change the labor-intensive process of translating a message into Morse code, then tapping, receiving, and retranslating back into ordinary language. A system to automate telegraphy would provide a fundamental advance, and this, too, Edison worked on.

The equipment that he invented to create an end-to-end system of telegraphic automation used a keyboard similar to that of a typewriter that composed messages on a long strip of paper, making small and large perforations that corresponded to Morse code. Once complete, the tape would be run across a drum that could send as many as a thousand words a minute. At the receiving end, a roll of chemically treated paper was drawn beneath a row of four styluses, each of which could be turned on and off rapidly dozens of times a second, forming roman letters that anticipated the dot-matrix computer printer of the twentieth century. The system did involve an extra step of preparing the perforated tape and was best suited for long messages such as news stories that had to be sent to many different locations. But Edison's automatic telegraphy not only dramatically increased the carrying capacity of the telegraph network, it also eliminated the need for skilled operators. Daniel Craig, a financial backer of Edison's, wrote him, "You captivate my whole heart when you speak of making machines which will require 'No Intelligence.' That's the thing for Telegraphers."

The next month, Craig wrote him, "If you should tell me you could *make babies by machinery,* I shouldn't doubt it." Automated baby production, however, was not on Edison's list of prospective projects in 1875 when he broke off from Murray. Edison wanted to leave manufacturing and pursue invention full-time—and without the encumbrance of a partner. He did not move far, establishing a laboratory for invention on a different floor in the same building in Newark.

Using his experience developing the machinery to perforate the paper tapes used for transmitting messages automatically, he came up with a handheld, battery-powered electric pen. This was Edison's first significant venture outside of the telegraphic field and would be the direct antecedent to the mimeograph machine: The pen had a sharp needle that moved up and down rapidly, creating a stencil master that could be used to run off hundreds of copies. Edison was sanguine about its commercial prospects. "There is more money in this than telegraphy," he wrote a colleague in September 1875.

Edison was content, however, to set up a separate company to handle the manufacturing and sales and other prosaic annoyances. It is likely that he, like his chief assistant, Charles Batchelor, envisaged no ongoing role other than receiving royalty checks. Batchelor, a British-born immigrant one year older than Edison, had come to the United States originally as a textile mechanic but had quickly acquired expertise in electrical engineering, too. He was smart, tireless, and modest to a fault in his personal ambitions. "We have now got the 'Electric Pen' fairly out on Royalty," Batchelor wrote his father in England, "and in a very short time I shall have nothing whatever to do for it except receive my share of Royalty." He also reminded his father that the last letter he had received had been misaddressed to Newark; Batchelor, Edison, and their families, along with Edison's laboratory and its staff, had recently moved to a new location, Menlo Park, New Jersey.

The casual mention did not highlight the significance of this move, quite different from the many moves that had preceded it. This time, Edison moved out on his own, without a partner in tow, and settled in a place so empty of dwellings that it resembled open frontier (Batchelor reported that the "good shooting" available had to be balanced with the snake infestations). The move was made possible by the patronage of Jay Gould and his Atlantic and Pacific Telegraph Company, which was keenly interested in Edison's ongoing work on automatic telegraphy. Consulting contracts and purchase orders had brought prosperous times again to the Edison household. In January 1875, Gould paid Edison $13,500, and Western Union delivered $5,000, and it seemed as if the family would never have money problems again. Bills were paid off, relatives received cash gifts and loans for business ventures, and Mary Edison felt free to shop and entertain without worries. Edison had gone shopping himself, for a new site for a laboratory, and had settled on land in Menlo Park, about thirty miles from New York. He spent about $2,700 to build a new laboratory structure, and in the spring of 1876 moved into a nearby house with his family, which was newly expanded with the arrival of a second child, Thomas Alva Edison Jr. (nicknamed "Dash" to match three-year-old "Dot").

A short train ride out from New York City, but half a world distant, Menlo Park was the site where a real estate developer's ambitions had ended in bankruptcy. It consisted of about thirty large homes spread out on large lots, connected by a boardwalk and dirt roads. No town hall, school, or church. One saloon.

William Preece, a telegraph engineer for the British Post Office, happened to pay a visit to Edison's new Menlo Park laboratory in May 1877 when the rest of the world knew nothing about Edison's existence, nor Menlo Park's. The town was too small to merit its own identifying sign at the train stop, and Preece almost missed it, hurriedly hopping off the train after it was in motion again. When he did so, he found himself at a desolate station in rural New Jersey. It was a blazing hot day and no porters were on hand.

Preece provides a unique account of one not-famous Englishman paying a call on a not-yet-famous American and fellow telegraphy expert. Before taking the train to Menlo Park, Preece had been most entertained in New York City by the nineteenth-century version of *The Fast and the Furious,* illegal street racing with lightly harnessed horses, roads lined with spectators, and frequent "collisions and rows" that brought unwanted attention from the police. In the little residential development of Menlo Park, however, such excitements were nowhere in evidence. Built up too recently to have the benefit of protective shade trees, the houses sat exposed to sunlight.

Starting from the Menlo Park station, Preece passed a substantial three-storied frame house, wide and shallow with cross-gables, that sat next to the tracks—this had been the sales office for the development and now was the Edison family's house—and climbed up to the top of a hill, which offered a prospect from which one could glimpse the spire of Trinity Church in New York City. On the hilltop sat a long, two-storied plain white building variously described as "an elongated schoolhouse" or a "country shoe factory." This was Edison's laboratory. On the outside, the bucolic setting was not wholly intact. At the rear of the building was an old apple tree, around which were arranged discarded barrels, wheels, and machinery. The second story drew in twelve telegraph lines that came up from the station. This was not incidental; discovering improvements in telegraphy was the laboratory's raison d'être and the primary interest of Preece.

The first floor of the laboratory was divided into a reception room, an office, a library, a machine shop, and a storehouse; the upper floor comprised one long room, filled with workbenches and machines, and lined with glass cases holding chemicals and sundry materials. A "spider web" of telegraph wires covered the ceiling of the laboratory's main room, converging on a large battery placed in the center of the room. The twelve or so workers on hand were directed by a disheveled figure of medium height. He had grimy hands, wore a collarless shirt and a seedy black jacket, and his hair was uncombed. Most striking were eyes that impressed visitors as penetrating, and later inspired flights of poetical description by hagiographers ("the fire of genius shone in his dark deep gray eyes"). The man was only thirty years old, but he carried an aura of authority and a tendency toward curtness that suggested advanced years. Thomas Alva Edison was already "the Old Man" to his employees.

The Menlo Park lab had not yet attracted the attention of the general press, so Preece's visit went unremarked. Nor did Edison record his impressions. The only notes are in Preece's diary, which is full of praise for Edison, whom Preece described as an "ingenious electrician." He goes on at great length about the train's whistles ("the most horrid howls—more like an elephant's trumpet than anything else") but has nothing in particular to say about the apparatus upon which Edison was working. What is most remarkable is how unremarkable Preece found the inventive activity there.

The isolation of the Menlo Park setting infused the laboratory with a feeling of unbounded creative freedom. It encouraged an outlook that saw far, which also meant that little interest could be mustered for fixing problems with older products like the electric pen. Royalty checks for the pen were not adding up as Edison had expected because it had been sent into the field without anyone at the laboratory noticing that it was rather difficult to hold and use. It was likened by one unhappy customer to holding "'the business end' of a wasp on a sheet of paper and letting the insect sting holes into the sheet while you move him back and forth." A sales manager reporting to Edison tried to strike an impossible balance of optimism and realism: "The thing is highly praised everywhere but it will be harder to sell than you anticipate." The fault, Edison was told by another manager, was with the customers' "prejudice and stupidity." (The pen would enjoy a second life years later, in the 1890s, when converted into the first electric tattoo needle.)

Despite the ideal conditions, big ideas did not materialize in Menlo Park. Instead, odds and ends were turned out and marketed by another company that Edison established for this purpose, the American Novelty Company. It sold duplicating ink, an electric drill, an electric engraving machine for jewelers, an electric sheep-shearing machine, and other oddments. At least it could be said that these used the laboratory's expertise in electrical engineering, even if they comprised an incoherent line of offerings. Still other curiosities were added to the mix, such as Batchelor's "Office Door Attachment," an exceedingly low-tech sign to show the occupant's presence or, if absent, time of return. An idea for a "Flying Bird," capable of flying to an altitude of a thousand feet or higher, and to be used as either "a pleasing Scientific Toy" or perhaps for "carrying communications short distance," was scribbled in a notebook, but never was worked up into a prototype. Having tried all sorts of products, and focusing on no single one, the American Novelty Company failed about eight months after it was incorporated.

Telegraphy trumped toys. Great sums of money would go to the inventor that solved the telegraph industry's most pressing need: finding ways to pack more messages into a telegraph line. Acoustic telegraphy, also called harmonic telegraphy, opened up a new way to send more than one message at a time. This approach took advantage of the fact that a tuning fork will respond to the vibrations of another fork with identical characteristics and ignore others. By utilizing in a telegraph network many pairs of vibrating reeds that acted like tuning forks—one of each pair placed at the sending station, the other at the receiving station—each set could be operated as a separate channel of communication, unaffected by the others.

It was while Alexander Graham Bell and his assistant were experimenting with acoustic telegraphy that Bell accidentally, and famously, discovered that the instruments could convey any form of sound. The precise moment of discovery, in June 1875, did not involve speech in crystalline form. Bell, with ear pressed against a vibrating reed, could hear the faint blurry sound of Thomas Watson's voice, but could not make out any words. This was sufficient to provide Bell with the insight that led to the telephone. (The more famous rendering—"Mr. Watson, come here, I want to see you"—came almost a year later, after Bell had filed the patent for the telephone and built a working model.)

Young Bell and Edison were the same age, each improving the major invention that the other had come up with first, Edison following Bell, then Bell following Edison. Edison, in fact, had been close to devising a working telephone himself. After Bell's success, the next best thing for Edison was to come up with an indispensable improvement, the carbon transmitter that captured the human voice far better than Bell's magnetic design. Edison also devised an entirely new kind of receiver based on his electromotograph, which involved a chalk cylinder, chemicals, friction controlled by varying current, and a hand crank; it would never prove to be a practical design for the ordinary speaking telephone, but it could reproduce music clearly and at an astounding volume. Initially, Bell and Edison were direct competitors in the brand-new telephone business, playing upon the public's interest in musical performance to show off their wares by holding telephone "concerts" in exhibition halls.

Bell lacked the gifts of the born showman, however. In May 1877, he offered a concert-lecture to an audience of three hundred who had gathered at Chickering Hall in New York City for an evening heavy on lecture, light on concert. The *New York Times* described Bell's presentation on "Sound and Electricity" to be "exhaustive"; the lecturer's supplemental visual aids were panned as "complex and not very intelligible." At last, the audience was treated to what we may guess they had been waiting for most eagerly, the novelty of hearing recognizable organ music, piped via telegraph connection, from a location miles away.

Edison was no showman, either, and, being partially deaf, hated speaking before a group. He could rely, however, upon an energetic promoter as his proxy: Edward Johnson, a former telegrapher himself (and former sales agent for the Inductorium). Johnson was technically knowledgeable, had his own ideas for invention, and possessed a gift for extolling the virtues of whatever was his preoccupation of the moment. (Johnson's excitability, on occasion, led to misplaced enthusiasm, such as his eagerness in April 1876 to persuade Edison to lend his name to Johnson's invention of an improved tobacco pipe that Johnson hoped to market as "Edison's Perpetual Segar.")

Edison, Batchelor, and Johnson oversaw preparations to launch their own concert tour of the musical telephone. About the time of Bell's concert-lecture in New York City, Edison and his assistants were still working out the kinks while giving concerts in nearby Newark. Edison had yet to show the public a telephone that conveyed human conversation in addition to music, but he had local boosters. The *Woodbridge Independent* confided, "We should not be at all surprised if Edison taught this child of his inventive fancy to talk." "Mr. Edison has been so often scoffed at," the *Newark Daily Advertiser* observed, "that it has no other effect upon him than to stimulate him to increased study and labor." In what readers of 1877 were expected to regard as a humorous touch, the reporter concluded that were Edison to succeed in devising a telephone for speaking, "what an instrument of torture it would be in the hands and at the mouth of a distant and irate mother-in-law."

The big-city debut of Edison's musical telephone was arranged for Philadelphia in mid-July 1877. A three-way contest was under way. Alexander Graham Bell's musical telephone had been eclipsed by the recent debut of a competing musical telephone developed by rival inventor Elisha Gray. Would Edison's, in turn, best Gray's? The competition was as keenly followed as a sports rivalry. The *New York Times* did not even wait for the formal debut of Edison's telephone; the paper dispatched a reporter to the public rehearsal held the day before.

The early *Times*'s verdict: awful. Compared to Gray's, Edison's telephone was not nearly as loud, its notes not as "sweet." It might work well as a practical instrument in sending telegraphic messages, the paper reported, but as a device producing sounds intended to please the human ear, it lagged the competition.

When Johnson saw the review, he was in Philadelphia overseeing preparations for the performance. He wrote Edison that "the N.Y. times [*sic*] man is a fool," but he was happy that the rehearsal had come off, period. His Edison telephone was behaving erratically, and he begged Edison to send him a new, more dependable one from the laboratory. He also had to pay off the newspapers, which had their hands out. The *New York Daily Graphic* explained that it was "customary" for subjects to order extra copies in order to indirectly reimburse the newspaper for the additional expense of providing engraved illustrations that would accompany the upcoming story. For the "Puff," Johnson agreed to take one hundred copies and asked Edison to sign up for a similar amount.

On the day of the concert, Edison responded at last to Johnson's pleas, and placed a new telephone on the 8:00 A.M. train bound for Philadelphia. Alas, when Johnson arrived at the Pennsylvania Railroad depot to pick up the package, it could not be found. It turned out to be in the hands of an express company and would not appear until too late that evening. In the end, Johnson had to use the defective equipment that had been used in the rehearsal.

The demo gods gave their blessing to the event, however, and now the *Times* was impressed in every aspect. The volume was excellent, the sound being easily heard by the crowd of 3,500 (Johnson, fond of exaggeration, boasted to Edison that the crowd was even bigger, six thousand people). The songs were deemed "musically enjoyable" and one even was "encored," though the performers were five miles away.

Johnson knew that "by the turn of a hair" the performance "might have been the most ridiculous farce ever heard of," yet the narrow aversion of disaster did not slow down his calculations of future profits to be earned charging admission to similar exhibitions. Johnson was as sanguine as any businessperson in the new telephone business about the commercial potential in using telephones to deliver music, but even he could not keep up with the general public. Let the credit for the most farsighted vision of that moment go to one Joseph Hipple, of Spruce Mills, Iowa, who in March 1877 had a fully developed scheme for piping music directly to the home rather than to exhibition halls. Hipple proposed that relay teams of musicians could perform at one central location during the late afternoon and evening hours, providing music on tap, "the same as water and gas." (Hipple's idea of music-on-demand was beautiful in conception but advanced no further than Hipple's exposition in a letter to the editor of the *New York Daily Graphic*.)

At that moment, when Edison's telephone was better suited for conveying music than the human voice, when the music-loving public was willing to traipse to a concert in which the players were not physically present and was willing to pay for the privilege (at least until the novelty wore off), when it was possible to imagine individual households paying for satellite-radio version 0.1, pre satellites, Edison was in the perfect position to realize the business potential in music. But he did not; telegraphy remained his principal interest. Around the time of the telephone concerts, he redoubled his efforts to complete a complicated contraption of thirty wheels that would convert taps on an alphabetic keyboard into unique vibrations for acoustic telegraphy. He did have a vision of delivering signals directly to households, but it involved sending the human voice, not music. By attaching telephones to gas pipes that were already in place in the home, Edison thought it should be possible to use the gas, instead of electricity, as a medium for conveying sound waves.

The musical telephone offered the opportunity to enjoy live music without being immediately present. The constrictions of geography were loosening, but not those of time: one could listen to performances only synchronously, that is, at the same time the players performed. In retrospect, one can see the need for an invention that permitted the enjoyment of music asynchronously, at a time of the listener's own choosing. Edison came up with the first gadget that would eventually fill this need. The process that produced the invention could not be called careful planning, but it was something more than pure serendipity. It was the by-product of working on state-of-the-art communications technology, while remaining receptive to chance insight and recombining bits of recently secured experience. Bell invented the telephone while tinkering with acoustic telegraphy; Edison invented the phonograph while tinkering with the telephone.

Initially, telephones were regarded as instruments to be used only by telegraph company employees. Instead of sending messages in Morse code, the operator would transmit the message verbally, but if the message had to be transcribed manually at the receiving end by a human operator, the capacity of the system to carry a given quantity of messages would be dramatically constricted. Some way needed to be devised to record the message mechanically—the practicality of the telephone appeared to hang in the balance.

The very variety of Edison's previous inventions served him well for tackling the problem of recording. His automatic telegraph used a stylus that rested on a strip of paper that ran continuously beneath it—that paper would be part of Edison's solution. For another project, making electrical condensers, Edison's laboratory staff had learned how to apply a wax coating to paper, and Edison had tried to peddle it as a sideline to food producers, with no apparent success (the New York Paper Barrel Company explained that the paper "must be <u>Sweet</u> & <u>Pure</u> free from oder [sic]," a tough requirement for Edison's grimy laboratory to meet). A legacy of this work in the laboratory was a cupboard well stocked with coated and uncoated paper, cut to various sizes.

A sketch and brief caption in a notebook entry dated 17 July 1877 recorded an idea for putting the paper to use on the telephone problem: Edison and his assistants sketched in bare outline a system that the telegraph company could use to record spoken messages. How exactly the recording would be accomplished was treated as incidental—the paper could be embossed, or perforated with needles, or inked using the electromotograph. The principal point was to enable the company to send the recording for playback and transcription by low-paid copyists, who could work at the rate of twenty-five words a minute, rather than have highly skilled—and highly paid—operators try to record the message in real time at one hundred words a minute as it arrived.

Another project under way was the laboratory's ongoing work on improving the quality of the telephone transmitter. Under Edison's direction, the laboratory was in the midst of testing different materials as experimental diaphragms that would vibrate when receiving sound waves. A partial list of candidates: glass, mica, hard rubber, celluloid, aluminum foil, parchment, pith, leather, chamois, cloth, silk, gelatin, ivory, birch bark, rawhide, pig's bladder, fish guts, and a $5 bill. To each, a mouthpiece was attached and then mounted in a frame for convenient handling. By holding the frame up and speaking in a loud voice while holding a finger on the rear of the diaphragm, one could detect the vibrations, all without the trouble of attaching it to a working telephone and applying electrical current.

No less important than the technical antecedents was the setting, this after-hours laboratory. When Edison was working long hours, which on occasion meant all-night work sessions, his assistants were expected to do the same. Early on, Edison established a tradition of providing a midnight dinner in the lab, brought up by the night watchman. The feast was accompanied by a convivial conversation that was the only time of the workday that Edison would allow himself to relax. An employee described the typical pattern: "Hilarity came with the filling of stomachs, bantering and story telling were interlarded, until Edison arose, stretched, took a hitch at his waistband in sailor fashion and began to saunter away—the signal that dinner was over, and it was time to begin work again."

The day after Edison had noted the idea for recording voice messages received by a telegraphy office, he came up with a variation. That evening, on 18 July 1877, when the midnight dinner had been consumed but the men had not yet dispersed to return to the work of comparing different types of diaphragms for the telephone, Edison entertained himself speaking into one, while pressing his finger on the rear surface, feeling the vibrations. After a while, he turned around to face Batchelor and casually remarked, "Batch, if we had a point on this we could make a record on some material which we could afterwards pull under the point, and it would give us the speech back."

As soon as Edison had pointed it out, it seemed so obvious that they did not pause to appreciate what Batchelor would later describe as the "brilliancy" of the suggestion. Everyone jumped up to rig a test. John Kruesi, the laboratory's chief machinist, took command of soldering a needle to the middle of a diaphragm; he then attached the diaphragm to a stand holding one of the wheels used in the automatic telegraph. Batchelor cut some strips of wax paper, and within an hour, they had the gizmo set up on the table, paper inserted on top of the wheel, and the needle adjusted so that it pressed lightly on the paper. Edison sat down, leaned into the mouthpiece, and while Batchelor pulled the paper through, he delivered the stock phrase the lab used to test telephone diaphragms: "Mary had a little lamb."

When they took a look, the paper strip, as expected, had irregular marks. Batchelor reinserted the beginning of the strip across the top of the wheel and beneath the needle, then pulled, trying to maintain the same speed as the first time. Out came "ary ad ell am." "It was not fine talking," Batchelor recalled, "but the shape of it was there." The men celebrated with a whoop, shook hands with one another, and worked on. By breakfast the following morning, they had succeeded in getting clear articulation from waxed paper, the first recording medium—in the first midnight recording session.

The all-nighter at the laboratory must have been a routine occurrence, for the discovery was treated surprisingly casually in the lab's notebooks. The entries for 18 July 1877 were extensive but focused on the telephone; only at the bottom of one page was the following brief entry:

> Just tried experiment with a diaphragm [sic] having an emboss-ing point & held against parafin [sic] paper moving rapidly the spkg vibrations are indented nicely & theres [sic] no doubt that I shall be able to store up & reproduce automatically at any future time the human voice perfectly

Though Edison used the first-person voice, Batchelor and James Adams, another assistant, signed their names to the page, too.

It was a singular moment in the modern history of invention, but, in the years that would follow, Edison would never tell the story the way it actually unfolded that summer, always moving the events from July 1877 to December. We may guess the reason why: in July, he and his assistants failed to appreciate what they had discovered. At the time, they were working feverishly to develop a set of working telephones to show to their best prospect, William Orton, president of Western Union, and Batchelor's diary shows entry after entry that July in which he dryly recorded varied phrasings of a single routine: "worked all day and night on Speaker telegraph." We can assume that Batchelor's assignments were tightly coupled with Edison's own experimental agenda of the moment, and the task that occupied the entire staff was to improve the telephone's ability to handle human speech rather than music. There was no time to pause and reflect on the incidental invention of what was the first working model of the phonograph.

Other potential distractions were shut out, too, such as suggestions from professional acquaintances to strike out in a wholly new direction. On the very day that the laboratory noted its breakthrough in recording sound, George Field, an early investor in Edison's telegraphy work, wrote him with a suggestion to take notice of the recent demonstration of electric streetlights in Paris. "I feel quite confident," Field said, "that if you will apply yourself to it that important results might follow." Edison was unwilling to change course—or even to give the phonograph sustained attention.

The first, brief public mention of the crude phonograph came in mid-August 1877, a month after the midnight birth (even then it still lacked a name). Edward Johnson told the *Philadelphia Record* that Edison had invented an instrument "by which a speech can be recorded while it is being delivered on prepared paper" and the same paper could "rede-liver" it at any time. Edison and Batchelor, focused as they were at the time on improving the telephone for speech, naturally thought that their device would be used for speech, ignoring music. But curiously, even Johnson, the impresario in charge of exhibiting Edison's musical telephone, failed to consider the possibilities for recording music, too.

It took a long while for Edison to decide what to call the contraption. By this time, "phonograph" had been jotted onto a laboratory note-book, but the word was in common usage at the time as a synonym for "shorthand." The invention continued to be labeled in the notebooks with the broader rubric "speaking telegraph," reflecting the assumption that it would be put to use in the telegraph office, recording messages. An unidentified staff member drew up a list of possible names for the machine, which included:

Tel-autograph
Tel-autophone
Polyphone = manifold sounder

Autophone = Self-sounder

Cosmophone = Universal sounder

Acoustophone = Audible speaker

Otophone = Ear-sounder = speaker

Antiphone = Back-talker

Liquphone = Clear speaker

Chronophone = Time-announcer = Speaking clock

Didaskophone = Teaching speaker = Portable teacher

Glottophone = Language sounder or speaker

Climatophone = Weather announcer

Klangophone = Bird-cry sounder

Hulagmophone = Barking sounder

Omphlegraph = voice writer

Epograph = speech writer

aerophone = air sound

phonomime

Ecophone

As he and his staff made progress on the telephone's speech capabilities, Edison kept Western Union's Orton briefed on the good news. The sensitivity of Edison's carbon microphone permitted the speaker to stand ten feet away from the speaking tube, he wrote excitedly, after another long night of experimenting. In September, Edison's telephones were placed in competition against Bell's in Orton's presence, and Edison won an immediate order for 150 sets. Edison wrote a colleague of Orton's surprise: "He had no idea that he could get it so loud."

The expense of maintaining the laboratory was considerable, the money Edison had received in 1875 was spent, and the initial order for telephones from Western Union did not immediately ease the cash shortage. In October 1877, he wrote his father that he was "at present very hard up for cash," but if his "speaking telegraph" was successful, he would receive an advance on royalties. The commercial potential of his still-unnamed recording apparatus remained out of sight. Edison seems to have been disappointed when he told Benjamin Butler, an attorney who had represented him in the past, that he had not yet achieved the goal he had mentioned to Butler: developing the ability to "print" the human voice on paper using a particular mark for a given sound, without prior recording, as one typesets a romanized alphabet.

Edison said that he could at least capture the human voice on paper by recording speech and then play it back "at any *future time*." Butler thought this so remarkable that "I do not understand it at all." However it worked, he told Edison, there was no need to go further in his experimental work (advice that ratified the Menlo Park crew's view that the human voice was the ultimate prize in recording sound). He sensed, correctly, that Edison did not appreciate the significance of his own discovery. "I need not say that you had better keep it perfectly secret," Butler advised.

A secret it remained, effectively, as the mention the previous month in the *Philadelphia Record* had been missed by other newspapers. But only two weeks later, Edward Johnson could not remain quiet, not when French rivals were getting attention for similar work. He was infuriated by an article in *Scientific American* describing C. L. Rosapelly and Étienne-Jules Marey's work on instruments for graphically—and cumbersomely—recording speech by simultaneously registering the movement of thorax, larynx, lips, tongue, and palate. Once recorded, those lines would somehow have to be translated into audible speech. If *Scientific American*'s respectful treatment of this path to failure was not exasperating enough to Johnson, the magazine had also voiced the prediction that it would lead someday to the recording of speech that could be transmitted electrically by wire. With Edison's permission, Johnson wrote to the editor of *Scientific American* to say there was no need to wait for the French to perfect their technique for capturing speech on paper—Mr. Edison had already achieved everything the French hoped for, and could use paper to reproduce speech long distances, too.

An engraved illustration accompanied Johnson's long letter, showing a strip of paper that ran along the top of two rollers, with a recording stylus and telephone mouthpiece suspended over one, and a playback stylus and a reproducer that looked from the outside just like the mouthpiece suspended over the other roller. A "boss," or protuberant line, ran the length of the paper, so the stylus, which rested on top, could easily make an indentation in response to the amplitude of the sound. The invention still lacked a name and was referred to as "the apparatus."

The editors of Scientific American were so excited—so emotionally moved, they confessed in an introduction, by the immediate prospect of being able to listen to the voices of the dead—that they jumped ahead to a list of possible applications of this new capability. Spoken messages might replace written letters. The words of history's greatest orators could be enjoyed in perpetuity. And "music may be crystallized as well."

The publication of Johnson's letter in Scientific American in early November set off a frenzy in America and Europe. The New York Sun was fascinated by the metaphysical implications of an invention that could play "Echoes from Dead Voices." The New York Times predicted that a large business would develop in "bottled sermons," and wealthy connoisseurs would take pride in keeping "a well-stocked oratorical cellar." To the English Mechanic, still absorbing the capability of the telephone, it appeared that Edison's new invention was "more remarkable still," for it could convey the human voice at any time, even "a hundred years hence." Such was the authority of Scientific American's imprimatur that all of this extraordinary attention was lavished not on the first working phonograph made available for public inspection, but merely on a description supplied by Edison's assistant.

No machine was ready for public inspection because just before Johnson wrote his letter describing how a paper strip served as the recording medium, Edison had shifted his experimental focus from paper to tinfoil. Instead of using a raised ridge embossed on paper as a soft surface that was easily impressed by the recording needle, Edison now conceptualized a one-foot-long cylinder, whose surface had been threaded, and upon which a sheet of tinfoil would be placed. By positioning the recording needle on the top of the cylinder at the beginning of the thread, it rested on a continuous groove below the foil's surface, easily impressing the foil just like the embossed ridge of the paper.

When setting down on 5 November 1877 the outlines of his design, Edison still conceptualized the device as a medium for speech. He estimated that a single sheet could hold about two hundred spoken words. But the next day, Johnson's letter to *Scientific American* appeared, and from that moment on, Edison no longer worked in obscurity. The permanence of this change was something that he, like anyone else, could not have appreciated at the time. But one immediate benefit of the press's marveling was that the extensive coverage supplied Edison with creative ideas about how the phonograph could be adapted for many more uses than telegraphy or senatorial speeches.

Years before, Edison had begun to systematically record all laboratory findings and the progress of his own thinking about the projects. His jottings in this period reflect the influence of speculations of strangers. By late November, Edison and his staff had caught on to the phonograph's commercial potential as a gadget for entertainment. On a page signed by Edison, Batchelor, Adams, and Kruesi, a list of possible uses for the phonograph was noted, assembled apparently by free association: speaking toys (dogs, reptiles, humans); whistling toy train engines; music boxes; clocks and watches that announced the time. There was even an inkling of the future importance of personal music collections, here described as the machine for the whole family to enjoy, equipped with a thousand sheets of prerecorded music impressed upon tinfoil, "giving endless amusement."

The design of a tinfoil phonograph had been conceptualized, then refined, and a myriad of future uses enumerated. The first actual model, however, remained to be built. John Kruesi took on the assignment. On 4 December 1877, Batchelor's diary laconically noted "Kruesi made phonograph today"; it received no more notice than the other entry, "worked on Speaking Tel," the invention that continued to be at the top of the laboratory's research agenda. Even the loquacious Johnson had little more to say when he received the machine in New York: "Complete success. Talks plainer than telephone."

It is not clear whether the decision to immediately display the new creation to the press was Johnson's or Edison's. What *is* clear is that the idea was not first vetted by a patent attorney—Edison would not get around to executing his first patent application for the phonograph until the next week. The one-week delay would later cause many difficulties in his efforts to secure patents in countries outside the United States. Given his immersion in patent battles in the telegraph industry, it is somewhat surprising to see Edison's lack of caution in proceeding with the phonograph's unveiling. The decision can be explained, perhaps, by the absence of a professional business structure and consulting counsel for the laboratory, by haste born of pride of accomplishment, or from underestimating the commercial significance of the invention.

However ill-advised, the debut came off not just smoothly but brilliantly. On 7 December 1877, Edison, Batchelor, and Johnson walked into the New York offices of *Scientific American*, placed a small machine on the editor's desk, and, with about a dozen people gathered around, turned the crank. "How do you do?" asked the machine, introducing itself crisply. "How do you like the phonograph?" It itself was feeling quite well, it assured its listeners, and then cordially bid everyone a good night.

To the editors of *Scientific American*, the performance was utterly astounding. How could such a small machine mimic so accurately the human voice? Even for someone thoroughly familiar with the science underlying the machine, "it is impossible to listen to the mechanical speech without his experiencing the idea that his senses are deceiving him." Edison's choice of favoring this journal with the demonstration was shrewd, as the editorial staff was familiar with the latest experiments that attempted to re-create the human voice. The state of the art was not impressive: large machines the size of a pipe organ, endowed with keyboards, pipes, and rubber larynx and lips were supposed to deliver a humanlike sound but were only able to reproduce what sounded like a single monotonous note of an organ. And yet somehow Edison could coax what sounded like a naturally inflected human voice from "a few pieces of metal, set up roughly on an iron stand about a foot square."

So enchanted were the editors that Edison was given credit for solving what had been seen as two separate problems, decoding the sound notations (misunderstood as "dots and dashes") that were recorded on the tinfoil, and then re-creating them. It was as if instead of having to read the individual words, one could drop a book in a machine and it would automatically read itself. In fact, Edison could not decode the scratches, and had failed in his attempt to solve the first problem, that is, translating the microscopic marks into a phonetic alphabet. But there was no need for anyone to break the recording down into analyz-able units; the phonograph automatically played whatever had been recorded, blithely insensible to differences in language, equally articulate in all tongues. It was already possible to project life-sized stereoscopic images of an individual upon a screen. "Add the talking phonograph to counterfeit their voices," the journal suggested, "and it will be difficult to carry the illusion of real presence much further." This was stop-the-presses news. *Scientific American,* which had been ready to publish its regular issue on the day of the talking phonograph's visit, delayed pub-lication one day so that an illustrated account could be inserted, a fact that pleased Johnson exceedingly.

Thanks to *Scientific American,* Edison would never again enjoy the sweetness of anonymous obscurity. "I want to know you right bad," the *New York Sun*'s Amos Cummings wrote him in early January, in quest of "something about the secrets of electricity and so on." Edison wel-comed Cummings, and William Croffut of the *New York Daily Graphic,* making them feel as if they were not just reporters but friends. Edwin Fox, of the influential *New York Herald,* was an old acquaintance who had originally known Edison when they were both telegraph operators; Edison granted him and other former operators access, too. The sensa-tional news of the phonograph's performance—so wondrous that the fact that the phonograph was wholly mechanical and had no electrical com-ponents or power was often overlooked—brought the press to Edison's doorstep, and he, in turn, intuitively cultivated the relationships, using the press's hunger for more sensational discoveries for his own ends.

The technique that Edison used most effectively in handling the press was the seemingly offhand disclosure about what he had discovered, leaving the impression that he was parting the curtain only enough to provide a glimpse of what he had actually achieved and withholding the remainder from public view. He left it to the reporters to draw their own conclusions. The *New York World* referred to Edison's telephone transmitter and speaking telephone, the electric pen and a sewing-machine prototype that was powered by tuning forks, as "a few selected from hundreds equally curious and of more or less practical importance." When the newspaper estimated the number was "hundreds," and regarded all to be equally significant, it was in effect creating a superhero, a man who was only thirty years old, lifted up to a plane above his contemporaries, including Alexander Graham Bell.

One cannot help but feel a little sympathy for Bell in the competition between the two men. The acclaim for his telephone was quickly superseded by the attention that Edison's improvements drew, and then by Edison's phonograph. This was especially galling because Bell had come so close to inventing the phonograph himself. He had understood how sound waves could be recorded on paper, and he also knew that the motion of one's hand could generate waves that produced similar sounds. Indenting a medium to save and then reproduce those waves had not occurred to him, however. "It is a most astonishing thing to me that I could possibly have let this invention slip through my fingers," Bell said in early 1878. He recovered sufficiently to imagine that he could improve on the phonograph without violating Edison's patents, using a technique "which can be turned to immediate account so as probably to realize a large fortune in a couple of months or so." Time would show that he really did have the germ of the idea for what would become formidable competition for the phonograph—his "graphophone" would play wax-coated discs rather than foil-wrapped cylinders—but it would be a long while before it was ready for market. No quick, large fortune for him, but none for Edison, either.

CHAPTER TWO

THE WIZARD OF MENLO PARK

AS A BUSINESSPERSON poised to bring the phonograph to market, Thomas Edison was hindered as much as helped by experience. Having long worked within the world of telegraphic equipment, he had been perfectly placed to receive the technical inspiration for the phonograph. But that same world, oriented to a handful of giant industrial customers, had nothing in common with the consumer marketplace. It was impossible for Edison to imagine the phonograph as the basis for a new home-entertainment industry. His lieutenants were slow to appreciate the possibilities, too. "The Phonograph is creating an immense stir," Edward Johnson wrote a business acquaintance, "but I think it impresses people more as a toy than as a practical machine." It was as a toy that Edison planned to first introduce the phonograph, but he favored a passive role for himself: let others do the manufacturing, worry about the sales, and send him a royalty check, leaving him free to pursue a life of ceaseless inventing.

In early January 1878, Edison signed a contract with Oliver Russell to bring out an array of toys—dolls, trains, birds—all of which would be endowed with the power of speech or sound effects, thanks to a hidden phonograph. To pursue opportunities for the phonograph beyond the realm of toys, music boxes, and clocks, Edison signed with a syndicate of five investors later that month who set up the Edison Speaking Phonograph Company. The syndicate gave him an immediate payment of $10,000 to "perfect" the instrument, that is, to complete the development work to ready the invention for the market. Edison would receive a 20 percent royalty on net proceeds. He insisted on embedding a clause in the agreement that protected his future royalty payments from price-cutting: phonographs had to be sold for $80 or more unless he personally granted an exception.

The investors feared that Edison would exhaust the $10,000 advance before the phonograph would be ready for the market. After the agreement was signed, they tried to arrange to have the money placed in a trust. Edison would not approve, feeling (correctly) that, as one of the investors wrote another, the proposed change "was a reflection upon his ability to take care of himself."

According to a psychological profile published at the time in the *Phrenological Journal,* his backers had to be flexible and patient, as Edison was apt to "show irritability and people who do not understand him may think he is impatient and fretful." The journal expressed concern that if Edison did not take proper care of himself, "he will become exhausted and break down."

Improving the phonograph's sound clarity, natural intonation, and volume of reproduced speech were Edison's principal concerns. Mechanizing the turning of the cylinder when it played back a recording seemed to solve many of the problems with quality. In his lab, he used an industrial belt to hook up a phonograph to the overhead shaft that was connected to a steam engine, the source of the power for his machine shop. The results were stunning. Edison wrote one of his representatives in Europe, "Letters can be dictated & copied *with ease.* The singing is beautiful in fact I am overjoyed."

The typical office or home parlor was unlikely to have an industrial steam engine already on the premises to provide steady power, of course, so Edison tinkered with a weight-driven clockwork mechanism, which replaced the hand crank and assured a steady rotation speed. Without mechanizing the rotation, the sound of the phonograph, whether for music or speech, left much to be desired. When Edison finally wrote to Preece about his invention in February 1878, he said that the machine had to be cranked at 120 turns per minute in order to achieve acceptable sound. A clockwork mechanism also made all the difference in comprehensibility when transcribing business letters that had been dictated.

Listening comprehension was influenced by subjective factors, Edison noticed. If a person who had never heard of the phonograph was pulled off the street and asked to listen to a recording of a simple sentence, he would not find it comprehensible, even if it were played a dozen times. If that same person were first told what he was about to hear, he would declare, after hearing it played, that it was a perfect reproduction. The same phenomenon was observed when novices first listened through a telephone. Edison speculated, "They do not expect or imagine that a machine can talk hence cannot understand it[s] words."

In his lab, Edison made good progress in increasing the phonograph's volume, using copper sheets for recording instead of tinfoil. If a speaker shouted into the microphone, Edison was able to make the playback distinctly audible at a distance of 475 feet. Shouting would not be practical in an office setting, but the progress encouraged him to find still better means of increasing playback volume. He got the idea that sound could be amplified by triggering a valve releasing steam or compressed air that would hit an enormous diaphragm, effectively sending a phonograph's sounds outward for miles. The idea was so novel that, at the Patent Office's urging, he separated the idea from his workup for the phonograph and filed a separate patent application, granted in early March 1878. He called this talking foghorn an "aerophone."

Outside of the lab, Edward Johnson was the first to successfully commercialize the phonograph, albeit only modestly, when he added it to his traveling "concerts" featuring the musical telephone. His prospectus promised that

> Recitations, conversational remarks, Songs (with words), Cornet Solos, Animal Mimicry, Laughter, Coughing, etc, etc, will be delivered into the mouth of the machine, and subsequently reproduced by the machine with such fidelity of tone, Articulation, emphasis, etc., as will kindle an enthusiasm as hearty as it

will be spontaneous. . . . The Apparatus is really a great discovery and not a mear [*sic*] trick or toy for producing deceptive effects—the known reputation of Mr. Edison as a producer of practical inventions is however the best guarantee I have to offer of the genuinness [*sic*] of this great discovery.

His show played in small towns in New York and Pennsylvania, where competition in the amusement business was scarce: Elmira, Cortland, Homer, Dunkirk, Fredonia, Jamestown, Lockport, and so on, each night a different locale. Local promoters were so pleased to receive Johnson and his assistant that they agreed to his demand of a guaranteed flat fee of $100 rather than accept a percentage of the gate receipts.

Johnson first had the telephone deliver piped-in music, saving the phonograph to close the show. "You should hear me bring down the House by my singing in the Phonograph when I failed to get a Volunteer," Johnson wrote a colleague. "The effect when they hear me is stupendous, but when they hear the Phonograph reproducing my song with all its imperfections they endanger the walls with clamor."

Johnson reported that he was paid promptly by the promoters, even though for them the concerts "had not been pecuniarily successful." Did Edison show him proper appreciation? He had not, Johnson groused, nor had Edison provided him with one of the newest phonograph models, instead sending him off to struggle with the oldest one on hand. Johnson assumed he had been deliberately slighted, and lobbied to attain higher standing in Edison's eyes. Others felt the same, jockeying for what they imagined was better position. But Edison did not give or withhold attention deliberately. He tinkered in the lab, oblivious to politics.

In February 1879, Edison sent out a premature announcement to an acquaintance that the phonograph was now *perfect,* underlining the word for emphasis. Perfection had not yet been attained, however, and Edison knew it. To another friend, he allowed it was "almost perfect," but felt it was not yet ready to release commercially. The investors in the Edison Speaking Phonograph Company were less fastidious about the issues of quality that concerned Edison. They pressed for a ship date, but Edison resisted release before the product was ready.

Bugs had to be removed. In Edison's time, the term "bugs" was used exactly as it is today. In the early 1870s, when Edison was working under contract on the quadruplex telegraph with a group of assistants, the work had established the proof of concept, but the prototype was not wholly reliable. For Edison, that was sufficient. "Boys," Edison told his underlings, "the principle is all right, and the sharps upstairs can get the bugs out of it."

In early 1878, Edison's laboratory was his alone. There were no "suits," as "sharps" would be called today, to foist a not-yet-bug-free product upon the public. But postponing release was difficult when the clamor of prospective customers was so loud. Most eager to get their hands on the new invention were college professors, who wrote Edison, pleading for the privilege of purchasing one. For example, Alfred Mayer, a professor of physics at the Stevens Institute of Technology, in Hoboken, New Jersey, flattered Edison with mention of "admiration of your genius." Mayer said that the phonograph "has so occupied my brain that I can hardly collect my thoughts to carry on my work." He and a colleague were writing a physics textbook, which would introduce students to "all really worthy American work" and would replace, they hoped, the European textbooks that everyone in their field used. Would Edison be willing to provide a phonograph for this noble endeavor? No one could resist such an appeal, combining the scientific and patriotic; Edison assented.

Wanting to please the impatient scientific community, but at the same time not wanting to endanger his own reputation by releasing the phonograph prematurely and allowing it to be scrutinized before it was ready, Edison found himself in an uncomfortable position. The pressure to ship applied by the investors added to his discomfort. In early February, he came up with what he thought was a plan that would please all parties. His clockwork-driven machine, which reproduced sound at about half the volume of the original, was showing sufficient promise that he would make it the basis for a commercial model to be released in April. In the meantime, he would rush out five hundred copies of a small, inexpensive model for those who could not wait. It would be hand-cranked, capable of recording no more than fifty words, and would be clearly advertised as nothing more than a novelty whose only purpose was to "illustrate the principle." His backers debated the proposal, but came around, agreeing with Edison that "a good deal of money could be made in selling these small traps."

Judging from the volume of correspondence coming in to the Menlo Park laboratory, the articles in *Scientific American* and reprints and secondhand digests of the articles carried in various newspapers had spread the word effectively. The task at hand was readying for the market the two models, one larger, one smaller. Edison must have slapped his forehead with irritation for having promised *New York Sun* reporter Amos Cummings a month earlier that he would be willing to sit for an interview. Cummings was comically self-deprecating ("I know no more about electricity or electrical machinery than a cow") and polite, but now he was also insistent in getting Edison to name a date for the promised interview. Edison put him off awhile longer, perhaps hoping Cummings would lose interest in the campaign. Cummings was not to be denied, however, and finally Edison capitulated. The inventor leaves no record that he had any inkling that the resulting story that appeared in the *Sun* on 22 February 1878 would change his life.

Below the comparatively restrained headline "A Marvelous Discovery" was a subheadline that nicely summarized the theme of the profile: "A Man of Thirty One Revolutionizing the Whole World." This was not the product of grandiosity on Edison's part, nor was he playing the public relations game with a master's touch. He was, in fact, entirely passive. He did not even go into New York to meet with Cummings. Edison interrupted his work at Menlo Park, answered his questions, and then resumed what he had been doing.

It was Cummings, his employer, the *New York Sun,* and its readers who jointly conspired to create a mythic inventor hero to suit their craving for a larger-than-life, yet accessible, figure. For everyone who was not an engineer, this was a time when technology seemed to be both overwhelming and increasingly incomprehensible. The cotton gin's workings had been transparent; the telephone's were not. If the latest technology itself could not be explained, at least the inventor could be rendered in terms that made him accessible and appealing as a person. At the same time, it was entertaining to view him as endowed with extraordinary power.

Permitting others to make him famous was easy. Drawing up realistic plans for marketing the phonograph was not. If any person in Menlo Park was in a good position to provide what we today would call a consumer perspective to help plan the introduction of the phonograph to the marketplace, it would have been the person who stood clear of the self-absorbed laboratory: Mrs. Mary Edison. She would have been ideally situated, that is, were she interested in offering advice, and were her husband interested in receiving it. Edison was not receptive to guidance from others, whether its nature was technical, strategic, or business. For the very shortest time after they were married, Edison had viewed his wife as his helpmeet in the lab. This was a short-lived idea—only a month later, Edison wrote in a laboratory notebook in an agitated hand: "My wife Dearly Beloved Cannot invent worth a Damn!!" He redefined their roles with a conventional boundary: his sphere was work; Mary's, the home.

In Menlo Park, the separateness of spheres remained intact even on Sundays, the only day of the week when the laboratory was nominally closed. After the Edisons' second child, Thomas Alva Edison Jr., arrived, Mary would leave Saturday evenings with the children to visit relatives in Newark, not returning until the wee hours of Sunday or even Monday. With his family away, Edison often spent Sundays at the lab.

One of the rare instances in which we have a glimpse of the two spending a free evening together is in January 1878, just when the phonograph's birth had been announced in the press. The Edisons joined the Batchelors for an evening's entertainment in New York, where they saw a magic show that was running on Broadway. The featured performer was Robert Heller, who claimed expertise in "necromancy and diablerie" and had unsettled clergy with posters commanding passersby to "Go to HELLer's." The evening's entertainment would be the first thing that came to Edison's mind when a reporter soon after asked Edison if he wasn't "a good deal of a wizard." Edison laughed, shrugged off the label, and suggested that no one deserved it. He recalled he had just seen Heller, all but one of whose illusions Edison claimed to have figured out.

For members of the general public, the advanced edge of applied science was not easily distinguishable from Broadway magic, creating the opportunity for someone like John Worrell Keely, an inventor—a title open to anyone—and a fraud. Claiming to have discovered a new physical force resulting from "intermolecular vibrations of ether," Keely in 1874 had built a machine that was supposedly powered by no other source, and invited the public to invest in the Keely Motor Company. He did not succeed in fooling all the people all the time, but he fooled some for decades. At the beginning of Keely's rise to fame, Edison had been intrigued and had visited Keely's workshop to ask some preliminary questions, intending to return with Batchelor for a round-the-clock vigil to watch the Keely engine in action. But when Keely balked at providing more information, Edison canceled his plans. "The one thing necessary for me to know," Edison later told a companion on a train ride in 1878 without saying what that one necessary thing was, "he refused to impart, and without this information I might as well look at a pile of broken machinery as at the motor." (After Keely's death in 1898, his workshop was examined closely—and the discovery of hidden tubes for conveying compressed air brought a posthumous end to Keely's dogged claims.)

Not so long before his visit to Keely, Edison had himself been at the center of a heated scientific controversy when he had made claims about the ether, too. The first time he had drawn attention to himself outside of the world of telegraphy had not been in 1877, with the phonograph's invention, but two years earlier, when he had publicly announced, overly hastily, that he had made a fundamental discovery in physics of the "etheric force." Having noticed sparks flying between parts of his telegraphic apparatus that were not conducting currents,

Edison carried out investigations that appeared to rule out scientific explanations based on conventional knowledge of electricity. He did not think he was on the threshold of a perpetual-motion machine, but he did think the etheric force could revolutionize telegraphy, making possible transmissions through uninsulated wire, whether on land or through sea. For a brief moment, Edison's claims were treated in some scientific quarters respectfully, even in the *Scientific American*. Refutation and ridicule followed. Edison was defensive, but was also embarrassed and chastened; he would never again make as large a claim of discovery in science again. (Years later, however, scientists came to realize that Edison had stumbled across high-frequency electromagnetic waves—the basis for radio, and ultimately an ironical coda for the inventor who would live long enough to personally witness the radio boom of the 1920s yet stubbornly dismiss its commercial future.)

Edison's unhappy experience in 1875 when he had announced the discovery of the etheric force prematurely drained his interest in taking an active role of self-promoter. But in early 1878 he was amenable to playing the passive role of principal subject in newspaper profiles, and Menlo Park was perfectly placed for this purpose. It was sparsely populated, as if it were a world removed from New York City, yet it was also conveniently located a short train ride away. It sat close enough to the city to be regarded proprietarily by New York–based reporters as their own. Had it been located, say, between Philadelphia and Washington, D.C., Edison's lab would not have received visits by representatives of the New York press, and without them, the story of Edison's lab would have remained one of merely local interest.

Amos Cummings jumped ahead of his rival reporters and put himself into the Menlo Park story he reported. He described in detail his arrival at the laboratory and initial impressions, including the setting itself as a member of the dramatis personae. The laboratory was depicted with imagery anticipating Henry Adams's later twin images of the Virgin and the Dynamo: the long wooden structure was likened to "an old-fashioned Baptist tabernacle," but on its roof were nine lightning rods, and on its side were the twelve telegraph lines.

Cummings walked in the front door and found himself stepping into an office, in which an unidentified man was studying a drawing. Having asked for Edison, he was told, "Go right upstairs, and you'll find him singing into some instrument." The rarity of a visitor such as Cummings is underlined by Edison's availability, uninsulated by a personal secretary or other gatekeeper. Up the stairs, and there "Prof. Edison" was, seated at a table. Grimy hands, uncombed hair, dirty shirt, muddy shoes, "he looked like anything but a professor," Cummings would write, forgetting that his subject was not, in fact, a professor. Edison was also described as utterly lacking pretentiousness. "A man of common sense would feel at home with him in a minute," Cummings reported, "but a nob or prig would be sadly out of place." This motif—the genius who spoke plainly—proved so irresistible that it became the one used in almost every profile of Edison for the rest of his life.

Edison had virtually no prior experience with a reporter who was about to make him the subject of a long profile, but he was naturally adept at steering the conversation in the direction he wished, which was to describe the future commercial possibilities of the phonograph. Even though he was privately focused on its use as a dictation machine in the office, he sensed that the general readership of a newspaper would be interested in other applications. The arias of opera soprano Adelina Patti could be recorded, Edison suggested, and enjoyed in the parlors anywhere, selling "millions." He lamented the lost opportunity to record the last benediction of just-deceased Pope Pius IX; the recording could have been easily duplicated for every Roman Catholic in the world. A great public service, and a great business opportunity, too. He did the arithmetic: at $5 each, "there was a fortune in it."

The more he talked, the more he looked out to the future. He was prescient in some cases: audiobooks ("Say I hire a good elocutionist to read *David Copperfield*"); Nixon's Oval Office recordings ("I could fix a machine in a wall. . . . Political secrets . . . might be brought to light"); movies with sound ("The pictures and gestures of the orator, as well his voice, could be exactly reproduced, and the eyes and ears of the audience charmed by the voice and manner of the speaker"). Edison also thought parents would hide recorders so that they could in the comfort of their own bed listen to "all the spooney courtship of their daughters and lovers."

Edison's talking foghorn, the aerophone, which conveniently remained unfinished, provided still more incredible possibilities. He suggested installing one inside the mouth of "the Goddess of Liberty that the Frenchmen are going to put upon Bedloe's Island that would make her talk so loud that she could be heard by every soul on Manhattan Island."

Cummings meekly took it all in, unquestioningly, and was so eager to depict Edison as a genius that he reported as fact details that were empirical impossibilities. In front of Cummings, Edison recorded his favorite ditty for a phonograph demonstration, "Mary Had a Little Lamb," played it normally, and then reversed the cylinder, which Cummings claimed then yielded the words in reverse order and distinctly: "Lamb little a had Mary."

When Cummings, the polite guest, asked Edison how he had discovered the phonograph, Edison concocted a great drama in the wrong place, not when he and his assistants had first tried to record on a strip of paper, but later, when he directed his chief machinist to build the first cylinder model, the successful testing of which was noted in the lab books with scarcely a yawn. Edison told the reporter that his lab mates "laughed at me" when he proposed making the cylinder, and bets involving cigars and cash showed that his belief in success was matched by his associates' skepticism that it would work in the first trial, which it did.

With Cummings faithfully recording his every utterance, Edison showed an impish side, recording serious verse, and then overlaying upon it jeers and gibes ("Oh, cork yourself!"). He saved the best part of the demonstration for the end, when he recorded "Mad dog!" a half dozen times "and then amused himself by turning the crank backward." Cummings does not spell out the profane result, but it was not, as he claimed to have heard before, the original words merely reversed.

Cummings headed for the train, leaving his readers with a final charming image of Edison, returning to work on his phonograph "like a delighted boy." The reporter had obtained materials for a flattering portrait; the inventor had lost only a few hours of work time. But when Cummings's story appeared in the *New York Sun*, the seemingly intimate portrait of the "genius" in his laboratory created a sensation, setting off a mad rush of reporters to Menlo Park to write their own profiles of the inventor in his lab. And with the reporters came others who wanted to see "the Professor" for themselves. "I find I cannot get away," Edison wrote one of his attorneys, complaining only semiseriously. "Every day a dozen of the heavy lights of literature and science come here."

The Edison stories served to whet readers' appetites for still more. The result was that Menlo Park became a place known far and wide around the world, and so closely was the place name associated with Edison's laboratory that it entered the nation's consciousness and stayed, even though Edison himself would live and work there only three more years, and would spend more than four decades at another location in New Jersey.

The more that Edison spoke with reporters about his ideas and plans, the more giddy he became. He was untroubled by doubt that he might lack the time and resources to accomplish all of the side projects that he mentioned, seriously or casually. Readers learned that he not only had invented a new painkiller cocktail, but also had invented a hearing aid for his own use. His "telephonoscope" was supposedly inconspicuous, yet enabled Edison to hear " a cow chew a quarter of a mile off." When letters came pouring in, imploring him to commercialize the invention, he announced that he had assigned two of his assistants to work on tests, and was confident he would have a hearing aid on the market within months.

His aerophone remained incomplete. But when Vanity Fair Tobacco and Cigarettes wrote "Prof. Edison, Menlo Park," asking if he could adapt his "airaphone" to proclaim "Smoke Vanity Fair," Edison wrote back that he could, though it would take him a while to "perfect" it. The aerophone made for wonderful copy, but reporters found it impossible to see it for themselves. "I am very sorry," Edison apologized to a *New York World* reporter in March 1878, "that I cannot show you the aerophone today. I have just sent the application for a patent to Washington, and have taken the machine I had here to pieces." The reporter said this was a "great disappointment," but Edison, "one of the most courteous gentlemen in the world," covered for the machine's absence with a detailed explanation of its supposed capabilities.

The aerophone and the telephonoscope could not materialize because Edison was woefully understaffed. Even though he conveyed to reporters the impression that his laboratory was home to a staff too large to name, in fact it was small. In early March, he hired a few more hands, but that gave him a total of ten or twelve assistants, eight of whom were working on the phonograph, and the others on the telephone. At the same time that Edison was working on a new version of the phonograph that employed a disc rather than foil wrapped around a cylinder, he was also serving as host to increasing numbers of reporters and visitors, performing the same parlor games, answering the same repetitive questions. In the transition from unknown to iconic figure, Edison still felt free to say whatever he wished, so one entertainment he concocted was a variation of the one in which he had heckled himself in an overlay after first recording a serious reading. In the new version, he mimicked a sermon, in a mock-solemn drawl: "Ladies and gentlemen, I have come—before you this evening—to deliver for your—benefit—a discourse on travels—in Bible lands. Allow—me before commencing—to sta-a-ate—" Then he stopped, returned the stylus to the beginning, and recorded a running commentary: "Oh, give us a rest! Oh dry up! Sit down! Put him out! Hire a hall! Oh, that'll do! Bah!"

When the *Sun*'s Amos Cummings had visited the Menlo Park laboratory in February, he was the only outsider on the premises. When his competitors followed him, however, they bumped into one another. Edison complained that "the reporters that come down here have already [so] unstrung my nerves that I think of taking to the woods," but this seems more a handy pretext rather than genuine complaint. He stayed where he was and left the door to his lab wide open. No one had to tell him that the feature stories were the best kind of advertising possible: disseminated for free.

If anything, the advertising was too effective, creating demand for the phonograph that caught the Edison Speaking Phonograph Company by surprise. Phonograph Company investor Charles Cheever wrote another board member in mid-March that "the tide has started itself so fast that I have been unable in spite of all that I can do to hold it back until we had the small Phonograph ready to sell." Cheever had helped whip up the public's interest by holding public exhibitions in New York City, packing in three hundred people each afternoon, and drawing in the influential figures who were concentrated in Manhattan. William Cullen Bryant was so tickled he asked to come again with friends. An Astor, whose interest was piqued by Bryant, would not deign to rub shoulders with hoi polloi in the public exhibition, but she did ask for a private exhibition for herself and forty friends.

Having received so much attention, gratis, the phonograph seemed poised for a sensational commercial launch. Gardiner Hubbard, the father-in-law of Alexander Graham Bell and another backer of the Phonograph Company, was so confident that demand would outstrip supply that he developed a plan for maximal exploitation of the imagined shortage. Why not announce that sales agents must place their orders—and pay in full—in advance? Figuring that each unit would only cost $15 to manufacture and would sell for $100, Hubbard gleefully rubbed his hands together, calculating paper profits. "We incur no risk," he wrote a fellow investor.

This proposal ran into opposition. Cheever was more concerned that early customers remain happy customers, and wondered aloud whether it would be better to lease the first small phonographs, once they were ready for release, rather than selling them. He knew that the shortcomings of the first-generation models would be a public embarrassment to the company as soon as the next-generation machine was released. Customers would naturally want "the most perfect one going and not a crude model." If the company put all the machines out on lease, then it could "call them in and smash them up." This praiseworthy idea disappeared.

The principals of the Edison Speaking Phonograph Company debated various business models, and counted in advance the coming profits, without asking Edison's opinion. They encouraged Edison to hasten his work on finishing the two phonograph models, and excluded him from their discussions about the business. Edison had opinions about everything, however, including marketing. When asked by reporters, he doggedly insisted that the phonograph be purchased by executives for dictating letters, which would be transcribed and dispatched by lesser-paid office boys. "They can thus save hundreds of dollars a year," Edison asserted, without explaining how exactly the savings would be captured by executives who were paid a flat salary, not by the number of letters sent out per day.

Editorialists and feature writers were not much interested in technical details; they credulously reported Edison's claim that he could record forty thousand words on a single disc when, in fact, he was nowhere close to being able to do so. They were more interested in projecting a heroic image of the inventor, "the Napolean of invention," as the *New York Sun* dubbed him. Convention demanded that he be given a tender, domestic side, too. A visiting reporter read much in Edison's pat on the head of "a bright little three-year-old boy who called him 'papa' with a genuine affection that showed, though the most remarkable inventor of the age, he is by no means dead to the less exciting episodes and battles of a domestic world."

Much was said about the phonograph as a source of humor, running along the lines that had been established from the beginning: It would be the bane of philandering husbands (surreptitiously recording, for example, "Hurry up, Betty, and give me a kiss before the old hen comes down") and a boon to sharp-tongued mothers-in-law. The *Washington Herald* described the phonograph (on 1 April 1878) as the "outside agent of the divorce courts" and urged the passing of a law "making it a capital offense to manufacture or sell this species of deadly weapon." Edison, too, was the subject of humorous editorials, vilifying him for inventing too many things. The *New York Times* said with a rather macabre sense of humor that "something ought to be done to Mr. Edison, and there is a growing conviction that it had better be done with a hemp rope."

The jokes and spoofs were entertaining, but the reader was susceptible to being confused, too. The phonograph, described in close detail in the *Sun*'s long profile "A Marvelous Discovery," which had started the stampede to Menlo Park, was regarded by many as fantastic. Edison received three hundred letters that denounced the reporter's mendacity. One professor urged Edison to protect his reputation and publicly disavow the claims that had been made in the article. "The idea of a talking machine is ridiculous, but the article is so ingeniously constructed, and some persons are so ignorant of the first principles of science, that they will be apt to believe it true, unless you deny it."

Truth appeared to be spoof; and spoof, truth. The *New York Daily Graphic*'s William Croffut wrote of a lunch that Edison had served him on a recent visit to Menlo Park, at the conclusion of which Edison explained that he made all of the food "out of the dirt taken from the cellar." In an almost plausible fashion, Edison provides a description of how he had found a way to speed up organic processes by inorganic means. Croffut was amazed: "This food machine is going to dispense almost entirely with farmers and stock-raisers, with millers and bakers—why it seems to me you are going to abolish all occupations except the manufacture of your machines." Oh, no, Edison replies, laughing. But he did modestly allow that it would "certainly revolutionize the world."

The publication date of 1 April for "A Food Creator" should have served to put readers on alert. And the final paragraph, in which the narrator is awakened by a train conductor, groggily realizing that he had been napping and was only then arriving at Menlo Park, clearly showed that the preceding story had been a parody of the boilerplate Edison profile. But just as some listeners failed to hear disclaimers that were interspersed in Orson Welles's 1938 broadcast of *The War of the Worlds*, so, too, some readers, and some newspapers, failed in 1878 to appreciate Croffut's nicely crafted spoof. Though the hoax was clearly revealed at the end, the *New York Daily Graphic* pointed out afterward, "a good many, with the careless American habit of hasty reading, seemed to have stopped short of that revelation."

Edison was tickled. He told Croffut the article was the "most ingenious hoax I have ever seen." Following its appearance, he received letters asking for the price of the food machine and the date when it would be ready for the market. While testing the telephone the next day, he playfully acted out his role in the parody in the presence of another visiting reporter, asking Charles Batchelor, "By the way, don't you want half a dozen of my latest? Invented since you left this morning. It changes fire clay into rice pudding and corn meal into gold dust. Warranted for nine hundred and ninety-nine years."

Ten days after his spoof appeared, Croffut published a serious profile of Edison that differed from the *New York Sun*'s only in its ingenuity in finding new ways to extol Edison's genius. It was Croffut who coined the new nickname "the Wizard of Menlo Park" (an improvement on Croffut's previous attempt at coining a new name for Edison: "the Jersey Columbus").

In Chicago, George Bliss, the head of the electric pen company, ribbed Edison that "the Mania has broken out this way—School-girls write compositions on Edison. The funny papers publish squibs on Edison. The religious papers write editorials on Edison. The daily papers write up his life . . . Why don't the Graphic fill up exclusively with Edison and [have] done with [it]." Croffut had similar news: "Every paper I take up is full of you—not less than 190,547 columns in American newspapers every day."

For Edison, these reports were entertaining, but they did not affect his life in any noticeable way. The only immediate change was the new need to devote time responding to correspondence from strangers. Referring to what he called "Begging letters," Edison wrote Uriah Painter, one of the phonograph company investors, "My god how they little suspect—" and left the thought unfinished; it was probably something like "—I have yet to secure my own financial security." In a recent profile, he had patted the phonograph in his lab, saying it was his "baby," and he expected that it would "grow up to be a big feller and support me in my old age." In the present, it still was an infant and was the one being supported.

Edison had no idea how greedily the public grabs for a piece of a person who has become famous—he thought he could personally respond to every stranger who wrote him for an autograph or for money. This quickly proved impractical. Six days after the publication of "The Wizard of Menlo Park," he told Painter he had written fifty-two letters that night and had sent twenty-three more to Edward Johnson to handle.

A "Begging letter" might begin with mention of some personal connection. Mrs. Andrew Coburn, for example, wrote Edison on behalf of her husband, who had worked for him ("you will remember") in his Newark shop. "I am entirely beaten down," she wrote, as she described her husband's confinement to bed with a fractured elbow that had become infected and now required amputation. Could he assist them? He sent her a check for $5.

But this was not the conclusion of the episode. A few weeks later, Mrs. Coburn was back with a request for $50 as a loan to start a sock-and-leggings business. Then Mr. Coburn dictated a follow-up letter, and separately the surgeon wrote asking for payment for the amputation. Mrs. Coburn followed the next month with a renewed plea for assistance.

Not all the begging was done by the less powerful. Edison received a plea for financial assistance from an official in a position of power over his professional future: Zenas Wilber, who was the Patent Office's chief examiner of electrical apparatus. He said he had to borrow $200 or $250 "immediately" and "confidentially." It placed Edison in a difficult position. He had Batchelor send Wilber $200 under a name and address that could not be traced back to Menlo Park.

Wilber would do Edison a favor weeks later when Edison made a rare foray outside of his laboratory and arrived in Washington, D.C., on 18 April for a two-day visit. He had accepted an invitation from Professor George Barker, of the University of Pennsylvania, to demonstrate the phonograph at the National Academy of Sciences meeting. Before the meeting, a reporter with a local paper happened to see Edison standing alone outside of the Smithsonian, looking around intently, apparently studying the rich foliage and taking in a beautiful blue sky. The reporter approached and, as a conversation starter, ventured, "Handsome grounds, these." "Yes," Edison agreed, then pointed to what he had been studying so closely: "What an immense stretch of telegraph wire without a support."

The phonograph demonstration was set up in the office of the academy's secretary, a place that did not accommodate all who wished to witness the performance. The double doors in the adjoining hall were removed so more people could crowd in for a peek. Edison sat at the secretary's desk, nervously twisting a rubber band, while Charles Batchelor recorded and played back the ditties and sounds that had become a routine. In the reception following, Edison was described as "shy and shrinking, and did not show off at all ornamentally." He confessed to a reporter that he did not like to be pressed by crowds, and he had not enjoyed the academy president's welcome because he had not been able to hear a word that was said.

Having come to town, there was no respite from the press of the curious. The demonstrations continued all day and into the evening, and continued later in the Washington office of the *Philadelphia Inquirer*. Finally, Edison was set free and joined academy members at the U.S. Naval Observatory for a look at the stars. It had been a long day, and was not yet over. It was only then that Zenas Wilber came up with a brilliant idea: President Rutherford Hayes should not miss out on hearing the phonograph for himself, and should get a demonstration before morning arrived. Calling up the White House was easily accomplished: Hayes liked to answer the phone himself (there were only a few dozen telephones in the entire capital at the time). Nor did Wilber, the patent examiner, have difficulty speaking with Hayes, the president: they were cousins. A command performance by Edison was quickly arranged, and he headed to the White House, arriving around eleven o'clock that night. He showed off the phonograph for the president for about an hour and a half. His country asked still more of him: the First Lady and several of her friends wanted a demonstration, too, so Edison had to run through the routine still one more time, finishing about 2:30 A.M.

The second day brought more attention. Edison, Batchelor, and the phonograph were installed in the office of the Senate's committee on patents, then the House's committee, attracting drop-in visits from members and leaving Congress without a quorum for nearly an hour. After Edison's return home, the press added new expressions to the lexicon of hagiography. Having been honored by the most distinguished men in the country, the *New York Sun* reasoned, Edison had received more attention than if Robert Fulton, Sir Isaac Newton, or Galileo had appeared. Beneath Edison's unassuming appearance, a reporter for another paper sensed something else hiding beneath his hat: "a kingly crown."

CHAPTER THREE

FLIGHT

MAY–AUGUST 1878

T HE PHONOGRAPH GAVE EDISON an opportunity in mid-1878 that would never reappear in his eighty-four-year-long life. With no other invention did he have as open a field without competition; he was perfectly positioned to move forward. He had become renowned. Financial backers were standing at the ready, impatiently waiting for the machine to be "perfected" and made ready for sale, and were willing to accept a small, toylike placeholder in the meantime. He had at his disposal his own development lab and complete machine shop, with a staff that took orders from no one but himself. He had all the materials that he conceivably might need at his fingertips. But just then, when the whole world seemed to be focused on him and his mechanical marvel, Edison simply could not muster the focus to complete its development. The moment passed before he realized it, and it would be ten years before he would return to work on what he called affectionately his "baby."

In retrospect, the late spring and summer of 1878 is a time easily overlooked because it is of interest for what did *not* happen. Put simply, Edison failed to read the market. Without question, he was distracted by the attention that came with celebrity. Some of his admirers sought to protect him from distraction and worry. He was publicly hailed in a letter to the editor of a Washington paper as a member of a class of "martyrs, being devoid of acquisitiveness" and ill-suited to "competing in the scramble for material wealth." The writer urged the federal government to provide Edison with the material rewards he could not earn himself, to save him from the fate of an Eli Whitney, "begging for bread," or a Charles Goodyear, dying in a poorhouse. Edison himself, however, never indicated he gave thought to, let alone desired, subsidy, nor did he see his work as a noble enterprise in service to humanity. Typical was his remark to an associate about Edward Johnson's traveling phonograph show: "I told him what he should go for [is] dollars & cents for the Phono Co as they wasn't after glory but the [money] of an admiring public."

Edison's own point of view was unabashedly commercial, but by temperament, he tended to flit from project to project. Most were minor in ambition and were left in an incomplete state. This had been his pattern when he was working in the field of telegraphic equipment, and the phonograph's own serendipitous invention came from a tangential observation that had led away from the original project. He did not impose upon himself limits to his inventive excursions. He would strike off from the main path, follow an interest, then branch off from that path, and then from that one, too. With the work on the main phonograph still incomplete, and with even the placeholder toys failing to work (the Edison Speaking Phonograph Company's Gardiner Hubbard lamented, "We shall not sell any of them"), Edison decided to renew experimental work on a commercial hearing aid. He had not actually built a working model of a "lap megaphone," but he was confident that he would be able to pick up a $10,000 prize offered by Joseph Medill, the editor of the *Chicago Tribune,* for the hearing aid that would best ameliorate Medill's deafness (Edison never sustained interest in ameliorating his own). That project was itself pushed aside, still incomplete, while Edison chased the invention of a microphone that he thought would serve as a successor to the stethoscope. Nothing came of either diversion.

The Edison Speaking Phonograph Company was a venture separate from Edison's own Menlo Park lab, which meant Edison could not be ejected. The Company's investors could, and did, beg and implore Edison to push on with his work on the phonograph, but they could not force him to heed their wishes or anyone else's.

Edison arranged his business affairs so that he could maintain complete independence, which required that those closest to him should not have strong opinions of their own. The composition of his inner circle of subordinates may not have been important in any case, as the best advice available to him outside of the lab was mediocre, too. Uriah Painter, one of the Speaking Phonograph Company's investors, led Edison to believe at the beginning of May that phonograph exhibitions would be wildly profitable. "*Your* receipts will be *immense,*" Painter wrote, double underlined for emphasis, as he made plans to hold a thousand public exhibitions of the phonograph within the next ninety days. Edward Johnson, however, who was the first one out in the field actually holding exhibitions, was finding the profits uneven and was tortured by the thought that he was so close, yet so far, from touching the "money floating all about just baskets full of it thrown into ones face." It would turn out that even though eighty men had paid the company $100 each for the privilege of undergoing training and heading out in the exhibition business for themselves, their efforts would result in total royalty payments to Edison of $1,031.91.

Imagining fabulous profits to be earned even from merely hawking Edison's portrait, Painter offered Mathew Brady exclusive rights to Edison's portrait, in exchange for a royalty of 25 percent. Painter had to persuade Edison to sign off on the arrangement and stop by Brady's Washington studio during his visit to the city. He assured Edison that 100,000 prints could be sold in the upcoming summer, pointing out that P. T. Barnum had sold 150,000 Brady prints of Tom Thumb. The best portrait that came out of the sitting shows Edison dressed in a dark, dignified suit, seated by a table upon which sits the phonograph, a metallic contraption that resembled a lathe. The inventor peers at the camera with no expression. Lacking anything that is visually striking, the photograph needed someone like Barnum to push its sales. But no one at the Edison Speaking Phonograph Company was much interested in this sideline, and even Painter, who was offered the opportunity to sell the prints, seems to have lost interest, too.

Edison could have used Barnum's talents to exploit the crowds drawn to Menlo Park, too. An increase in visits to the lab by tourists and self-invited, self-designated VIPs suggested Edison's celebrity was growing. Work at the lab could not proceed smoothly, however, when interrupted by the arrival of groups of outsiders in quest of entertainment. On a not atypical day, a group of thirty businesspeople, inhibitions loosened by a "bucket of punch" they had brought along, took possession of the laboratory, leaving Edison no recourse but to disappear, wondering what he was going to do when a party of one hundred more visitors, on their way down from Boston, arrived. Editorial writers began to notice and speak out on his behalf. A Newark paper sensibly suggested that he limit visitors' access to the lab—"the electrical Mecca"—to just one day a week. Another paper suggested that a separate building—"a theater or entertainment hall"—be built on the laboratory's grounds for accommodating visitors and sparing Edison the indignity and waste of his own time when he had to spend "hours each day shouting and singing into a phonograph for the amusement of a crowd of unscientific people."

Edison had not plotted a course to obtain attention; the attention had come to him. True, when it arrived, he had swung the door open to receive it. The problem, he was now discovering, was that once open, it could not be shut, even if he sincerely wanted to do so, and he was ambivalent in any case.

Edison was cooperative, for example, when William Croffut asked him for a letter praising his paper, the *Daily Graphic,* suitable for publication. The letter from Edison that was subsequently published was not typeset but reproduced photographically, keeping intact Edison's best calligraphy. "Dear Sir, I feel inclined to thank you for the pleasant things you have said about me and the Phonograph," the letter read, going on to single out Croffut's April Fool's Day hoax for special praise. It appeared to be a sincere testimonial, written by a new celebrity who also was able to work in mention of coming improvements to his phonograph that "will soon justify all the hopes of its friends." What the letter did not disclose was that Edison had agreed to Croffut's request, but only on condition that Croffut write the letter that would appear in Edison's name. Croffut had sent his draft with polite noises ("bless you! don't follow a word if it seems not quite the thing"), and Edison had recopied it in his own hand without a single modification.

Croffut, on his part, acted less as a reporter than as Edison's unofficial amanuensis, recording whatever Edison claimed without independently sorting through Edison's pronouncements to distinguish truth from wishful thinking. An example of Croffut's apparent gullibility: While giving Croffut a tour of the lab, Edison had told the story of a dog that had wandered up to the lab's door and whose bark was then recorded. "We have hung up that sheet yonder," Edison said, "and now we can make him bark any time." Not true. Edison could not make the dog bark again, and he knew it, because once the foil was removed from the cylinder, it could not be reinstalled on the cylinder in playable form. This problem rendered the tinfoil phonograph virtually useless, except for the limited purpose for which it was being used, that is, as a machine permanently in demonstration mode. Croffut was silent, either because he was completely credulous, or perhaps because he knew of this problem but calculated his own career was best served by preserving the mythic image he was working so hard to create.

When Edison had been an unknown inventor who specialized in the telegraphic equipment business, reporters had not sought him out and begged him for an opportunity to become his friend. Now, however, in early May 1878, sycophantic journalists led him to believe that he was wise in all manner of subjects, far afield of the electrical business. If they wished to listen to his opinions, and they did indeed, he was glad to hold forth on any topic, such as the relationship of diet to national destiny, a lecture delivered over lunch while digging into strawberry shortcake, strawberries and cream, and an apple dumpling.

> I have a theory of eating. Variety—that is the secret of wise eating. The Nations that eat the most kinds of food are the greatest Nations. . . . The rice-eating Nations never progress; they never think or act anything but rice, rice, rice, forever. Look at the potato and black-bread eaters of Ireland; though naturally bright,

the Irish in Ireland are enervated by the uniformity of their food. . . . On the other hand, what is, take it all in all, the most highly enlightened Nation, the most thrifty, graceful, cultured and accomplished? Why, France, of course, where the cuisine has infinite variety. When the Roman Empire was at its height the table was a marvel of diversity—they fed on nightingales' tongues, and all sorts of dainty dishes. . . . Some say I get the cart before the horse, and that the diversified food is the result of a high civilization rather than its cause, but I think I am right about it.

This was a role, pontificating on demand, that was quite agreeable to him. As the years passed, it came to supplant the actual work of inventing. His thinking about an ideal diet for himself would change radically, however. In 1878, he said he wanted to live up to his own theory about the salutary benefits of variety and "live so that I could change my diet a thousand times a year." This gave way in his later years to ever more restrictive diets, each change publicly chronicled as no alimentary detail was too private for the reporters who would always attend to him, from when he was thirty-one until he died at the age of eighty-four.

Following his sensational April visit to Washington, D.C., he was deluged with invitations to make personal appearances for sundry groups and occasions. He told a visiting reporter that he had no interest at all in making such appearances. ("You shouldn't have become famous, if you didn't want to be talked about and bored by strangers," the reporter replied.) Edison turned down the invitations across the board, but he made two exceptions when he was still glowing from the warm reception received in Washington. The unsatisfying results in both cases served to show him that the role of traveling celebrity was not to his liking.

In May, he accepted an invitation to speak at the Academy of Mount Saint Vincent, a Catholic girls' school on the Hudson River, as a favor to an old telegrapher friend. His hearing disability loomed as a larger issue when he was on the road. His hosts did not know how best to overcome its isolative effects (and Edison had yet to finish that "lap megaphone" he had been talking up with the press). When he was taken to the chapel during Mass, he strained to hear the celebrants' words. (When the priest touched his arm to let him know it was time to go, Edison misinterpreted the gesture, thinking it was a rebuke for not showing proper reverence, and stooped down almost to his knees, remaining with bowed head. No one knew how to clear up the misunderstanding with the service still in progress.) Before Batchelor began the phonograph exhibition conducted before the students, Edison took a seat on the platform, "instantly becoming absorbed with some train of thought," and apparently heard little or nothing of the school's welcome. For him, the highlight of the day appears to have been at the end when he and Batchelor, after saying their good-byes, raced each other down the hill, oblivious to the rain and the propriety expected of the eminent inventor and his assistant.

A few weeks later, Edison was lured out of the lab one more time, for an invitation-only appearance at a reception held after a public exhibition of the phonograph in New York City. He was introduced by Hilbourne Roosevelt—organ builder, investor in the Edison Speaking Phonograph Company, and first cousin of Theodore—who said he "had almost been obliged to use force to drag the inventor from his work." The occasion was what a political campaigner today would call a meet and greet, and only the professional pol could be expected to have the stomach for it. At midnight, Edison excused himself, explaining he had to "get home and work."

As for family matters, hagiographers did not hesitate to see Mr. and Mrs. Edison as a perfect couple. One journalist described Mary as "a charming woman, and is evidently the counterpart of himself, and one would know, the moment he put his eyes on both, that they were exactly suited to one another." This scene, painted by a stranger with a ripe imagination, was based on nothing at all. Edison's almost total withdrawal from the family's domestic sphere was the leitmotif that would be the one Edison and his assistants chose for Edison's life narrative: the tireless inventor. Edward Johnson pretended to confide to a reporter that Edison's "only bad habit" was work, so consuming that it constituted "a dissipation." For the last ten years, Johnson said in 1878, Edison had averaged eighteen hours a day at his desk. So immersed in work's demands, he "does not go home for days, either to eat or sleep," even though his house was only a few steps away. On another occasion, a reporter observed that when his five-year-old daughter Marion came to the lab to fetch him for dinner, Edison had told her he would "be along in a minute"—and then had become engrossed in something else in the lab. "That's nothing," Batchelor had explained when the reporter commented on Edison's susceptibility to distraction. "When we get interested in a thing here we stay all day and all night sometimes, and Edison hardly stops to eat even if they send his meals to him." What Mary Edison thought of her husband's absences was not recorded. She was only rarely included in the standard newspaper profile, and even then, merely as the ornament.

Whether it was for a banquet in the city or supper at home, it was difficult to extract Edison from the lab. As the months passed following the phonograph's first public exhibitions in early 1878 and he failed to produce a production model, Edison remained maddeningly blasé. He puttered and procrastinated, his attention flitting from one side project to the next.

The "telescopophon" was one of the distractions that held his attention, but not long enough, it would turn out, for it to ever reach commercial release. This was a giant megaphone that performed marvelously when used as a pair, one for speaking, the other for listening, placed a mile apart on hilltops. Reporters were invited to try it themselves—one claimed he could hear a voice that was two miles away and out of sight—an entertainment so diverting that no one bothered to ask Edison details of how he was going to miniaturize it to make good on his claim that this nonelectrical mechanical device would enable the partially deaf to "hear every whisper on the stage of the largest theater," yet be so small that it could be used "without your next neighbor knowing that you have one."

Any sense of urgency was blunted by pleasing news arriving from Paris, where the phonograph's exhibition was drawing large crowds. Theodore Puskas, Edison's business agent in Europe, had had to overcome the skepticism of the French Academy of Sciences, to whom he had first presented the machine. The scientists thought the machine's playback was a ventriloquist trick and insisted that Puskas leave the room while they listened again and were finally convinced.

Puskas secured a coveted place for a machine at the Paris Universal Exhibition. He cunningly chose to leave the machine inert and silent, without giving visitors the opportunity to hear it. At the same time, he leased a private hall on the Boulevard des Capucines, where he charged an admission price for phonograph demonstrations that ran three times a day, bringing in $200 daily. Edison called this "the sharpest kind of an advertising dodge," which was high praise. Edison attributed Puskas's inspired arrangements to ideas Puskas had picked up while in the United States.

One of Edison's associates on the ground in Paris wrote Charles Batchelor that the phonograph drew crowds that were overly enthusiastic and difficult to dislodge. A dispatch from Paris reported, "So we can only show it once and cover [the machine] up until the crowd gets away so as to give some one else a chance."

In the newspapers, Edison's own name had become so familiar to readers that humorists could invoke it without having to provide any background. Typical was this brief item that appeared in several newspapers in June: "Edison has not invented anything since breakfast. The doctor has been called." In Menlo Park, Edison could read these items and smile; they were harmless. But by July, he had passed through the exhilarating novelty of being well known; now he was weighed down by an accumulation of irritations. The stream of letters from strangers was holding steady at about seventy-five or eighty a day, coming from people whom Edison described as "the deaf, dumb, halt, blind, lame and all sorts of people." This one, with failing eyesight, wanted Edison to invent a "blindoscope." That one, a phonograph for advertising purposes, even though the machines were not being mass produced. Many wanted only one thing: cash.

His correspondents included new acquaintances who held positions of power, and they too made requests of him. An example: John Vincent, the cofounder of the Chautauqua program based by Chautauqua Lake, New York, which offered summer programs for families that combined religious and secular education, invited Edison and his family to participate. Edison agreed, making plans to stay three weeks in August and offer a demonstration of what Vincent poetically described as "all the marvels of electricity which you can evoke and exhibit."

Vincent undoubtedly had no idea what a coup he had scored, obtaining atheistic Edison's assent to being cooped up for weeks in a family-oriented church camp far from his lab. Vincent pressed on. He had a brother, who had a friend, who would like to rent a phonograph—that is, the machine that had yet to enter production. Could Edison oblige? And another thing. Vincent suggested—no, he *instructed*—Edison to change the name from "phonograph" to "tautophone." When Edison politely replied that he thought that "phonograph" was known so widely that it was probably too late to change, Vincent was unmoved. He informed Edison he was going to write an article about the machine, calling it by what he regarded to be its proper name, and expressed the hope that Edison would correct his patent records accordingly.

Edison's family plans for Chautauqua in August had been arranged early in the year, when August was distant; then, the correspondence with the insufferable Vincent followed. By July, Chautauqua in August was looming. William Croffut was also proving rather pushy, inviting himself and his wife for an overnight visit at Edison's house. At the lab, Edison continued to flit from one workbench to another. The work, such as it was, continued to be interrupted by uninvited visitors and their expectations that he follow his self-assigned role in the trained-seal-with-phonograph act. Painter urged Edison to close the lab's doors to visitors entirely and "only show your hand when you are ready for the market & then its [sic] too late for thieves to get your things." Edison had not yet been convinced that he had to abandon the open-door policy, and letters from Painter were a reminder that the principals in the Edison Speaking Phonograph Company were waiting impatiently for the machine that they could sell in volume. At home, Mary Edison was pregnant with their third child, due in October.

By all the evidence, Edison felt he was being crushed by demands on him, from strangers, reporters, associates, and family. He responded by acting on a threat he had made in jest a few months earlier of curing his "unstrung nerves" by "taking for the woods." He abruptly accepted the invitation of his biggest admirer in academe, Professor George Barker, to embark upon a one-month trip to the West. The official purpose of the trip was to observe a total solar eclipse on 29 July from the best vantage point, near Rawlins, Wyoming. The eclipse provided unimpeachable justification for why Edison had to embark right then, absenting himself from lab associates, business partners, and pregnant wife and forcing cancellation of the Chautauqua trip. At the Wyoming site he could test his new "tasimeter," a scientific instrument for measuring the temperature of the sun's corona that he had thought up while he was working hard on not working on the phonograph. It was Barker's inspired idea that on their way back they could stop in St. Louis and attend the annual meeting of the American Association for the Advancement of Science, where Edison would read a paper that Barker was ghostwriting for him. It was apparently Edison's idea, however, to extend the trip to California before turning around for St. Louis and the return.

Edison and Barker left on 13 July, and the timing of his escape was fortuitous, Edison being absent when, a week later, a new problem popped up back at the lab. *Scientific American*, which had taken the lead in introducing the world to the wonders of the phonograph, continued to do so. The journal told readers, "The Phonograph, truly wonderful as it is, is exceedingly simple and may be made at a slight expense." It published detailed instructions so that anyone could build a machine without waiting for Edison and the Edison Speaking Phonograph Company to finally make good on their promises to the public.

Flouting the phonograph's patents presented the Menlo Park lab with a crisis. In Edison's absence, it was left to Batchelor and Johnson to decide how to respond. Reflecting their different personalities, Batchelor's first reaction was to write Edison for instructions, and Johnson's, to prepare a take-no-prisoners counteroffensive. He prepared a circular warning of the patents that protected the invention and spelled out what would happen to anyone foolish enough to infringe.

> The manufacture, sale or use, of a patented article without the consent of the owner of the patent is an infringement, and subjects the infringer TO AN ARREST or prohibition from the employment of his machinery, shop, works, or men, in the production of the article. The infringer is also LIABLE TO BE MULCTED IN TREBLE THE AMOUNT OF DAMAGES AWARDED BY THE JURY, TOGETHER WITH THE SUM TOTAL OF THE COSTS. . . . Ignorance of the law or of what the patent covers cannot be pleaded in Court . . . the Company are [sic] satisfied that upon an examination of the law, anyone desirous of having a Phonograph will find it the cheapest to procure it in a *legitimate way.*

Johnson also protested to *Scientific American*'s editors, but the journal did not back down. "Investigators have rights as well as patentees," a long editorial explained, and among those rights was the one that permits making a patented article for one's own tests. Anticipating contemporary debates about an individual's right to make copies of copyrighted music or television programs for noncommercial purposes, the editorial argued that only if a self-assembled phonograph were offered for sale, depriving the patent holder of his "lawful reward," would the action be rightfully treated as illegal. With phrasing that could have been lifted from a blog, *Scientific American* in 1878 declared, "Unfortunately, the purchasers of patents are too apt to construe their rights so as to make them cover pretty much the entire universe."

Meanwhile, Edison had left the phonograph with the rest of his cares back in Menlo Park. He was determined to see all that could possibly be seen on his trip, and he secured the very best position to do so, obtaining permission to ride at the very front, on top of the locomotive's cow-catcher, with the help of a letter from Jay Gould, with whom he had developed a relationship years earlier when Gould had used his railroad interests to gain control of Western Union and Edison was the telegraphic equipment expert of the day. The train traveled at a top speed of twenty miles per hour. The only time he felt he was in danger was when the locomotive hit an animal—Edison thought it may have been a badger. Upon impact, the animal was thrown up against the locomotive, just below the headlight, but Edison at that moment was leaning on the side, hanging on to an angle brace, and suffered no harm.

Edison's party arrived well in advance of the eclipse, but after the solar event Edison took a dilatory four weeks to return home. What he enjoyed most talking about when the journey was complete was not the eclipse but his adventures as a white tourist in a West whose native inhabitants were in the process of being violently removed. A visitor to Wyoming in 1878 saw terrain similar to that Custer had seen only two years before at the Little Bighorn in Montana. After the eclipse, Edison, Barker, some railroad officials, a U.S. Army major, and some soldiers embarked on a hunting trip that took them one hundred miles south of the railroad into Ute country. A few months later, the same major and thirty soldiers were attacked and killed by Utes near the place Edison had camped, or such is the story Edison later told.

Edison had left behind *Daily Graphic* reporter William Croffut, but he had not shunned the company of reporters entirely. The *New York Herald*'s Edwin Fox was on hand for the eclipse, and became Edison's roommate and hunting companion. When the two men went off on short hunting trips as a twosome, locals spared Edison the worst pranks directed at tenderfeet from the East, though he was the butt of a mild ruse when he was fooled into taking some shots at a jackrabbit that happened to be near a remote rail depot. The rabbit didn't move; he advanced closer, and shot again, with the same result. When he got close enough to see that the rabbit was dead and had been stuffed, a crowd of onlookers did not hide their amusement. Fox, however, suffered more when a stationmaster loaned him his "fine Springfield musket" when Fox had run out of cartridges for his own rifle. Inexperienced, Fox failed to notice that the musket had been run over by a rail handcar and was ever-so-slightly bent. Upon firing, the recoil drove the gun against his shoulder with such force that he had to be treated at a hospital.

Edison did not fully appreciate the reach of the media and the diffusion of his own name until late one night, after he and Fox had gone to sleep in their hotel room in Rawlins. The two were awakened by a loud knock. In walked a man who introduced himself as "Texas Jack" and said he had read about Edison in the newspaper and wanted to meet him. The hotel proprietor appeared and attempted to intercede on behalf of his guests; Texas Jack tossed him into the hallway and resumed his self-introduction. He had just arrived in town from a hunting trip and boasted of his marksmanship. To illustrate, he pulled out his Colt, pointed it through the hotel window, and fired at a weather vane that sat on top of the town's freight depot. The shot hit its target and awakened the townspeople, adding to the commotion. Edison, pleading fatigue, tried to coax his new friend to leave, but he did not succeed until he promised he would see him in the morning.

These and other picturesque encounters provided abundant potential material for colorful letters if Edison had written home, but he and his wife did not correspond. Edison kept in touch with his assistants at the laboratory, but the only time he heard news about his pregnant wife was when his secretary, Stockton Griffin, wrote him on August 5 with a report that she was not well.

> Mrs. E's health is not of the best—She is extremely nervous and frets a great deal about you, and about everything—I take it to be nervous prostration—She was so frightened yesterday for fear the children would get on the track that she fainted—This morning I telegraphed Dr. Ward who came at noon. . . . She needs a change and right away, as the [train] cars keep her awake at night and this causes her to lose strength.

Neither Griffin nor the doctor urged Edison to cut his trip short; Griffin ended his letter with the reassurance that "there's nothing serious in this," and that is how Edison received it. It would be three more weeks before he arrived back in Menlo Park.

He and Barker had just finished a three-day visit to San Francisco; ahead was a tour of Yosemite; a visit to mines in Virginia City, Nevada; hunting and fishing in Wyoming; and then the appearance at the American Association for the Advancement of Science meeting in St. Louis. Barker formally presented Edison as a new AAAS member, with a soaring introduction that asserted theirs was a time when "the practical man has found science too slow, and has stepped in and discovered for himself." On that day, Edison was not only feted by the august body of scientists, he also received word that the Paris Exposition had awarded the grand prize to the phonograph.

A perceptive newspaper reporter noticed upon Edison's return to Menlo Park that blurring of boundary separating the private and the public that we now understand as accompanying the arrival of celebrity. "The people have come to regard him as public property, and were almost jealous of the little time he found to give his family," said the *New York Sun*. "Little knots of people came and went all day long, and took possession of him and his office and shop as if they had been personal property."

Nothing at all seemed to bother Edison, however. He was tanned, positively exuded health, and beamed when interviewed. His trip had been "bang-up": "It was bully. I never saw such a country in all my life. That's the place to go to. What with following trails, and tumbling down precipices, and riding over alkali deserts and keeping cool at 125 degrees in the shade, a person couldn't help enjoying himself." His freshly obtained imperturbability was put to the test by yet another stack of begging letters. But even when he read a letter from an inventor who claimed to have invented a "fluid resistance neutralizer" and a "gravimotor" and asked for $1,000 ("It shall be returned to you by God, through me, more than a thousand fold and that shortly. You will greatly oblige, for I have a family. Yours In Christ . . ."), he simply handed it to a reporter and said, meditatively, "There could be an awful good story made out of the letters I get."

During his first interview after his return, with the *New York World,* Edison, the raconteur, told an entertaining story about his encounter out west with a pony that resisted his directions. The next beat, he became Edison, the absentminded scientist, falling silent as he became engrossed in a journal that was on his desk. When his daughter wandered in, "he looked at her for a moment as if trying to recollect who she was and then exclaiming, 'Why, Dot, is that you?'" She had just returned from vacation herself and this was the first time father and daughter were reunited. After kissing her a half dozen times, he slid her from his knee and returned to his reading.

If his riding on the train's cowcatcher was a metaphor for his desire to see opportunities before others, Edison had been successful. He returned with lots of dazzling ideas for new investigations into fields wholly new to him. He spoke confidently of using electricity to evaluate the value of ore deposits, of applying cottonseed oil to the walls of underground mines to control moisture problems, of devising ways to reduce the teeth-rattling noise of New York's elevated railway. The blind would benefit from his discovery of an ink that produced raised letters, and the partially deaf from that ear trumpet he had been promising for a while (and whose completion date he candidly said he could not even guess).

His experience on the trip had sharpened his creative faculties, but he had never suffered a lack of promising ideas. His principal problem prior to the trip had been his inability to remain focused on completing the phonograph, the single most promising invention he had ever devised. Now, after the trip, his mind was agog with new projects of which he spoke enthusiastically. He gave no indication that he had developed during his trip to the West an ability to designate some projects as more important than others, and the phonograph as the most important of all.

In retrospect, the most interesting aspect of the interviews that followed Edison's return to Menlo Park was the deliberate way he misled the reporters about his plans. "Did you get any new ideas out there, Mr. Edison?" the *New York World* asked. "No. That's not a place for ideas," Edison replied. "It's perfectly barren." The West offered splendid country for a summer vacation, he said, further deflecting attention from inspiration for a new project that he did not want to disclose. He spoke of the barrenness of the West on August 27, the day after he had returned. It was also the very day he, along with Batchelor and Kruesi, signed and dated a page in a laboratory notebook containing three sketches. They were labeled "Electric Light."

CHAPTER FOUR

GETTING AHEAD

A U G U S T 1878–O C T O B E R 1879

EDISON'S INVENTION OF the electric light is as embedded in national mythology as Columbus's discovery of America. The invention of the one and the discovery of the other are also similar in that they indisputably occurred, but their mythic significance requires ignoring preceding history in both cases.

When Edison in 1878 began to look in to 'inventing" electric light, Europeans had a seventy-year lead. In 1808, Humphry Davy in England had employed a large battery to demonstrate for the Royal Society how light could be produced with electricity in either of two ways: by inducing a strong current to leap across a gap, which created a bright arc, or by heating an element until it glowed white-hot—incandescent. Arc light proved to be the easiest to render into practical form. An experimental installation on the streets of Lyon, France, in 1855, dazzled pedestrians who, at nine in the evening, were bathed in what a local newspaper called "a flood of light that was as bright as the sun." Birds were confused and began singing; ladies opened up umbrellas to shield themselves.

Creating bright light was accomplished relatively easily. What was difficult was moderating the intensity. First used in lighthouses, then mounted on high lampposts on the streets of European cities, the arc light was powerful, but it lacked a dimmer switch. Genealogically, the arc light was much more closely related to the modern arc welder than it is to the household lightbulb. Nineteenth-century passersby did not have welder's masks to protect their eyes, leading Robert Louis Stevenson to write: "A new sort of urban star now shines out nightly, horrible, unearthly, obnoxious to the human eye; a lamp for a nightmare!"

Stevenson's was a minority opinion. For most people, the "artificial sun" provided by arc lights at night was welcomed. In the early years, however, they required frequent maintenance while in use. The lights used two carbon rods placed vertically, one above, one below, whose tips were kept at a set small distance apart in order to achieve the arc. As the carbons burned away, however, adjustment was needed in order to maintain a constant distance. Automatic regulating mechanisms that eliminated the need for maintenance men to make the rounds were tried, but their complexity and unreliability introduced new problems.

When an inventor came up with an ingeniously simple, reliable electromagnetic device that kept the gap between the rods at a fixed distance while they burned two inches an hour, arc lighting was no longer a high-maintenance proposition. That inventor was Charles Brush, and he would become a very wealthy man. In April 1878—when Thomas Edison was still touting his yet-to-be-completed phonograph and months before he had gone west and returned thinking about the electric light—Brush was shipping arc lighting equipment to paying customers who were installing his lights indoors, as well as out. His lights were also garnering flattering attention from the press. The *New York Times* described a demonstration that Brush set up in a manufacturer's space in his hometown of Cleveland providing "a pure white light" that was "unexpectedly soft and endurable to the eyes." This latter description is not credible, however. For the demonstration, each of two floors had been provided with two three-thousand-candlepower lamps—the gas jets that they replaced were only ten to twenty candlepowers each—so the arc light's sheer candlepower in a confined interior space made another description in the same article more accurate: "the effect was most brilliant." Needless to say, the bulk of Brush's sales would be for street lighting.

Incandescent lighting, the other possible form of electric light that Davy had shown to the Royal Society, offered a tantalizing prospect of light that truly would be "soft and endurable to the eyes." Since Davy's day, many fine minds had tried different approaches toward realizing the potential. Frederick de Moleyns, an Englishman, received a British patent for an incandescent bulb in 1841, six years before Edison was born. In addition, an American, J. W. Starr, received patents for two different kinds of incandescent bulbs in 1845 and traveled around England giving exhibitions. He died at the age of twenty-five.

An incandescent bulb required a filament that would glow brightly without melting. Starr had worked with the two materials that showed the most promise: carbon and platinum. Carbon did not melt at high temperatures, but it burned up too easily. Platinum had drawbacks, too: It was extremely expensive and it was difficult to bring to the point of incandescence without reaching the slightly higher temperature at which it melted. In 1878, at least twenty different individuals had tried to make a practical incandescent bulb, or were still engaged in the quest, and no one had succeeded in producing a bulb that was ready for service outside of a laboratory.

Edison had tinkered with both arc and incandescent lighting in the past, using batteries, and on his trip out west, his traveling companion, Professor Barker, had called his attention to the potential for unlimited electrical power from waterfalls, which could be applied to mining, a field in which Edison was interested. While traveling, Barker had also urged Edison to visit the workshop of William Wallace, in Ansonia, Connecticut, to see what Barker himself had seen: a dynamo that Wallace had designed with the inventor Moses Farmer and built at his own foundry, which powered an arc lighting system that Wallace had set up. Barker offered to make the arrangements for a visit to Connecticut, and two weeks after returning home, Edison made the trip.

Edison was accompanied by Barker; another professor, Charles Chandler, of Columbia University; and Edison's chief assistant, Charles Batchelor. The party included one more member: a reporter for the *New York Sun*, whose observant eye captured an Edison who moved separately from his companions, standing apart due to deafness and personality quirks. Barker and Chandler exchanged jokes that Edison could not hear. Occasionally, Batchelor would repeat a choice anecdote in Edison's ear, and Edison would laugh appreciatively, and then quickly lapse into "deep meditation." Edison also expressed a curiously ghoulish thought when Wallace showed the group his invention for use in mining that directed a stream of water with such force that it could tear flesh from the hand. "Barky," Edison suddenly said to his friend, "if a person could cut a man's throat with such a stream of water, I don't believe a jury could be found that would convict him of murder."

For Edison, the highlight of the visit was seeing the Wallace-Farmer dynamo in operation. The inventor fell in love.

> Mr. Edison was enraptured. He fairly gloated over it. Then power was applied . . . and eight electric lights were kept ablaze at one time, and each being equal to 4,000 candles. . . . This filled up Mr. Edison's cup of joy. He ran from the instruments to the lights, and from the lights back to the instrument. He sprawled over a table with the simplicity of a child, and made all kinds of calculations.

Everything that Edison said and did on the day of the visit to Ansonia convinced him that the electric light was easily attainable. This required a fertile imagination. What he had seen in Connecticut was a powerful electromagnetic generator, a form of power vastly superior to batteries. But it powered four-thousand-candlepower arc lights that lacked a filament—it did not suggest a way to find a durable filament suitable for a sixteen-candlepower incandescent lightbulb. Edison thought he saw the perfect opportunity: others had solved the problem of power, and he would add a solution for providing a reliable bulb, which he told the press soon after was "so simple that a bootblack might understand it."

A simple solution should have presented no serious problems to the great inventor. Once uttered, however, the announcement of a solution could not be retracted, not when a celebrity has spoken. Edison was not necessarily more careless about making empty claims than his contemporary inventors in the electric light field; he simply was more exposed.

Many ideas, until practically realized, will seem grandiose; but the inventor's own interest in a given idea often disappears as quickly as the inspiration arrived. Out of public view, these brief enthusiasms cause no embarrassment.

Before Edison had made members of the press his personal friends, he was free to think aloud, try out an idea, and drop it. In 1871, he recorded his excitement about adapting a new electric motor "so as to obtain the resquisite [*sic*] strength and still be of extreme lightness—and combined with suitable air propelling apparatus wings parchoutte [*sic*] etc. so as to produce a flying machine of extreme lightness & tremendous power." On the next page of the notebook, he had returned to the ongoing work of designing a new telegraphic printer.

By 1878, however, he was the Wizard of Menlo Park, the famous inventor of the phonograph, who had willingly given up the privacy that kept momentary enthusiasms out of public view. Before the invention of the phonograph, he had shown an underlying streak of vanity in his assiduous stockpiling of patents in his name. Now, he set a far more ambitious goal for himself, confiding that he "wished to produce something at least as good as the phonograph every year." That the ambition was shared not with a friend but with a reporter is telling.

"Subdividing" light was how reducing the intensity of arc light was referred to. If Edison attained it in 1878, following the invention of the phonograph in 1877, the feat would double his fame and keep him on pace for achieving technological breakthroughs annually. True, the task would usurp the work of making the phonograph a practical appliance, but a past triumph held less interest. He leaped at the opportunity to move quickly on to another great invention. The electric light was a tantalizing object for another reason: Unlike the phonograph, which did not exist before Edison's invention, the incandescent bulb had been pursued by many of the world's best electrical engineers and resourceful inventors. When the self-trained Wizard stepped over the failures of others to enter what for him would be a new field, using technical knowledge that bore no relationship to the phonograph, the satisfaction was immense.

"I don't care so much about making my fortune," Edison said in an interview, "as I do for getting ahead of the other fellows."

So great was the anticipated satisfaction that Edison convinced himself that he had succeeded in the "subdivision of light" within a week. He had visited Connecticut on Sunday, 8 September 1878. On the following Saturday, Edison told the *New York Sun* that he had only needed "a few days" to learn how to apply electricity for indoor lighting. "I have it now!" he claimed, though he was unwilling to provide specifics, other than to say that "scientific men" had not thought to investigate his approach and "everybody will wonder why they have never thought of it, it is so simple."

Edison had also somehow found time to conceive of a detailed vision of how he would first install his "light centers" in Lower Manhattan, connecting central power stations with individual businesses and houses by running insulated wires underground like gas pipes and converting the gas burners and chandeliers that were already in use into lightbulb receptacles. The same wires could also provide power for elevators, sewing machines, and stoves. Not as prescient were his cost estimates; he thought his electric lights would be one-tenth the cost of gas. Furthest off was his one-word prediction of when he would provide a public exhibition: "Soon."

In his private correspondence, Edison spoke in the same giddy fashion, blurring the distinction between what he hoped for and what he had achieved. He wrote Theodore Puskas in Europe, "Have struck a bonanza in Electric Light." Prospective investors quickly approached Edison, relying upon the successful entrepreneur's past record to project new triumphs with still-to-be-proven technology. Several Western Union directors were keen to form a new company around Edison, and the company's attorney, Grosvenor Lowrey, served first as intermediary, and then as Edison's trusted adviser.

Lowrey quickly learned how difficult it was to persuade Edison to disrupt his routine at the laboratory, even for the purpose of gaining financing. When Edison missed a meeting that Lowrey had set up in New

York City with interested investors, Edison's secretary explained that Edison had worked all through the night and the morning, breaking off only at ten o'clock—and forgot the meeting. When Lowrey tried again to make arrangements, Edison wrote him, "If I come to New York I lose the day—time valuable on light please come out."

What Edison did not explain to the investors knocking at his door was that he had run into some serious difficulties. The approach that he had initially proclaimed to be "so simple" was complex in the extreme: He was attempting to use platinum as the filament and was devising regulators to automatically break the circuit when the temperature edged too close to the melting point. This had been tried by many inventors before Edison, and he had discovered for himself how elusive was a design that actually worked. Drawing on his experience with multiplex telegraphic equipment, he came up with various complex combinations of electromagnets, switches, and levers to regulate the temperature of the filament, to no avail. He had not yet succeeded in building a single light whose platinum filament could remain intact for more than a few minutes. Eventually, Edison was forced to abandon altogether his attempt to regulate the temperature.

In October 1878, when corresponding with his most trusted associates, he began to rein in his optimistic predictions a little bit. He cabled George Gouraud in London: "I have only correct principle. Requires six months to work up details." At this point, he could have begun tempering the public's expectations, too, which he had stoked by his premature "I have it" announcement a few weeks earlier. Having experienced the thrill of power from his celebrity—Gouraud told Edison of a "panic in gas shares" in London when word was received of Edison's announcement of success—Edison could not bring himself to concede publicly that he had been too hasty in his claims.

Gouraud sent Edison a continuous flow of reports from Europe that would have stimulated the imagination of any inventor, even one without a weakness for the grandiose. Gouraud wished he "had had my wits about me" when he had first received word of Edison's invention of a new approach to the electric light: "I might have made you a clean million as it played the very devil with stocks all over the country." The British equivalent of $1.36 billion was "trembling in the balance," Gouraud wrote in another letter, while British scientists tried to determine whether Edison's "alleged" discovery was genuine. Gouraud urged Edison to form an electric light company in England, without delay, to take advantage of "universal free advertising such as cannot be bought for money under any circumstances."

In the excitement of the moment, Edison was unable to remain quiet. He once again invited members of the press to his laboratory, one by one, not to bring them up to date on the technical difficulties that he and his staff had encountered, but to quell any doubts that his announced success was complete. When the *New York Herald* arrived, Edison had a demonstration set up, showing a bulb that was lit for three minutes, not long enough to expose the short life of Edison's platinum filaments. The reporter was impressed. When arc lights were the principal competition, Edison's incandescent bulb drew praise simply because "it did not pain the eye."

Running the sham demonstration for the representative of a second newspaper, Edison flipped a switch, and he and the reporter waited while the filament began to glow and finally reached incandescence. Sitting in front of the bulb that would burn out in a couple of minutes were he to leave it on beyond the brief demonstration, Edison was asked, "How long will it last?" He answered, "Forever, almost."

When the reporter from a third newspaper paid a visit for the same demonstration, Edison was asked point-blank if he had yet encountered any difficulties. "Well, no," he replied with a straight face, and then claimed that the very absence of setbacks was "what worries me." For another newspaper, he asked the public to be patient—not for the perfection of the "subdivided" electric light, which was complete, but for his phonograph, which he granted was viewed by many as a toy of little practical use. He was making daily improvements, he claimed, and it would eventually take its place "in the niche of public utility in good time."

Little attention was spared for readying the phonograph for the mass market, however. The time sheets from his laboratory for this period show that five staff members devoted about sixty hours to the dictating phonograph in October 1878, an insufficient investment to produce an affordable model that would supplement the expensive model sold to commercial exhibitors. The exhibition model's best month had been in May, when it sold forty-six units; in July, the number had dropped to three; in September, it had recovered slightly, to reach the lofty level of sixteen units, netting Edison a commission of $461. The treasurer of the Edison Speaking Phonograph Company told him that these paltry sales would soon disappear altogether and that he looked forward to the introduction of a "'Standard machine' which I understand you are perfecting." But even the minimal ongoing work on the phonograph would be pushed aside by the launch of frenzied efforts to find a way to fulfill Edison's premature public claim that his electric light was working. A couple of months later, when asked in an interview about the state of his phonograph, Edison replied tartly, "Comatose for the time being." He changed metaphors and continued, catching hold of an image that would be quoted many times by later biographers: "It is a child and will grow to be a man yet; but I have a bigger thing in hand and must finish it to the temporary neglect of all phones and graphs."

Financial considerations played a part in allocation of time and resources, too. Commissions from the phonograph that brought in hundreds of dollars were hardly worth accounting for, not when William Vanderbilt and his friends were about to advance Edison $50,000 for the electric light. Edison wrote a correspondent that he regarded the financier's interest especially satisfying as Vanderbilt was "the largest gas stock owner in America."

In mid-October, the American Gas-light Association, the industry's principal trade group, met in New York and took stock of the threat posed by the claims issuing from Edison's laboratory in Menlo Park. Gaslight monopolies had few friends outside of the ranks of shareholders. At the beginning of the nineteenth century, gaslight had been viewed as pure and clean; seventy years later, its shortcomings had become all too familiar: it was dirty, soiled interior furnishings, and emit-

ted unhygienic fumes. It was also expensive, affordable for indoor lighting only in the homes of the wealthy, department stores, or government
buildings. The *New York Times* almost spat out the following description of how gas companies conducted business: "They practically made
the bills what they pleased, for although they read off the quantity by
the meter, that instrument was their own, and they could be made to tell
a lie of any magnitude. . . . Everybody has always hated them with a
righteous hatred."

Edison credited the gas monopoly for providing his original motiva-
tion to experiment with electric light years before in his Newark laboratory. Recalling in October 1878 his unpleasant dealings years earlier
with the local gas utility, which had threatened to tear out their meter
and cut off the gas, Edison said, "When I remember how the gas companies used to treat me, I must say that it gives me great pleasure to get
square with them." The *Brooklyn Daily Eagle* printed an editorial titled
"Revenge Is Sweet" in which it observed that the general public greatly
enjoyed the discomfort of the gas companies, too: "To see them squirm
and writhe is a public satisfaction that lifts Edison to a higher plane
than that of the wonderful inventor and causes him to be regarded as a
benefactor of the human race, the leading deity of popular idolatry."

The gas interests had been dealt a number of recent setbacks even before Edison's announcement of a newly successful variant of electric light.
An "enormous abandonment of gas" by retail stores in cities, who now
could use less expensive kerosene, was noticed. The shift was attributed
not to stores' preference for kerosene but as a means of escaping "the
arrogance of the gas companies." Arc lights had now become a newly
competitive threat, too. The previous month, Charles Brush had set up
his lights in an exhibition hall in New York and then added a display in
Boston. Sales to stores followed in several cities; then, as word spread,
other establishments sought to obtain the cachet bestowed by the latest
technology. William Sharon, a U.S. senator for and energetic booster
of California, retrofitted the public spaces of his Palace Hotel in San
Francisco with arc lights that replaced 1,085 gas jets. The gas-industry

conventioneers preferred to talk about the failed installations of arc lights, such as in textile factories, in which the dark shadows cast by the light made it difficult for loom operators to distinguish threads.

Speakers at the gas-industry convention explained that Edison's light did not pose the potent competitive threat to gas that had been described in the press. (Edison had sent Charles Batchelor to attend and enjoyed hearing Batchelor's account that showed "they talked in the dark.") While the popular image of Edison was of a wonderful man who "could accomplish almost anything he undertook," sober scientific authorities were shaking their heads doubtfully about Edison's claims of success.

One independent observer, Albert Salomon von Rothschild, in Vienna, had had his interest piqued, and he wrote an American colleague for an impartial assessment of whether Edison's invention would "allow electric light to be henceforth employed everywhere just as gas-light, and not only in very large rooms or places, as is now the case [with arc lights]." Rothschild made clear that he had never joined the cult that idolized Edison, whose most recent inventions, including the phonograph, "however interesting, have finally proved to be only trifles." Still, he did see that if Edison's technical claims were to prove valid, the business implications could not be overstated.

Edison did not publicly divulge the details of his electric light experiments, of course, so no external authorities could know for certain that his attempts to devise a lasting filament—which he was trying to do with platinum and thermal regulators—were as ill-fated as those of his many predecessors. He blamed his reticence about the electric light on his past experience with the phonograph. The premature publication of technical details in *Scientific American* had been translated, via French, into German, causing endless difficulties with foreign patents. He had a letter from Lemuel Serrell, one of his attorneys, to show to a skeptical reporter, in which Serrell lectured Edison, "The confounded newspaper men are doing you more harm and producing more trouble than they are worth."

Not so easily put off was his friend and supporter, Professor George

Barker. As the person who had encouraged Edison during their shared trek out west to revisit the project of developing incandescent light, Barker had been thanked with a promise of six working sets of bulbs when Edison thought he had easily found a simple, but complete, solution in platinum. Relying on Edison's word, Barker had announced he would present a public lecture on the state of the art of electric light, complete with a demonstration. The newspapers carried the announcement, and Edison had promised to leave his laboratory for the occasion and make an appearance himself. Only after Barker had set about making arrangements did Edison realize how woefully unready he was to unveil his short-lived platinum bulbs. First, he begged off from making the trip himself, and then he told Barker that though he personally wanted very much to provide lights for the demonstration, he could not because the directors of the new Edison Electric Light Company would not allow him to do so.

Barker was astonished and angry in equal measure. He did not know that the company that Edison invoked as the villainous party in the matter had not yet signed an agreement with Edison. The prospective investors apparently had been told little about Edison's setbacks in his electric light research, and Edison understandably was not eager to make a public display of his yet-to-be-reversed failure in the laboratory. "Positively No Admittance" was now posted at the front door of the laboratory. "What is that inhospitable sign for?" a reporter asked Charles Batchelor, who gallantly took responsibility for the change of policy. Edison "doesn't want to bar anybody out, so he lets all sorts of inquisitive people come here and occupy his time." Batchelor said he and the other assistants had prevailed upon him to keep the curious out. Closing the front door also served to restrict the outflow of information, too, in this delicate time of arranging financing.

Professor Barker would not be denied without a protest, however. If Edison would honor his promises for the lecture, Barker would go to New York and personally ask individual company directors to give permission. The thought of giving a lecture on the electric light without having one of the Edison lights that had been advertised would put him in a position in which "I would rather lose my right hand than occupy." In the event, he did not have an Edison bulb for a demonstration in his survey of the state of the art, but Charles Brush's company also failed to show. It had asked for, and secured, a place in Barker's program, then the company had suddenly begged off only twenty-four hours in advance. Barker forgave Edison for his breach of promise, and publicly covered for him at the demonstration by saying that Edison's London attorney had advised against a public showing quite yet. Afterward, he privately indulged with Edison in the pleasure of knocking Edison's arc light rival ("not always fair in their statements or scrupulous in their dealings").

At the same time that Edison was careful not to let outsiders see the true state of his electric light research, he continued to accept cheerfully individual requests for interviews from the major newspapers. He conveyed complete confidence in his still-secret solution, and charmed reporters with his disdain for conventional formality. The press was fascinated with Edison's fondness for chewing tobacco—the Professor tore into a "yellow cake as large as a dinner plate" while being interviewed by the *New York Sun,* as he talked on without end about the advantages of indoor electric light and the imminent test of lights in every home in Menlo Park in order to "keep the bugs out of the invention."

Talking at such length in the *New York Sun* was hurtful to Edison's public image, advised another reporter-friend, Edwin Fox, who wrote Edison with unsolicited advice about proper management of Edison's celebrity. "Keep yourself aloof and reserved," Fox said, like the extremely reserved, and much-loved, General Ulysses S. Grant (Fox had no way of knowing in 1878 that Grant, pressed by financial need, would drop his reserve at the end of his life and write two volumes of bestselling memoirs, published in 1885–1886). In Fox's not unbiased view, the image of Edison that came through in the competitor's interview was abhorrent. "Holding you out to the world as a chewer of tobacco and all such trash . . . is really too bad." For his own reporting, Fox said he had always "sought to keep you on a high pedestal."

Days after he wrote this, however, Fox sought intimate access to Edison and the laboratory, so that he could write about everything: "how you act, talk, live, work, and look—the struggles and obstacles attending the completion of your chief inventions." Showing a sure, and strikingly modern, understanding of the popular appeal of fly-on-the-wall journalism, Fox said he planned to spend at least a week living in Menlo Park, dropping into the laboratory "when the spirit moves" to fill his notebook with "fresh crisp data." This was the only way to do justice to his subject, did not Edison agree, "my esteemed manipulator of the fiery lightning"? Fox's flattery is not especially noteworthy; not just Edison, but his wife and children, too, received uncommon compliments on a daily basis. A speed record in sycophancy was established when a story in late October reporting the birth of the Edisons' third child, William, credited the newborn with "indications of precocity" and "intellectual independence" because he had kicked mightily as he was dressed for the first time.

Members of the press, academics, investors—everyone made their own individual appeal for access to Edison. At the same time, he had nothing to show them that would withstand scrutiny. Edison's position must have been uncomfortable, and all the more so because he had no close friend in whom he could confide. Stress may have played at least some role in a severe attack of neuralgia that kept him in bed on 23 October. Without being privy to a complete view of Edison's predicament, Barker ascribed the attack to overindulgence in work. "Be regular about your meals and sleeping hours," the amateur doctor advised, "or some day you will break down entirely." Edison had a different theory about the cause of his malady: on seven successive nights he had looked too long into arc lights that he had set up. "I think electricity burned me," he said. "I shall not repeat that trick." When he recovered, he wore a floppy black sombrero in the lab for protection.

In the eyes of an entirely neutral party, the credit-reporting agency of R. G. Dun & Company, Edison was seen as "an untiring genius apt to run from one effort at invention to another without fully completing the work he is on." His world renown was acknowledged; so, too, was a history of commercial disappointments: "the financial fruits seem to be mainly plucked by other hands." The report summed up rather nicely Edison's reputation and prospects:

> Now claims to have solved the problem of furnishing cheap Electric light to dwellings & places where multitudes of single lights are required at less cost than gas. His claim is not yet demonstrated to be good, but if he is successful this time his ability to pay need not be questioned. He is reported to be a thoroughly honorable steady & industrious man. He must have some means but probably all his ready money is continually being planted in the expenses of his experimenting. It is impossible to Estimate his worth, or in fact to say that he has a class of assets valuable as a basis for credit.

Edison was not much interested in what a credit-reporting agency had to say about him, as he was not interested in obtaining commercial loans. When R. G. Dun wrote him a few years later for information about one of his companies, he scrawled some basic information in the margin as his reply, closing with "hope nobody will ever give us any credit." What he sought were passive investors who would provide his laboratory with the funds necessary to make good on the breakthrough he had thought he had obtained in early September. He left negotiations to Grosvenor Lowrey, saying he did not care about the details, he simply needed money to "push the light rapidly." In fact, he was in no position to do anything rapidly with the electric light; he first needed the money to make his incandescent filament durable.

Lowrey, in turn, told the senior executives at Western Union; Drexel, Morgan & Company; and his fellow law partners, all of whom wished to invest in Edison's electric light venture, that "all serious difficulties have been overcome." Lowrey knew just what to say to bring investors on board, letting them know that some refinement was still needed, but not letting them know so much that they were scared off. On 15 November, the newly formed Edison Electric Light Company gave Edison an advance royalty payment of $30,000, of which $25,000 was to go for work at the laboratory for "further necessary investigations and experiments" related to the light.

A few days later, some members of the company's executive committee paid a visit to Menlo Park, and Lowrey did his best to convince Edison that such visits were helpful in making their expectations of progress more realistic. "It is all the better that they should see the rubbish and rejected devices of one sort and another," Lowrey wrote Edison. When other company directors made another visit, Lowrey again labored to convince Edison that it was good that the backers had had "their imaginations somewhat tempered." He wrote Edison: "They realize now that you are doing a man's work upon a great problem and they think you have got the jug by the handle with a reasonable probability of carrying it safely to the well and bringing it back full."

In a matter of just a few weeks, Edison had spent $19,000 of the $25,000 advance on a new laboratory building. When directors showed up at Menlo Park when the move was in progress, and Edison himself was not present to offer reassurance that all was well, the visitors saw "general dilapidation, ruin and havoc." Lowrey met with the executive committee and shared with them what he later described to Edison as a "very good natured laugh over their disappointment at their visit." Edison was fortunate that the committee members were so willing to tamp down their rising concern.

While Lowrey undertook the education of the company's trustees, Edison continued to release little puff balls of news and anecdotes for the general public that were meaningless at best and outright misleading at worst. In his telling, work at the laboratory was going so well that he could not do anything, even clumsily dropping a tool, without improving his electric lightbulb. He claimed he had doubled the intensity of light in one of his platinum filaments after a screwdriver was accidentally dropped and bent it. From now on, he declared, he would make all of his filaments in the same misshapen form. Edison packaged this and other entertaining partial disclosures as if he were being candid to the point of being imprudent. "I have begun by taking the public into my confidence," he told the public in December 1878, "and I don't propose to keep from them anything I know, or propose to do, if I can help it."

One blemish-free story was fed to the press for the public; another, more candid version went to the investors; and an uncensored version was provided only to his most senior, trusted employees. There were no financial conflicts-of-interest regulations in Edison's era. In January 1879, when the Edison Electric Light Company issued 500 shares, there were only ten shareholders. One was Edison, who received 219 shares; but, significantly, one was Edwin Fox, of the *New York Herald,* and another was William Croffut, of the *New York Daily Graphic,* who received 8 and 5 shares respectively as gifts from Edison. Not having heard acknowledgment that Croffut had received his shares, Edison sent a follow-up note and received the following effusive reply:

> My Dear Edison,
>   Yes! Bless you, yes, of course I got the five shares of stock and have been commercially ecstatic ever since. You are a brick. If I can do anything in the world for you at any time, order me up & I'll go it alone.

The thank-you note that Fox sent to Edison treated the gift as recognition of past services rendered (it made Fox "truly sensible of the pleasing fact that my friendship is not unappreciated"), but he, too, served up fulsome flattery, closing with the wish that Edison continue in his "triumphal march to undying fame."

Edison misled the general public, and, in more sophisticated fashion, the outside investors of the Edison Electric Light Company, not to effect a stock swindle but to buy precious time so that he could work his way out of the corner his premature boasts had backed him into. He did not confide to a diary or in letters how the discouraging results in the laboratory little resembled the daily miracles he publicly claimed or hinted at. But the mood in the lab is chronicled in the letters written home by one of Edison's new hires, Francis Upton, a twenty-six-year-old physicist from Peabody, Massachusetts. Upton came from a background of privilege and formal academic training, different from Edison's in every imaginable way. He had studied at Bowdoin College, in Maine, then at Princeton, and had done postgraduate work under Hermann von Helmholtz at Berlin University in Germany. Before being invited to Menlo Park, he had been a temporary subcontractor doing a patent search for Edison in the Astor Library in New York City. In November 1878, Edison offered him a permanent position, which Upton accepted without even knowing what he would be paid. Excited about the prospect of having his first real job, he wrote his father, "I cannot really believe that I am earning money."

Upon arrival in Menlo Park, Upton was brought into Edison's inner circle, even as he was referred to by some colleagues as "the mathematician" rather than by name. Edison, Batchelor, Upton, and three other assistants worked from 7:00 P.M. to 7:00 A.M.—a schedule necessitated by the well-intentioned visitors who made work during the day impossible. Edison complained that they would appear as a line of heads coming up the hill in the morning, "devour" his time, and then "pay for it with expressions of admiration." When a tornado and fierce rain hit the area in early December, Edison and his staff were glad for the storm, as it kept the curious away for a day.

Upton arrived just at the moment when Edison was coming to the realization that he and his staff would never be able to make a durable electric light based on platinum. This conclusion, accepted most reluctantly, meant starting over. Alternative filament materials, which could reach incandescence without soon melting, all shared a similar vexing attribute: In the presence of oxygen, they oxidized, ruining the light. To prevent this, they had to be placed in a high vacuum that was difficult to achieve even with the best technology available at the time. It was the troublesome vacuum that Edison had thought he could avoid when he had rashly seized upon platinum as the "simple" solution.

Contrary to his published avowal that he would be perfectly candid with the public about the progress on the electric light, Edison did not tell reporters that he had hit a dead end. Even when he decided to tell the Edison Electric Light investors in late January, he had Stockton Griffin, his secretary, go into New York to deliver the news. Edison had no patience for attending personally to the care and feeding of his backers; that was for minions like Griffin or his attorney, Grosvenor Lowrey, to take care of. The most striking thing about how the investors received the news was their meekness—no one demanded that Edison appear to explain his failure to secure the first principles for a working incandescent bulb. On 25 January 1879, when Lowrey visited the offices of Fabbri & Chauncey on the same day that Griffin had come and gone delivering the news that Edison had been forced to abandon the platinum filament, the Edison Electric shareholders gathered around Lowrey and jokingly asked him if he knew anybody who would want to buy their shares. Lowrey did what he was supposed to do, dispensing homilies as Edison himself did, saying that doubt and tribulation accompanied any great accomplishment, and "this was just the time when we must all stand by the inventor."

The investors did stand by the inventor, which was important to young Francis Upton, who, like any new hire at a start-up that was in trouble, spent much time wondering if he had made a mistake. In late February, Upton, reasoned, "I am learning a great deal and nothing will be likely to take that from me," even if the venture ran aground. At times like early March 1879, when Upton wrote his family marveling that he was actually paid $12 a week for labor that "does not seem like work but like study and I enjoy it," he seemed younger than his twenty-six years. A few weeks later, however, he had worked up the courage to ask Edison for a raise. Edison ruled that out, but offered to provide him with the fees Edison would receive for publishing magazine articles if Upton would serve as the ghostwriter who would "dress his thoughts for the press." Flattered, Upton accepted the offer.

In May, when Upton was visiting his home in Peabody, he heard about a mill owner in Lawrence who was unhappy about paying $30,000 a month for gas lighting and interested in trying Edison's light in his mill. He wrote Edison excitedly, offering to investigate the opportunity, and doing the arithmetic for his employer: "Three or four hundred thousand dollars a year are not to be sneezed at." Inexperience with the world of business must have contributed to Upton's failure to see that he was working with the wrong numbers. The mill owner paid the gas company $30,000 *yearly*, not monthly, Upton sheepishly had to inform Edison.

Upton's value was revealed not in business development but in the experimental work in the laboratory. In early June 1879, Edison offered to provide his young assistant a 5 percent share of equity in the Edison Electric Light Company. Edison made his offer to his protégé on an either/or basis: salary *or* equity, not both. At the time, Upton had not yet married and was childless, but he knew his financial obligations would soon become considerable. He was engaged and would be married later that summer when his fiancée returned from travels in Europe. He could see that the electric light was "far from perfection," and there was no way of predicting when it would ever be ready for commercial introduction. Edison had difficulty letting go of his original design based on platinum, which served only to delay the inevitable day when all of his focus could be trained on alternatives.

In writing about his quandary to his father, Upton preserves the jumble of conflicting feelings he had at that moment. On the one hand, he wondered if he should ask Edison for 7.5 percent of the company instead of 5 percent, as Edison was anything but stingy when making such allocations. On the other hand, it was generous of Edison to have offered 5 percent, without requiring any contribution from Upton other than forgoing wages of $600 a year. Upton wrote, "I think it is not becoming in me to try and jew him."

Upton's father urged him to choose the salary, but Upton elected in July 1879 to take the offer of a 5 percent share of the company. He reasoned that a salary was ultimately dependent on the success of the electric light anyway, so he might as well select the option that provided the largest potential gains. He immediately felt a freedom as "master of my own time," free to come and go as he pleased, confident that Edison trusted him that "I should know what is best." As time passed, however, uncertainty about Edison Electric's prospects grew. On 19 October, he wrote home, "The electric light goes on very slowly." It was impossible not to think about the fact that if it were to succeed, "the money will come in enormous amounts." But if the efforts were to end in failure, Upton said he would be "contented with the experience I shall have, though of course very much disappointed at not having the money."

He did not foresee that the very day he was drawing up this somber assessment, Sunday, 21 October 1879, his laboratory colleague Charles Batchelor spent ten hours evacuating the air in a bulb with an untested filament, a carbonized sewing thread. That night, the bulb was placed on a test stand and the power was switched on. The bulb burned on and on, passing the twenty-four-hour mark. Bets were laid down, and the round-the-clock vigil continued for a second night. It stayed on into the afternoon of Tuesday, having performed admirably for more than forty hours, when Edison decided to end the endurance test under normal conditions and increased the voltage until the bulb turned into a ball of dazzling white, and then—pop—burned out.

In retrospect, those forty hours would be looked upon with fondness as the first successful test of a durable incandescent filament, a breakthrough, but the laboratory records at the time show a laconic reaction. Batchelor wrote without affect that "we made some very interesting experiments with cotton thread," but he was also testing at the same time fishing line, paper, cardboard, and other materials. We might guess that Edison's premature declaration of success with platinum the year before made everyone at the laboratory wary of committing the same mistake again.

Edison could not trumpet the promising results in public because he had maintained all along that the necessary technical innovation had been accomplished in short order at the beginning of the initiative. He did tell the *New York Times* in a story published on 21 October 1879 that "the electric light is perfected," allowing that unspecified problems "which have been puzzling me" had now been solved. Francis Upton had already learned, however, that Edison used "perfect" as verb or adjective without regard for conventional definitions, and it was best not to be carried along by his optimism. Upton discounted Edison's claim that the Edison Electric Light Company stock was now worth a thousand dollars a share. "He is always sanguine," Upton wrote his father about Edison, "and his valuations are on his hopes more than on his realities." A couple of weeks after seeing the cotton-thread bulb burn steadily, Upton's spirits had fallen again. "Continual trouble" continued to dim the electric light's prospects, as "we cannot make what we want." He acknowledged, and mocked, his own disappointment when it appeared that he and his fellow experimenters would never "see the untold millions roll in upon Menlo Park that my hopes want to see."

And then, in mid-November, the work in the laboratory produced new excitement, when carbonized paper, bent into the shape of a horseshoe, was tested as a filament and proved more durable than the cotton thread had. Finally, Upton said, "we now know we have something." He could not yet say whether the economics of electric light would make it competitive against gaslight, but at least the laboratory had a working prototype. By the end of November, private trading of shares of the Edison Electric Light Company had sent the price upward to vertiginous heights. No one associated with Edison's laboratory then foresaw that commercial introduction of the electric light would still be three long years away. Upton, however, did not have to wait to enjoy pointing out that Father had not known best, that in giving up less than $300 in wages at that point, Upton's shares were already worth more than $10,000. He told his father, "I cannot help laughing when I think how timid you were at home." Already forgotten were his own doubts about the venture that had left him depressed only a few days before.

CHAPTER FIVE

STAGECRAFT

NEWSPAPERS AND MAGAZINES had made Edison famous with portraits created with words, not cameras. Were Edison to leave his laboratory for a rare trip to New York City, he could do so without attracting attention to himself. Occasionally, on a Saturday night, Edison would go into the city with Francis Jehl, a young assistant, taking in lowbrow theater, or a boxing match, or a streetside phrenological exam. As the two strolled at leisure, taking in the sights of card hustlers, street vendors, and quack doctors, Edison "enjoyed being incognito," Jehl recalled in his memoirs. It is indeed remarkable that Edison could move in public with such ease, at the very time that one New York paper asserted that the general public discussed at greater length the probable life span of Edison than most anyone else in the world, "outside the crowned heads." Edison was in possession of "more inventions than any man living," and was all of thirty-two years old.

When Edison announced the perfection of his electric light, one fan expressed a wish to meet the great man and got her wish. But then, Sarah Bernhardt always got her wish. Bernhardt, a French actress and singer, enjoyed a movie star's celebrity decades before movies were invented (and when they did arrive, Bernhardt became the medium's first star). In December 1879, as she completed a run of stage performances in New York, Bernhardt was only thirty-five and, like Edison, a prodigy in her profession. But having made her acting debut at the age of eighteen, she had much more experience than he in the management of celebrity and was quite expert in the art of drawing attention to herself. She moved with an entourage as large as a contemporary hip-hop star's posse. The juxtaposition of Bernhardt and Edison exposed their differences: he, uncomfortable with celebrity; she, fully in her element.

Bernhardt's original plan was to pay a visit to Menlo Park in the early evening of 4 December, after giving a matinee performance in New York City, her last before traveling to Boston the next day. The plan failed to account for the delays caused by her overly appreciative fans. When her carriage arrived at the theater before the performance, a crowd of autograph seekers was waiting; it took twenty-five minutes to get from carriage to stage door. After the third act of *La Dame aux Camilias,* her American audience insisted on seventeen curtain calls, and then after the final act, another twenty-nine. She dispatched her sister out the rear door of the theater where Bernhardt herself was expected, then snuck out the front unnoticed. On her own, it took an extra hour to return to her hotel. By the time she and her party were ready to depart, it was ten o'clock. The train was a local doing a milk run; it took hours to deliver them to Menlo Park.

Upon arrival at the depot near Edison's lab, Bernhardt, her furs, and her retinue were loaded into carriages and headed up the hill to Edison's house. It was 2:00 A.M., and waiting for the visitors in the bitterly cold night were four men, two women, and a girl. Never having seen a photograph of Edison, Bernhardt felt a moment of panic: Which one was he? When she leaped out of the coach, she received a bouquet of flowers from Mrs. Edison, she presumed. But she still could not figure out which of the four men, all of whom moved closer to her, was Mr. Edison. Then she picked him out: he was the one blushing slightly, and in his eyes she saw traces of irritation. With a start, she realized that her visit was bothering him: "He saw in my visit only the banal curiosity of a foreigner drunk on publicity. He already foresaw the interviews the day after, and the stupid remarks that would be put in his mouth. He suffered in advance for the ignorant questions that I was going to put to him, and the explanations that politeness would force him to give me; and for a minute Thomas Edison disliked me."

Bernhardt then called upon "the full force of my seductive power to conquer this wonderful shy scientist," and in her memoirs claims that they were soon "the best friends in the world." Her credibility on what she observed during the tour of the laboratory and dinner served afterward is shaky—she described Edison's electric light as so dazzling as to create "an impression of full daylight." What Edison recalled about the visit in the interviews late in his life that serve as his memoirs was Bernhardt's interest in everything she saw; her long dress that one of Edison's assistants was assigned to watch carefully so that it was not caught in a machine; and the cumbersome process of translating everything from English into French. Ultimately, Bernhardt chose to treat him the same way as a member of the general American public did, idealizing the person whom Bernhardt called "this King of Light."

Two years before Bernhardt's visit, Edison had begun his own career in stage business, when he had brought a single prop—his new phonograph—to the offices of *Scientific American*. He subsequently had favored the use of his Menlo Park laboratory as his preferred stage, and, with the professionalism of an actor in a Broadway hit, had performed the same play, with the phonograph as costar, hundreds of times. During the whole of 1879, Edison had built his presentation around the electric light, but short-lived bulbs could not be displayed for long, so the performances were brief and infrequent. With the cardboard filament proving to be longer lived, however, Edison had begun taking steps in preparation for a full demonstration to the general public when Sarah Bernhardt had paid her visit. By that time, he had illuminated the front rooms of his and Upton's houses with electric light, utilizing the gaslight fixtures. Bernhardt's visit, which went well, served to bolster everyone's confidence and speed preparations for lighting up the laboratory and opening its doors again to the public.

A month before, in November 1879, one of Edison's reporter-friends, Edwin Fox of the *New York Herald*, was given exclusive access to the laboratory and to Edison for two weeks, while forty bulbs and fixtures were being installed throughout the laboratory buildings. As a condition of giving access, Edison had asked Fox to embargo his story until the date that Edison would provide him, when tests and preparations were complete. Fox accepted the arrangement and worked on the story; Upton helped with revisions.

On Sunday, 21 December 1879, the *Herald* published "Edison's Light," catching Edison by surprise and infuriating him. The article was flattering in the extreme, however, describing the completed light as a "little globe of sunshine," without giving off gases, smoke, or odors. It gave all credit to one person, Edison. But as Edison knew full well, the publication of an article reporting the "perfection" of the light would bring yet another onslaught of curious visitors, for which preparations were not complete. He also knew that his reputation, already damaged during the previous year, would be irreparably harmed if the public once again expected to see a durable light and was again disappointed. A *New York Herald* editorial, "Edison's Eureka—the Electric Light at Last," spoke of how the public's faith in the Wizard of Menlo Park had grown "feeble" when silence had followed the announcement the previous year of Edison's invention. Now, the newspaper said, Edison finally had the goods to make the gas companies quail. For Edison, receiving such highly visible support was helpful to the cause, but the timing was hardly ideal.

The *Herald* article also made public all of the technical details that Edison's many competitors in the incandescent light field could have hoped for. William Sawyer, for example, immediately fired off letters to the major newspapers, claiming that Edison was infringing on a number of his own patents. And when Edison was not infringing, Sawyer said, he was hawking technology that simply would not work. He dared Edison to run one of his bulbs three hours, explaining that even if Edison achieved a perfect vacuum inside the bulb, it would not last ten minutes. Edison returned the challenge, daring Sawyer to reach three hours with his own bulb. Sawyer responded by saying that the publicity that Edison was so skilled at generating for himself was a transparent ploy to raise money in the capital markets.

A conservative response to this provocation would have been for Edison to put off the demonstration until ready, placating newspapers with descriptions of the longevity of the latest bulbs built in the laboratory. At that time, Edison bragged that he had a bulb that had burned 108 hours; with assumptions that favored his case, he stretched this into a claim that this would provide a family with light for evening hours for twenty-four days. But stung by the skeptics and challengers who spoke up after the *Herald* article, Edison felt strongly that he now had to show, not tell. He responded with a public promise: In short order, no later than the end of that week, he would light up ten houses in Menlo Park with his electric light, and set up ten electric streetlamps.

When Egisto Fabbri, one of the directors of the Edison Electric Light Company, learned of Edison's plan, he was aghast. On 26 December, Fabbri tried to find just the right tone to head off a premature demonstration. "I am much older than you are *and* a friend," he wrote Edison, covering all angles, going on to suggest that it would be best if Edison were to first try out the electric lights, indoors and out, for one continuous week before inviting the public in. Fabbri made a good argument: "As long as you are trying private experiments, even before 50 people, partial failure, a mishap, would amount to nothing, but if you were to express yourself ready to give a public demonstration of what you considered a complete success, any disappointment would be extremely damaging, and probably more so than may appear to you as a scientific man."

Edison was not accustomed to receiving suggestions from anyone, even key investors. He did not openly defy Fabbri, but instead of taking a week to carry out a nonpublic test, he devoted only one evening to the trial run. For a group of invited friends, he set up bulbs in the laboratory for a showing, from 6:00 to 10:00 P.M. Each bulb gave about the same illumination as a gas jet, and there were no mishaps. The next night, on the twenty-eighth, uninvited strangers "of all classes" came to Menlo Park to see the light, said one newspaper account, and more arrived the next night. Those who "hold that Rome was built in a day" were disappointed that the lampposts that had been set up in a field as if they lined a real street still lacked electric lights, which awaited the arrival of another generator.

Two and then four more streetlamps were electrified. The boarding-house of Edison's neighbor Sarah Jordan was outfitted with lights and opened up to visitors. Just as quickly, the stream of tourists descending upon Menlo Park grew, with hundreds arriving in the daytime, even before nightfall. The laboratory itself was opened to the public, too. The number of people crowding into the limited space made work impossible; the laboratory assistants found themselves fully occupied answering questions, and trying to protect the equipment from damage. "Requests and notices not to touch or handle were unavailing," said one report, and one of the best vacuum pumps was broken by some strangers who had given themselves permission to conduct their own experiments.

Edison was not, as his rival Sawyer charged, attempting just then to raise capital on Wall Street—the Edison Electric Light Company had been recapitalized just the previous month. But an incidental effect of placing his electric light in public view in Menlo Park was to excite the interest of traders. Company stock now was changing hands for $3,500 a share. Francis Upton received, and gladly accepted, an offer for five of his shares, at $5,000 a share, a tidy windfall for someone who had been paid $12 a week earlier in the year. The spike in prices did draw the censorious attention of the *New York Times*, which wrote in an editorial that "a suspicion arises that much of the appearance of success may be factitious and intended for stock-jobbing uses."

On New Year's Eve, extra trains were run to bring the curious to Menlo Park, and the laboratory added new stunts to the show. One bulb was submerged under water in a large glass jar, amazing onlookers with its ability to function. Across the room a lab assistant manually flicked one light on and off rapidly, as many times, it was claimed, as a household would switch a light on and off over the course of thirty years, and on it burned. Edison made himself available, putting on a performance on his own terms, wearing a rough suit of work clothes, and impressing the *New York Herald* as "a simple young man attired in the homeliest manner, using for his explanations not high sounding, technical terms, but the plainest and simplest language."

The next day, however, on New Year's, the numbers of visitors increased to the point that the crowd became unmanageable. The willingness of Edison to turn his laboratory into a public theater had succeeded, only too well. When he appeared, a shout, "There is Edison!" rang out, causing a surge of bodies in his direction. One report claimed that the crowds "more than once threatened to break down the timbers of the building," a statement that may not have been hyperbole; the lab assistants were convinced that collapse was possible and hurried outside, bolstering the floor supports below with telegraph poles and lumber. Where the realm of science ended and that of entertainment began could no longer be distinguished, judging by the printed condemnation of the behavior of a minority of the visitors who "cared nothing for science, who regarded the laboratory as they would a circus."

In the laboratory itself, the lights were arranged on a table to resemble a miniature layout of Menlo Park, and Edison had assigned assistants on all four sides to look out for sabotage. Their vigilance was needed that day, as one man was caught applying a jumper wire that ran under his clothes and down both sleeves, deliberately short-circuiting four of the lights. He turned out to be an electrician employed by the Baltimore Gas Company and was marched out, with language ringing in his ears "that made the recording angels jump for their typewriters," Edison later recalled.

Early in the evening of New Year's Day, as order in the laboratory gave way to chaos, Edison sought refuge in his private office. But distinguished visitors would show up, insisting that they see the great man himself, and he would have to appear, answer the same questions that he had already addressed countless times before. Seeing this reluctant showman forced to work the crowd, the correspondent for the *New York Tribune* described Edison with tenderness: "Edison is one of the most retiring of men, detesting all pomp and show, resembling the ladies in his desire to get away into the forests of solitude." The next day, on 2 January, Edison ordered that the lab be closed to the general public so work could resume.

The public-relations benefits from the Menlo Park demonstration proved short lived. Without the rollout of commercial service in New York or another city, the show ended without disarming the skeptics who said that Edison's lighting system had yet to be tested outside of his cozy laboratory and own home. An English critic described Edison's many announcements with acidic sarcasm:

> What a happy man Mr. Edison must be! Three times within the short space of 18 months he has had the glory of finally and triumphantly solving a problem of world-wide interest. . . . If he continues to observe the same strict economy of practical results which has hitherto characterized his efforts in electric lighting, there is no reason why he should not for the next 20 years completely solve the problem of the electric light twice a year without in any way interfering with its interest or novelty.

The price of Edison Electric Light Company stock quickly fell from $4,000 a share to $500.

Edison was reminded daily that as the world-famous inventor, he had to defend himself daily against attacks that his counterparts who labored in obscurity could never imagine. This was especially the case when the commercial potential of the invention was clearly visible to all. The phonograph had not caused him similar tribulation. Two years after its public debut, it was not regarded as a potentially lucrative invention, even by its progenitor. At this moment Edison had been observed to treat the phonograph "with the same degree of interest as a boarding school miss would allude to a discarded doll," in the view of the *Philadelphia Record*. The latest attempt by a licensee to make a business out of it was in the form of a toy, but those machines were so flawed that no distributor would accept them. Edward Johnson sighed: "The trouble with them is, not one person out of 50 has mechanical skill enough to adjust them as per instructions." Edison took what solace he could in the observation that at least no one was bothering him with claims of inventing the phonograph twenty-five years previously. But the moment an inventor "has perfected something of commercial value, something that will conflict with the interests of long-established monopolies," he told an interviewer, "then there is a general rush to endeavor to pull him down."

Closing the laboratory to the general public was one way to protect himself and the electric light from industrial spies. For those who had an academic or business interest in the experimental work and made arrangements in advance, he remained welcoming—too much so. A professional snoop who purported to be interested in licensing Edison's technology for manufacturing purposes quickly won Edison's confidence and was provided a tour of all of the facilities with Charles Batchelor as his guide. The visitor published a pamphlet based on the tour, intending to discredit Edison, but he had seen nothing that was serviceable for this purpose. Instead, he saw that the incandescent lights worked well. The worst he could say about them was that each light could be turned only on or off; an intermediate level of brightness could not be set. He was told that some of the bulbs burned continuously for eight hundred hours, but that they would be tested for eight more months before the system would be introduced for public use.

The company directors were willing, however, to put the electric light to an immediate test in the real world for Henry Villard, one of the company's investors, as long it was done out of public view, in case the test went awry. Among Villard's other financial interests was the Oregon Railway and Navigation Company, which had given John Roach, a leading shipbuilder, a commission to build a new 334-foot steamship, the *Columbia*. Impressed by the exhibition of the electric light in Menlo Park, Villard decided that to fulfill his wish that the *Columbia* be outfitted with state-of-the-art equipment, it should have electric lights, too. Over Roach's objections that the light should be proven on land before tried on the sea, Villard gave Edison a contract for the work. Power for the lights would be supplied by the ship's steam plant. Francis Upton was assigned the task of hand-carrying to the shipyard a basket with a delicate cargo—the lightbulbs, wrapped in cotton batting—while dodging traffic on the city streets, as no one wanted to test whether the bulbs would survive a crosstown trip on a wagon.

The *Columbia* sailed on its maiden voyage in May 1880, carrying locomotives and railcars around Cape Horn and then up to Portland. The electric lights did well on their first practical test outside of Menlo Park, but the designers thought it best to have a professional control the lights in the individual cabins. The ship's steward had to be called to unlock a box outside each stateroom and throw the switch whenever a passenger wanted a light turned on and off.

In reality, Edison's electric light had yet to be tested in a setting that resembled its intended destination, in a commercial urban district. But in the imagination of his associates, it shone brightly, at least when described to lovers. Grosvenor Lowrey, the Edison Electric Light Company's attorney, can be forgiven for concocting mumbo jumbo for impressing his fiancée: "Be thou to me, my love, a low resistance lamp! Be a voltaic arc! & not a nasty *high* resistance continuous conductor." Lowrey also told his beloved that spending time with Edison had improved Lowrey's spirits. "Perhaps I'd better marry him, since he cures me," he teased her.

When Lowrey showed Edison a miniature photograph of her, Edison offered a compliment about her looks, but then asked him, "Why is it, Lowrey, that so few women *have brains? Men* of brains it is easy to find, but *women*—" Edison's own wife was almost completely invisible in contemporaneous accounts of his life written by his closest associates. When she appears, it is as a foil for a tale of how Edison could not abide her concern for middle-class appearances and propriety. A man who did odd jobs around the Menlo Park lab, for example, tells a story of how Mrs. Edison managed to get Mr. Edison home, where she "dolled him up in a fifty-dollar suit." Edison stayed put for a short while "looking pretty," then fled for the lab. In the tale, Edison was found at the lab two weeks later, still wearing the same suit, having not been home the whole while. The suit, covered in grease and dirt, was ruined, a fact that went unnoticed by its wearer.

Edison knew how to mimic the sounds of a pragmatic businessperson, but the decisions he made then, as well as throughout the remainder of his life, favored new projects over near-term payoff of old ones. After countless performances of "Mary Had a Little Lamb," the novelty of the phonograph had worn off, and he had failed to sustain his interest long enough to see the machine's development through to commercial introduction of a model for the mass market. Still, as he and his laboratory staff brought the electric light into viable form, it is striking how Edison's interest waned here, too. Despite his avowed near-term pragmatism, Edison got excited about another idea of his: electric trains.

The idea originated in his interest in mining, and when in the spring of 1880 he first sketched out the electric train that he had in mind, it was capable of astounding feats. He thought electrical power could give a train's wheels the ability to grip the rails as if clamped upon them, enabling the train to run up and down steep mountains. There would be no need to drill tunnels again, he said in an interview published in the *Denver Tribune*. No need for human engineers or brakemen, either. Freight trains could be controlled by telegraph.

This project hardly offered prospects of meeting the criterion he had vowed to use, that is, likely to "pay in the near future." But there was another aspect that made it attractive: It would make a terrific show for the public. In April 1880, Edison ordered workers to lay down a half mile of track in Menlo Park for his electric railroad prototype, equipped with a modified dynamo as its motor, with current supplied by the rails. It was the picture of a freckle-faced boy, working under a hot summer sun, that left an indelible picture in the mind of David Trumball Marshall, a laboratory associate, who, many years later, wrote a memoir about his experiences. The unidentified boy had to dip each railroad tie into hot, liquefied asphalt, to render it nonconducting were it to get wet. Day after day, the work went on with melancholy repetition. "It takes brains and brawns to perfect inventions," Marshall observed, and it was that boy who "furnished some of the brawn."

Upon completion, the track was extended across the hilly country-side, and a ride on the little railroad became the new novelty for visitors. Edison took strange enjoyment in his own ability to remain unaffected by conditions that made others around him physically queasy. In previous summers, when he had taken his laboratory assistants fishing on the banks of the Atlantic, and rough seas had driven the others to the bottom of the boat, immobilized with seasickness, Edison thought it amusing to swing a piece of rancid pork across the noses of his suffering men. "The smell was terrific," said one account, "and the effect added to the hilarity of the excursion."

Offering rides on the train offered opportunities for more "hilarity." In early June, Lowrey wrote his fiancée with an account of his ride at forty miles an hour through sharp curves, protesting that the speed was not safe, while Edison brushed his concerns aside. Then the train jumped the tracks, throwing the temporary engineer from the track, face down in the dirt, "and another man in a comical somersault through some underbrush." Edison hopped off, but instead of rushing to the aid of the two, he was described as "jumping & laughing & declaring it a most beautiful accident." The foreign-born engineer managed to stand up, though clearly shaken up, and with face bleeding, mimicked Edison's earlier reassurances to everyone: "Oh, yes, *pairfeckly* safe!"

Work proceeded on the electric light at the same time. In July, the laboratory began experimenting with bamboo for use as a filament in place of cardboard. This created the need for "bamboo hunters" to search out the varieties with characteristics most suitable for the purpose. The first bamboo hunter dispatched was John Segredor, who was a laboratory staff member known for his fierce temper. His lab mates liked to provoke him just for their own entertainment. On one occasion, they were rewarded richly when Segredor told the group, "The next man [who provokes me], I will kill him." The threat was received as entertainment and instantly forgotten. The next day, a colleague directed a sarcastic remark at Segredor as before, but this time, Segredor left without a word and was next seen marching back up the hill toward the lab with his gun (the building quickly emptied). This brought an end to the sarcasm. In late August, Edison sent Segredor first to Georgia and Florida to collect bamboo specimens, and then on to Cuba, turning botanical research into an adventure. For Segredor, the adventure did not last long. He arrived in Havana on a Tuesday; that Friday, he died of "the black vomit" (yellow fever). Edison placed the blame on the victim himself, writing a mutual friend that he had cautioned Segredor "about his diet and about drinking cold drinks but as you say he was very self-willed and would always do in these respects about as he pleased and this I doubt not caused his death."

Edison decided against sending a replacement to Cuba, but sent another emissary, William Moore, to Japan and China, and an indefatigable traveler, John Branner, to Brazil. Traversing Brazil's interior by canoe and foot, Branner collected many specimens during a two-thousand-mile journey, but none was the equal of a certain Japanese variety that Moore had found. Moore arranged to have one Japanese farmer supply all of the bamboo that Edison would ever need, an arrangement that must have been satisfactory to all parties as it would last many years.

Edison designated Menlo Park itself as an outdoor annex for his work and prepared to expand the real-world demonstration of his bulbs by laying out a grid of wires through the fields, along imaginary roads, to support three hundred or four hundred streetlights. The work was well advanced, with more than five miles of wire placed underground, when Upton began testing the insulation and discovered that it was defective. Even at the time, there was considerable head-scratching among Edison's colleagues about how Edison could have permitted the project to advance so far without anyone testing the circuits as work proceeded.

Perhaps the explanation is a simple one: The overly hasty rush was the consequence of Edison's desire to retain the attention of the press so that his electric light would not be outshone by those of competitors. As the months passed, more disturbing news about the competition came in. In October, Edwin Fox, the reporter, wrote Edison from Manhattan that as he sat at his desk and looked out the window of his skyscraper office and peered into the window of the office in the next building, he saw about twenty individuals busily at work—making electric lightbulbs. Fox was certain that they were baldly infringing upon Edison's patents.

It happened that Fox was peering into the office of the United States Electric Lighting Company, which made an incandescent bulb based on the design of Hiram Maxim and was immediately identifiable by a filament that resembled the letter "M." As far as Edison was concerned, the bulb was a "clean steal" of his own cardboard-filament design, thinly disguised by the cutesy "M." When interviewed, he professed to be unconcerned. "I do not worry about them, or a hundred like them. I always expected them and there will be more of them." But United States Electric had not merely begun manufacturing, it had already installed a working exhibition of 150 bulbs in a basement reading room of the Equitable Building, the home of its Manhattan office. Edison's laboratory could argue the technical merits of its newer bamboo filament, but in the image game, it was now behind. United States Electric had got the jump on Edison Electric by being the first to establish a presence in New York City. Its lights soon were installed in several other offices and the post office, powered by generators on the premises in each case. Edison must have been upset, too, by the way that George Barker, his friend at the University of Pennsylvania, seemed to have switched allegiance, writing him that Maxim's bulbs were brighter than Edison's, an observation that Barker felt he had to share with Edison because "my own self-respect requires me to be honest, even with a friend, like yourself."

Edison also had to contend with a new manifestation of hostility: cartoons that turned the image of the Wizard of Menlo Park into a charlatan. In one cartoon that appeared in 1880, captioned "The Decadence of the Wizard of Menlo Park," Edison is depicted as a con man, playing a shell game with nonsensically named inventions, offering to show "the Great Invention Trick." Place your money on the table, receive a share of stock, then "now you see them, and now you don't see 'em!"

Edison would not be able to quell the criticism, nor best Maxim and other competitors, by means of technical specifications. Nor was the competition to establish the electric light one that would be fought primarily in the courts. Rather, Edison was the reluctant participant in a contest of marketing strategies. The bigger the stage, the better. The Edison Electric Light Company urgently needed to complete Edison's original plan of introducing his electric lights in Lower Manhattan, connected to what would be the first system of centralized power generation. To lay the electrical lines, however, the company needed the permission of the Tammany-dominated city government, one of the most corrupt governmental bodies in an age defined by political corruption.

The Brush Electric Light Company, having negotiated an understanding with the city well before Edison's company was ready, was the first company to be able to flip the switch, in dramatic fashion, sending power from a central station to lights installed along Broadway, between Fourteenth and Twenty-seventh Streets, at 5:25 P.M. on 20 December 1880. Brush had arranged with the city's Department of Public Works to secure permission for a two-week trial in the city. In doing so, the company had shown its willingness to take on considerable financial risk in order to obtain the opportunity to show its lights in the most coveted location in the country. Not only did it offer the service to the city free of charge, it had to accept a provision that gave the department the right to order that the streetlamps be taken down on a day's notice.

The debut of Brush lighting went well. The lights were mounted on corrugated iron posts that stood twenty feet tall, double the height of the gas lamps (they, too, were turned on that evening, permitting a side-by-side comparison). The arc lights were sufficiently bright that a newspaper could be read while standing 150 feet away from a post. One account described an "artistic effect" produced by the contrast of brilliant white and deep black, as in the sight of white horses attached to an elegant carriage standing outside of Tiffany's, surrounded by an impenetrably black background. As bright as the arc lights were, however, this stretch of Broadway was already well lighted by gas lighting in the shops. When the city cut off the gas streetlamps at six o'clock to see how much light was supplied by the arc lights alone, the ambient light thrown out by the shop windows made it hard to even notice that the gas lamps on the street had been turned off. Still, the drama of the electric light display was heightened, albeit artificially, by the presence of ten uniformed policeman assigned to stand along the route of the Brush Electric Light Company's wires (whether to guard against sabotage or to serve as ornamentation was not explained).

In making arrangements with the city to lay wires for his service, Edison had not pursued a contract for street lighting. He knew his bulb was ill suited for the purpose, and even were that not the case, he expected to be fully occupied initially with supplying individual businesses with service. Even as a private businessperson, however, seeking to provide service to other private interests, he had encountered substantial bureaucratic obstacles. The Department of Public Works tried to apply the same terms to Edison Electric as it had to Brush Electric, insisting that the city could withdraw permission with only one day's notice. Edison countered that he could justify making the considerable investment in laying lines only if he were provided with irrevocable permission that would extend a full year. This seems to have been a reasonable request, so Public Works could say nothing other than that it was powerless to bestow a utility franchise of such duration, and pushed the problem upstairs, to the city's Board of Aldermen.

Edison himself had neither the experience nor the temperament to work with a group of professional politicians known for being more attentive to personal pecuniary interests than to the public weal. Fortunately, Grosvenor Lowrey knew that this was the time to step forward and propose a modus vivendi that did not involve bribes, but did involve currying of favor from political operators. Lowrey obtained Edison's consent to provide a special performance of the Menlo Park magic light show for the New York Board of Aldermen.

It's impossible to determine whether Lowrey was supernaturally savvy, or just plain lucky, but the evening he set for the demonstration in Menlo Park for New York's City Fathers was 20 December, the very same evening that Broadway would be transformed into the Great White Way by Brush Electric. The aldermen missed the spectacle in New York, pulling in to Menlo Park on a private train provided by the Pennsylvania Railroad exactly at the moment when Brush Electric made its Broadway debut. Edison Electric attempted to put on a show of equal dramatic power in Menlo Park, having installed three hundred streetlamps in a double file up the hill. All were alight when the visitors from New York arrived, and the press accounts praised their "soft, mellow" light. No one pointed out—in print, at least—that Edison Electric was not planning on competing head-to-head with Brush for the street-lighting business and that this display was decorative but effectively useless. Unlike Brush's two-thousand-candlepower lights arrayed along Broadway, Edison's sixteen-candlepower incandescent bulb was of use only indoors. When placed outside it did little but illuminate the protective white globe within which it sat.

Two years before, Grosvenor Lowrey had overridden Edison's objections and insisted that Edison spend a portion of his advance payment from the Edison Electric Light Company on a separate two-story brick building to serve as an office and library. Edison had argued that his little office on the ground floor of the laboratory was sufficient for his needs, but Lowrey had countered that he must have a suitable place to receive distinguished visitors, one that projected an image of financial solidity. A new freestanding office was built, and on Lowrey's orders Edison had purchased the finest cherry furniture, identical to the pieces in Lowrey's own offices in the Drexel Building in New York City. These proved to be farsighted preparations for this moment, when the party of visitors climbed the hill and stepped into Edison's richly appointed office.

Edison was haggard in appearance, with uncombed hair, and as he greeted each person with a handshake, one reporter described Edison as wearing "a forced look of pleasantry." Just as Edison had been expected to perform the same routine ad nauseam when the phonograph was unveiled, now he was called upon to do parlor tricks with the electric lights, though the possibilities for a variety show were limited. Leading his visitors to the laboratory, he had them look out the windows when, with a signal to an assistant, the power was cut to the twin lines of outside lights. The visitors began to applaud, and then, in a twinkling, the lights were brought back on. "That's the last of the lamplighters, if we have the electric light in New York," one of the visitors said to another. The city's savings in labor costs resulting from the dismantling of gas streetlamps maintained by humans was not viewed by this group as purely positive, however. A city commissioner recalled that a machine sweeper had once been introduced to Central Park: "'What do you think of it, Pat?' he asked a sweeper employed there. 'It's a wonderful thing,' said Pat, 'but yer 'oner,' he added archly, 'devil a vote it can cast.' The Mayor took the hint. The force was retained, and the machine received no endorsement."

It was a moment of awkwardness for Edison and his associates, and could easily have been avoided. After all, his light was not going to be marketed for use as street lighting, so there had been no need to allow the aldermen to worry about the potential loss of patronage. It fell to Lowrey to keep the guests moving toward the evening's final act, following the tour of the laboratory and the machine shop: a feast catered by New York City's Delmonico's Restaurant (birthplace of baked Alaska and lobster Newburg). The spread was laid out in the laboratory, tended by gloved waiters in formal evening wear who did not stint when pouring champagne.

Edison did not know the protocol for such occasions—he ate and drank oblivious to the fact that he was still wearing his sealskin hat—but Lowrey was an adept master of ceremonies. After allowing his guests time to fill themselves and let the ample quantities of alcohol take effect, he rose to give the first after-dinner speech. He began with compliments for the mayor, and then for the aldermen, and only after warming up his audience did he launch into a talking advertisement for Edison and his great enterprise and the difficult challenge of making the light not brighter, but less bright, into a "soft, mellow light, which was adapted to commercial needs." Edison's was the "perfect light."

Edison was strongly averse to speaking in public and allowed Lowrey to speak on his behalf. The guests then followed with perorations that became more ornate as one followed another. The champagne flowed, "Menlo Park" became "Melno Park," and the drinking continued even after the aldermen boarded their train at ten o'clock for the return home. The effects of the alcohol produced the impression, recorded by the reporter for *New York Truth,* that "each alderman looked as though he thought himself the Mayor of New York." The paper declared Edison's demonstration a "decided success, especially of his guests' capacity for Champagne."

When the aldermen woke up the next day, the convivial feelings for Edison with which they had left Menlo Park were replaced by hangovers. Negotiations resumed and the aldermen would not back down from onerous terms, asking the Edison Electric Light Company to pay ten cents a linear foot for the privilege of laying wire. With wires running in parallel along both sides of every street, this charge would run about $1,000 a mile. The city also wanted 3 percent of gross receipts after the first five years. Outraged, Edison made the terms public in January 1881, seeking support for terms more favorable to the company. Brush Electric had not had to pay the city anything for the privilege of operating, Edison pointed out. He also made noises that if he could not obtain reasonable terms, he would take his business to a more hospitable place, such as Newark or Philadelphia.

Edison's public airing of his grievances over proposed terms did not result in any noticeable strengthening of his bargaining power. His representatives and the city government would wrangle for four more months before settling upon five cents a linear foot as a franchise fee. In the meantime, however, Brush Electric had adroitly moved from brief free demonstration, to free demonstration of longer duration, and then to a profitable city contract to light a number of important locations in addition to Broadway. Well positioned on the most visible streets, the company was asked to light hotels and theaters, providing lighting that also met "commercial needs," the segment of the marketplace that

Lowrey had attempted to position the Edison Electric Light Company as uniquely capable of addressing.

Menlo Park had been the perfect locale for Edison's laboratory when the quest for novelty would bring eager feature writers to Edison's door, happy to describe whatever was put on display. But now that Edison Electric had formidable competition that was well entrenched in the most visible part of the most visible city, a rural train stop was no longer the best-placed stage. A member of the Edison Electric Light Company board came up with an intriguing idea: leasing a four-story brownstone residence in Manhattan to house the company offices, strategically situated in a prominent location, on Fifth Avenue, just south of Fourteenth Street. With the installation of a gas-powered power plant in the basement and two hundred incandescent lights throughout the building, 65 Fifth Avenue could serve as a glowing advertisement for the company's lighting on display every night, indoors, where it was designed for use, yet in a location easily visible to the passersby and open for visitors to tour.

For the company to fully exploit the potential of offering attractions at 65 Fifth Avenue that could not be found anywhere else, Edison himself would have to be installed there along the with the two hundred light fixtures. He would have to be willing to spend more time glad-handing visiting strangers than had ever been the case in Menlo Park, where he had been protected by the relative isolation of the laboratory. Yet in early 1881, when his business interests required a personal sacrifice on his part, moving into an almost full-time role as greeter, he did a brave thing: He accepted the responsibility to contribute in whatever way would most help the business, regardless of how much he loathed the role, and how reluctantly he relinquished control of the miniature universe embodied in the Menlo Park laboratory. In early February 1881, Edison began to spend his daytime hours at the Fifth Avenue office, returning to Menlo Park at night. At the end of the month, he moved his family into a hotel across the street from the office. He now could make himself available to personally receive the lines of visitors, including scientists, financiers, actors, diplomats, and sundry royalty (afterward, in private, he would do wicked impressions of the famous for the entertainment of the staff). In its first year on Fifth Avenue, the company rarely closed its doors before midnight.

The Menlo Park laboratory was emptied, with just his junior assistant Francis Jehl left there to perform whatever miscellaneous tests of equipment he was asked to do. Jehl was certain that Edison would never close the laboratory completely, and would eventually return there after the temporary need to be in New York City had passed. But just three months after Edison had moved himself and his family to Fifth Avenue, he sent Jehl a short note telling him to pack up the remaining equipment and join him in New York. In Jehl's memory, the orders were a surprise and meant he would have to give up the "soothing seclusion in God's open country, away from the beaten tracks of men." In retrospect, he should have taken heart in Edison's example: Edison had the most reason to appreciate the seclusion of Menlo Park, and yet he acquiesced when necessity tapped on his shoulder, calling him to center stage.

CHAPTER SIX

IMMERSION

W HEN THOMAS EDISON MADE plans to build his first centralized power plant in Lower Manhattan, the city had many
surprises in store for him. Real estate presented the first
problem. Edison must have been the last person in the country to notice
that Manhattan is an impossibly expensive place to be. Only "the very
rich can afford the expense," said an observer—in 1882. Oblivious,
Edison had drawn up blueprints for an installation that would require a
single floor about two hundred feet square. He assumed that by selecting a "slum street" near the waterfront with the most dilapidated properties, he would be able to pick up the property he would need for
about $10,000. He was way off the mark, however. The available prop-
erties were four-storied industrial buildings that were only twenty-five
feet across, not two hundred, and only eighty-five or one hundred feet
deep. Edison purchased two adjacent buildings on Pearl Street, which
cost not $10,000 but $155,000. With much less space with which to
work, he replaced the plan of his original layout with a creative revi-
sion. Gutting one of them, he reconstructed the interior with structural
steel, building up instead of out.

He took in stride his first serious financial setbacks. When the directors of the Edison Electric Light Company declined to invest in facilities
for manufacturing the dynamos whose spinning generated electricity,
Edison founded a new company, the Edison Machine Works, to take on
the responsibility, and took over shipbuilder John Roach's Etna Iron

Works on the Lower East Side. Acting with admirable boldness for some-one without adequate liquid assets. Edison directed George Gouraud, his representative in Europe, to unload Edison's holdings in various tele-phone interests, such as the Edison Telephone Company of Glasgow. He wrote Gouraud that he would sell all his holdings before touching his shares in Edison Electric, which he wanted to hold "as long as pos-sible." (He eventually succeeded in getting the Machine Works funded without touching his prized shares in the light company.)

The directors of Edison Electric wanted nothing to do with the manu-facture of lightbulbs, either. Edison and his closest associates—Charles Batchelor, Francis Upton, and Edward Johnson—pooled $35,000 of their personal resources to found the Edison Lamp Company ("lamp" referred to bulbs). Edward Johnson, along with former Edison associate Sigmund Bergmann, founded still another company that would manu-facture light fixtures, switches, sockets, and related hardware. Bergmann was a German-born machinist who had run his own machine shop after leaving Edison's. A few years earlier, Johnson had provided Bergmann's shop with a contract for small demonstration phonographs, a line of business that had not been successful but had brought the two men closer, leading now to the establishment of Bergmann & Company. The two partners decided it would be in their best interests to add Edison as a third equal partner. When they asked him if he were interested in joining them, Edison inquired, "For how much?" Without consulting his part-ner, Johnson said, "For nothing but goodwill," and the deal was sealed on the spot with a handshake. Bergmann later said ruefully that he and Johnson left money on the table: "Edison would have been glad to pay us fifty thousand dollars."

In the push to commercialize his electric light, Edison had never taken on so much work, so much risk, and right in the center of the media capital of the country. Technical problems, business issues, per-sonnel headaches—the obstacles in Edison's path were of a size he had never encountered, yet he moved them out of his way, one by one. This was real-time invention and problem solving, in every imaginable tech-nical and nontechnical domain, on an impressive scale. One reporter marveled at Edison's quick recovery from dyspepsia that had briefly confined him to bed: "What a wonderful amount of nervous energy there is in this man."

Edison's energies continued to be applied exclusively to his business interests. The family doctor was concerned about Mary Edison's state of mental health, but as had been the case before, Edison did not change his own plans to attend to her. "She seems very nervous and despondent and thinks she will never recover," the doctor wrote Edison in January 1882. He suggested that Edison take her to Europe for a few months; at the least, "something ought to be done."

Edison remained immersed in his work, however. He spent most of his time at the Pearl Street station, or nearby. Often he napped on the premises, sleeping on top of an electrical conduit that was stacked in the cellar. It was both cold and damp, but Edison did not mind. Later, he recalled that two Germans who were employees who worked in the cellar doing tests caught diphtheria there and died, but he was never affected.

One component of the project was designing, then building and installing, the dynamos for the Pearl Street station. He insisted on custom building a dynamo far larger than the ones he had used before, conceived on a scale that required special tools. Another component was laying the lines that Edison was determined to place underground, a more difficult undertaking than stringing them overhead, where there already existed a tangle of lines owned by Brush Electric and a multitude of telegraph, telephone, and fire alarm companies. Edison had originally planned to offer service to the entirety of south Manhattan, south of Canal Street and north of Wall Street, but engineering considerations forced him to carve out a smaller district, bounded by Wall, Nassau, Spruce, and Ferry Streets. Still, his company had to place underground some eighty thousand linear feet of electrical wire. This had never been attempted before, so it should not have been a surprise when H. O. Thompson, the city's commissioner of public works, summoned Edison to his office to explain that the city would have to be assured that the lines were installed safely. Thompson was assigning five inspectors to oversee the work, whose cost would be covered by an assessment of $5 per day, per inspector, payable each week. When Edison left Thompson's office, he was crestfallen, anticipating the harassment and delays ahead that would be caused by the inspectors' interference. On the day that work began, however, the inspectors failed to appear. Their first appearance was on Saturday afternoon, to draw their pay. This set the pattern that the inspectors followed as the work proceeded through 1881 and into 1882.

The public was reminded of the lethal potential of electricity while Edison's crews dug up the streets. They read in the newspaper that a thirty-year-old dock laborer who was touring the Brush Electric Light Company's Buffalo plant had leaned over a railing and gripped two hanging wires. He dropped onto the railing, dead. In England, a series of fatal accidents to workmen drew remarks about how "the electric Frankenstein turns now and then upon the magician who has raised him." About the same time, a German proposed building an electric chair for executing criminals, which would bring death "instantaneously." He tried out the concept on dogs, a horse, and an ox.

Edison's company did its best to distance itself from Brush and the other arc light companies, arguing that the others used a form of electricity that was as dangerous as Edison's was harmless. At this point, before the "battle of the currents" had formally begun, the public was not informed what exactly distinguished Edison's direct current from arc light's alternating current. Direct current flows in the same direction; alternating current flows in one direction, then reverses and flows in the other, continuously changing. Both forms of current could electrically shock a human being, causing sustained contraction of muscles. Alternating current poses an especially dangerous risk, however, because its rapid discontinuous movement—flowing in this direction, then that one—is more likely to scramble the neural subsystem that serves as the heart's guiding metronome. Once the signals are scrambled, fibrillation follows: rapid, ineffective contractions of the heart muscles that fails to pump blood as it should. Alternating current's propensity to induce fibrillation gives direct current an edge in terms of safety.

Even if comparatively safer, however, direct current was capable of inducing harmful, even fatal, shocks, too. Edison Electric was not wholly honest with the public about its own safety issues. When the Pearl Street station was running tests prior to the official launch of the service, a police officer noticed that horses that passed a certain spot near the corner of Nassau and Ann Streets would bolt, or drop to their knees, or perform "certain equestrian antics such as had never before been witnessed," wrote Francis Jehl. Almost inevitably, a crowd gathered for the free entertainment. When a horse-drawn wagon approached the place where the electrical "juice" was leaking, the people who stood on either side maintained blankly innocent expressions for the wagon driver, silently urging him to proceed. Then the horse was shocked and bounded off, out of control. The police officers present also thought the horses' reaction was highly entertaining. Only when the crowd of onlookers grew too large did they tell Edison Electric to cut the power and find the problem. Edison went to see for himself and thought the shocks amusing, too, even as he directed a crew to locate the leak. The next day, a visitor came to his office wishing to buy apparatus that he could install at a horse market, where, in Edison's description, he "could get old nags in there and make them act like thoroughbreds."

As soon as the newspapers had received word of the Nassau Street shocks, reporters headed to the Pearl Street station to ask questions. Charles Clarke, a Bowdoin classmate of Francis Upton's who had joined Edison's staff in 1880, served as reluctant spokesperson. "We have no evidence that the shocks, if there were any, came from our station," Clarke said cautiously, having delayed answering by taking off his glasses and rubbing the lenses for a long while. The reporters pressed, and Clarke ended up conceding that it was theoretically possible, and even drew a sketch of how the leak may have occurred.

The president of Edison Electric, Major Sherburne Eaton, resorted to what appeared to be the easiest course: emphatic denial of a problem. He explained that he himself had "taken the full force of the entire current with my naked hands, and have seen hundreds of others do it, both men and women, and always without the slightest shock." Eaton was publicly expounding upon the impossibility of Edison Electric's current producing a shock at about the same time that Edison was privately telling Charles Clarke that, yes, the company's workers had accidentally spiked one of the electrical tubes in that spot, and the current was not dissipated harmlessly through the earth, as Eaton was telling reporters would be the case even had a rupture occurred.

The Edison Electric Light Company in 1882 launched a counter-offensive to direct public attention to its most vulnerable competitors: the gas companies. The arc light companies could not be attacked without hurting the image of everyone in the electric power business; the lay public could not readily distinguish between direct and alternating current. The threat to public safety posed by gas, however, was easily understood. The *Bulletin of the Edison Electric Light Company* devoted considerable space to reports of devastation and death caused by gas. A man was found dead in his hotel room—with the gas turned on. Two young girls found dead in bed—gassed. An explosion blew out heavy plate glass from windows in a downtown office building—again, gas. Standing alone in a room lit with gas was no different from standing "immured with 23 other persons all taking oxygen from the atmosphere," according to the author of an article titled "How to Escape Nervousness." After several hours of oxygen deprivation, was it a surprise that "your nerves should rebel as far as their weak state permits, and that your head should ache, your hands tremble, and that your daughter's playing on the piano almost drives you wild?"

Gaslight customers could appreciate the simple physical fact that an electric light did not affect the quality of the air, nor generate heat in a room. The gas industry, however, slyly instilled fear, uncertainty, and doubt among customers who were considering an alternative. The public was warned that the electric light projected a toxic ray that would turn the complexion of survivors green—and swell the death rate. Those claims clashed with positive ones issued by entrepreneurs touting the healthful benefits of electricity. An electric corset, for example, was advertised that would "cause the wearer to grow plump and to enjoy the very best of health."

The prospective advantages of replacing gaslights with electric ones were clear enough to the warden of the Maryland state penitentiary in

Baltimore, who had seen the electric lights in the Menlo Park demonstration and was eager to install them, "without any red tape," he promised. This would have entailed installing a small power plant, like the one serving the laboratory in Menlo Park or the company's office in the brownstone on Fifth Avenue. Such installations, which Edison Electric called "isolated lighting," did not help the company advance toward its strategic aim of building an electrical utility that served an entire city, however. Edison asked that word be passed on to the state penitentiary that his work was organized to build a complete system. He acknowledged the paradox that "I could very much easier light up a square mile with 1500 to 2000 houses than I could a single building."

One New York company, the lithograph firm of Hinds, Ketcham, succeeded in buying its own power plant from Edison Electric. The electric light was much superior to gaslight for work that required distinguishing colors, and the firm provided a testimonial that the light was "the best substitute for daylight we have ever known, and almost as cheap." The Blue Mountain House, a hotel that sat thirty-five hundred feet above sea level in the Adirondacks, got an Edison power plant, too. Located forty miles from the nearest railroad, the machinery had to be packed onto the backs of mules, and once installed the boilers were fed by wood. With a printing firm grateful for the quality of the light, and the resort hotel grateful for electric light of any form, these early installations offered Edison Electric good references from customers less concerned about the economics than others would be.

Well before Edison's Pearl Street station was ready, Brush was selling its arc lights to businesses for interior use, too, with power supplied from its own central station. In December 1881, the only thing that kept Brush from moving faster was a shortage of machinery needed to expand its generating capacity. Its system in Manhattan supplied 550 lights, outdoors and indoors, and could have supplied light to more offices if it had had more power to distribute in the late afternoon and early evening. In winter, its outdoor lights uptown along Broadway came on while downtown offices were still open, creating peak demand for electricity that exceeded the limited supply of power.

While Brush was hampered by insufficient capacity and the gas companies were unable to persuasively portray electric light as intrinsically more dangerous than their own, Edison Electric could have grabbed all the business it could handle by responding to requests for lights powered by on-site plants. In the three months following the Menlo Park demonstrations, the company received three thousand to four thousand separate applications—so many it had lost accurate count. Thomas Edison's determination to spurn these opportunities to quickly commercialize the electric light, and instead to remain focused on the more difficult, but ultimately more significant, task of launching his own central power system, proved to be a brilliant stroke. It was not the result of formal study, or broad consultation with his lieutenants. Instead, it was an intuitive hunch that demonstrating the viability of a centralized system would be strategically more important to the business than accepting orders from individual customers.

The laying of the mains had begun in April 1881, but by December, only one-third of the district had been wired. Work was slowed by shortages of wire and the iron pipe through which it was threaded. Suppliers reneged on contracts signed before inflation had sent prices higher, and Edison filed lawsuits to enlist the authority of the courts to enforce the earlier agreements. In addition, the lines could advance only at night because the city prohibited work during daylight hours so that traffic would not be disrupted. Work stopped completely when winter set in and the ground froze. Edison Electric had to issue a disappointing announcement: Downtown would not be lighted until the spring.

Incandescent lighting did not hold the nation's interest during the hard slog beneath New York's streets. For the city that sought the latest lighting technology—and what city did not?—a new possibility had appeared the previous year: placing arc lights high enough to project an intense light for many blocks in all directions. In Wabash, Indiana, four enormous three-thousand-candlepower arc lights were suspended in 1880 from a flagstaff atop the courthouse. The light was said to be bright enough to throw shadows of cows standing five miles away. Other cities followed, mounting lights upon iron towers that rose hundreds of feet above the central business district. In San Jose, California, the publisher of the local newspaper raised cash contributions from the general public for the erection of a four-legged, 237-foot monster of a light tower, believed to be the tallest in the country. (Wild fowl crashed into its upper structure and dropped into the street below, providing an income supplement to police, who sold the birds to local restaurants.) In Detroit, the Brush Electric Light Company built 142 masts, each 200 feet high (and when it lost its contract with the city, refused to turn them over to the successor contractor, which added another 100 towers to the blight). A British observer marveled at Americans' tolerance for such breathtaking ugliness, "the most defiant appearance of utter disregard for every other claim except utility."

The foreign observer did not understand the competitive metabolism of local city boosters in America, determined to outhustle, outdo, outbuild every other city. Wabash, the pioneer, bragged that it had earned headlines like "Wabash Enjoys the Distinction of Being the Only City in the World Entirely Lighted by Electricity." It was not just small three-thousand-person towns in the Midwest that regarded aerial lights as an easy shortcut to electric lighting for a city. In Los Angeles, editorial writers advocated construction of multiple light towers atop the hills surrounding the city and provided poetic descriptions of the benefits. The lights "shall search the roads, alleys and corners, the streets will be safer and iniquity of all kinds will decrease. The brighter the light the better for truth, purity and honor, and the worse for fraud and all that fearful spawn of evil which flourishes in the darkness. Up then with the graceful and generous towers!"

The towers in Los Angeles were never erected, averting certain disappointment. A source of powerful light mounted so high created a glow that stretched in all directions, sufficient to cast shadows at great distances, but not strong enough for the light to be of useful intensity. When a history of Detroit that was published in 1923 looked back upon the city's tower lights, which by then had been dismantled, it described them as "more spectacular than efficient."

The initial sensation they had stirred upon their introduction, however, had drawn attention away from Edison and his light. In a contest, incandescent light could never match the sheer candlepower of arc light. The only way Edison Electric could regain some attention for itself was to come up with an entirely novel use of its low-candlepower light, a feat accomplished by William Hammer, formerly the chief engineer of the Edison Lamp Works and lately dispatched to London. In February 1882, Hammer unveiled at the Crystal Palace Electric Exhibition an electrified sign. It was about ten feet in length, spelling out "Edison" in foot-high letters, using about a dozen sixteen-candlepower bulbs for each letter. By means of a hand-cranked drum that was out of sight, the letters of "Edison" were illuminated, one by one, then all at the same time. With this, Americans introduced to the world the first electrified advertisement.

While work on Pearl Street was in progress, Edison was able to test his newly designed electric light equipment in a full-scale, real-world demonstration—in the heart of London. Along a half-mile route following the Holborn Viaduct, streetlamps and interior lights in adjacent hotels, restaurants, shops, and offices were installed, including in part of the General Post Office. It was a technical success, impressed the newspapers of Fleet Street, which were nearby, and provided valuable experience that would be used in readying the Pearl Street system. But it was merely a demonstration, not a commercial operation, and so could not answer the critical question: Would Edison's centralized system of supplying electricity for incandescent lighting be able to match the low price of gas lighting?

Edison deployed a large battalion of canvassers to go house to house in the Pearl Street district, noting the number of gas jets, the usual hours of use, and their cost. He also learned which establishments had manufacturing operations in which a motor could be applied. Within the district, the researchers found some eighty horses who provided motive force by stepping on treadles in the top stories of buildings that they were never permitted to leave until death. The locations of prospective electricity customers were easier to determine, however, than the future cost of delivering power to them, generated in an untested centralized system likely to entail high distribution costs.

The passage of time did not serve to bolster the public's confidence in Edison's system. In May 1882, when completion seemed too far off to be within view, share prices of gas utilities advanced to great heights. Edison was unable to remain silent. Concerned that he was losing the public's support, Edison called in the newspaper reporters and predicted that his system would within a few years completely eliminate gas as a source of lighting. He was so confident that customers would prefer his light, "better, cleaner, purer, and more wholesome," that he could charge $1.50 for electric light equivalent to that produced by one thousand cubic feet of gas, even if the gas companies lowered their price to a penny.

Edison also boasted of his company's considerable experience in the electric light business, pointing to the "isolated" site-based plants that the company had tried its best to avoid building while the Pearl Street project remained incomplete. The sheer volume of requests had worn down Edison's resistance, and he had been least opposed to requests that had come in from overseas. By agreeing to build and supply the miniplants in places such as Italy, Austria, Finland, and Chile, Edison Electric was able to quickly establish its name in far-flung locations. By May 1882, two hundred of these small plants were in operation.

As engines of publicity, the miniplants potentially could most help when they became highly sought after by the wealthy for use in their own homes. This required, however, that they supply electric light without mishap. William Vanderbilt was the first to place an order for his own personal power plant and lighting system for installation at his house under construction on upper Fifth Avenue. Having seen the electric light on display at Edison Electric's offices, Vanderbilt turned the responsibilities of general contractor over to his son-in-law, who was acquainted with technical issues as the head of the telephone department of Western Union. Edison was present on the evening that the system was turned on for the first time. The test went well, and Vanderbilt, his wife, and his daughters joined Edison in the main parlor, admiring the light. Almost immediately, however, signs appeared of a smoldering fire within the wallpaper, which apparently had a fine metallic thread in its weave. Edison ordered the system shut down and was pleased that no flames had appeared. Mrs. Vanderbilt, however, "became hysterical," according to Edison. She wanted to know where the fire had started. The electrical plant in the cellar was described, but the more that was explained, the more upset she became. She had not been told before then that a boiler for the power plant had been installed in the house. On her orders, the entire installation was removed.

The unhappy ending to this first installation swiftly became public knowledge, and the gas utilities were glad to help spread the news. Edison did his best to minimize the problems that had been revealed. When asked whether it was true that Vanderbilt had ordered Edison's electric lights to be removed from his new house because they did not work well—and had set fire to the woodwork—Edison declared, "It is false." True, the lights had been removed, but they were not "our" lights, Edison maintained. "Our" lights will be those powered by the central station on Pearl Street. Mr. Vanderbilt had been so impatient, however, that he had insisted on installation of an individual power plant, which Edison appeared to disown. As for the report of a fire that had been caused by the lights, this, too, Edison tried to spin to his advantage. He told a reporter that one of the electric light wires had come in contact with a burglar-alarm wire, become overheated, and charred a few gold-thread wires in the cloth wallpaper, nothing more.

Undeterred by Vanderbilt's unhappy experience, J. P. Morgan wanted Edison to build a system of lights and self-contained power plant for his house, too, at 219 Madison Avenue. He directed that the plant be installed at a distance, however, in a cellar excavated for this purpose beneath the stables, which were at the rear of the property. A subterranean conduit, built of brick, ran from the plant to the house and wires were run through the gas conduits. The power plant was staffed with its own full-time engineer, who came on duty at 3:00 P.M. and fired up the boilers so power would be ready by 4:00. He completed his shift at

11:00 P.M., a fact the members of the Morgan household sometimes forgot when the house was plunged into darkness in the middle of a late-evening card game.

The generating plant was situated far enough from the main house of the Morgan property that its presence did not annoy members of the household—the Morgan household, that is. Near the Morgan stables was the house of Mr. and Mrs. James Brown, however, and Mrs. Brown complained that the vibrations of the dynamo made her house shake. Pierpoint Morgan had rubber pads installed beneath the machinery and sandbags placed along the walls of the cellar to reduce the noise and vibrations, appeasing Mrs. Brown only somewhat. Fumes and smoke, she said, were penetrating her house and tarnishing her silver. Noise pollution in the neighborhood returned when stray cats in the neighborhood discovered a toasty place to gather and yowl in the winter: on the conduit that ran between the power plant and the Morgan house.

Morgan prized being ahead of everyone else, and the next year was concerned that his plant was already less than state of the art, a suspicion that was confirmed when he persuaded Edison to send Edward Johnson to the house for an evaluation. Johnson was instructed to upgrade the equipment and also to devise a way to provide an electric light that would sit on Morgan's desk in his library. At a time when the very concept of an electrical outlet and detachable electrical appliances had yet to appear, this posed a significant challenge. Johnson's solution was to run wires beneath the floor to metal plates that were installed in different places beneath the rugs. One of the legs of the desk was equipped with sharp metal prongs, designed to make contact with one of the plates when moved about the room.

In conception, it was clever; in implementation, it fell short of ideal. On the first evening when the light was turned on, there was a flash, followed by a fire that quickly engulfed the desk and spread across the rug before being put out. When Johnson was summoned to the house the next morning, he was shown into the library, where charred debris was piled in a heap. He expected that when Morgan appeared, he would angrily announce that the services of Edison Electric were no longer needed.

"Well?" Morgan stood in the doorway, with Mrs. Morgan standing behind him, signaling Johnson with a finger across her lips not to launch into elaborate explanations. Johnson cast a doleful eye at the disaster in the room and remained silent.

"Well, what are you going to do about it?" Morgan asked. Johnson said the fault was his own and that he would personally reinstall everything, ensuring that it would be done properly.

"All right. See that you do." Morgan turned and left. The eager purchaser of first-generation technology handled setbacks with equanimity. "I hope that the Edison Company appreciates the value of my house as an experimental station," he would later say. A new installation with second-generation equipment worked well, and Morgan held a reception for four hundred guests to show off his electric lights. The event led some guests to place their own orders for similar installations. Morgan also donated entire systems to St. George's Church and to a private school, dispatching Johnson to oversee the installation as a surprise to the headmistress. The family biographer compared Morgan's gifts of electrical power plants to his sending friends baskets of choice fruit.

Every such gift basket sent by Morgan represented a mix of good and bad news for his supplier, Edison Electric. Keeping its most important investor happy was good; diffusing the company name into places likely to impress influential individuals was also good. But the self-contained plants were a distraction that required a diversion of precious talent and diffusion of focus while the main project, the centralized station at Pearl Street, was still unfinished. Outside of the New York City area, Edison Electric had obtained contracts to build centralized systems in other municipalities whose officials were willing to believe that the technology had been proven adequate in the demonstrations, without waiting for the real-world test in New York. In Appleton, Wisconsin, for example, the lighting system had been purchased by a local industrialist who was so thoroughly sold on the technology during a fishing trip with an Edison salesman that he had placed an order without even seeing a demonstration. It could have been ready for operation before New York's Pearl Street, but Edison forbade its operators from progressing beyond the test stage so that Pearl Street would receive the publicity from being first.

By August 1882, the underground conductors for the Pearl Street district were in place, and all that remained was to connect the street mains with the individual buildings, rewire the interior fixtures, and install meters. The very last step was the inspection of each customer's premises by the city's Board of Underwriters, a slow process as it had only one inspector. Kinks in the system were ironed out by tests that covered different portions of the district. By the end of the month, service to a few customers had begun unofficially. Though not all portions of the district had received underwriter approval, Edison decided the time had arrived for an official beginning. On the afternoon of 4 September 1882, he, Bergmann, Kruesi, and a few other Edison Electric staff members went to the offices of J. P. Morgan in the Drexel Building at Broad and Wall Streets. At 3:00 P.M., a switch was ceremoniously thrown, and Edison's electric lights came to life.

No throng of reporters was on hand to commemorate the event. It received the most complete coverage from the *New York Times*, but that was to be expected: The *Times* itself received service in the Times Building for the first time—a long-anticipated dividend from Edison's decision to place the first central station where it was. The light was described as superior to that of gas by "men who have battered their eyes sufficiently by years of night work to know the good and bad points of a lamp," said the *Times*. The comparison between electric and gaslight favored the former, but the differences were subtle. The shades on the electric light fixtures made them resemble gas fixtures, and "nine people out of ten would not have known the rooms were lighted by electricity, except that the light was more brilliant and a hundred times steadier." The newspaper had not fully committed to switching to electric lights — only fifty-two of a possible four hundred or so lights in the building had been electrified—so the first evening of service did not mark a clean, dramatic beginning of a new era.

The official beginning was covered more objectively by the *New York Herald,* which itself used five hundred incandescent bulbs in its offices in the evening, but these were supplied by power from its own plant, the largest on-site power plant in the city. Its report was a positive one, noting that the Pearl Street machinery worked well and about three thousand Edison Electric customers were ready to receive service, out of five thousand when all of the installations in the district were completed. Some customers were "a trifle disappointed at first" when they saw the soft electric light, but supposedly soon realized that a softer light was best for interior lighting and would be easiest on the eyes.

The *Herald* reporter portrayed the moment as a satisfying denouement to a long-running drama involving unfulfilled promises and a loud chorus of skeptics. After recounting the various difficulties that had slowed the realization of the vision, the story said "many people shook their heads at [the] failure of the promised radiance and believed something was amiss." Edison and his company had persevered nonetheless and now "the Edison light had a very fair degree of success." This was the most generous review that the new service received.

The launch of commercial service was not criticized so much as it was greeted with a yawn. It was not regarded by contemporaries as the red-letter date in the history of progress that would be featured in the textbooks assigned to later generations. Most of those people who the *Herald* said had shaken their heads skeptically no longer took an interest in the venture. It had taken four long years after Edison's announcement in 1878 about inventing a new electric light to bring the complete system into operation. By 1882, the flighty public had moved on to other diversions. The technical community had had their doubts about the feasibility of the system, but demonstrations and awards in London and Paris had eliminated their interest at the same time that the doubts were removed. The only group that had cause to pay close attention was the small group of Edison Electric investors, and they could not yet relax because they still did not know whether this novel system would turn out to be profitable.

At the time of the first announcement in 1878, Edison had painted a picture of electric lights in houses that also included electric meters. After a few weeks of experiments, Edison had declared that he did not think it necessary to measure the amount of electricity used; he proposed instead a simpler system, charging a flat rate for every light fixture (which he anachronistically referred to as a "burner"). "If I find that this works an injustice," he said, "why I shall try to get up a meter, but I fear it will be very hard to do it." Planning for flat-rate pricing had ended almost immediately, however, and he returned to working on a chemical meter. Reading the meter involved removing a metal plate and taking it to the central station to be weighed—measuring the quantity of zinc that had been deposited on it indicated the amount of current that had passed through. Characteristically, Edison announced that he had completed work on the meter well before he actually had. But his design eventually did turn out well; the mechanism was simple and accurate. To ensure that it worked well in winter, too, a lightbulb was added below the bottles that held the chemical solution, providing heat to keep them from freezing. The only shortcoming of the chemical meter, and it was not a small one, was that the customer could not verify its accuracy and had to trust the company that its reading was correct.

Edison Electric did not charge for its service the first four months. Its initial customers were treated to a beta test, offered without charge while bugs were identified and eliminated. Short circuits were difficult to track down, especially in the underground feeders. Often employees at the station had no way of identifying the location of the problem, other than to walk the streets, looking for smoke coming up from the paving stones.

Edison Electric had done everything it could to make it easy for prospective customers in its Pearl Street district to switch from gas to electric lighting. It had wired the homes and businesses of its customers for free, and provided bulbs without charge. It also guaranteed that its electric lights would be cheaper than gas. Still, it proved difficult to enlist the cautious prospects who had not signed up before service started. Some customers seemed to Edison determined to "prevaricate" when demanding discounted rates, claiming that their electricity bill was greater than their gas bill had been.

Some of the early customers expressed appreciation of Edison Electric's inaugural service. One such customer in the liquor business put in an order for 250 lights, placing one light in each of 250 barrels of cheap whiskey, believing that the light took "the shudder out of it." He was always prompt in paying his bill.

J. P. Morgan was not so cheerful about his own bill, however. He complained to Edison that the meter was inaccurate, favoring Edison Electric. Edison was unwilling to concede any problem with his meter and outlined a method of checking its accuracy, to which Morgan agreed. Cards were printed and hung on every fixture in Drexel, Morgan and Company's offices, which noted the number of bulbs in each fixture and the time they were to be turned on and off each day. At the end of the month, a clerk collected the cards and calculated the total number of lamp hours consumed. When the number was compared with the bill, the results confirmed the overcharge. Morgan was happy, Edison was not. Edison suggested that they continue the test for a second month. When it yielded similar results, he was nonplussed. Determined to uncover a problem at Drexel, Edison visited the offices, inspected the wires and fixtures, and reviewed the cards recording usage. He then asked that the janitor be summoned. Upon questioning him, Edison discovered that he used the electric lights while he worked but did not record the hours—no one had asked him to. The test was run another month, with the janitor's participation. With his hours added to the total, the calculated sum came within a few cents of the amount based upon the meter. Morgan was said to have been pleased to find that the meter stood up better to interrogation than others whom he suspected of bilking him.

The story—a parable—was retold with pride many times by Edison and his associates. The lesson it was intended to impart was that Edison Electric had begun its service in an exemplary way. The system worked, and worked well. Judged on its technical merits, the accomplishment was no less than what the company claimed. But as a business that intended to operate in the black, it was less impressive. For once, this could not be blamed on Edison's inattention to business considerations. He had not pursued the light for the sake of intellectual curiosity; his interest in electric light was nakedly commercial. He had entered the field because of his belief that he could produce a profitable service superior to gas and to the other electric light entrepreneurs. Prior to the start of Pearl Street's service, he could only estimate and guess and hope, filling notebooks with speculative figures. The definitive answers could be obtained only when real customers paid real money for what he offered. The initial data produced by actual service were disappointing. At the time the company began assessing charges, it had a modest number of 231 customers. It operated at a loss.

Before the switch had been thrown at the Pearl Street station in 1882, Edison had been consumed with the work, technical and non-technical, necessary to launch the service. But with consummation of the goal, and with it, the conquering of the major technical challenges, his psychological state changed just enough to break his concentration. He had said the previous year that he planned to begin work "immediately" on a second district in Manhattan, bounded by Twenty-fourth and Thirty-fourth Streets, excited at the thought of supplying electricity that would replace not only forty-two thousand gas jets but would also power forty-four hundred sewing machines. But he had not started work on it then, nor could he do so when Pearl Street service began, not when the business had yet to be proven as sound as the technology upon which it was based.

Edison had launched the service believing he could move easily between laboratory and front office, going wherever outstanding problems needed his attention. Two months after Edison Electric began collecting from its first customers, Edison told a reporter that he was going "to be simply a business man for a year," taking a "long vacation" from inventing. And when he did return to the lab, he said, he would give his attention wholly to electricity; "no more phonographs or things of that kind."

Acting as "simply a business man" did not satisfy him, however, nor could he take pride in seeing the company prosper. After a year, Pearl Street had merely doubled its customer base to 455 and was still running at a loss. To Edison's credit, he acknowledged the necessity of bringing in a professional manager, offering Charles Chinnock $10,000 if he succeeded in making the Pearl Street operation profitable. Chinnock was able to do so within the second year of operation. According to company legend, Edison paid Chinnock the promised bonus out of his own pocket.

Expansion in New York proceeded slowly. The uptown station that Edison the year before had claimed that he was about to begin work on was not constructed that year, or the year after. The second district, based at a station on Twenty-sixth Street, did not commence service until 1888, six years later. Coverage in the original downtown district was not expanded until 1891.

Outside of New York, Edison Electric sold a smattering of central power systems to small towns, but these did not serve as showcases. The second plant opened was the one hastily built in Appleton, Wisconsin, by the licensee who made his riskiest investment decisions while fishing. It was the nation's first hydropower plant, but lacked voltmeters, ammeters, lightning protection, and fuses. Its poorly insulated wires shorted out frequently; its managers were unacquainted with cost accounting and set rates below cost. Operating expenses were paid for by ongoing issuance of company stock.

Six months after the start of business at Pearl Street, Edison Electric had failed to convert its establishment of central service in New York into a base for a growing business that sold similar systems to other large cities. The only line of products that sold well were the ones that Edison disdained, the on-site power plants. The company had sold more than 330 plants, some of which were larger than those installed in central stations. Edison Electric's backers, who had waited patiently for four years and were now eager to see a return on their investment, urged Edison to promote the product line that customers were most interested in, the on-site plants. Edison sought vindication of his belief that centralized power generation was superior to distributed generation, but he acknowledged that here, too, he needed help to make a success of the central-station business. He appointed his own personal secretary, twenty-three-year-old Samuel Insull, to take charge of the campaign. Insull had immigrated from England two years before to work for Edison, and his employer had come to view him as indispensable. In his new position, Insull quickly closed sales in small towns in Ohio, Pennsylvania, Massachusetts, and New York.

For Edison's grandly conceived central stations, this was as good as it would get, it appeared: success gained one sale at a time, each on an exceedingly modest scale. He had the patience for a long campaign, if it were technical in nature. But for the slow process of winning customers, he was not well suited temperamentally. He needed technical mysteries and skeptical onlookers and drama. He was an impatient spectator, as when he was invited to Boston to attend a special performance at the Bijou Theatre, marking the debut of its newly installed electric light system. In the course of installing the new lights the theater had taken the daring step of removing the backup system, its gas fixtures. Power was supplied by a neighboring printer, which had installed the largest on-site power plant in the country. The governor was in attendance, and Edison brought along his closest associates, including Johnson, Bergmann, and Insull, all of whom arrived in formal evening dress. The performance began and all seemed well at first. Then Edison noticed that the stage lights were growing progressively dimmer. He and Johnson left their seats to investigate. At the printer's, they discovered that the boilerman had been absorbed in repairing a steam leak, neglecting the boiler fire. When other members of the Edison Electric delegation arrived to see what was the matter, they found Edison and Johnson shoveling coal into the firebox. When the fire was stoked, they picked up their swallow-tailed coats and high hats and returned for the remainder of the performance.

The grander the scale of Edison's ambitions, and the greater the skepticism that he had had to overcome, the happier he had been. Once the electric light had been introduced, however, he found himself in a difficult position. How could he possibly sustain the pace of accomplishments of the previous five years? He could not shrug off the expectation that the Wizard of Menlo Park could accomplish anything. He was thirty-five years old, and the rest of his long life was devoted to attempts to make the inspiration that brought the phonograph and the electric light return.

PART II

Life After

1883–1931

CHAPTER SEVEN

STARTING ANEW

THE MAN WHOSE public image was of a wizard who could conjure whatever he wished faced daily at home his actual powerlessness: He could not make his wife well. She was plagued by headaches, panic attacks, and severe fatigue. In the summer of 1884, she insisted that the family move from their New York apartment at Gramercy Park back to the family house at Menlo Park. She died there on 9 August 1884, at the age of twenty-nine, succumbing to what her doctor termed "congestion of the brain."

Edison was not prepared. His daughter Marion would later recall the image of her father "shaking with grief, weeping and sobbing so he could hardly tell me that Mother had died in the night." Mary's mother, Margaret, had already become the principal care-providing adult for the three Edison children. After Mary's death, the two younger boys, Tom and Will, did not spend time with their father, but their daughter Marion, who was now twelve, became Edison's constant companion. He removed her from Madam Mears's Madison Avenue French Academy and continued her education at home. The curriculum was simple: He had her read ten pages daily from an encyclopedia. This freed her to accompany her father on horse rides, or visits to the theater. She also attended board meetings of the Edison Electric Light Company and stayed with her father until the wee hours of the morning at Delmonico's.

Professionally, Edison was drifting, without an all-consuming project to blot out everything but the work itself. The electric light no longer needed him, and he did not know what to do with himself. Mercifully, his floundering took place out of public view, as newspapers and magazines had swiftly lost interest in him. His boast that electric lighting would replace gas lighting in homes had been more credible before Pearl Street had begun its service on a modest scale. A book about prominent New Yorkers that appeared that year noted how swiftly his public image had flipped, from that of a prodigy to a failure, an illustration of "the fitfulness of the fever of fame."

Electric light had become more of a curiosity than an epoch-defining change. It was used to add novelty one evening to a parade sponsored by the Blaine-Logan presidential campaign of 1884. With Edison's blessing, Edward Johnson and Charles Batchelor designed helmets equipped with lights that were worn by Edison Electric Light employees who marched down Madison Avenue on behalf of Blaine. Each marcher was connected by wires to a portable generating plant that accompanied the group, along with supporting coal and water carts for the steam engine.

In Philadelphia, the light-equipped helmets were put to another use when Edison's company presented to the public the "Edison Darkey." This was the name given in a caption in *Scientific American* to the African American men who were hired to hand out flyers at the 1884 Philadelphia Electrical Exhibition. They wore helmets that were wired to copper spikes on the heels of their shoes and drew power from electrified copper strips placed on the floor of the hall. One report said that they drew crowds of such size that their movement in the hall became impossible.

For a technology story to be interesting to the lay public, novelty was a prerequisite, and that became ever harder to supply. Longtime Edison associate William Hammer succeeded in garnering attention for a New Year's Eve "electrical dinner" that he threw for guests at his home. Electricity was used throughout, beginning with invitations that had been written with an Edison electric pen. At Hammer's house, the approach of a guest on the steps sent electrical signals that lit the veranda, rang the doorbell, and swung open the front door. Electricity supplied the power for self-operating bells, alarms, telephones, cigar lighters, phonographs, fans, musical instruments, and a lemonade pitcher equipped to deliver a nonlethal shock to the unwary person who picked it up, and other curiosities that served to give the house a haunted feel. "It seemed unsafe to sit down anywhere," said one visitor. The party was intended to provide guests with a peek into the future, as if "they had been living half a century ahead of the new year."

Even a good technology story, however, can never match the appeal of a good financial scandal. In 1885, John Roach, the shipbuilder who had worked with Edison to outfit the *Columbia,* tumbled into financial ruin and public humiliation. Roach had once been the preeminent shipbuilder in the country but had become overextended. It was he who later had leased to Edison the building in Lower Manhattan that Edison used to establish the Edison Machine Works. Edison was appalled by the callous mistreatment of Roach by his creditors. Roach was a fellow self-made man, who had been responsible for "feeding innumerable families," and was deserving of respect, not persecution. Edison wrote privately, "For people who hound such men as these I would invent a special Hades. I would stricken [*sic*] them with the chronic sciatic neuralgia and cause them to wander forever stark naked with the arctic circle."

Reading a headline such as "John Roach Embarrassed" in the *New York Times* must have given Edison a scare about his own situation. Just a year before, his own pinched finances had forced him to ask for Roach's indulgence when Edison failed to pay rent on the Machine Works property. Edison blamed tardy payments from his foreign customers and his own costly experimental work. "I am desirous you should do me this favor," he wrote Roach.

At the time of Roach's financial collapse in 1885, one newspaper published rumors that Edison was himself financially hard-pressed. Neither Edison nor his associates deigned to publicly respond, but they did not need to. William Croffut, the reporter who had written many fawning articles about Edison over the years, wrote a piece claiming "personally to know that Mr. Edison is to-day what most people would call a rich man."

The investors in Edison's Electric Light Company, however, did not feel rich. They were grumbling that the price of the company's shares had tumbled to levels that were a fifth or a sixth their peak value, attained when Edison's electric light existed only as an announcement and long before it was introduced as reality. In 1885, three years after the start of service at Pearl Street, a director of the company who chose to remain anonymous complained to the *Philadelphia Press* that Edison insisted on taking an active part in the management of the company "although he is not a bit of a business man." He gave an example of Edison's poor judgment: Edison had proposed installing a new cable in Manhattan that would cost nearly $30,000 a mile, oblivious to the fact that Western Union had one with similar capacity in operation that had only cost $500 a mile. "If he would leave it to practical business men to make money out of it and stick to his inventions," the director said, "the company would in time become very rich."

For Edison, "sticking to his inventions" full-time would mean relinquishing control of Edison Electric, which was anathema. Managing his company did not engage him half as much as creating it, but he could not bring himself to let go of the captain's chair. Edison's intellectual interests, however, wandered from one minor project to the next. He had always done best when attempting something both entirely new and gargantuan in scale, but in the mid-1880s he could not find a suitable project. Around this time he asked his old friend Ezra Gilliland, who was a senior executive at the American Bell Telephone Company, what he should work on now that the electric light was "practically" out of his hands. Gilliland suggested that he return to the phonograph and make it "a practical instrument," but Edison was unable to muster interest. An alternative area that Gilliland mentioned, train-based telegraphy, did not address a potential mass market of comparable size, but Gilliland had done work in this area himself and Edison leaped at the idea.

In short order the two men founded the Railway Telegraph and Telephone Company, and Edison tinkered in a small lab he set up on Avenue B. William Croffut obligingly offered "the Wizard Edison" the opportunity to publicly tout his latest enthusiasm without waiting to put laboratory work to a test in the real world. The article was based solely on one visit to Edison's lab—and on what Edison said about his work, uncomplicated by independent verification. Pointing to a long board covered in tinfoil and suspended from the ceiling with ropes, Edison said that the device permitted him to "make electricity jump 35 feet through the air, carrying the message without spilling it." The plan would be to install foil-covered boards lengthwise atop railcars so that telegrams could be sent and received by trains while passing by stations without stopping.

After Croffut's puff piece appeared, Edison directed Samuel Insull to send Croffut fifty shares of the Railroad Telegraph company. Even judged by the looser journalistic ethics of that day, the gift was apparently deemed best delivered outside of the office (it was sent to Croffut's home). In his note of thanks to Insull, Croffut wrote, "That's what you wanted my private address for, is it, you rogue?" He asked Insull to pass on his appreciation to "Mr. Edison for his continual kindness."

Edison had sent the shares with the message that they "may be worth something some day." The new technology did not work well, however, and the company's prospects diminished accordingly before "some day" could arrive. Put simply, the company was headed toward oblivion. Insull soon concluded that its prospective customers, the railroad companies, were unlikely to "adopt it with much of a 'rush'" and tried to unload his own allocation of shares at a decent price, urging Edison to do the same.

The Railroad Telegraph did not occupy Edison the way that Pearl Street had in the years before service was launched in 1882. Now, nothing in his life did so. He wanted a wifely helpmate, and it is this that commanded his attention more than anything else the year following Mary's death. Ezra Gilliland, and his wife, Lillian, would be a great help to Edison in this quest.

In February 1885, Edison had traveled to New Orleans to visit the World's Industrial and Cotton Centennial Exposition. A world's fair was a splendid place to show one's wares, and Edison Electric had obtained the coveted contract to illuminate the fair's main building, which covered thirty-three acres and was said to be the largest wooden structure in the world. While in New Orleans, thirty-eight-year-old Edison met nineteen-year-old Mina Miller, daughter of Lewis Miller, an Ohio industrialist whose agricultural machinery was on exhibit. Miss Miller had graduated from a Boston seminary the year before and while a student had been a frequent guest at the Gillilands' home. (The circumstantial evidence suggests that Edison met the Millers, father and daughter, in New Orleans by the matchmaking designs of the Gillilands.)

The Gillilands had a summer house on the north shore of Boston Bay, which served as a place for Edison to try out a new sociable persona in the summer of 1885. Edison invited Insull, who was also single, to come up and join the group: "There is [sic] lots [of] pretty girls." Edison himself had already fixed upon Miller as his choice for future wife, and Miller was spending the summer not on Boston Bay but with her parents at the Chautauqua Institution, on Chautauqua Lake, New York—the very place Edison had been scheduled in 1878 to present a talk before he canceled and fled on his trip west.

Chautauqua had been founded by two people. One was John Vincent, the insufferably self-important person who had pressed his uninvited opinions too hard on Edison in the early days of the phonograph. The other cofounder was Lewis Miller, Mina's father. In 1885, Edison understood that Mina Miller was bound closely to Chautauqua, and he would have to make an appearance there during the summer program.

Edison spent the weeks preceding his first Chautauqua visit at the Gillilands' to get comfortable with the new version of himself that he was trying on: a gregarious bon vivant, uninterested in work, filling summer days with frivolous entertainments such as boat rides, card games, and a variation of Truth or Dare for middle-aged participants. He seriously considered buying a yacht, before he came to the realization that his self-transformation was still incomplete—he recognized that he still lacked the ability to disregard the frightful expense.

One of the pastimes organized by the Gillilands was having the guests maintain individual diaries, which were to be passed around among the guests for the entertainment of the group. Edison was willing to go along, making entries for ten consecutive days in July 1885. The calligraphy is impeccable and the grammar without fault, suggesting the final version of writing had passed through at least one preliminary draft. The entries provide a window into what Thomas Edison wanted others—in particular, Mina Miller—to see as his inner feelings. The first entry established that Miller was the very first object of his thoughts upon waking that day; a later entry claimed that "it would stagger the mind of Raphael in a dream to imagine a being comparable to the Maid of Chautauqua."

Edison reported that his daughter Marion invited him one day to toss a ball with her for the first game of catch he had played in his life. His receptiveness to new experiences extends to accepting the dress code of polite society—he wore a clean, starched white shirt, explaining that he submitted out of fear of the disapproval of Mrs. Gilliland. He picks up a book by Hawthorne but fails to be engaged, the reaction to be expected, he self-mockingly says, of a "literary barbarian."

In a newspaper Edison read of two suicides, which he describes in his diary with cold eyes: "Among the million of perfected mortals on Manhattan Island two of them took it into their heads to cut their navel cord from mother earth and be born into a new world." The sarcasm works to better effect in his description of a clerk he encountered when he went into town on errands: "A drug store nowadays seems [to be . . .] in the charge of a young man with a hatchet-shaped head, hair laid out by a civil engineer, and a blank stare of mediocrity on his face."

Edison's trip into town had come close to being fatal, he says in the diary, because he "got thinking about Mina and came near being run over by a street car." He further embellishes the tale: "If Mina interferes much more will have to take out an accident policy." Though he did not address Mina directly, he knew that she would soon read what he wrote, and clumsily joked about marriage. When Marion showed her father her notes for a novel she was planning to write that touched upon the subject of matrimony, Edison writes that he told her "in case of a marriage to put in bucketfuls of misery; this would make it realistic."

Marion Edison could see that her father, joking aside, would soon marry again, and her stepmother would be the person whom her father was incessantly talking about and who was only seven years older than herself. In his diary, Edison thinks Marion's jealousy of Mina, whom he regards as "the yardstick of perfection," was quite amusing. He writes that Marion "threatens to become an incipient Lucretia Borgia."

In August, the Edisons and the Gillilands traveled to Chautauqua and spent a week with the Millers. Edison did not possess the religiosity of Lewis Miller, but the two men did share experience as commercially minded inventors. Miller had experience, too, as a publicly known figure, more so for his work for the Chautauqua Institution than as a principal in an agricultural machinery firm. Edison had noticed earlier that summer that when he picked up a business bestseller titled *How Success Is Won,* both he and Miller were mentioned. (At the time, Miller would have been the wealthier of the two men. A contemporary newspaper placed his net worth at $2 million, or about $38 million in today's dollars.)

The first meeting went well enough for Mina Miller to receive her parents' permission to accompany Edison, Marion, and the Gillilands as they traveled farther upstate in New York and then over to the White Mountains of New Hampshire. Looking back on the trip years later, Edison recalled it as a time in which he and Mina enjoyed an intimate privacy while in the same carriage as the three others. He had taught Mina how to use Morse code as a private language tapped out on the hand of the other person. Private endearments were exchanged in the carriage without risk of being overheard. A story from family lore is that Edison was sitting in the Gilliland family parlor with a number of other people present when Mina suddenly stood up and rushed upstairs without saying a word. Concerned about her sudden exit, Lillian Gilliland went up after her. "What in the name of goodness is the matter?" she had asked. Mina said, "Why, Mr. Edison has just proposed to me across the living room floor." This version of the story does not make clear how Miller had responded at the time, but Edison said that Miller tapped back, "Yes." He would retell the story many times to illustrate why he regarded his deafness as a help in winning Mina as his wife. "If she had been obliged to speak it," Edison speculated, "she might have found it harder."

Upon returning home, Edison formally wrote Mina's father seeking his approval of the marriage. Seeking to show that he was a suitable, sober husband-to-be, he referred to his professional accomplishments—and fame—as his qualifications. "I trust you will not accuse me of egotism when I say that my life and history and standing are so well known as to call for no statement concerning myself." Edison probably sounded more presumptuous than he intended when he closed, "I trust my suit will meet with your approval." Miller received the letter happily, invited Edison to visit the family home in Ohio, and bestowed his blessings on the couple.

The wedding was held at the Miller home in Akron in February 1886. Reporters were present not only at the wedding but also on the train trip south to the honeymoon in Florida. Edison showed off his irrepressible nature as the inventor who never goes on holiday, telling the *New York World* midjourney that he had just been inspired to sketch out the design of a machine that "will pick cotton without trouble." When Edison had first become famous almost ten years previously, he had been complimented with mock editorials calling for action to stop the flow of his inventions; now, Edison was playing to his audience, showing off his legendary mind that could not be switched off, even when traveling with his new bride.

Mina Edison, who still was only twenty years old, did not register a complaint about having to compete with the mechanical cotton picker for Edison's attention. From the beginning of her marriage, she was Mrs. Edison, wholeheartedly devoted to helping her husband, the inventor. While they stayed in Fort Myers, Florida, where Edison and Gilliland had recently purchased adjacent lots and put up vacation houses, Edison shared his unceasing brainstorms with her. His new ideas were recorded in notebooks, each entry dated and signed first "TAE," then "Mina." When they returned home, she commuted daily with Edison for a brief time to his laboratory at the lightbulb factory and assisted in experiments there.

Mina Edison's work at the lab workbench did not last much longer than had Mary Edison's, but the domestic arrangement that succeeded it would turn out to be durable for decades. Edison was the inventor, Mrs. Edison the household manager whose responsibility was to keep her husband insulated from distractions. Later, after almost forty years of marriage to the man whom a clever magazine editor referred to as "the most difficult husband in America," Mina described her auxiliary role without a hint of complaint: "We have always put his work first, all of us. And we have tried to organize our home and our home life to give results just as much as the laboratory."

When Edison and Mina were engaged, Edison offered her a choice of two houses: one in Manhattan on Riverside Drive, the other in a suburb in New Jersey. She weighed the advantages and disadvantages of each by considering which location would be most ideal for Edison's creative work, quiet and free from interruption by visitors. She chose the suburban house, and there she would preside as the chief executive of the household for the duration of his and her lives.

The house Edison purchased was a twenty-three-room Queen Anne–style mansion. It was set amid thirteen and a half sylvan acres in Llewellyn Park, in West Orange, New Jersey, a stunningly beautiful planned suburban community, the country's first. The house had been built and occupied by Henry Pedder, a department store clerk with a modest salary who had discovered that he could afford the good life by embezzling funds from his employer. His bookkeeping exploits had been exposed two years before. When arrested, he promptly turned over title to the property to his employer as partial restitution. The house remained unoccupied but just as it had been, stuffed with Pedder's furniture. The real estate agent who spoke with Edison estimated the combined value of the house and furnishings at $400,000, and initially offered it to Edison for half that if he wished to purchase it furnished. Here was a large estate with collections of exquisite art and furniture and a five-thousand-volume library, the product of ten years of what Edison admired as "enthusiastic study and effort," available at half price—or less. So eager was the department store to unload the property that it eventually lowered its asking price to $125,000. After Mina had made it her choice, Edison took pains to say publicly that he himself was not interested in its luxury. "It is a great deal too nice for me," he said, "but it isn't half nice enough for my little wife here." The Edisons would call their estate Glenmont.

Edison could have viewed the house as an exhibition space to be used for semipublic demonstrations of the fruits of his latest experiments, just as his own associate William Hammer had done with his all-electric house. Edison, however, took little interest in using his own home in this way. Chandeliers had gas burners as well as electrical bulbs. Speaking tubes—interconnected pipes like those used in ships—served as the house's unelectrified intercom system. ("They don't break down," a member of Edison's family would later say in the electronic era.)

Edison found himself with a new home, a new wife, and he would have another daughter, Madeleine, and two sons, Charles and Theodore, who followed. (This matched the pattern of his three children from his first marriage: daughter, Marion, followed by two sons, Thomas and Will.) What he still lacked, however, was the dream laboratory, one that would exceed the humble dimensions of the one he had abandoned in Menlo Park when he moved to New York City to install his first electric light system. His plan was to provide himself with the means to recapture the magic of Menlo Park, which he was already viewing through the gauze of nostalgia. He wrote in his diary, "Everything succeeded in that old laboratory." The limitations of its equipment had not prevented him from enjoying his two biggest triumphs in invention, the phonograph and the electric light. But he thought he could accomplish even greater feats in better appointed surroundings. By building a new lab from scratch that was state of the art, he could tackle any and every kind of problem that struck his fancy and surpass his previous entries in the annals of invention.

The five-building complex for which he drew up plans would be the largest and best-equipped industrial laboratory in the world. He picked out a site in Orange, New Jersey, a short distance from Glenmont in Llewellyn Park. The three-story main building would extend 250 feet in length and include a machine shop staffed with fifty machinists at the ready waiting for his instructions, a stockroom that would have "every conceivable material of every size," and an enormous library with shelves extending from the floor to the 40-feet-high ceiling. The remaining buildings would house specialized labs. In Edison's mind, the complex would enable him to "build anything, from a lady's watch to a locomotive."

So excited was he by his vision that he began construction without waiting to arrange for financing. When the project neared completion in August 1887, Edison was still scrambling to sign outside investors. He hoped to raise $1 million, offering to form an industrial research company in which he would hold half of the equity. No less grandiose were his plans for factories that would be built in the valley to produce his inventions. These, he predicted, would eventually employ fifteen thousand people and return 500 percent to the pioneer shareholders.

Edison acknowledged that his relationship with Edison Electric's board of directors had become less than amicable and he conceded in a letter to a prospective backer that "my place is in the Laboratory." He was confident that by outfitting the lab in advance with everything he could possibly need, it would produce "10 times as much" as a lab with empty shelves, dependent upon ordering materials, castings, or machinery when a particular need came up. He wanted to be ready whenever inspiration paid a visit. He expected to have thirty or forty projects going simultaneously, all profitable yet none as "cumbersome" as the electric light.

Edison had a knack for coming up with memorable images. Newspaper reporters who came by especially liked the one about ladies-watches-to-locomotives. It was used for years even though neither watch, nor locomotive, nor anything close to either would emerge. The only people who were not immediately charmed by Edison's vision were the prospective investors. When his fund-raising efforts petered out, Edison quietly dropped his plan to organize a separate company to oversee the intellectual property that he expected to produce. He ended up being the sole owner and merged his own personal bank accounts with those of the lab. Contract work for other companies provided much needed cash, but also kept Edison entangled in the agendas imposed by others. Freedom to do exactly as he pleased in his laboratory turned out to be elusive.

The shortage of cash affected Mina, who was given responsibility to manage Glenmont while Edison gave his undivided attention to launching his new laboratory. About this time she directed a salaried household staff that included a waitress, cook, maid, and laundress, as well as various gardeners and stable hands. Earlier, in 1887, when construction on the laboratory was beginning, Mina's father, Lewis Miller, wrote to his daughter and reviewed the financial difficulties Edison had found himself in, having begun erecting the lab so soon after stretching his finances to purchase the Pedder mansion. The shortage of capital had made Edison "cautious" when it came to budgeting for household expenses, making newlywed Mina's life as chief household executive rather "hard." Miller praised her for handling the challenges well, but he also told her she should expect to be on her own in doing so, as he thought that Edison "did not care much to hear about home affairs."

After spending about $180,000 on the new lab, Edison had everything he could imagine ever needing. He was not going to squander splendid facilities merely to refine what was already in existence, however. Only projects that had yet to be realized would do. By January 1888 he was still pursuing Henry Villard as a possible investor, offering him the opportunity to own a half share in his new inventions for covering the $60,000 he estimated the lab's operating expenses would run annually. On the list of projects he planned to pursue was the mechanical cotton picker, the inspiration he had brought home from his honeymoon, and the hearing aid, the invention he had delayed working on ever since the news of the phonograph's appearance had brought mail bags full of entreaties from strangers. Other interests included using electricity to cut ice; sheet glass; "artificial ivory"; and railroad signals.

When Edison subsequently revised the estimated annual expenses for the lab upward 50 percent to $90,000, Villard declined the invitation to invest. This left Edison without outside financing—and without outside guidance. By beginning—and then completing—construction of the lab complex prior to arranging the commitment of investors, Edison made sure that the project would go forward without compromises, exactly as he had dreamed, whether others believed in him or not.

At precisely the time he was readying his lab, circumstances forced him to return to the one older invention he had been least interested in working on again: the phonograph. In the early 1880s, he had been embarrassed by the mechanical problems of the tinfoil phonograph, its modest sales, and the damage to his reputation. In 1884, *Off-Hand Portraits of Prominent New Yorkers* said that "the failure of the phonograph did much to destroy the popularity of Mr. Edison." But by 1887, a new rival, the American Graphophone Company, whose wax-coated cylinders could be removed without damage to the recording, which was not possible when using tinfoil, was poised to make a success where he had met with failure. Edison, who was as competitive as anyone, could not abide the prospect of being passed by others. The fact that his old nemesis Alexander Graham Bell was a member of the three-person group that had invented the graphophone raised Edison's ire to the point that he could think of nothing else but joining battle.

Edison's phonograph patents offered no protection, as they had been filed tardily, after foreign patents had been obtained by others. After reviewing the legal issues, Edison explained to Edward Johnson, "We cant [*sic*] stop anybody." The Graphophone Company, for its part, approached Edison with conciliatory offers that were unnecessary given its strong legal position. The company flattered him as the "real" inventor of the talking phonograph (one of the earliest graphophone recordings ended with this concise autobiography: "I am a graphophone and my mother was a phonograph"). It offered to turn over the graphophone and its improvements to him, to pay the costs of any additional experimental work that might be needed, and to grant him half interest in the merged companies, gratis. Company officials tried to persuade Edison's London representative, Colonel Gouraud, to consider a senior position in their company and to approach Edison about accepting a "complimentary" equity position, were Edison willing to approve use of the Edison name on the product.

Edison would never agree to share the mantle of Papa of the Phonograph with anyone else. He fired off a tart note to Gouraud: "Under no circumstances will I have anything to do with Graham Bell [or] with his phonograph pronounced backward." Edison claimed to have come up with a wax-cylinder machine that was better than Bell's and pointed out he was already building the factory that would enable him soon to "flood" the market with them at "factory prices."

Gouraud congratulated Edison for coming up with a "practical" machine and announced he would side with Edison and drop his proposed affiliation with the American Graphophone interests. He was considerate of Edison's feelings and did not mention that it was only the goad of competition that had motivated Edison to return to his work on the phonograph. Alfred Tate, a senior manager who worked for Edison at this time, would later confirm that it had been the Graphophone Company's overtures to Edison that had "shocked him into action."

Edison spoke dismissively of Bell and his Graphophone associates, whom he described as "pirates attempting [to] steal my invention." After being rebuffed, the American Graphophone Company dropped the polite ritual of paying tribute to the Wizard. A story made the rounds about the time when Charles Sumner Tainter, Bell's colleague and the principal inventor of the graphophone, was asked about future collaboration with Edison. Tainter had replied, "Thomas A. Edison can go to Hell! He hasn't got anything that he didn't steal from me."

Edison personally did not have the financial resources to build out his manufacturing capacity and distribution system so that he could go head to head against the Graphophone Company, which had a sizable lead in the race to get machines to market. For a single, promising business opportunity like this, he could still get the attention of the wealthy angel investors who had passed up his earlier invitation to fund Edison so he could play in his new laboratory. A group of four agreed to come to Orange to see a demonstration of Edison's "perfected" phonograph.

When his guests were gathered around him, Edison spoke into the tube and recorded a speech he had prepared. He then stood back confidently to listen to the playback. The words could not be heard, however, over a continuous hissing sound. Edison was visibly perplexed; the machine had worked perfectly only fifteen minutes earlier. He changed the wax cylinder, made another recording, and played it back. The hissing returned. Alfred Tate described the scene.

> Edison was bewildered. There was no possible way in which he could account for such a result. Again and again he tried to get that instrument to talk, and again and again it only hissed at him. The time of our guests was limited. They had apportioned one hour for the demonstration, ample time had the instrument functioned. Mr. Dolan and Mr. Cochrane had to catch a train for their homes in Philadelphia and their time for departure came while Edison still was engaged in a futile effort to reproduce his own voice. Most courteously these gentlemen promised to return to the laboratory when Edison had discovered and corrected the obscure defect in the instrument. They left. But they never came back.

The malady was eventually traced back to the ill-timed decision by one of Edison's assistants to swap, just before the guests arrived, a critical part used for reproducing the sound. He thought he had installed a superior part but it was just a bit wider than it should have been, producing disaster.

The flubbed demonstration turned out to have irreversible ramifications. Edison would not have another opportunity to obtain funding to support his own phonograph company. He was subsequently saved from financial ruin by a member of the nouveau riche, Jesse Lippincott, who had made a fortune making glassware and had lately taken an interest in the thrills of building up the phonograph business. His North American Phonograph Company, which took on the distribution of Edison's phonograph, would prove to be woefully undercapitalized. Edison, however, could not be picky; financially, he was out of options and agreed to the arrangement through gritted teeth. (Lippincott's company simultaneously distributed the Graphophone, too.)

Ezra Gilliland played an instrumental role in the negotiations between Lippincott and Edison. Because Gilliland enjoyed an unusually close personal relationship with Edison, he spoke with more candor than other business associates. The Edison phonographs that were produced in trial manufacturing runs were riddled with defects, and Gilliland did not hide his displeasure. The machines that Gilliland had looked at "would not compare favorably with the graphophone." He went on to warn Edison about steering clear of shoddy business practices: "I have never felt that you would put it upon the market in that condition."

Edison needed to hear straight talk about problems, but unfortunately Gilliland was soon out of the picture, his relationship with Edison ending abruptly on bad terms. The split came when Edison discovered that Gilliland had negotiated a side deal with Lippincott at the time that Gilliland was representing Edison's interests in the negotiations with Lippincott's North American Phonograph Company. In consideration of Gilliland's transfer of his "agency" rights for the phonograph that Edison had given him earlier, Gilliland and Edison's attorney took two-thirds of the $125,000 cash that Lippincott paid for the distribution rights to the phonograph. The two men arranged for the payment to themselves without telling Edison.

Lippincott was unaware that Edison had not been consulted and happened to mention the details of the deal to Edison only after it was completed. When the press heard about the affair, it depicted Edison as a dupe who had been "razzle-dazzled" out of $250,000 by Gilliland, his trusted confederate. Edison was shocked by the revelation and responded with a lawsuit, but was unsuccessful in pressing his claim that the money paid for agency rights was properly due him. The episode made Edison even more withdrawn. With Gilliland, he had allowed business matters and personal life to commingle, and it had come to this regrettable end. (He would not let down his guard again until late in life, and then, only with a friend whose much greater wealth removed concern that Edison would be taken advantage of: Henry Ford.)

Having retained control over design and manufacturing, Edison was responsible for delivering the finished product to Lippincott. The inventor, now settled in his completed lab, could not resist tweaking the final design, and tweaking it some more. Even though Edison announced the completion of his "Perfected Phonograph" in May 1888, he continued to tinker, supervising 120 lab personnel who were pursuing sixty separate experiments related to the phonograph. The remainder of the year passed, and he still was not satisfied and refused to release the first machines for sale.

It was not until the spring of 1889 that Edison reluctantly began to ship the Perfected Phonograph. Even then he grumbled privately he had been so rushed that the battery design remained unsatisfactory. He did not seem concerned, however, about what would happen when customers made the unpleasant discovery that the batteries in their new phonograph were the same ones that Edison privately told Batchelor were "not of much value." (The graphophone, which had gone on sale eighteen months earlier, had a more reliable source of power—a foot treadle—but it too had its own shortcomings.)

Upon its release, Edison's Perfected Phonograph was immediately scooped up by the individuals who leaped to be among the first to possess newly available technology. The governor of Wyoming purchased three phonographs so he would have one on hand for dictating correspondence wherever he happened to be. A distributor in New York noticed the beginnings of the extended workday for executives, as the phonograph made dictation at home feasible. Recordings made in the evening could be brought to the office in the next morning for transcription by a "type-writer" (the person shared the same name with the machine).

Unfortunately for the North American Phonograph Company, and for Edison, the Perfected Phonograph was far from perfect, and not really functional. The wax cylinders were fragile, the mechanical works prone to breakdown. The phonograph required a resident expert to keep it properly adjusted. The *Atlantic Monthly* said that "trusting its manipulation to the office boy or the typewriter girl, that is out of the question for the present." The intelligibility of the recorded voice was unpredictable, "something of a lottery."

Edison, however, was exasperated by the complaints of customers, whose own incompetence he blamed for failing to get satisfactory results. After the first reports of defects came in, he dictated to Charles Batchelor four single-spaced typewritten pages in response to a single field report, ending his reply with "I could go on for a week answering this kind of a letter." What was the point, he wondered aloud, when the complaining customer was someone "who does not know how to work the machine"?

While Edison continued to use his own human amanuensis for dictation, he installed a phonograph in the office of Alfred Tate. "I was the 'dog' on which this novel method was tried out," Tate wrote in his memoirs. For Tate, using the phonograph to carry out his work was an exercise in frustration. He noticed that acids in the wax coating on the cylinders corroded the steel stylus, making playback unreliable. He also did not like having to stand in one place, speaking into the tube, preventing him from pacing the office to "clarify and accelerate thought." Whenever he shoved the phonograph aside and called in a stenographer to take a letter, Edison would choose that moment to happen by, poke his head in the door, and say disapprovingly, "Aha! Shoemakers' children never wear boots."

Eight thousand Edison machines with the defective steel styluses were returned to the factory, arriving without protective packing material. They were in such poor shape that they could not be refurbished and had to be junked. Quality problems afflicted the graphophone, too. Lippincott's company tottered on the precipice.

All was not bleak, however. Everyone who tried out the phonograph— everyone but Edison, that is—was struck by its beautiful reproduction of music, which it handled far better than the sound of the human voice. The same article in the *Atlantic Monthly* that had pointed out the machine's shortcomings as a device for office stenography also heaped praise on its ability to magnify musical sounds without distortion. Although there were very few recorded songs available for sale, the reports from the field showed avid interest among consumers. At the first convention of phonograph dealers in 1890, one distributor reported that one customer was "a crank on the subject," spending as much as $100 a week for musical cylinders (about $2,000 in current dollars).

Tate and other Edison associates did their best to persuade Edison of the commercial potential of a phonograph marketed for entertainment purposes, but Edison was so attached to his original notion that the phonograph was best suited to office dictation that he could not let go of it. He also did not give the business issues as much attention as the technical issues. As always, nothing gave him as much pleasure as notching more patents to his name, and with his vastly larger lab space and staff working at his behest, the temptation to accumulate patents by the bushel was irresistible. In the course of three years, 1888–1890, he was granted seventy-six related to the phonograph alone.

Tate speculated in his memoirs afterward that Edison was reluctant to accept the phonograph as a machine for playing music because he did not want his phonograph associated with wind-up music boxes. Edison was dedicated to bringing out "useful" inventions, a mission that would be sullied by its association with something as frivolous as Victorian "toys" marketed to adults.

Children's toys, however, were a different matter. Even as the North American Phonograph Company was spinning down the drain, Edison also worked on a separate venture: a talking doll. He had licensed rights to the concept when he had invented the phonograph a decade earlier and nothing had come of the deal. Now he had the laboratory of his dreams and all things seemed possible. In the spring of 1890, in the factory he had built adjacent to the laboratory he employed hundreds of girls for recording, again and again, the nursery rhymes for each doll. He had not yet come up with a way of reproducing a recording from a master, so each cylinder had to be recorded individually. He and toy distributors looked forward eagerly to Christmas season sales. Advance orders far outstripped the factory's capacity.

These dolls, the first-generation ancestors of Chatty Cathy, did not prove capable of being very chatty. Every one was tested at Edison's factory before being shipped, but in the course of the journey to stores, the internal organs of almost every single doll suffered injuries that left it capable of emitting nothing but discordant squeaks. One dealer found that of the first 200 dolls sold, 188 were returned. At that point, he told prospective customers that his remaining stock of dolls was for sale only on an as-is basis, without guarantee. He then learned what the modern parent knows all too well: The hot toy of a given season must be obtained by any means necessary (and in any condition). His customers continued to buy up the doll.

After the 1890 Christmas season had passed, and the tears of disappointed children dried, Edison shrugged off blame and distanced himself from the party that was least responsible, the company to whom he had licensed the marketing rights. With the loss of Edison's name, the company died and the talking dolls' fiasco was complete. On a parallel track, the North American Phonograph Company similarly failed to survive while handling Edison's far-from-Perfected Phonograph. The Phonograph Company's principal owner suffered, too. Lippincott fell behind in his payments to Edison, suffered a paralyzing stroke, and died soon after.

These ventures were the first ones that Edison mounted after building his new laboratory complex. Their unhappy endings suggest that Edison was mistaken in thinking that expanded space, new equipment, and large technical support staff were everything he would need to succeed in his ambition to eclipse his own earlier achievements in Menlo Park.

Two years before, soon after the lab had begun operations, Edison had declared publicly that his inventions should be judged only on the basis of commercial success. This had come about when a reporter for the *New York World* had asked him a battery of questions that threw him off balance: "What is your object in life? What are you living for?

What do you want?" Edison reacted as if he'd been punched in the stomach, or so the writer described the effect with exaggerated drama. First, Edison scanned the ceiling of the room for answers, then looked out the window through the rain. Finally, he said he had never thought of these questions "just that way." He paused again, then said he could not give an exact answer other than this: "I guess all I want now is to have a big laboratory" for making useful inventions. "There isn't a bit of philanthropy in it," he explained. "Anything that won't sell I don't want to invent, because anything that won't sell hasn't reached the acme of success. Its sale is proof of its utility, and utility is success."

He had been put on the spot by the reporter, and had reflexively given the marketplace the power to define the meaning of his own life.

CHAPTER EIGHT

BATTLE LOST

B Y THE EARLY twentieth century, Edison had earned a reputation as "the world's greatest inventor and world's worst business-man." The phrasing, attributed to Henry Ford, is memorable, even if both characterizations as greatest and worst are too extreme to be accepted literally. The range of Edison's technical interests was enormous, but it is hard to separate cleanly his accomplishments from those of his assistants. His standing as a businessperson is not aptly described in extreme terms, either. He never passed through bankruptcy, nor lost ownership of Glenmont or his Orange laboratory. In fact, he was a genuine millionaire at the time of his death in 1931. Still, Ford was correct, Edison was the "world's worst" businessperson if one compares what Edison himself earned from his most significant inventions to the far larger sums earned by his contemporaries who profited from Edison's original work. The dismal commercial beginnings of Edison's phonograph business provide materials for one case study; the shaky start of electric light service provides materials for another.

The central irony in Edison's biography is that his electric light became the foundation of a viable business, eventually known as General Electric, only after Edison yielded control of its management. Samuel Insull, Edison's young assistant, deserves credit for his role in guiding the electric light business through the transition from Edison era to post-Edison. Insull was precociously self-assured. He spoke well, dressed well, and made sure that everything was handled just so. Edison gave him genuine decision-making authority because Insull was preternaturally adept at management and yet, because of his youth and lack of technical background, he could never be Edison's peer, drawing public attention away from Edison. Technically gifted individuals who arrived at the Lab with their own strong opinions, such as Nikola Tesla and Frank Sprague, clashed constantly with Edison and left. Insull had strong opinions, too, but he stuck around longer than the engineers. He had begun as Edison's private secretary—the cocky lad, then only twenty-one years old, had insisted that he be appointed to the position as a condition of his emigration from England—and was soon taking care of whatever Edison needed, from buying clothes to arranging for financing for Edison's businesses. Edison no longer needed to sign his own checks; Insull wrote them. As for handling correspondence, Edison merely scribbled a *yes* or a *no* in the margin of a letter that had arrived, and Insull would figure out how to compose a detailed response to the correspondent. (Insull's talent for creative writing makes it likely that he was a collaborator in, if not the author of, Edison's formal letter to Lewis Miller, seeking his blessing for Edison's marriage to Mina.)

What is most surprising about Insull's relationship with Edison was that it was not at all sycophantic. He was the only member of Edison's inner circle who was unafraid to tease Edison publicly about sensitive subjects, such as Edison's heavy reliance on staff members in the invention factory. One evening, Edison, Insull, and others were sitting around in the office, bantering, when Edison teased Insull about his comically extreme self-confidence in his expertise in business. Insull retaliated, telling everyone present how Edison really worked: In the evening, Edison would hand out various assignments to his lab assistants, who were expected to toil through the night. He would then lie down and sleep. In the morning, he would arise, have a good breakfast, and exclaim, "What a wonderful night's work I have done." This was daring—everyone present knew well that it was not far from the truth. At first, Edison showed irritation, but then regained his equanimity and laughed with the others.

There was precious little else to laugh about, after all. After Pearl

Street's launch, Edison's various electric light businesses struggled to remain alive. The Edison Electric Light Company failed to win contracts with large- or even medium-sized cities, so Edison decided to add another company to his portfolio, the Thomas A. Edison Central Station Construction Department, which offered to build turnkey power-and-light systems. The business it attracted turned out to be meager. Instead of relieving Edison's financial difficulties, the Construction Department only exacerbated them.

The financial reports that came in from the municipal licensees show a painfully slow process of winning customers. The Edison Electric Illuminating Company of Jackson, Mississippi, which could boast of $100,000 in capital stock, reported profits of $139 for the first four months of 1886. For the first nine months of that year, the electric company in Cumberland, Maryland, reported profits of $282. Des Moines earned $426 for the first eight months, and New Bedford, Massachusetts, $155.

One wag wrote a mock letter to the shareholders of the Edison United Manufacturing Company: "We wish to impress the fact indelibly on the minds of our stockholders that our object is not to make money. This fact once accepted will prevent much dissatisfaction and many unpleasant explanations."

Samuel Insull was Edison's right-hand man—and left-hand man—when Edison's finances were in their most parlous state. One night, the two hunched over the books, mulling over schemes to put off the creditors of Edison's Construction Department. In matters of finance, Edison deferred to Insull, but Insull himself later said that he himself "knew little or nothing" about the subject. Edison's assets were tied up in the various companies that supplied Edison Electric. He had no cash and was embarrassed that he could barely meet his household expenses. Only royalties from some hitherto-forgotten telegraphic devices saved him from worse. Insull was personally getting by with loans from Edison associate Sigmund Bergmann and credit extended by Delmonico's, where Insull ate two meals a day. The situation seemed so hopeless that Edison, the irrepressible optimist, was wondering aloud that night what would happen to them. "This looks pretty bad," Edison confessed to Insull. "I do not know just how we are going to live. I think I could go back and earn my living as a telegraph operator."

It was the only time Insull ever saw Edison betray deep discouragement. The moment passed. Revenues in the other companies began to increase, the Construction Department was liquidated, and prospects for Edison's electrical interests began to look up. Insull played a major role in the turnaround. Edison can be credited with being willing to turn over major operational responsibilities to Insull, which he did only because, by chance, a labor dispute created the opportunity.

In Edison's view, his troubles with his workers at the Edison Machine Works on Goerck Street began when he was too generous.

> It seems I had rather a socialistic strain in me, and I raised the pay of the workmen twenty-five cents an hour above the prevailing rate of wages, whereupon Hoe & Company, our near neighbors, complained at our doing this. I said I thought it was all right. But the men, having got a little more wages, thought they would try coercion and get a little more, as we were considered soft marks. Whereupon they struck at a time that was critical.

In his recollection in an oral history he prepared years later, Edison regarded the incident as amusing. The strikers did not realize that Edison's company happened to be so short of cash that it would have difficulty meeting its next payroll. Edison decided to use the strike as an occasion to catch up on other matters, and when a committee representing the strikers appeared at the company's offices to begin negotiations, the office was empty. For two weeks, Edison and his managers found other places to be. When they finally returned, they were pleased to discover that "the workers were somewhat more anxious than we were." There were no more demands for raises.

The strike by the Machine Works personnel had ended with a victory for management, but the experience gave Edison an excuse to find a new location far away. More spacious quarters were needed in any case.

The Machine Works was so cramped that lathes had to be placed on the sidewalk, powered by belts that came through the shop windows. At the time of the strike, the company had already purchased a piece of property in Brooklyn and was about to let contracts for construction of a new factory. But in the strike's aftermath, Edison decided to quit the city and leave its workers behind. Charles Batchelor heard of a possible site in upstate New York, in Schenectady. A locomotive works with two large buildings situated on a ten-acre site, adjacent to rail tracks and the Erie Canal, was available for less than the property alone in Brooklyn. "And we will have no more trouble there from strikes," said Batchelor to reporters, speaking exaggeratedly of *strikes* in the plural. Edison appointed as general manager of his relocated machine works none other than Samuel Insull, who had just turned twenty-seven years old.

The new position in Schenectady meant greater responsibility and diminished income; Insull could no longer supplement his modest salary by serving as a secretary to the boards of other Edison companies. It rankled him that he was not given an allowance for entertaining and had to personally maintain a stable of horses for the sporting pleasure of guests of the company. He had never asked Edison for a raise, however, and he decided to "leave these things to [Edison's] own good judgment to deal with them whenever he thought it advisable."

Insull began with two hundred employees in Schenectady and immediately obtained improved results, building up an electrical supply business that was not dependent upon the sale of turnkey systems. He oversaw newly brisk business in almost all lines: electrical conduits, dynamos, motors, pulleys, and wire insulation. Discarding slack operations and sloppy accounting, he reorganized the office so that statements to customers went out on time, invoices were paid promptly, and letters handled professionally. By the fifth of each new month, he knew exactly how all the accounts stood. He even introduced the novel concept of sales goals. By "pushing" the department responsible for wire insulation, for example, monthly sales increased within a year more than tenfold. Within sight were annual profits of $100,000 a year for the combined departments.

After his first year was complete, Insull came down from Schenectady and paid a visit to Glenmont to report to Edison in person. Pleased with what he heard, Edison rummaged in his waistcoat pocket and pulled out a piece of paper that he handed to Insull. It represented stock warrants in the company, which would be worth $75,000 when Insull cashed them in. Edison also wanted to know who had paid for company-related entertainment. When Insull said he had absorbed the cost himself, Edison awarded him on the spot a substantial raise in salary and a separate entertainment allowance. Insull's decision to trust that Edison would eventually reimburse him was vindicated.

Insull was engaged in an ongoing campaign to modernize business practices in Edison's offices, a campaign that brought him into conflict, at times, with other senior managers and with Edison himself. For example, he berated Alfred Tate, who was in Orange, in a letter with an unmistakably sharp tone. Insull wrote that in the future whenever he asked Tate about a particular matter "what I want you to do in these days of cheap telegraphic rates is to leave nothing to my imagination" when replying. When he noticed that Tate had made a withdrawal depleting Edison's account the day before Edison had a note of $1,600 due, Insull was furious. "Don't you realize that the first thing in business should be to meet a man's notes and let everything else wait?"

Poor Tate—he was merely acting at Edison's behest. Edison treated the Schenectady shops as a handy source of funding for his lab complex. The more the shops prospered, the more boldly Edison, through Tate, siphoned off the profits by overcharging the Schenectady factory for lab services. In his second year in Schenectady, Insull noticed that when the lab transferred materials up to the shop, the lab billed at double the rate that the shop collected when the same materials moved down to the lab. In January 1888, Insull openly defied Tate and Edison, refusing to pay any more of Edison's laboratory bills until he could tote up the outstanding liabilities. Insull wrote Tate: "The large and rapid calls that [Edison] has made upon us for money simply puts me in the position of being compelled to refuse to assume any further liability." In July, furious at new charges assessed by the lab that Insull felt were "simply outrageous," he threatened to bring the paperwork down to

Glenmont and "see Mr. Edison personally about them." This was bluster: Tate had done nothing without Edison's approval.

Under Insull's management, the Schenectady workforce grew from two hundred to eight thousand in just six years. Looking back, Insull attributed his success during this time to simple geography: "We never made a dollar until we got the factory 180 miles away from Mr. Edison."

Insull did not oversee the marketing of the Edison power and light system, however. That remained under Edison's direct purview. Edison's conviction that his direct-current system was vastly superior to the alternating-current systems of his competitors was unshakable. But it would have been better for the business if he had been willing to pay attention to what the market was telling him. Customers favored the system that served a wide area. To avoid prohibitively high costs, Edison's direct-current generating station could only serve a small district, like Pearl Street's. Edison sales agents in the field felt helpless as they lost municipal contracts again and again in competitive bids against rivals like Westinghouse, which offered an alternating current system, and Thomson-Houston, which offered customers a choice of alternating or direct current systems. A frustrated sales agent wrote the home office: "Are we going to sit still and be called 'old fashioned,' 'fossils,' etc. and let the other fellows get a lot of the very best paying business?" Edison's longtime lieutenant Edward Johnson corroborated the reports from the field, telling Edison that until the company had a system that could compete on price with alternating-current, "we may as well accept the fact" that the company would not win business in its targets. Edison paid no attention. He was convinced that his system was technically superior, end of discussion. "If our patents were public property," he wrote an acquaintance, "you wouldn't find an alternating man in the US."

Our view of a battle over two competing technical standards is colored by our knowledge of the outcome. In retrospect, alternating current appears fated to best direct current, just as VHS video recording would best Betamax, and Edison appears naive in his faith that his direct-current system would eventually triumph. In this case, however, he was not as naive as it may appear. He believed his technology would triumph for a perfectly good reason: Edison's technology did not kill utility workers; the competition's did.

"Killed By an Electric Shock" was a headline that ran frequently in any city newspaper. A sample story from October 1887: A superintendent for Brush Electric in Detroit clambered up a pole to find out what was wrong with a streetlight and set to work too hurriedly, neglecting to put on the rubber gloves that were in his pockets. A police officer who happened to be walking up the block saw the man fall unconscious, draped across the wires. Firemen were called, he was brought down, and carried into the drugstore. No bruise or mark left visible evidence of his electrocution. Eulogized as a "careful man" who had been a longtime employee, the victim also happened to be engaged to be married. The news story provided one more horrible detail: "When his body was carried into the drug store last night his fiancée by some strange chance was at the counter making some purchases. Her grief was most heartrending and moved some of the spectators to tears."

These stories invariably commented upon the paradox: The electrical current was lethal, yet did not leave visible marks that were proportionate to its power. When a manager of an electric light company in Lyons, New York, stopped for a moment on his way home to tinker with a malfunctioning arc light on the street, he was fatally felled, but the only mark was a small hole in his thumb where it had come in contact with the alternating current. In another incident, reported under the headline "Struck Dead in a Second," a superintendent of the United States Illuminating Company in New York was called upon to snip wires that were interfering with firefighters who were trying to extinguish a fire in the commercial district. He received a fatal shock. When rushed into a nearby store, the crowd of curious onlookers who followed were mystified by the invisible nature of the force that had killed him. "His features were not in the least distorted, and death might have resulted from heart disease."

Passersby occasionally were victims, too. In April 1888, a seventeen-year-old boy walking down Broadway was killed when he brushed against a telegraph wire that dangled overhead, crossing two wires from the United States Illuminating Company. The *New York World* worried that "right on Broadway, where thousands and thousands of people are passing during all hours of the day, scores of wires are swinging in mid-air, any one of which is likely to become dislodged." An alert person could avoid being run over by a careless driver, but "no amount of agility will be of any avail to him when a deadly arc-light current is conveyed without a note of warning into his anatomy."

The lethal potential of electricity caught the notice of New York state legislators in Albany who were interested in utilizing electricity for capital punishment. A commission was appointed to look into the matter. It surveyed judges, district attorneys, sheriffs, and doctors, and found slightly more respondents favored electrocution than hanging (though five held out for the guillotine and four for the garrote). One physician pointed out that little was actually known about the effects of strong currents on the body, and "if lightning [does] not always kill, surely we cannot expect death to result from artificial electricity." Nevertheless, the commission decided to recommend using "current of electricity" as the means of execution, replacing hanging.

When Edison first introduced electric light service in New York City, his primary competition at the time had been the gas utilities, so he had done his best to call public attention to the dangers of gas. But when Westinghouse and other well-capitalized competitors entered the power-and-light business, Edison began instead to talk of the dangers of alternating current. The state's consideration of adopting electrocution for executions gave him an opportunity to point to the inherently dangerous nature of the competition's technology. Edison personally favored abolishing capital punishment, but as long it remained in place, he advocated using the technology that was most lethal and thus would inflict the least amount of suffering: alternating current. He told the New York advisory commission that the best machine for this purpose was the standard dynamo manufactured by "Mr. Geo. Westinghouse, Pittsburgh."

Edison was also more than happy to give thought to devising a new word for this new form of capital punishment. One associate suggested a new verb for execution by electricity, "to westinghouse," and also a new noun, as in "such and such a man was condemned to the westinghouse." Dr. Guillotin had been so honored; why not give Mr. Westinghouse "the benefit of the fact in the minds of the public"? To his credit, Edison was not so crass and instead favored "ampermort," "dynamort," or "electromort." The *New York Times* did not spell out which word it favored, but expressed emphatically its opposition "to 'electrocution,' which pretentious ignoramuses seem to be trying to push into use."

By the time George Westinghouse had entered the electric light business in 1886, he had already made his first fortune from his invention of the air brake for railroads, and he was no slouch himself in piling up hundreds of patents as an inventor. In Edison's view, however, Westinghouse did not pose a serious threat in the power-and-light business because he used the relatively more dangerous alternating current, certain to kill one of his own customers within six months.

Edison's conviction that direct current was less dangerous than alternating current was based on hunch, however, not empirical scientific research. He, like others at the time, focused solely on voltage (the force that pushes electricity through a wire) without paying attention to amperage (the rate of flow of electricity), and thought it would be best to stay at 1,200 volts or less. Even he was not certain that his own system was completely safe—after all, he had elected to place wires in underground conduits, which was more expensive than stringing wires overhead but reduced the likelihood of electrical current touching a passerby. Burying the wires could not give him complete peace of mind, however. Privately, he told Edward Johnson that "we must look out for crosses [i.e., short-circuited wires] for if we ever kill a customer it would be a bad blow to the business."

The Edison system was spared the scandal of causing accidental deaths, which gave Edison all the more reason to feel confident that customers would very soon see the differences in systems. He coined an infelicitous slogan to describe his own: "High Economy, No Risk." Surely customers would reject Westinghouse's and embrace his. But it did not happen. The accidents involving alternating current were not frequent enough, nor was responsibility for the deaths publicly pinned on Westinghouse or any single company.

Westinghouse's alternating current was superior to Edison's direct current if considered from a strictly business perspective. Alternating current could be distributed much more economically, and to greater distances from a generating plant, than could direct current. This gave Westinghouse's company the ability to undercut Edison's prices; by 1887, it was expanding quickly all over the map, as if no competition stood in its way.

Cooperation between rivals was another possibility, one that occurred to George Westinghouse. Antitrust restrictions did not exist—this was two years before the Sherman Anti-Trust Act was enacted and many more years would pass before the federal government began to enforce it. In June 1888, Westinghouse took the initiative and wrote Edison a warm letter, exploring the possibility of rapprochement. He said that it must have been others who had sought to drive a wedge between Westinghouse Electric and Edison Electric. He, for his part, was most appreciative of the hospitality that Edison had shown him when Westinghouse had paid a visit to Menlo Park, shopping for a power plant for his own house before he had entered the business himself and even before Edison Electric had formally launched its own service. It would be a pleasure, Westinghouse wrote, if Edison would visit him in Pittsburgh where "I will be glad to reciprocate the attention shown me by you." Edison turned down Westinghouse's overture, however, claiming that his work in the laboratory forced him to turn over all business matters to others. He would later say to a colleague that Westinghouse's "methods of doing business lately are such that the man has gone crazy over sudden accession of wealth or something unknown to me and is flying a kite that will land him in the mud sooner or later."

Westinghouse's invitation had arrived just as Edison was directing lab experiments whose purpose was to undermine Westinghouse's reputation, namely, how much electrical current was needed to execute a human being? Stray dogs were used as surrogates at the lab, which offered to boys in Orange a bounty of twenty-five cents for each hapless dog delivered to its gates for the advancement of science (and intercompany competition). Edison told the *Brooklyn Citizen* how the effect of direct current left the dog subjects unchanged in appearance, and then, after a minute, they would tumble over dead. Alternating current, however, killed in as little as one-tenth of a second. This impressed the lab assistants, who took care to wear rubber gloves even when writing in the lab's notebook, Edison said "with a grin."

Edison's bounty offer was so successful that soon no more canine volunteers could be had. The very day after he had curtly turned Westinghouse away, Edison wrote to the Society for the Prevention of Cruelty to Animals to augment his local supply. Anticipating that mention of capital punishment was unlikely to elicit the desired cooperation of the SPCA, Edison blandly explained that he was looking into determining the exact quantity of electricity required to kill dogs, work that would incidentally help to safeguard the lives of linemen in the electric power business. Would the SPCA be so kind as to supply some "good-sized" animals as soon as possible?

Henry Bergh, the society's president, could not understand how Mr. Edison, whom he regarded as a "genius" who had "conferred such great and lasting benefits upon humanity," could have so misunderstood the mission of the SPCA. The dogs placed in Edison's care would be subjects in experiments that entailed suffering, not instantaneous death. And the great scientist had to be told that any data that he collected at his lab would have no value for his avowed purpose, saving the lives of linemen, given the disparity in electrical force required to kill humans compared with small animals.

Such was his celebrity and presumed expertise that no one pointed out that it was strange that Edison was experimenting with small mammals months after he had spoken with such certainty about the effects of electrical currents upon humans. It had been his letter—the one recommending generators made by "Mr. Geo. Westinghouse, Pittsburgh" to "inflict the least amount of suffering upon its victim"—that had persuaded one member of the New York commission to shift his support from morphine executions to electrocution, making the panel's recommendation a unanimous one. Its report, in turn, led directly to passage of a new capital punishment law in New York State, changing the method of executing criminals from hanging to electrocution.

Perhaps the state had acted a bit too hastily. The first person to be sentenced under the new law was one William Kemmler, a Buffalo resident convicted of murdering his female companion with an ax. He lacked sufficient education to do more than mark an X on his confession, but the world took notice of the case when he was sentenced to death by electrocution, making him a human guinea pig. His plight drew attention and a new attorney who volunteered to press his appeal, arguing, "We hold that the state cannot experiment upon Kemmler."

The judge who heard the appeal understandably blanched at upholding the constitutionality of the new law without assurance from the scientific community about the humaneness of electrocution. Hearings were ordered up, and the leading experts were deposed. The star witness was the world-renowned authority on all matters electrical. "How long have you been engaged in the work of an inventor or electrician?" Edison was asked. "Twenty-six years." What would happen if current—not that from Edison's system, but the competition's—were applied to Kemmler for five or six minutes? Would he be carbonized? Edison was asked. "No," he replied, "he would be mummyized. All the water in his body would evaporate in five or six minutes." The tone of peerless authority, which was Edison's public style, remained intact even when he was cross-examined. The Wizard, who was chewing an unlit cigar, received a light and was dismissed; Kemmler's initial appeal was not successful. New motions were filed, but the appointed day of execution neared.

Edison's campaign to link in the public's mind alternating current with fatal consequences, whether accidental or intentional, was gaining momentum. George Westinghouse stepped forward to counterattack, his words thrown against those of Edison's and the other proponents of electrocution.

Westinghouse wielded a variety of arguments in defense of alternating current. Its low cost brought incandescent lighting within the reach of the multitude, and its low voltage within the house—lower than Edison's—made it safer, he claimed. The package also included his own pseudoscientific theory, with no more substance than Edison's, that an alternating current was inherently less harmful because its momentary reversal of direction "prevents decomposition of tissues." No discussion was complete without argument by anecdote, and Westinghouse was not remiss. A lineman had accidentally grabbed hold of a live wire with one thousand volts of alternating current and held on for three minutes. Yes, the man was shocked insensible, but not only had he lived, he "in fact was able to go on with his work after a short period."

This was a reassuring tale, uncomplicated with details that would permit it to be independently verified. Westinghouse could not provide such a comforting coda to another accident involving a lineman, however. On 11 October 1889, John E. H. Feeks, thirty-two, was engaged in cutting down dead telegraph and alarm wires on a pole in downtown Manhattan for Western Union when the accident occurred. The time and location made it visible to many people: just after one o'clock in the afternoon, near Chambers and Centre Streets, in the shadow of the city offices, with hundreds of people hurrying below on the sidewalk. Astride a crossbar, Feeks was reaching out for a wire that he intended to cut when he appeared to shiver and tremble. Putting out his right hand, he seized another wire as though to steady himself—and sparks and blue flames shot out of his hand. He fell forward, and was held aloft by the dense bands of wires that ran across lower crossbars, suspended some forty feet above the ground. With flames seen coming from his mouth and nose and feet, and blood dropping and pooling on the sidewalk below, this tableau could not have been more ghastly. The crowd swelled, and police had difficulty clearing space for the rescuers. It took thirty long minutes before the body could be brought down.

Court officials and members of the Board of Aldermen were among the witnesses, and the very public nature of Feeks's death brought impassioned calls for swift action to bring the company responsible to account. Responsibility could not be easily assigned, however. The pole upon which he was working did not have any wires that belonged to an electric light company. The United States Illuminating Company ran wires elsewhere on the street, but though it was reasonable to assume that one of its wires was improperly insulated, the fatal current could not be traced with certainty to a particular point of contact. Without question, moving all power lines to underground conduits, as in Edison's system, would eliminate the danger in running them overhead amid tangles with others. Demands for requiring electric light companies to move their lines underground became conspicuously louder following Feeks's death.

Edison did not add his support to these proposals, which he faulted for not going far enough in addressing the danger posed by alternating current's relatively higher voltage. He told a reporter that insulation on wires buried in the ground provided no measure of safety—the current would burn through the insulating fibers, and then "the dangerous current will creep into your house, and will come up the manholes." In October 1889, he urged the readers of the *New York Evening Sun* to press the mayor and the Board of Health to enact regulations that would curtail "deadly currents" within the city's boundaries. He reasoned, "Is there not a law in New York against the manufacture of nitro-glycerine?"

The only purveyors of "deadly currents," of course, were Edison's competitors. The battle of the currents was so important to Edison that he made publicly disparaging comments about his rivals as persons, not just as vendors of inferior technology. This, in turn, left his competitors wondering why he had cast off the restraint expected in civilized competition. When George Westinghouse read in the newspaper that Edison had called him a "shyster," Westinghouse's feelings were "very much hurt," or so he said when he bumped into Edison's attorney.

Westinghouse faced a genuine crisis. Feeks's death, the calls for burying power lines, and Edison's personal attacks added up to a public relations mess for his company. Rather than remaining quiet and hoping that this bad weather would blow over, Westinghouse decided to speak to the press and try to put a better face on his business than Edison had drawn. He could not avoid talking about Feeks, so he argued that direct current, which was used on telegraph wires, was fully capable of inflicting the horrible burns suffered by the unfortunate lineman. The danger came not from the particular form of current but from inadequate insulation. If properly shielded, overhead wires were perfectly safe, he said. The public had been stirred up by "the active work of the managers of the Edison Company and of Mr. Edison, who have sought to turn the present situation to their advantage."

The defensive position that Westinghouse found himself in is illustrated by the way he contradicted himself as he tried to defend overhead wires. The wires that were supposedly safe were also the same wires that he had to admit, yes, posed dangers, yes, but dangers of various kinds had to be accepted throughout the modern city. Westinghouse said, "If all things involving the use of power were to be prohibited because of the danger to life, then the cable cars, which have already killed and maimed a number of people, would have to be abolished." Say good-bye to trains, too, he added, because of accidents at road crossings.

Westinghouse was not able to form these few off-the-cuff remarks into a fully developed response. Edison, however, seized an opportunity to further strengthen his position with a long article titled "Dangers of Electric Lighting" that was published under his name by the *North American Review,* which had invited the piece. It repeated the same arguments that he had been making and is notable as the zenith of Edison's influence in the battle of the currents. At that point, he was fully justified in believing that he had the ear of the world and could make everyone understand the superiority of his system of power and light.

His apparent mastery of the debate was short lived, however. The next month, the *North American Review* gave Westinghouse an opportunity to respond. Having gained some experience in public combat, and with some time to do a little research, he brought new material and fresh counterarguments to the debate. Statistics bolstered his case. In 1888, sixty-four people were killed in streetcar accidents in New York, and twenty-three in gas-related accidents—and only five by accidental electrocution. He pointed out that within an individual's own home, "there is not on record a solitary instance of a person having been injured or shocked from the consumers' current of an alternating system." Don't underestimate the power of direct current, he warned readers; he had personally "witnessed the roasting of a large piece of fresh beef by a direct continuous current of less than one hundred volts within two minutes." He invited readers to connect a tin pan to the electrical wires of a home supplied by Edison's company and reproduce the experiment for themselves.

Westinghouse also dredged up an old interview with Edison and found this quotation: "I don't care so much for a fortune as I do for getting ahead of the other fellows." Westinghouse suggested to readers that it was this, not the supposed merits of Edison's own system, that drove Edison to exaggerate the dangers inherent in the systems of others and to minimize them in his own.

The most damning argument against Edison's system was what the marketplace said about the relative merits and shortcomings of the two rival systems. Those customers who had a choice were voting in favor of alternating current, the less-expensive option. In only three years of operation, Westinghouse's company had five times as many customers as Edison's older company, testimony to the public's view that Westinghouse offered lighting that he described as "safe, cheap, efficient."

American consumers ignored the question of whether alternating current was truly "safe." As historian Mark Essig points out, the public simply became blasé about the accidents that continued to occur. Even in the 1920s, when electricity finally became widely available in homes, "about 1,000 Americans died annually from electric shock." Notwithstanding, the appeal of "cheap" electricity was powerful, and alternating current was considerably cheaper because Edison's direct current required progressively more expensive investments in copper wiring the farther the system extended out from the generating plant. In 1889, customers were voting every day, and the results showed a landslide victory for Edison's new competition.

It is probably not mere coincidence that 1880 was also the year that Edison began to withdraw his own financial stake in the industry he had founded. Starved for cash, he was receptive to an offer to gain liquidity, selling his stake in the electric light to a syndicate of investors led by Henry Villard and financed largely by German concerns. What the public saw was a newly formed company, the Edison General Electric Company, which consolidated into a single organization the Edison Electric Light Company and Edison's various manufacturing companies that supplied the industry.

For his stake, Edison was given shares valued at $3.5 million. In his official biography written decades later, Edison depicted the episode as coming about from being too successful; orders had simply swamped his undercapitalized company. Insull had suggested that they might run into difficulties because of lack of capital, so when the offer to be bought out came, "we concluded it was better to be sure than be sorry, so we sold out for a large sum." When Insull had his own turn to talk about the same events in his own memoirs, he termed the value of the shares granted to Edison as "a small amount compared to the great value to the world at large of the work done by Mr. Edison" in the field.

The shares in the new company gave Edison an opportunity to cash out, and he did so, liquidating 90 percent of his stake. Why did he divest almost all of his holdings, rather than simply sell slowly, diversifying at a steady rate that would, at the same time, reassure investors that he had not lost faith in the company? He wrote Villard afterward that he had cashed out because he had been "under a desperate strain for money for 22 years." Even as he continued to bark in public as loudly as ever at alternating current, he was poised to enter "fresh and more congenial fields of work," he told Villard. Iron-ore mining was going to be his new passion. Insull wrote a colleague that Edison was "practically intoxicated by the business."

Villard had tried to persuade Edison to agree to merge his electrical companies with alternating-current rival Thomson-Houston. The two companies' patent holdings were complementary and consolidation in the industry seemed inevitable. But Edison could not accept it, for reasons that were not obvious. It was not the thought of joining hands with the very interests he was campaigning against that was too much to bear. Nor was he passionately committed to his own company, even though this served as a convenient pretext to object to a merger with a better-managed, better-capitalized company. Were Villard to proceed, Edison told him "my usefulness as an inventor [would be] gone," arguing that it was the spur of competition that provided the fuel he needed to persevere.

In fact, Edison was not interested in sticking around, merger or no. His direct current was going to lose the battle of the currents, and he could not accept graciously a prize for first runner-up. He had cashed out his own personal position and was ready to move on to new projects, but he wanted to leave on his own terms, not someone else's. He also wanted to make certain that his Orange laboratory would continue to receive financial support. Consolidating his various companies into one, while spurning the Thomson-Houston offer, allowed him to do what he wished.

The new Edison General Electric Company appointed Villard as president, and Insull as vice president and, effectively, the chief operations officer. Edison had assumed that his laboratory would be supported as it had been previously, receiving $250,000 annually from his various companies. But after Edison General Electric was organized, the multiple sources of funds were reduced to a single company, and that one was willing to pay only $85,000. Edison told Villard that the shortfall "has produced absolute discouragement."

By withdrawing his own financial stake in the industry, Edison discovered too late that he had lost considerable power in directing his own affairs at the lab, too. As a contract researcher, he had to do the bidding of others. When the Association of Edison Illuminating Companies, which were the Edison system's licensees, convened in the summer of 1889, the members spoke in the hoarse voice of the desperate: They begged Edison General Electric to supply association members with an alternating current system as soon as possible, within six months at the latest. Insull was fully supportive and assigned the task of developing the system to the person who was under contract to perform research and new product development: Thomas Edison, the world's most vociferous opponent of alternating current.

One year after agreeing to deliver the new system within six months,

Edison had failed to do so. Insull, not bothering to hide his anger, wrote Edison with the tone used when addressing a subordinate whose recent performance was wanting: "I would like to know definitely from you what I can promise to our District Managers throughout the country." He was not going to accept hollow assurances that would not be fulfilled. "I think that it is particularly important that in our new organization any promises I make to our people should be absolutely adhered to, and I shall be glad if you will bear this in mind when you reply to this letter." Edison did not like being spoken to in this manner. He had his secretary write a short note saying that he had perused it but was "unable to reply fully to it at the moment."

Edison was working on the project, albeit slowly. He may have dragged his feet hoping that the first state-sponsored experiment in electrocution would publicize the menacing aspect of alternating current, making it possible to imagine that its triumph was not certain after all. The convicted murderer William Kemmler exhausted his appeals, and the date of his execution was set for 6 August 1890. Here, at last, was the moment Edison had anticipated: the lethal nature of alternating current would be demonstrated in dramatic fashion. Only the warden of the state prison in Auburn and the individuals he had invited as official witnesses would actually see the execution, but reporters and crowds showed up anyhow. To accommodate the press, Western Union set up a temporary dispatch office at the freight station. Curiosity seekers gathered around the prison walls, and atop trees, rooftops, and telegraph poles, hoping to catch a glimpse of the condemned man.

"They say I am afraid to die," Kemmler said to one of his jailers after breakfast that morning, "but they will find that I ain't." Indeed, when he was led to the room with the chair constructed to bring his life to an abbreviated end, he remained calm. As the warden adjusted the headpiece and the eleven straps that crossed his body and limbs, Kemmler tested each one and advised the jailer when a strap needed adjustment. "Warden, just make that a little tighter," he asked at one point. "We want everything all right, you know."

When the electrodes had been attached and preparations were com-

Edison in 1880, at the age of 33.

Mary Stilwell Edison, Edison's first wife, in 1871, the year of their wedding.

The first-generation tinfoil phonograph in 1877.

Opposite: Edison in Mathew Brady's Washington, D.C., studio in April 1878, posed with a second-generation tinfoil phonograph.

Edison in 1888, at the age of 41, posed after spending 72 straight hours working in his West Orange laboratory on his "perfected" phonograph.

Edison with his second wife, Mina Miller Edison.

Edison's Black Maria movie studio, mounted on turntable and equipped with hinged roof to utilize direct sunlight.

A man posed with a kinetoscope in 1895: Ear tubes provided sound that was synchronized with the images viewed from the peephole mounted on the top of the cabinet.

Advertisement for the
Edison Concert Phonograph
in 1899.

Thomas Alva Edison Jr., at
the age of 21, in 1897.

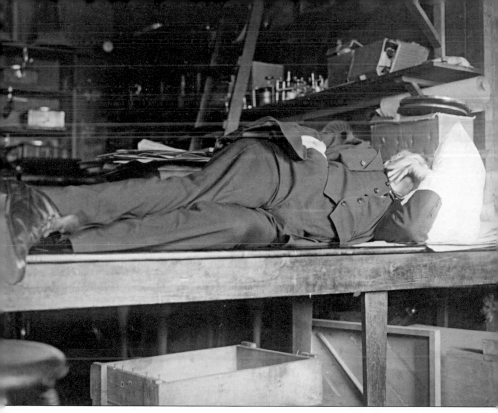

Edison asleep on a laboratory bench in 1911.

In Vermont in August 1918, Edison poses with other members of camping trip (left to right): Edison, young Harvey Firestone Jr., R.J.H. Deloach (seated), John Burroughs, Henry Ford, and Harvey Firestone.

Edison ceremonially punches the laboratory's time clock on his 74th birthday in 1921.

Mourners lined up outside the West Orange laboratory to view Edison's bier.

plete, the warden said, "Good-bye, William." This was the signal for the assistant to throw the lever. When the circuit closed, Kemmler's body convulsed and then froze as rigidly as if bronzed. After seventeen seconds, the presiding doctor declared Kemmler dead, the warden signaled for the power to be cut, and the seated witnesses stood up, exhaling with relief that the ordeal was apparently over.

"Great God! He is alive!" someone cried. "Turn on the current," implored another. The warden, who had been detaching the electrode on Kemmler's head, stopped momentarily, then hastily reattached it. Everyone could see that Kemmler's chest was rising and falling. The doctor told the warden to switch the current back on. The signal was given and the lever was thrown again. The witnesses were so aghast, the sight of blood drops that appeared on Kemmler's forehead so horrifying, the stench of singed hair so strong, that no one present could later say with certainty how long the second attempt at execution lasted. After this indeterminable period, the doctor again signaled for the current to be shut off, and the witnesses stumbled out, all but a few retching.

One of the first individuals to leave the prison was the electrician who had set up the apparatus. He went immediately to the telegraph office and sent a message to Westinghouse: "Execution was an awful botch. Kemmler was literally roasted to death."

"Far Worse Than Hanging" read the headline in the *New York Times,* which characterized Kemmler's execution as nothing less than "a disgrace to civilization." When asked for his reaction, George Westinghouse drily remarked, "They could have done better with an axe." The public could place the blame where it belonged, he said, and "it will not be on us."

Westinghouse's prediction proved accurate: Blame did not attach to his company. Nor did blame attach to the concept of an electric chair, only on those who had handled the arrangements and done the testing. After the U. S. Supreme Court refused an appeal of another person, Shibuya Jugiro, convicted of murder and headed for death by electrocution, the electric chair got another chance. Shibuya was one of four who died one morning in 1891 at Sing Sing. By the end of the century, more than fifty had died in the chair. More than four thousand followed in the twentieth century, before lethal injection became an alternative to the chair, if not its replacement, in all states but one (Nebraska). The shift away from electricity shows that a century of experimentation was insufficient to realize Edison's claim, made before the first execution, that electric current was sufficient to kill the condemned person painlessly "in the ten-thousandth part of a second."

Unaffected by this experimental work that state prisons undertook in the early 1890s involving human subjects and lethal (or not-quite-lethal) electricity, the adoption of alternating current in the wider society accelerated and the future for direct current dimmed. Edison General Electric was the sales leader among the three largest power-and-light concerns, but its costs were much higher, and its strategic positioning and growth prospects the weakest. It was up against competitors that played by their own rules (historian Forrest McDonald describes Thomson-Houston's tactics pertaining to intellectual property as "scarcely distinguishable from theft"). Samuel Insull appreciated the necessity of merging with Thomson-Houston, even if Edison still did not. While Insull carried out negotiations with the prospective merger partner, and at the same time tried to coax Edison to acquiesce, he found himself politically isolated at Edison General Electric. He was only thirty-two and had not yet mastered the more subtle techniques of persuasion; by his own admission in his memoirs, he had made "a good many enemies." For a few weeks, Edison himself was "prejudiced" against him and the merger, but Edison came around and the two men repaired their relationship.

In early 1892, the deal was done: Edison General Electric and Thomson-Houston merged as nominal equals. The organization chart, however, reflected a different understanding among the principals. Thomson-Houston's chief executive, Charles Coffin, became the new head and other Thomson-Houston executives filled out the other positions. Insull was the only manager from the Edison side invited to stay, which he did only briefly. From the outside, it appeared that Thomas

Edison and his coterie had arranged the combination from a position of abject surrender. Edison did not want this to be the impression left in the public mind, however. When the press asked him about the announcement, he said he had been one of the first to urge the merger. This was not close to the truth, and is especially amusing when placed in juxtaposition to Alfred Tate's account of the moment when Tate, hearing news of the merger first, had been the one to convey the news to Edison.

> I always have regretted the abruptness with which I broke the news to Edison but I am not sure that a milder manner and less precipitate delivery would have cushioned the shock. I never before had seen him change color. His complexion naturally was pale, a clear healthy paleness, but following my announcement it turned as white as his collar.
>
> "Send for Insull," was all he said as he left me standing in his library.

Having collected himself before meeting with the reporters, Edison could say with sincerity that he was too busy to "waste my time" on the electric light. For the past three years, since he first realized that his direct-current system would ultimately be driven to the margins by alternating current, he had been carting his affections elsewhere. The occasion of the merger did shake him into a rare disclosure of personal shortcoming: He allowed that "I am not business man enough to spend time" in the power-and-light business.

Edison found himself staring from the outside looking in, as others who had the business acumen to extend electric light with newer technology, unconstrained by the orthodoxies written by a direct-current zealot, capitalized on the opportunity. In addition, Edison lost the services of Insull, who realized he had to leave Edison in order to work unfettered as a chief executive.

At the time of the 1892 merger, Edison's name disappeared when the new organization, the General Electric Company, was christened. Whether this was by his own choice is not clear. Years later, Insull said that Edison refused to permit the Edison name to be associated with the new entity. It is not difficult to picture Edison acting spitefully, angry that his namesake company could no longer remain independent. When Edison's own children grew to be adults, however, they told a very different story, of his lifelong disappointment that "Edison" had been stripped from the new company's name against his wishes. Both versions can be accommodated: Perhaps Edison refused to allow the use of his name in 1892, then, after the company narrowly escaped bankruptcy in the Panic of 1893 and grew into a far larger business, and the passage of years tempered his earlier ire, he came to feel regret about his decision—and came to think of it not as his decision but that of an ungrateful Wall Street. By that time, he had forgotten that he had become so discouraged about the commercial prospects for his electric light, outshone by the new entrants to the business, that he had given up on it.

CHAPTER NINE

FUN

HOPPING INTO A new field and betting almost everything he owned, Thomas Edison set off in a quest to make a name for himself—in mining. The effort cost him five years of living apart from his family and ended without success. But he enjoyed the experience immensely and walked away without regrets. It was the one time in the fifty years he lived as a public figure when he ignored what was expected of him. It was also the one time when the man who seemed cold at his core recorded in letters his affectionate feelings for his wife.

Edison's adventure in mining began when he anticipated losing the battle of the currents. He was weighed down with self-doubt, telling an assistant that he had come to the realization that others on his staff knew more about electricity than he did. He went even further, morosely saying that he had never really known anything. But that did not matter because "I'm going to do something now so different and so much bigger than anything I've ever done before people will forget that my name ever was connected with anything electrical."

He had long been excited by the idea that electrically charged magnets could be used to process iron ore, separating the iron from other material. In Menlo Park, more than ten years earlier, a laboratory notebook recorded experiments he had personally conducted to test the concept. Other inventors had also worked on "magnetic concentration," as this process was called. Edison had never had the chance to devote sustained attention to it, however, and the idea had been stuck into a cubbyhole. Now he was ready to pull it out and put it into practice. New Jersey, New York, and Pennsylvania had considerable quantities of low-grade iron ore, but it was so costly to refine by conventional means that it drew few or no buyers. Edison was convinced that he would be able to build a system of magnetic concentration that would make easily mined, low-grade ore economically competitive with hard-to-extract, high-grade ore found elsewhere. In 1889, when he cashed out his interest in the newly formed Edison General Electric, he had the financial means to put his ideas to a real-world test. This money did not stay in his pockets for long. He bought the Ogden iron mine in rural northern New Jersey, about two miles south of Ogdensburg, and began to erect a concentrating works of his own design to process ore.

The Edison system was designed to handle the iron-laden rock in as large a chunk as the largest steam shovel of the day could bite off. Rather than blowing it up using explosives, it would be sent to the works to be crushed by rollers, breaking the rock into particles small enough to be separated by magnets. In making his plans, Edison con-catenated three seemingly obvious insights that no one else had thought to put together. First, it was cheaper to break up ore using the energy provided by coal, which cost $3 a ton, rather than dynamite, at $100 a ton. Second, a five-ton chunk of rock could be pulverized into powder if the crushing rollers were built sufficiently large. Third, the rollers could do their work at low operational cost, relying on centrifugal force after steam power got them spinning at high speed. The scale of everything was outsized.

Edison happily embraced a thousand and one problems encountered in implementation. The rollers, for example, did not actually crush the rock as much as knock it into smithereens with knobs that were at-tached to chilled iron plates bolted to the curved surfaces. The rock turned out to be stubborn; its submission to the process required trial and error. The technical issues were primarily mechanical in nature; Edison had no claim to special expertise or advantages in this area, but he relished this opportunity to play in a field entirely new to him.

When he bought the Ogden property in 1889 and assigned staff to begin building the new concentrating works, he had not anticipated that he would move to the mine site himself. He had a new wife, a new estate, and a new laboratory in Orange that placed at his disposal everything he had ever desired. He had a newborn child, Madeleine, and another, Charles, would be born the next year, in 1890. Yet in 1891, when he had to accept the loss of control of his power-and-light businesses, Edison could not enjoy his blessings at home and at the laboratory. He had resolved to make his mark in mining and prepared himself to invest whatever it would take, and spend as much time away from his family as required. This was the venture that he was determined to make "so much bigger than anything I've ever done before."

It is hard to imagine a more stark contrast between the otherworldly luxury of the Glenmont estate and the frontier-town conditions at the Ogden site. At the mine, there was no town, so Edison and his lieutenants crowded into an old farmhouse, sardonically referred to as "the White House." There were no amenities, no amusements, just work. In the winter, the room temperature fell below freezing; washing up in the morning required first melting the ice that had formed in the pitcher on the nightstand. In the summer, temperatures were hotter "than the seventh section of hades," reported Edison, who added that the humidity was "so thick that some of the fish from the Hopewell pond swam out into the air." Ambient dust made life miserable, to the point that Edison had difficulty retaining workers until he put a crew of seventeen to work to control the problem. Convincing Mina to move up to the mine, along with the children and the servants, was out of the question. So Edison took up a routine of taking the train up early Monday morning, then returning home on the last train Saturday night. One year turned into two, and still the work was unfinished. It lasted five years.

The bare facts suggest that Edison was doing his best to avoid his second wife and young children, that this was a repeat of his earlier flight to the western states in the summer of 1878, only in extreme form. The reality was something different. For most of his life, Edison did not record his feelings about personal matters, but the circumstances he found himself in during the Ogden years were an exception. He was at the mine, Mina was at home in Glenmont, and they lived at a time when the personal letter had yet to be displaced by the phone call. So the normally taciturn Edison, who usually gave nothing away about his innermost thoughts, wrote daily letters to Mina, whom he addressed by the pet name "Billy." They are attentive, funny, and loving—unabashedly so ("Darling Sweetest Loveliest Cutest . . ."). Upon occasion, they are quite explicit. "Last night I felt blue without you," he wrote Mina in 1895. "With a kiss like the swish of a 13 inch cannon projectile I remain as always your lover."

Edison's letters to Mina reveal an aspect of his personality that would not otherwise have been visible: his personal philosophy concerning mental well-being. To Edison, unhappiness could be vanquished by sheer force of will. In August 1895, when Mina and the children were at Chautauqua, and he was at Ogden, he responded to Mina's expression of the "blues" with empathy, and tried as many therapeutic approaches as his philosophy permitted. He humored her with stories about the dust ("some smart weed seeds have commenced to sprout out of the seams of my coat"). He teased her that she was blue because of her disappointment in him. He praised her intelligence ("There can't [be] 1 woman in 20,000 that is really as smart as yourself"). He lectured her on the medical basis of depression ("blues are from disordered liver"). He teased her in a way that would make a mental-health professional today cringe (referring to her in a babyish third-person voice: "I wonder if Billy Edison truly loves me or does she just say so at times to keep me deceived. If she really loved, why should she get the blues"). He advised her to stay away from novels, take up newspaper reading, and "have all the fun you can."

He himself looked for fun in only one place—at work. He enjoyed himself immensely at the mine, even when his colleagues' spirits dragged as the years passed, the money disappeared, and customers for what turned out to be expensively priced briquettes of processed iron ore failed to materialize. His chief assistant, Walter Mallory, was "the most dejected man you ever saw," Edison wrote Mina, but "your lover [is] as bright and cheerful as a bumble bee in flower time."

Edison took great pleasure in the novelty of the technical challenges and in the opportunity to redeem his reputation as a savvy business-person, even though redemption never came. The low-grade iron ore in New Jersey did not have a competitive chance once huge reserves of high-grade ore were discovered in the Mesabi Range of northeastern Minnesota; the Mesabi ore was easily mined near the surface and close to economical shipping on Lake Superior. Well after the first Mesabi mine opened in 1890, Edison remained pitiably hopeful about his Ogden mine, even when objective facts made the future of its business appear bleak to anyone else. In 1897, when failure was inevitable, he refused to acknowledge the facts. Edison wrote a colleague, "My Wall Street friends think I cannot make another success, and that I am a back num-ber, hence I cannot raise even $10,000 from them, but I am going to show them that they are very much mistaken. I am full of vinegar yet."

Edison was not so emotionally invested, however, that he sold all of his other assets in order to keep the business alive. Glenmont and his laboratory remained untouched, and he was proud that the mine en-joyed a top credit rating because he would not permit it to take on a penny of debt, even when it had exhausted his ready cash and the last of the General Electric shares that he had held. He had to close the mine repeatedly, then reopen when money from an unrelated line of business came in, only to exhaust the new funds. The enterprise did not turn out to be a complete waste: The rollers that were developed at the mine were moved and adapted for use in a new line of business—producing cement. For a while it would become a viable business, which Mallory headed, but not an innovation in the same class as electric light.

In 1902, at a time when General Electric shares were trading at a his-toric high and well after Edison had sold his, Mallory happened to be traveling with him and saw in the newspaper the eye-popping closing price. Edison asked what his stake would have been worth had he held on to it. Mallory quickly worked out the number: over $4 million. Hearing this, Edison remained silent, keeping a serious expression for about fifteen seconds. Then his face lit up and he said, "Well, it's all gone, but we had a good time spending it."

The story would be retold by Edison's hagiographers many times. The evidence suggests that Edison did have a jolly time, which, to him, was well worth the $4 million. He did not include in the calculations, however, the opportunity that he lost to profit from his own inventions, beginning with the phonograph that would bring into being the modern entertainment industry. It would be others who began to make money offering to the public recorded entertainment. Edison, distracted in the pursuit of his own fancies, was slow to observe the limitless business opportunities made possible by the commercialization of fun.

Edison could not take the pulse of a public from which he was isolated. First, cloistered within Glenmont and his new lab in Orange, and then even more isolated in unpopulated mining country, Edison was not well situated to listen to a mass consumer market clamoring for the opportunity to spend money on popular music. Work was the only form of fun he was personally familiar with; it took him a long time to even consider marketing the phonograph as a device for entertainment. As late as 1892, he told Alfred Tate, "I don't want the phonograph sold for amusement purposes." Tate explained in his memoirs that Edison was "unable to visualize the potentialities of the amusement field." By the next year, Edison had begun to relent, but only a tiny bit. He was able to picture the phonograph being marketed to the individual household for the "best in Oratory and Music."

The masses did not want to turn their parlors into a music appreciation class—they had neither the parlors nor phonographs, which were still expensive, nor hunger for classical music. But entrepreneurs materialized to give the people what they wished to hear. They added a gizmo to the Edison phonograph and came up with the "nickel-in-the-slot" machine, the earliest coin-operated jukebox. It only played a single selection, but many machines could be placed in a saloon, hotel lobby, or amusement hall. Each was equipped with rubber listening tubes that were placed in the ears of the paying patron, which permitted an individual to enjoy music in public space without disturbing others. Public health authorities worried, however, that the listening tubes were "disease breeders"; the park commissioners in Philadelphia ordered the machines removed from park grounds for this reason.

Phonograph dealers who invested in the machines discovered that the nickels added up to considerable profits, even after they turned over 50 percent of revenues to the patent holder, the Automatic Phonograph Exhibition Company. A San Francisco distributor said in 1890 that he collected more than $4,000 in about six months. That money was not earned from the "best in Oratory and Music." The impresarios of the nickel-in-the-slot machine provided whatever was not classical: popular music supplemented with programs of prurient storytelling that brought occasional censorship.

Even before others had found a way to earn profits from recorded music, Edison had begun thinking about a machine that did more. The "Kinetoscope Moving View" would do "for the Eye what the phonograph does for the Ear." The first version was modeled on Edison's phonograph, and was rather too ambitious, attempting to provide not only images but synchronized sound. This very early progenitor of modern cinema—only one of many that tinkerers around the world were working on—did not come close to resembling the machine that would cast mesmerizing images that filled large screens, for it was conceived on a microscopic scale. One cylinder was used to play back sound and a second one to provide visuals with thousands of tiny images, each taken as an individual photograph by a conventional camera and painstakingly mounted on the cylinder, one by one. They were arranged in a spiral so that they could be viewed continuously through a microscope. In theory, it was a clever arrangement; in practice, however, it was impossible to make the images lie flat and appear clearly.

Edison did not have time to work out solutions to the problems as he had done when the incandescent light was his top priority. He conceived of the kinetoscope just as he decided that ore milling was going to be his main project. Edison reassigned one of his principal assistants at the mine, William Kennedy Laurie Dickson, whom Edison knew was also a talented photographer, to head up work on the kinetoscope. It was Dickson who would advance the project with myriad contributions—and continue to do so after he parted with Edison on less-than-amicable terms in 1895 and put his talents and experience to work for competitors.

No one had yet figured out how to rapidly open and close the camera's shutter—dozens of times a second—while capturing crisp images on film that was in constant motion. A much improved camera was invented, but not by Edison or his assistants. Etienne-Jules Marey, the same distinguished French scientist who earlier had worked on recording human vocalization, had designed an ingenious camera: It recorded sixty images a second on a long continuous strip of film, which was pulled by a cam in a deliberatively jerky fashion to stop the film momentarily, so that light could saturate the film and capture motion. Not only had Marey made these crucial advances, he was happy to share what he had learned with the scientific community. When Edison visited Paris in 1889 for the Paris Exposition, he was cordially received by Marey and was presented with a copy of Marey's book, which detailed in French his recent photographic work. Dickson, who had remained back at the laboratory in New Jersey but was fluent in French, likely had learned of Marey's most recent work by reading French periodicals that he bought for the laboratory.

In Dickson's account of the events of that year, Edison does not play much more than an honorific role. While Edison was in Paris, Dickson readied a prototype system that was far ahead of its time—projecting images upon a screen with synchronized sound. Upon the inventor's return to the lab, Dickson appeared on the screen, raised his hat, and said, "Good morning, Mr. Edison, glad to see you back. I hope you are satisfied with the kineto-phonograph."

This feat was accomplished by using a tachistoscope, which used a stroboscopic light and a revolving disc that could only hold a few images. It would not serve as the next step in the technical evolution of moving images, but it did show Dickson's talents. Edison took no immediate notice, however, and temporarily shifted Dickson back to the mining project. Another month went by before Edison returned his attention to moving images and drew up a preliminary patent application for a motion-picture system that replaced the cylinder with a filmstrip, like Marey's. But mining remained his pet project. Two more years passed before a working prototype was ready for a public demonstration.

The kinetoscope that was unveiled in 1891 was a console made of wood, about twenty inches square and standing four feet high, that resembled its older sibling, the nickel-in-the-slot phonograph. On top was mounted an eyepiece for the peephole, through which the viewer saw a moving image, backlit and magnified, as the film moved past the opening. The film was spliced together as one continuous fifty-foot loop, arranged on rollers. The film feed was powered by a battery-powered electric motor. In all, it was a mechanical marvel. Still, what the eye saw fell well short of a sensual feast. The images were small, and the first commercial film, *Blacksmith Scene,* ran only twenty seconds.

The machine was a novelty item, and Edison did not accord it much commercial potential. When he filed for a patent in the United States, his attorney urged him to file for foreign patents, too. Edison decided not to do so, however, when told it would cost $150. Legend has him saying at the time, "It isn't worth it." Without the protection of patents in other countries, however, he was vulnerable to legal attack. Patent disputes quickly flared and would last for more than twenty years.

When Edison visited Chicago in May 1891, reporters asked him if he was preparing to exhibit an "electrical novelty" for the World's Columbian Exposition that the city would host in 1893. This was going to be the largest—and the most influential, it turned out—of the nineteenth-century world fairs. (Its White City would provide one visitor, children's writer Frank Baum, the inspiration for the Emerald City of Oz.) This inquiry handed Edison an invitation to talk up his kinetoscope, which, even if not yet ready for commercial release, seemed certain to be complete within two years, well in time for the fair. He chose instead to play the role of the Wizard, promising the never-before-conceived. "My intention," he declared, "is to have such a happy combination of photography and electricity that a man can sit in his own parlor and see depicted upon a curtain the forms of the players in opera upon a distant stage and hear the voices of the singers." What he is describing—color visuals and audio, capturing a performance in a distant locale, in real time, projected upon a large flat surface—seems rather close to what we would come to know as color television. Edison declared he was confident that it would be "perfected" in time for the opening of the fair.

Such a claim might appear to be the product of the feverish, and incorrigibly self-deceiving, mind of the Wizard of Oz. But Edison's expectation of the perfection of color television was more a case of absentmindedness—he was not immersed in the work on the kinetoscope as Dickson was. Standing at a distance, and preoccupied with mining, Edison gave his own motion pictures and sound only a half glance. If he did not face the practical issues on a daily basis himself, he was inclined to assume that the difficult was easy, and that the impossible took just a little bit longer.

The responsibility of readying the kinetoscope for the Chicago fair fell squarely upon Dickson's shoulders, and the burden proved too much to bear: Soon exhausted, he was unable to work at all for almost three months. At the same time, the Panic of 1893 imperiled Edison's ore mill; he had no time to return to the kinetoscope. In the meantime, Tate had proceeded on the assumption that all would be ready in time and had organized a syndicate, including a brother-in-law of one of the exposition's commissioners, that secured a coveted concession to operate twenty-five machines on the grounds. The fair opened in May 1893 and introduced to the world wonders such as the Ferris wheel, Cracker Jacks, and Juicy Fruit gum. Before closing in October, it drew 27.5 million visitors. Those 27.5 million visitors did not get a look at Edison's kinetoscope, however, as the machines were not completed until the next year, too late for the fair.

The development of the machines could have been accelerated, but only if Edison relinquished his notion that they were only a novelty. In February 1894, he wrote the photographer Eadweard Muybridge, "I have constructed a little instrument which I call a Kinetograph, with a nickel and slot attachment and some 25 have been made but I am very doubtful if there is any Commercial in it and fear they will not earn their costs."

Astute observers noticed at the time that Edison had made the wrong call about the future of the phonograph, too. "The wizard Edison's idea" that the phonograph would be adopted as a machine for office transcription "has not proved to be the success which its famous creator thought it would be," the *New York Morning Advertiser* noticed. But as a source of amusement, it was doing well. One entrepreneur, Charles L. Marshall, had installed five thousand nickel-gobbling machines in phonograph parlors. He had developed a simple rule of thumb: Give the public what it wanted, and that meant avoiding what he called "classical songs" like "Thou Art Like Unto a Flower." Music that appealed to a less-refined sensibility—he singled out "Throw Him Down, McCloskey" and "One of His Legs Is Longer Than It Really Ought to Be" as exemplars—brought in fifteen times as much revenue per day.

It was clear to everyone but Edison that the kinetoscope, once it was finally ready for release, would be a tremendous source of fun of all kinds—the silly, the spectacular, and the ribald. Even before the kinetoscope was released, an Albany newspaper reported on rumors that it would be perfectly suited for recording a boxing match, permitting hundreds of thousands to witness a match within a week after the event. Edison, however, continued to lecture the public in a churchy voice about the machine's suitability for performances at the Metropolitan Opera House in New York.

His sermonizing did not guide actual practice back at the laboratory, however, which was in the hands of Dickson. On the laboratory's grounds, Dickson had directed workmen to build the "Black Maria," a long, oddly shaped movie studio covered in black tarpaper ("Black Maria" was a slang expression for a police wagon, which the studio resembled). It had a retractable roof and was mounted on a turntable so that the studio could be moved in tandem with the sun. Significantly, the first celebrity visitor Dickson invited out to be filmed was not a prima donna from the Met but rather "Sandow, the Strongman." The bodybuilder had agreed to come for a $250 fee, which he offered to waive were he granted the privilege of shaking the hand of the great Edison himself. Edison appeared after Sandow and his entourage had arrived and did his assigned part, and Sandow did his, striking various poses that showed off musculature that is preserved for the ages thanks to the new invention. It does not, however, include a picture of Edison "feeling Sandow's muscles with a curiously comical expression on his face," as reported by the *Orange Chronicle*. Nor does it capture Sandow's enjoyment of his own strength. He asked one of the laboratory assistants if he would mind being "chucked" out of the door while the cameras ran. No thanks, the assistant demurred, but Sandow proceeded anyway, grabbing him with one hand and sending him airborne through the door—too quickly for the cameras to capture. In other short features, Dickson and his helpers offered a little suggestion of sex, in the flashing legs of a Spanish dancer *(Carmencita)*, and a good helping of violence *(Cockfight)*. They were clearly not constrained by Edison's high-minded goals for the new medium.

Alfred Tate saw the commercial possibilities that Edison could not, and invested in the first kinetoscope parlor, set up in a small space, 1155 Broadway, that had been a shoe shop. In April 1894, he and his brother received ten machines, arranged in two rows. These early machines did not have coin mechanisms, so Tate planned on offering patrons a ticket for twenty-five cents that would entitle the holder to look at the programs running in five machines in one row. In his memoirs, he tells of a great opening day.

It was two o'clock on Saturday afternoon; the machines had just been installed in preparation for the shop's planned opening on Monday. In the meantime, Tate had placed a small printed announcement in the store window, along with a plaster bust of Edison. As he sat with his brother and the parlor's mechanic, a small crowd gathered outside to look at the bust of Edison. Tate impulsively decided to open the shop for a few hours and see if they couldn't pull in enough money by dinnertime to treat themselves to an elaborate spread at nearby Delmonico's.

Tate volunteered to man the ticket booth at the front. The doors were opened—and what followed was a blur of feverish business with no time for dinner. They could not get the place cleared before 1:00 A.M. on Sunday, and had to look for an all-night restaurant. Without advertising, they had taken in $120 on the first day.

The tale does not reveal, however, whether a given patron would clamor to see the same twenty-second film multiple times. Novelty only went so far. On the movie-production side, Dickson and his associates were limited by their own creative resources and, even more, by the limits of the technology. Simply put, the short filmstrip did not have enough capacity to offer a narrative. How profitable a business could be built upon such a base, unable to tell a story of any kind, limited to showing a glimpse of a bodybuilder, an acrobat, or a dancer?

Edison and his circle could not see how to advance the medium beyond a proof-of-concept novelty. It was a group of young entrepreneurs who had no prior affiliation with Edison's laboratory who eventually pulled the industry forward. Two brothers, Grey and Otway Latham, and their college friend Enoch Rector, visited Tate's kinetoscope parlor not long after it had opened in April 1894, and emerged with a vision for building a business not upon acrobatic exhibitions but upon prize-fights. They intuitively understood the critical component of a boxing match: It was a self-contained narrative, with a beginning, a middle, and an end. Sandow, preening before the camera, lacked a story; a boxing match, however, was a story that played out within a roped-off rectangle, in fast-forward mode, completed in a matter of minutes.

If the Latham brothers and their friend could persuade the Edison Manufacturing Company to film actual matches exclusively on their behalf, they had no doubt that the exhibition, delivered by kinetoscopes, would be a smashing success. After securing preliminary encouragement from Edison's company, the group, along with another partner, formed the Kinetoscope Exhibiting Company for the express purpose of showing boxing matches.

No fight could be presented in full using twenty-second reels, however. Rector, who had a background in engineering, worked with the personnel at the Edison laboratory to adapt both the camera and the display box to accommodate a reel that was three times as long, with three times the playing time. With a capacity of sixty seconds, an entire, albeit shortened, round (the standard round was three minutes) could be captured, with a beginning and an end.

The new equipment was put to work in the Black Maria almost immediately. On 15 June 1894, Michael Leonard, an established fighter, met the lesser-known Jack Cushing for a six-round bout that was filmed by Dickson and his assistant, William Heise. In order to fit the cameras into the small space, the ring was only twelve feet square. In between each one-minute round, the fighters enjoyed seven minutes of rest, while the camera operators changed the film. This was pronounced a "great and glorious idea" by one sportswriter, who observed that the long interval between rounds enabled the fighters to recover their breath and "start to work each time fresh and nimble as though nothing had happened."

A prizefight did not help to advance high culture, but Edison took great personal interest in the event nonetheless. He was the official master of ceremonies (even though boxing was illegal in New Jersey), and an enthusiastic spectator, feinting and "punching" along with the others who were on hand, fighting a "battle in pantomime, after the fashion of all novices," said one account. The *New York World* did its part to pique the curiosity of prospective kinetoscope customers by reporting that in the excitement there was confusion about the outcome of the fight. Afterward, Leonard landed a good verbal punch, saying he would have hit Cushing more but "Mr. Edison treated me right, and I didn't want to be too quick for his machine." Cushing claimed that he was too busy looking at the camera, trying to keep a pleasant expression on, to pay attention to what Leonard was doing. It didn't matter, he said, because Leonard was not "muscular enough to fold towels in a Turkish bath."

Each of the six rounds of the fight was placed in a separate kinetoscope, which had been enlarged to accommodate the 150 feet of film that rested in vertical coils. Patrons were charged ten cents for the privilege of seeing one round, and if all went well, true fight fans would pay to see all six. The plan went well indeed. When the Kinetoscope Exhibiting Company opened for business on Nassau Street in Lower Manhattan in August 1896, the storefront was packed with eager throngs on the first day. On the second, lines formed into the street, prompting a call to the police for help in crowd control.

The success proved the drawing power of boxing for the new medium, and the Latham brothers moved quickly to arrange for another match, with a bigger name. They approached James Corbett, the reigning heavyweight champion, and offered him the opportunity to earn a sizable prize against a local patsy, Peter Courtney. It would be a "finish fight," going however many rounds were needed before one of the combatants was knocked out or unable to rise from his stool. Both the sponsors and Corbett showed considerable sophistication in working out the details of the arrangement. The Lathams insisted that Corbett grant to their company exclusive film rights; Corbett, on his part, demanded, and received, a clause specifying royalty payments for every set of film prints that would be put on exhibition; this proved a brilliant stroke on his part.

Like a modern-day fight promoter preparing a pay-per-view event, the Lathams worried about the possibility of a quick knockout—this would keep only a single kinetoscope busy instead of a line of machines for each round. They also did not want a fight that went on too long; a finish that came in the thirtieth round would come well after the pocket money, if not the patience, of the average fight fan would be exhausted. From a strictly commercial perspective, they decided the ideal length would be six rounds. But how could a genuine "finish fight" last a predetermined number of rounds? Simple: The remuneration offered to the dominant fighter was structured to achieve the desired result. The Lathams offered Corbett $4,750 of the $5,000 purse, but in order to collect he had to knock out his opponent in the sixth round—not earlier, not later. "You can bet I'll do the trick, too," Corbett predicted prior to the event, "for it's too much money to let slip out of one's grasp."

Corbett was a good choice to serve as the leading man in this drama. He was a professional actor as well as fighter, performing on Broadway

204 / The Wizard of Menlo Park

at the time in *Gentleman Jack*. He had become so accustomed to drawing attention to himself that he had lost the ability to become publicly
invisible, which was now a problem. Local police had been angered by
the flagrant violation of the state ban on boxing when Edison's laboratory had hosted the first filmed fight a few months earlier. On the day of
Corbett's fight, 7 September 1894, when he and his large retinue caught
the Christopher Street ferry for New Jersey, they were supposed to do
their utmost to travel incognito to avoid being arrested. Upon disem-
barking from the train station, he and his entourage did divide up into
two groups to evade detection on the last leg of their journey to the
Black Maria. But Corbett could not resist displaying his customary sar-
torial splendor (natty checked-cloth suit; immaculate white shirt; dia-
monds nestled upon black tie) and flashing the three jewel-encrusted
rings worn on his right pinkie.

As before, the Black Maria had room only for the makeshift ring and
a few invited guests. The photographic equipment was much improved:
One account said that the rounds lasted ninety seconds, with only a
one- to two-minute interval between each. Corbett was careful and
made sure that the fight lasted exactly as long as the sponsors had requested. He knocked his opponent down in the third round and could
easily have put him away then, but he backed off so that the show could
go on. A bit later, Corbett connected with a left to the jaw, then with a
right, landing on the same spot, and Courtney went down. He tried to
get up, then pitched forward, unconscious. The referee counted off ten
seconds and the fight was over. Wonder of wonders, this "finish fight"
finished in the sixth round.

Afterward, when a local judge heard about the event, he charged a
grand jury to investigate. Edison was summoned to appear, but Mina
told the authorities that he was up at Ogdensburg, working at the mine
site (the documentary record leaves open the question of where Edison
was on the day of the fight itself). The local law-enforcement apparatus
soon found other matters of greater interest, and no charges were
pressed. But the fact that Edison was indeed spending most of his time
at the mine is important because it goes a long way in explaining why

he committed the single largest blunder in his career as inventor-cum-businessperson. He failed to see what was needed to fully realize the commercial value of the Corbett-Courtney fight that had just been filmed. It had a professional actor as its star performer; it had drama with a satisfying denouement; it was the right duration to maximize box-office revenue without antagonizing patrons—it had everything but a means of presentation that could handle large numbers of customers simultaneously. For that, the images had to be freed from the confined space of the kinetoscope box. They needed to be projected so that a roomful of people could enjoy them at the same time. Anyone who spent time with the exhibitors would have seen the problem in an instant. Edison, who had seventy-ton rollers on his mind, missed it completely.

The Latham brothers, however, saw immediately the need for a projection system. As pleased as they were by the profits they collected from exhibiting the Corbett-Courtney fight in kinetoscopes, they felt even a greater degree of frustration in the inefficiency of a display that could only serve one patron at a time. The young men invited their father, Woodville Latham, a professor of chemistry at West Virginia University, to visit their Nassau Street parlor and render a scientific opinion: Was there any way they would be able to project the miniature images upon a sheet? Optics was not the elder Latham's academic field, but he told them that he was certain that any photographed image could be projected on a screen. His interest piqued, he joined them in launching a crash project to develop movie projection. Rather than working with Edison's laboratory as the Latham brothers had done earlier when they wanted to increase the running time of a kinetoscope reel, this time they set off on their own. A small room, twelve by fifteen feet, was rented to serve as the new lab. Eugene Lauste, an expert mechanic and former employee of Edison's, was the first person hired. The tiny space became still smaller when Lauste set up his cot and took up residence there.

The Lathams were not the only exhibitors frustrated with Edison's kinetoscope, and the others urged Edison to introduce a projection machine. Edison was adamant: no. He reasoned that the peephole machines were selling well and at a good profit. The problem with projection was that it would work all too well—if he replaced the inefficient kineto-scope with projection systems that could serve up the show to every-one, "there will be a use for maybe about ten of them in the whole United States." He concluded, "Let's not kill the goose that lays the golden egg."

At Edison's lab in Orange, without his boss's approval, W. K. L. Dickson carried out research on film projection on his own and shared his findings with a friend who was a keen listener: Otway Latham. And when Dickson accepted an invitation to try a projection experiment in a physics laboratory at Columbia, who should show up but Otway's father, Professor Latham. The Lathams made an offer to Dickson—come join us and we'll give you a quarter-share interest in the business—but Dickson was unwilling to make the leap. When Edison got word of his fraternizing with the Lathams, however, and failed to reassure Dickson that he believed Dickson's dealings had been perfectly honorable, Dickson felt he had no choice but to resign. The exact chronology of what he did and what he knew at various points preceding his resignation would be the subject of much litigation that followed. But regardless of intellectual-property issues, Edison lost the one person on his staff who would have been most valuable to him in developing a projection system.

The Lathams and Dickson had discovered that sending a bright light through a moving strip of film did not project satisfactorily because any given image did not absorb enough light before it sped on. The Lathams came up with a partial solution, which was to make the film wider, providing more area for the light to catch as each image went by. The projected images were about the size of a window and good enough to unveil publicly. Professor Latham gave a demonstration of his newly christened Pantoptikon to reporters in April 1895.

Press accounts were less interested in the pantoptikon than in Edison's critique of it. Here was an opportunity for Edison to offer a few gracious words to the competition, a modest outfit that only had financial resources to produce the one demonstration unit and not much else. And still Edison could not bring himself to tip his hat. Going solely on what the reporter described to him, Edison claimed that a kinetoscope could do everything that the Latham machine purported to do. Why was everyone making such a fuss about projecting pictures? He'd done that long before, but the pictures had been crude. Wait two or three months, he promised, and "we will have the kinetoscope perfected, and then we will show you screen pictures." Professor Latham wrote a letter to the editor in response that took Edison's self-flattering account apart, point by point.

A few weeks later, the Lathams, no longer dependent upon the Black Maria, photographed a boxing match on the roof of Madison Square Garden, and on 20 May 1895, offered the public the first showing of motion pictures on a screen. The Lathams' projector, now renamed the Eidoloscope, provided a "Life Size" reproduction of the fight, and a broadside printed for the occasion promised, "During the Exhibition the Audience will be Comfortably Seated." This was not a claim that Edison could ever make for his peephole machines, which required standing, stooping, and squinting. And if this was not galling enough, newspapers around the country seemed to be reveling in Edison's eclipse by unknown newcomers. "Edison Not in It!" shouted one headline in a Chicago paper, followed by "Kenetoscope [sic] Outclassed by Prof. Latham's Newest."

By the time the Wizard came down from the mountain and noticed what he had missed, he was too late. Not only in the United States, but also in France, England, and Germany, inventors were attacking the screen-projection problem simultaneously. In the race in the United States, the Lathams appeared to be in the lead. But they failed to understand that the wider film used in their eidoloscope could not draw in enough light to provide an image that was bright and large enough to be of commercial service. The fundamental problem that bedeviled all of the early attempts at projection remained: insufficient light. Two inventors who lived in Washington, D.C., Thomas Armat and C. Francis Jenkins, were the first to figure out the solution—the moving images needed to stop momentarily, so that enough light could pass through to produce a clear image, just as when filming, the camera had to stop momentarily to allow the light that came in through the aperture to produce a photo-chemical reaction and register. Their projector, the Phantascope, moved the film in the only way that could produce bright pictures and smooth-appearing action: by stopping each frame as it passed by the lamp.

Only in folklore does the world beat a path to the inventor of the better mousetrap. In September 1895, the world simply shrugged when Armat and Jenkins publicly unveiled their new machine in a corner of the Cotton States and International Exposition in Atlanta, Georgia. A local paper gave it brief mention, but only a few visitors stopped by, and the inventors had nothing to show for their first attempt at marketing. The two soon quarreled over assignment of the patents—given the dismal state of their business, this showed a hardy optimism—and dissolved their partnership.

Edison's largest kinetoscope distributor, Raff & Gammon, begged Edison in early October to complete the "Screen Machine" that he had promised them. The next day, Edison personally handwrote a letter that showed what was currently most on his mind. It was addressed not to Raff & Gammon, but to the Ingersoll-Sergeant Drill Company: "Gentlemen, We are using six of your drills at our mine and find them perfectly satisfactory." One cannot help but admire the obstinate way in which Edison refused to let go of his failing mining project. He jeopardized his own role in the commercialization of fun because he was having a great deal of fun himself, pursuing at his ore mill his own bliss, in his own way. He was happily immersed even though it entailed living for long, lonely stretches up at the mine without Mina. (His letters reveal his loneliness. They also provide a tiny contribution to the history of sex. In one letter, he tells her a joke he had just heard: How can one recognize the modern woman, or so-called Coming Woman? "The answer is 'Quite easily by their panting or short breaths.'" Concerned that she would not be able to "study out the joke," he told her not to show it to just anybody "because it is *bad*.")

While Raff & Gammon beseeched Edison to invent a Screen Machine, young Armat, realizing he lacked the means to get the attention of the marketplace, approached Raff & Gammon about acting as his distributor. He received a skeptical reception—Edison himself was unable to produce a projection system that worked, so how could an unknown inventor succeed? Armat offered to pay Raff & Gammon's expenses to come visit him in Washington to see for themselves. The phantascope proved to be all that Armat had claimed, and his patent solid. Raff and his partner prepared to abandon Edison and his instantly obsolete kinetoscope, if they could not persuade Edison to lend the one asset that he possessed that remained valuable: his name. Their plan also required Armat to swallow his pride and accept a marketing plan that depended on his remaining invisible. Explaining that they assumed that "you, like ourselves, have gone in this thing with a view to making all the money possible," they explained that many people had been waiting for the past year for Edison to perfect a projector and would continue to hold off purchasing a machine offered by anyone else, no matter what its virtues. "In order to secure the largest profit in the shortest time it is necessary that we attach Mr. Edison's name in some prominent capacity to this new machine. . . . We regard this as simply a matter of business and we trust that you will view it strictly in the same light."

Armat accepted the arrangement, and, more surprising, Edison did too, showing a willingness to use his name to market a better invention than he had been able to produce. He had not been willing to do the same when approached by the graphophone interests. To obscure its origins, the phantascope was given a new name, the Vitascope, and when it made its debut at Koster and Bial's Music Hall in New York in April 1896, projecting life-sized images on a screen twenty by thirteen feet, it was described as "the ingenious inventor's latest toy." Edison followed the script to which he had agreed and remained silent.

In July, Los Angeles showed an appreciation of the vitascope that exceeded even New York's. The inaugural film program offered a dancing sequence, then melodrama involving Uncle Sam knocking a diminutive bully, John Bull, to his knees, street scenes from New York, more dancing, and then the first medium-range close-up of a kiss. The *Los Angeles Times* said "the audience fairly shrieked and howled approval" and called the vitascope "an instantaneous success." Sports programming demonstrated the technology's capabilities in most thrilling fashion. At another site, the Corbett-Courtney fight was offered in a size that for the first time was like "actual life." In the first week in Los Angeles, some twenty thousand people saw a vitascope program, and another ten thousand had to be turned away.

The vitascope's success was credited to Edison's ingenuity, which gave a bright luster to his star. Edison also could derive pleasure as the head of a new business that had not existed before: film production. One of the prerogatives as studio head was the ability to sign off on the creative agenda. In 1897, one of his company's twenty-second features, *Mr. Edison at Work in His Chemical Laboratory,* had a cast consisting of just himself, playing the role of wizard, missing only a costume and pointed cap. It was filmed in the Black Maria, which had been outfitted with shelves filled with glassware and with a workbench overflowing with retorts and burners, everything needed for a fake laboratory. By donning a costume—a white lab coat—and doing nothing but dash from one end of the stage to the other, moving this piece of lab equipment here, and then there, pretending to be engaged in an experiment so demanding that he had no time to look up from his work and peer directly into the camera, Edison could fully inhabit the persona that had been placed upon him twenty years earlier, when he more closely lived the part. He intuitively understood the way invisibility heightened celebrity, but it could not be taken to an extreme; he needed to make rare appearances, too. For the public hungry to see the man at work, the film appeared to give them exactly that, albeit a glimpse that only lasted twenty seconds.

CHAPTER TEN

KINGLY PRIVILEGE

THE PUBLIC'S INTEREST in Thomas Edison's inventions rose and fell, as announcements of coming wonders would pique interest and then delays in the delivery of those wonders would disappoint. Over time, however, his fame acquired an indestructible sheath and eclipsed the attention accorded to the individual inventions themselves. It was Thomas Edison, the person, to whom the public became most attached during his lifetime. Edison realized this, and worked unceasingly to protect the most distilled expression of his person: his name. "Thomas A. Edison" was an estimable invention, too.

In the public's view, by the late 1890s anything associated with Edison's name was presumed to be blessed by the inventor's brilliance. The passage of time worked in Edison's favor, erasing from collective memory the earlier disappointments that had followed hyperbolic predictions. So positive was the association with his name that it was attached to a boggling array of goods, such as those offered by the Edison Chemical Company, a manufacturer of printing ink. If customers failed to make the connection between the name and the famous inventor, they could not miss the "Wizard" that was featured in its advertising. What the company did not draw attention to was this fact: The Edison Chemical Company had no tie to Thomas Edison. Its founders had found a man with the last name of Edison—one C. M. Edison, no relation— who was willing to license marketing rights to his name for a fee.

This had vexed the other Edison, Thomas, who won a court order that enjoined the company from using his surname. The matter did not end there, however. The Edison Chemical Company reorganized itself as the Thomas A. Edison, Jr., Chemical Company, having enlisted the famous man's twenty-five-year-old namesake son.

Thomas Edison Jr., Edison's second oldest child from his first marriage, had left St. Paul's preparatory school without a diploma, hoping to become an inventor, too. His father had created positions for him at the West Orange laboratory and up at the Ogden mine, but Junior felt extreme frustration with his father for not recognizing his inventive talents. He was also frustrated with himself, for being intimidated by his father and remaining mute. In May 1897, then twenty-one-year-old Junior wrote Mina, his stepmother, from the mine about his relationship with his father:

> I probably never will be able to please him, as am afraid it's not in me. But I shall never give up trying. If I could only talk to him the way I want to, perhaps everything may be different. I have many ideas of my own, which sometimes—yes—I may say on all occasions I would like to ask him or tell him about but they never leave my mouth, and are soon forgotten, perhaps where they belong, perhaps not. This I would like to have him to decide.

Later that year, writing from a hotel in New York City, Junior again confided to his stepmother that his father often told him that he was "impractical." He vowed to do his best to become a practical person, "but it is a difficult matter to change one's nature in a short time." His ambition to become an inventor remained firm.

Within a few days, his dream was realized: He became a famous inventor, at least in the eyes of the *New York Herald,* which ran a long, credulous profile titled "Edison, Jr., Wizard." The young man was credited with inventing an incandescent bulb superior to his father's and "developing a formidable rivalry to his illustrious parent in his own line." The powerful effect of his name mesmerized the *Herald*'s reporter, who took on faith Junior's claims about his invention, about financial backing from unnamed powerful figures, and about his autobiography (he claimed he had left school at the age of eleven and subsequently continued his education at his father's elbow).

Junior's claimed invention and related business interests were not verified by independent sources. He discovered, however, that his fame, even if inherited, led to new opportunities. He soon landed a publicly visible role at the Electrical Exhibition staged in Madison Square Garden in 1898. The position did not come with major responsibilities—he was head of the decoration committee, whose largest contribution to the exhibition was an illuminated fountain—but Junior used the opportunity to speak to the press about the life he led as inventor. A small accident that damaged his desk, caused by a fireworks-sized explosive used in an exhibit of miniature gunboats, gave him the opportunity to set his jaw bravely and proclaim his lack of fear as he persevered down the dangerous path he had chosen. "I never expect to die a natural death," he said in an interview; "I feel confident I will be blown up some day."

In fact, Junior was not actually staring down death in dedicated pursuit of new inventions. His assignment was to design the arrangement of decorative electric lights for the exhibition's fountain. The most plausible explanation for why the exhibition's sponsor had hired Thomas Edison Jr. is that he possessed a brand name suitable for marketing the show, which immediately followed another show in the Garden that pioneered the exploitation of famous names, Buffalo Bill's Wild West Show. Thomas Edison Sr. would have been the best draw, perhaps even better than Annie Oakley, but he was not available; the next best thing, therefore, was Thomas Edison Jr. So it was he, and only he, who was mentioned by name in the *New York Times* as the guest celebrity on hand at the exhibition, sipping tea that had been boiled on an electric range, a novelty, and munching a tiny biscuit cooked in an "electrically heated oven," another novelty. This time he was not credited with anything but being the son of the "Wizard."

When the exhibition closed, the spotlight moved on, and Junior had to find another sponsor who would pay him for the aura of fame attached to his name. Fortuitously, investors appeared to form the Edison Jr.

Steel and Iron Process Company, providing the younger Tom Edison with one-third of the company's stock. Edison Sr. was outraged that his ne'er-do-well son continued to exploit the Edison name and broke off communication with him, letting his next-eldest son, Will, deliver the news. Tom Jr. wrote his father in reply that he intended to "go on just as I have been doing." He maintained that his family name had been a "detriment" to his business career, as no bank believed Junior's claimed need for credit. "If my name was Smith," he said, "I would be a rich man today." He added a gratuitous insult about his father's bumbling in business. "You should have been—'ask any body'—a millionaire ten times over if you knew how to handle your own achievements."

The Edison Jr. Steel and Iron Process Company was followed by the Thomas A. Edison, Jr. and William Holzer Steel and Iron Process Company, which also failed. Junior was married, then swiftly not married, to a woman whose profession (chorus girl) was mentioned in newspaper accounts as a compact summary of her character. Her former husband's family viewed her as a gold-digging strumpet who had entered marriage with nothing but avarice in her heart. If the unflattering characterization were true, it suggests her eyesight was poor—Junior possessed no gold to be dug. His brother Will reported to the family that Tom Jr. had had to leave town to escape thousands in debts and a pursuing sheriff. "He is the laughing stock of business men," Will said.

Unemployed and estranged from his father, Tom Jr. was exactly the person that the Edison Chemical Company was looking for. Yes, a court order had forbidden the company from using the Edison name, but what if, instead of relying on C. M. Edison to justify use of the name, it could use that of Thomas Edison's own eldest born, who had been endowed at birth with a name that was now world renowned? Tom Jr. was agreeable, believing that his own inventive talents would finally be recognized. He had come up with a "Magno-Electric Vitalizer," a remarkable device that cured "Paralysis, Rheumatism, Locomotor Ataxia, and Nervous Prostration," and all other maladies that Junior called the "so-called 'incurable' complaints." The company added the Vitalizer to its line of wares, including the "Wizard's Ink Tablets," and renamed itself the Thomas A. Edison, Jr., Chemical Company. Junior was provided a vice president's position, a $5,000 initial payment, a monthly stipend, and royalties.

Edison Sr. was upset beyond measure. He communicated his feelings to Junior, and Junior's resolution to make his way on his own crumbled. In December 1902, he wrote his father with an offer to give up "all future rights to the name of Edison for the purpose of obtaining money," and left the monetary terms of the agreement to be set by Tom Sr. In the father's retrospective account of the episode, reconciliation with his son came about because it was he who offered his son "more money than the men he was associated with would pay him."

Having paid for the cooperation of his son, the elder inventor then filed a lawsuit against the company for use of the Edison name and for the moniker "Wizard." A press account in a local newspaper described it as "one of the most peculiar suits in the history of the court," as it featured a dispute that centered around protecting the inventor's name by restricting commercial use of the son's.

Edison's attorneys had a more difficult case to make against the Thomas A. Edison, Jr., Chemical Company than they had had against the Edison Chemical Company. They offered two arguments. First, customers were being misled to assume that Edison was the inventor of the Wizard's Ink Tablets and the Magno-Electric Vitalizer. (The future would bear this out: Years later, customers would still send to Edison's laboratory their Vitalizers for recharging—and the lab would send them right back, untouched, with a note explaining "we know nothing whatever about them and have no way of charging them.") Second, Tom Jr. could not legitimately claim to be an inventor. To bolster this contention, Tom Sr. supplied an affidavit that said Junior had no regular occupation, had never produced a single practical invention, and—this must have hurt—was "incapable of making any invention or discovery of merit."

Edison was more concerned about his name than about the commercial fate of any of his inventions, none of which had ever moved him to say anything equivalent to what he told a reporter in 1904: "I'll protect my name if it costs me every dollar in the world I possess." Having extracted his son from the Thomas A. Edison, Jr., Chemical Company, he did not have to spend more of his own money, however, to end the company's poaching of his good name. Contending that selling the Vitalizer perpetrated a fraud upon the public, the U.S. Postal Service halted delivery of all mail to the company, which had to close its doors.

This should have brought this public unpleasantness for the Edison family to a close. But the usually taciturn Edison had much still to say, including his thoughts about the shortcomings of his hapless son. He told the *New York American* that Tom Junior was incapable of building a Magno-Electric Vitalizer. Or anything else; he simply had no inventive talent. "I could not get him to attend school because he wished to become famous and have it said that he, too, never had attended a college." His son would struggle to support himself for the remainder of his life, but the lack of a college education would turn out to be a lesser problem than alcoholism and mental illness.

During the fight over use of the Edison surname, when Tom Jr. had flung the charge that his father did not know how to convert technical achievements into commercial success, his criticism had been spot on. As time passed, his father subsequently did no better in the timing of his launch of new business ventures. He followed the debacle of his ore-milling venture with a new obsession, electric cars. In 1900, and ahead of Henry Ford, Edison articulated an ambition to make automobiles "the poor man's vehicle." Edison's vision, however, centered upon using improved batteries to make electrically powered vehicles superior to gasoline-powered ones. Eking out greater range from batteries became his new, all-consuming preoccupation. By 1901, he had a prototype electric car that could reach seventy miles per hour, offering a ride Edison called "the sport of kings." By 1902, he claimed his car had a range of eighty-five miles without recharging, and he expected to have a battery on the market within months, just as soon as final road tests were complete. He predicted, "It will be but a short time before demand for storage batteries will create one of the most enormous industries in the land."

His battery was released, but its performance was less than he had led everyone to expect. His experiments continued and improved batteries followed, but the electric car remained a novelty. This did not cause him to alter his predictions for the car's future dominance, however. Ten years after his first pronouncement, he was excited to see that the sales of "family electric carriages" were increasing "very rapidly" and predicted that their lower maintenance costs would lead to their "probably" displacing gasoline-powered cars.

At the very moment Edison was rather too optimistic about the prospects for the electric car, he was insufficiently appreciative of the commercial potential of the music business. As always, it was technical problems that interested him more than commercial ones, and it was the challenges in the laboratory that kept him absorbed in batteries, to the exclusion of other possible business opportunities. His personal interest in working on the phonograph had waned, then returned, and then waned again. The technical advances that would finally, three decades after its invention, make it a commercial success were a reliable spring motor and the manufacturing technology for making multiple duplicate copies of a musical recording from a single master. Even before these pieces were in place at the very end of the nineteenth century, and sales of phonographs and recordings zigged skyward, Edison was puttering elsewhere in the laboratory, at work on his automobile batteries.

The public had no reason to doubt that Edison was giving anything but his full attention to the phonograph. His imprimatur was critical to its marketing, and retail distributors relied upon his celebrity. Prospective customers were told that the Edison phonograph had received the great man's "constant care," the only invention of his to receive this favored attention. In at least one instance, a Des Moines, Iowa, retailer went too far, appending a counterfeit "Thos A. Edison" signature to a typewritten letter sent out in a mass mailing that requested that the recipient send in his or her impressions of the latest Edison phonograph. "Will you drop me just a line—address it to me personally and mark it care Edison Laboratory, Orange, N.J.?" When the letters came into the laboratory, Edison's staff was so aghast that his name had been borrowed by one of his dealers that they held off mentioning the matter to him. They also knew that the letters came with idiosyncratic requests (one man, writing from Marcus, Iowa, was quite particular: He wrote Edison that he wanted "a personal letter from you, not a type written letter, but just a good plain written letter written with your own hand"). William Maxwell, the vice president for sales, wrote the Des Moines dealer, "You can readily see that it will not do at all to have people writing in here to Mr. Edison" and demanded an explanation of the dealer's presumptuousness. The dealer replied, not very credibly, that he had simply forgotten to get permission to use the facsimile of Edison's signature.

Edison had retained the patent rights and business stakes in the phonograph, so when the business came into its own, he approved the construction of expanded manufacturing facilities adjacent to his laboratory to handle the orders that poured in. This was followed by still more growth, and more building: An entire block adjacent to the laboratory was filled with five-story hulks. By 1907, as the company erected its sixteenth building, Edison boasted of "the largest talking machine factory in the world." All the buildings were built with concrete, which, Edison proudly pointed out, was "absolutely fireproof."

Edison and his copywriters were inclined to say too much when extolling the virtues of the Edison phonograph. A pithy rubric, like "Made in America in 1888—Made Perfect in 1914," would be dwarfed by long columns of text that brought out every subtle advantage to be gained by the consumer who chose the Edison machine. The praise in an advertisement that ran in the *Detroit Times* went on at such length that Maxwell wondered if it was a bit much. "I wish I knew whether people will read that much copy. Farmers will, we know—but do city people?"

Once Edison's marketers squarely addressed the urban middle class, they devised advertising that made prospective customers feel as entitled to enjoy the pleasures of recorded music as anyone. "When the

King of England wants to see a show, they bring the show to the castle and he hears it alone in his private theater." So said an advertisement in 1906 for the Edison phonograph. It continued: "If you are a king, why don't you exercise your kingly privilege and have a show of your own in your own house."

Other advertisements developed the theme of the phonograph as the great leveler. In 1908, a man in formal wear and his slender wife stood on one side of a table, upon which sat a phonograph; on the other side stood four servants, wearing smiles and expressions of curiosity. The caption said that the Edison phonograph had brought the same entertainment enjoyed by the rich within the range of all. The credit for making the phonograph "the great popular entertainer" was to be bestowed upon Thomas Edison. "He made it desirable by making it good; he made it popular by making it inexpensive." Another advertisement promised that the phonograph would "amuse the most unresponsive," adding reverently, "It is irresistible because Edison made it."

In truth, the Edison phonograph fell short of being irresistible; nor did it lead the industry in technical innovation. It was the Victor Talking Machine Company that made discs a practical medium. The disc's flat dimensions offered a more convenient means of storing many songs than the three-dimensional Edison cylinder. It was Victor that came up with a disc that offered four minutes of capacity when Edison's cylinder's had only two minutes. And it was Victor that introduced the pricey, and very successful, Victrola, which hid the horn of the phonograph within a wood cabinet, transforming it into a piece of fine furniture—and a very profitable item for its manufacturer.

Edison's offerings may have lagged, but such was the demand for kingly entertainment enjoyed at home that the Edison Phonograph Works prospered along with Victor and Columbia, the two companies that with Edison comprised the dominant three in the industry. Edison's cylinder, which cost about seven cents to manufacture, sold for fifty cents, providing a nice gross margin that covered all manner of strategic missteps. One of those was Edison's conviction that there was no need to switch to discs. When he finally gave in and brought out discs, he could not bring himself to relinquish cylinders, so resources had to be spread across two incompatible formats. Nor would he permit his standards for sound quality to be compromised. He insisted that his discs be twice the thickness of those produced by the competition and much heavier, which provided for better sound but made them far more cumbersome.

Edison was adamant that Edison recordings would be played only on Edison phonographs. His competitors, Victor and Columbia, shared the same playback technique, etching a laterally cut groove that sent the needle moving horizontally as the record played. Their recordings could be played on one another's machines. Edison, however, adopted his own design, a groove that varied vertically, called at the time a "hill-and-dale" cut. An adapter permitted Victor records to be played on an Edison Disc Phonograph, but Edison forbade the sale of an attachment that permitted his records to be played on the machines of the competition.

Edison had never shown a talent for strategy, and he did not give the subject close study. He spent most of his time working on problems related to industrial chemistry, principally, those related to batteries, and secondarily, those related to mass production of cylinders and discs. Yet he did take time to make decisions about music, personally approving—and, more often, disapproving—the suggestions of underlings about which performers should be recorded. His dislike of various musical genres and artists was strong and encompassed almost everything. Popular music—"these miserable dance and ragtime selections"—had no chance of receiving his blessing. Jazz was for "the nuts"; one performance reminded him of "the dying moan of dead animals." But he was no elitist. He also dismissed the members of the Metropolitan Opera House as lacking tune. Sergei Rachmaninoff was just "a pounder."

In 1911, Edison wrote a correspondent that he had had to take on the responsibilities of musical director for his company because the incumbent had made what Edison deemed to be awful decisions, permitting players to play out of tune and, most egregiously, tolerating a defective flute that "on high notes gives a piercing abnormal sound like machinery that wants oiling." How these dissonant sounds had escaped the notice of others is a question that Edison did not address.

Edison approached music as if it were a cryptographic puzzle to be solved; musical composition was merely a matter of formula, and in most cases, in his judgment, was unoriginal (he did except Beethoven from this criticism). His daughter Madeleine recalled in 1972 an occasion when she was a young girl, growing up in Glenmont, when her father was determined to personally select waltzes that would be recorded by his company. He hired a pianist and had her play loudly no fewer than six hundred. The experience was not enjoyed by Madeleine and the other members of the family. She remembered, "We just about left home that time."

To Edison, the technical problems posed in recording sound by purely mechanical means, prior to the development of the microphone, were far more absorbing than business issues. He allocated his time accordingly. He spent a year and a half overseeing research on how to record and clearly reproduce the word "sugar" perfectly. Two more months were needed to master "scissors." He wrote, "After that the phonograph would record and reproduce anything." This was not wholly true. Recording an orchestra with pre-electric acoustic technology presented insoluble problems. He did his best, ordering the construction of the world's largest brass recording horn, 128 feet long, 5 feet in diameter at the end that received sound, tapering down to ⅝ of an inch at the other. Its construction required thirty thousand rivets alone, each carefully smoothed on the interior surface. It was a marvel of metalwork, but as an instrument for recording sound, it never worked very well. (It did serve its country well, however, being sent off for service in World War II in a scrap drive.)

Edison's partial loss of hearing prevented him from listening to music in the same way as those with unimpaired hearing. A little item that appeared in a Schenectady, New York, newspaper in 1913 related the story that Edison supposedly told a friend about how he usually listened to recordings by placing one ear directly against the phonograph's cabinet. But if he detected a sound too faint to hear in this fashion, Edison said, "I bite my teeth in the wood good and hard and then I get it good and strong." The story would be confirmed decades later in

Madeleine's recollections of growing up. One day she came into the sitting room in which someone was playing the piano and a guest, Maria Montessori, was in tears, watching Edison listen the only way that he could, teeth biting the piano. "She thought it was pathetic," Madeleine said, "I guess it was."

Edison, though, was undaunted by the limitations of his hearing, which would make for an inspirational tale, were it not for the fact that he was the self-appointed musical director of a profit-seeking record business, whose artistic decisions directly affected the employees of the Edison Phonograph Works. His judgments and whims met no obstruction. One employee, A. E. Johnson, recalled the disillusionment that followed his being hired. He said of Edison, "I found out that he could make awful mistakes, and I also found it didn't pay to tell him about his mistakes. Let him find them out himself, and if you did that cleverly you were all right." Workers spread word daily about Edison's mood. "The Old Man is feelin' fine today" was welcome news. But if the word was "the Old Man's on the rampage," employees dove for cover, "as in a cyclone cellar, until the tempest was over."

Not just his employees, but also the general public, angered Edison. He was exasperated by a public that clamored, he said, "for louder and still louder records." He believed that "anyone who really had a musical ear wanted soft music." And it was those customers, the "lovers of good music," who Edison in 1911 said would be "the only constant and continuous buyers of records." This was wishful thinking. What was plainly evident to everyone else was that the only constant in the music business was inconstancy, the fickle nature of popular fads. The half-life of a commercially successful song was brief. By the time Edison's factory shipped the first records three weeks after recording, the flighty public had already moved on.

Even then, in the founding years of the recorded-music business, the economics of the industry was based upon hits, the few songs that enjoyed an unpredictably large success and subsidized the losses incurred by the other releases. On rare occasions, Edison grudgingly granted this. Then he would concede that the popular music he disdained was in most demand, and he took what comfort he could in the thought that the "trash" his company reluctantly released did help to sell phonographs and indirectly help him to provide "music of the class that is enjoyed by real lovers of music."

This business was not so easily mastered, however, and the contempt with which Edison regarded popular music did not help him understand his customers. They would purchase the records of particular performers whom they had heard of but shied away from the unknown artists. Decades later, economists who studied the workings of the entertainment industry would identify the winner-take-all phenomenon that benefited a handful of performers. The famous become more famous, and the more famous, the richer. Everyone else faces starvation. This was the case at the turn of the twentieth century, too.

The management of the Victor Talking Machine Company understood these basic market principles long before Edison absorbed them. Shortly after the company's founding in 1901, Victor signed Enrico Caruso to an exclusive contract, paying him a royalty that was rumored to be 25 percent of the $2 retail price of a Caruso record. His estimated annual earnings from royalties in 1912 was $90,000, at a time when the second-most-popular singer only earned $25,000. The others whom Victor signed were notables, too: Farrar, Schumann-Heink, Galli-Curci, Ponselle, Tetrazzini, Melba, McCormack, Paderewski, Cortot, de Pachmann, Heifetz, Elman, Kreisler, Zimbalist, Toscanini, Stokowski, and Muck.

At the same time Victor was writing checks for the leading talents of the day, Edison brought out his checkbook reluctantly and rarely. One exception was when in 1910 he signed the woman who way back on a wintry night in 1879 had visited his Menlo Park laboratory: Sarah Bernhardt.

In the *Edison Phonograph Monthly,* the company's internal trade organ, much was made of the difficulties that had had to be overcome in order to land an artist such as Bernhardt. She had had to be persuaded to discard her "professional aversion to exploiting her talent in this manner." The monetary terms supposedly were not an issue ("Bernhardt is an extremely rich woman"). The sticking point was her concern that crude recording technology would leave posterity with a sound inferior to her voice. According to the company's publicists, a demonstration of the phonograph persuaded her that Edison would produce "perfect Records." The company urged dealers to write their local newspapers and reap free publicity: "No paper will refuse to publish the news, as everything that the Immortal Bernhardt does is eagerly seized upon by the press."

We do not know whether Bernhardt ruled out commercial considerations (she did endorsements for commercial products like a dentifrice for a fee, but she did draw the line when P. T. Barnum offered her $10,000 for the rights to display a medical curiosity: her amputated leg). We do know that Edison hated the negotiations with recording stars, which entailed monetary demands far in excess of what Edison considered reasonable. He complained that despite their talk about their love for their art, "it is money, and money only, that counts." Even the large sums paid to the most famous failed to secure their loyalty. He grumbled that artists would bolt "for a little more money offered by companies whose strongest advertising point is a list of names." When Edison read that Stravinsky had written "the tempo of America is greater than the rest of the world. It moves at a wonderfully swift pace," Edison added in the margin: "Yes, with a metronome of money."

Edison convinced himself—without consulting others, in typical fashion—that he could simply opt out of competition for stars. He tried a small-budget alternative, scouting undiscovered voices among local choirs in Orange and Newark. He wrote a correspondent in 1911, "I believe if you record Church Choir singers and Musical Club, Glee Club, etc., singers, that we shall be able to discover a lot of talent just suitable for the phonograph." He was pleased to have found locally two tenors that "can beat any Opera tenor except Caruso." Over time, Edison did add Anna Case, Sergei ("the Pounder") Rachmaninoff, and a few others. But he permitted competitors to snatch up other talented performers, like Louis Armstrong, Bessie Smith, Fanny Brice, and Al Jolson. The first record to sell 1 million copies was Vernon Dalhart's hillbilly ditty, "The Prisoner's Song." Not surprisingly, it was a Victor recording, not an Edison.

The fame of the performers whom Victor Talking Machine astutely signed did more than bolster record sales; it also added great luster to Victor's brand. "Victrola" soon replaced "phonograph" as the generic term, a development that caused Edison considerable distress. His office would receive letters from confused customers who assumed that Edison had introduced the Victrola. In 1912, the chairwoman of the Immigrant Aid Department of the Council of Jewish Women wrote to ask Edison to donate a Victrola for placement on Ellis Island. It would offer a little cheer to the immigrant detainees awaiting processing—and in some cases deportation. In the margin of the letter, Edison drew a line near the reference to the Victrola and scribbled a note of irritation to his secretary: "Here is another of the innumerable instances where the public misunderstands." He directed that the correspondent be referred to the Victor Company.

Edison dealers grumbled among themselves, too. The Topeka agency, for example, complained in early 1915 to the one in Des Moines, "We have no artists of any note on the Edison." It fell to Edison's salespeople to explain their absence on the Edison label. A sales manual from this time laid out the company's defense, which directed the public's attention to "the great Wizard" who personally tested voice samples using techniques of his own devising and selected "those voices which are most worthy of Re-Creation by his new art." Only the voice, not the reputation, mattered to the Wizard.

So determined was Edison to strip artists of their vanity and unreasonable demands that he refused to print the name of the recording artist on the record label. When one of his dealers, the Santa Fe Watch Company, of Topeka, Kansas, asked him to reconsider, Edison let loose a torrent of pent-up opinion:

> I am sure you will give me the credit of having put a tremendous amount of thought into the Phonograph Business after the many years that I have been engaged on it. Not alone to the

technical side of the business have I given an immense amount of thought but also to the commercial side, and I want to say to you that I have most excellent reasons for not printing the name of the Artist on the Record. Your business has probably not brought you into intimate contact with musicians, but mine has. There is a great deal of "faking" and Press Agent work in the musical profession, and I feel that for the present at least I would rather quit the business than be a party to the boasting up of undeserved reputations.

Edison wrote this in 1913, when he was sixty-six years old. His confidence in his business acumen had, if anything, grown over time. And in taking this stand, he reveals a nature that could not see the inconsistency: Here his own companies used his fame as the Wizard to market his inventions, prominently displaying his name and driving off anyone who threatened to infringe the trademark. But he could not abide others—in this case, his own recording artists—using fame, even though much more modest, for their own commercial interests.

Victor was especially receptive to the fads of popular music. The company immediately responded to a dance craze around 1910, in which taxi dance halls opened, school proms multiplied, and lodge cotillions drew avid attendees. Victor signed the ballroom dance stars Vernon and Irene Castle to oversee all of the company's dance recordings. Columbia Records issued and promoted dance records, too.

Edison, however, stood aloof. He continued to follow the marketing plan with which he had begun, which was to make his phonograph the centerpiece of a home entertainment center, eliminating the need to go out in search of fun. Without mention of "cocooning," the Edison marketers in the early twentieth century tapped a preference for private consumption of entertainment, a preference that is only now, a century later, finding full expression in the installation of high-definition television sets and multichannel sound systems. One aspect of Edison's advertising campaign that does not have a contemporary ring is its depiction of married life: "When a man leaves home in the evening it is because he seeks amusement. The best way to keep him home is to give him the amusement there. Make home a competitor of downtown, the club, the cafe, the theatre and the concert hall. No such thing will furnish so much amusement for so many people, so many times, and in so many ways as the Edison phonograph."

The voice that is speaking is smooth and omniscient, wise in all domestic matters. It is not Thomas Edison's real-life voice, however, that had the burr of irritation when swatting away the complaints of his dealers. If one complained about the poor quality of the finish on the phonograph cabinets, Edison twisted the complaint into something else, a wish to have a $150 cabinet provided for a $100 machine. If he complied, "I would have to go out of business," he condescendingly explained to one dealer. As for his reasons why he did not affix the price on the face of the record, he wrote that he did not have time for "lengthy explanations," but there was a good technical reason that should have been taken on faith. The Wizard could not understand why his dealers refused to acknowledge his competence to make such simple decisions: "I should be credited in cases like this with as much intelligence as the general average of the genus homo."

His voice was more often than not tinged with irritation about the exasperating tastes of the public, too. A typical letter that he dictated in 1914 went on at some length about the regional variations in musical taste and the difficulties this created for his company. He did not display any interest in the New Englanders' objections to "ragtime and Coon Songs"; it was just one of many mysteries about likes and dislikes, conveyed to him in sarcastic letters. He claimed to be so discouraged by the hostility that these correspondents expressed that had he known about the differences of opinion, he never would have entered the music business.

Edison invested so much time personally managing every aspect of his music business that it is easy to forget that in this same time period he was principally concerned with work on automobile batteries. Music was merely a sideline. He launched other projects, too, such as promoting the sale to the working class of all-concrete houses, designed by Edison (but not adopted as a replacement for his own house at Glenmont). The project that was most ahead of its time was the home movie projector, named the Home Projecting Kinetoscope, that he introduced in late 1911. It was both an engineering marvel and a commercial flop. The film's frames were tiny: three-sixteenths of an inch high and a quarter of an inch wide. When the image was projected upon a six-foot-tall screen, each was enlarged about 120,000 times. In order to keep the dimensions of the unit small and its weight to twenty pounds, Edison and his assistants designed the projector to accommodate filmstrips that were only eighty feet long, but it was effectively triple this length because the film was composed of three narrow ministrips, mounted side by side. The film would be run through once, showing the images on one edge, then the film-transport mechanism would be shifted so that the images in the middle, which ran in the opposite direction, would be visible, and then the home projectionist would adjust the projector one more time to project the third row. This arrangement yielded a show that ran sixteen minutes.

Along with the home projector, the company introduced a central clearinghouse for used films, which offered customers a way of replenishing the family's entertainment supply by using the postal service to swap titles with others for a nominal processing fee. Edison, however, wanted to use his projector not for entertainment but for education. For preschoolers, his idea was nothing less than brilliant. For teaching the alphabet, Edison explained in an interview, "suppose, instead of the dull, solemn letters on a board or a card you have a little play going on that the littlest youngster can understand," with actors carrying in letters, hopping, skipping, turning somersaults. "Nothing like action—drama—a play that fascinates the eye to keep the attention keyed up." (A prospectus for *Sesame Street* could not have made a better case.)

And it wasn't just the youngest students who would benefit by adoption of the new medium; Edison was convinced all students would. He compiled a list of subjects suitable for his new pedagogical tool—the total came to four thousand, and he vowed in 1912 to "make films of them all." His marketing pitch to school systems was simple: He would rent a set of educational films to a school for $8 a week. "You couldn't hire much of a teacher for $8 a week, could you?" he chortled. "And then think of the saving—you won't need any truant officer. No, siree! Every little toddler in the district will just want to scoot to school!"

A year after the release of his home projector, Edison offered only twenty-five feature titles, including the scintillating *Manufacture of Paper, Apple Pies,* and *Modern Weapons for Fighting Fire.* It was not a catalog large enough to draw significant numbers of customers, nor was it sufficient to keep the clearinghouse well supplied. In 1913, two years after the debut of the projector, all owners received a letter from the company imploring them to send in any "idle films" for exchanges. The venture languished.

No critic at the time apparently commented on the outlandishness of Edison's carelessly announced ambition to radically remake American education—and in his spare time. The side projects multiplied, each initial announcement bringing reporters running and forcing Edison to dilute his attention.

When he plunged into a campaign, no subordinate would have any grounds to tease him for working less hard than anyone else. When a business colleague in 1912 wrote him and casually asked how he was feeling, Edison replied, "Well, I worked 122 hours in six days last week, hence I must feel fine—and do." The next month, he had a time clock installed in the laboratory, which permitted him to document his hours and call in reporters to let the world know that he outworked everyone. The first week the clock was in operation, Edison logged ninety-five hours and forty-nine minutes, or, as one story put it, "nearly twice as long as any of his 5,000 employees who enjoyed an eight hour day." His recorded hours would have been longer had he been able to log in properly on the first day, as he had been working all night and left the building at 8:15 A.M.

Five years earlier, on the occasion of his sixtieth birthday, Edison had told reporters that he was retiring from business and would spend all of his time in the laboratory, pursuing pure research. His self-exile from business matters ended, however, almost as soon as it had been announced. He felt compelled to personally oversee—and personally decide—everything, as he was wont to do. He drove himself hard, as hard in his sixties, seventies, and even eighties, as he had ever worked as a younger man, because he felt a burden that was uniquely his to shoulder: protecting the public image of "Thomas Edison," omnipresent and omniscient, the Wizard with a magical touch ("It is irresistible because Edison made it"). Protecting the brand required the deployment of lawyers to warn off anyone who attempted to trade on the Edison name. Brand protection also required that Edison remain personally involved in everything, trying to live up to the legend. He did not regard this as a burden. On the contrary, it was the very thing that gave his life meaning. As long as he was the one who made the decisions, he was happy, no matter what consequences followed for his businesses.

Edison had the ability to remain imperturbably content even when disaster struck. In the early evening of 7 December 1914, an explosion rocked his film-finishing building, part of the complex of buildings surrounding his laboratory. The building was swiftly evacuated, just ahead of the fire that swept the two-story structure. As the film stock fed the flames, the fire jumped to the surrounding buildings, where it was fed by the rubber and chemicals used in record manufacturing. These buildings were made of reinforced concrete, the material that Edison had boasted was completely fireproof. Their combustible contents, however, fed conflagrations whose temperatures melted the floors, and soon the walls collapsed. Even the newest building, less than two years old, and said to be state of the art in fireproof construction, succumbed when its contents—phonograph records—caught fire. Liquid chemicals poured down the sides of the building as streams of flame. The high temperatures rendered the efforts of the firefighters, who had been summoned from six neighboring communities, largely ineffectual. Ten to fifteen thousand people gathered to watch.

The fire had broken out at the dinner hour, when Edison happened to be at home. He was one of the first to get to the scene. Neither he nor his assistants thought that the fire would spread to the neighboring concrete buildings, and no one initially took action to save what they could. When Mina arrived, she rushed in and out of the company's general offices, carrying papers out of harm's way while Edison stood by and watched the firefighters. Her rescue efforts ended only when the flames reached that building, too. For seven hours, the firefighters did their best in the bitterly cold night, but the fires claimed ten of the eighteen buildings of the complex. Miraculously, the disaster claimed only one victim, William Troeber, an employee who had rushed back into a building with a fire extinguisher under his arm, believing, erroneously it turned out, that some of his coworkers were still inside.

The facilities for phonograph and record manufacturing were lost. The estimated damage was $3 million to $5 million, of which, the company told reporters, insurance covered about $3 million. This latter number appears to have been dispensed in order to give employees, jobbers, dealers, and customers reassurance that the Edison works would have no difficulty recovering. A private letter, however, suggests that the insurance coverage was minimal, as Edison had been supremely confident when he began to build concrete buildings that coverage for fire damage was superfluous.

Once the embers were cool and company managers could take stock, they discovered that in some ways the fire had been considerate, skipping over two thousand gallons of high-proof alcohol that came through undamaged. They also discovered that all of the master molds of the company's recordings were undamaged—and they would receive a kind offer of the loan of record presses from Victor. But on the night of the fire, when none of this was known, when the fire had yet to be contained and was still hopping from one building to the next and when the prospects were the bleakest, Edison's equanimity was put to a test. His immediate reaction? He cracked jokes, laughed, and declared, "Although I am over 67 years old, I'll start all over again tomorrow." Nothing could rattle him.

The striking absence of visible discouragement on Edison's part inspired a *New York Times* editorial titled "Abnormality Like His a Blessing." The *Times* ascribed Edison's "abnormality" to his temperament, a new concept that was explained as being beyond the control of an individual's will. (At that time, temperament was said to be controlled by the thyroid and pituitary glands.) Some "abnormality" should have been expected, however, from the abnormal experience of playing for thirty years the role of the celebrated Wizard. His fame had been built on his work, then reinforced by his eagerness to be the hardest-working man in the invention business. Edison reacted to the disaster as if it were a tonic: "It's like the old days to have something real to buck up against."

"I never intend to retire," Edison said in an interview in 1911. "Work made the earth a paradise for me." Not merely *made,* past tense, but *continued to make* for him a paradise. He voiced heresy when he said that he did not believe that a paradise awaited in the afterlife. He was speaking, however, as a man who experienced paradisiacal pleasure every moment he was at work. No wonder he could not imagine doing anything else.

CHAPTER ELEVEN

FRIEND FORD

I N 1896, WHEN Thomas Edison first met Henry Ford, Edison was
famous, and Ford was not. If Edison failed to remember the encounter afterward, the likely reason is not self-absorption but lopsided arithmetic: one luminary, many strangers clamoring to meet him.
The occasion was a convention of the Association of Edison Illuminating Companies held at a beach hotel near Coney Island. Edison was attending in an honorific role, having sold off his electric light interests
and thrown himself into his mining venture. It was not his customary
practice to spend time outside of his own workplace, but for three days
he settled into the role of passive conventioneer.

At dinner on the first day, Edison found himself seated at a large oval
table with senior representatives of various large electric utilities. The
conversation centered on the bright prospects for the industry, poised to
supply the power for electric cars that would replace horses. In the midst
of these happy speculations, the superintendent of the Edison Illuminating
Company in Detroit, Alexander Dow, spoke up to mention a curiosity.
Dow's chief engineer, thirty-three-year-old Henry Ford, whom he had
brought along with him, was an amateur inventor who had just built
a cart that was powered not by electricity but by a gasoline-powered
engine. It was equipped with four bicycle wheels; Ford called it a
Quadricycle.

Asked to explain how his carriage was powered, Ford addressed
everyone at the table and Edison cupped his ear, trying to catch Ford's

words. A man seated by Edison offered to change places with Ford so that Edison could hear better. Once the switch was effected, Edison peppered Ford with questions; Ford sketched out his answers. Then came the moment that Ford would say changed his life: "Young man, that's the thing!" Edison told him, pounding the table for emphasis. "Electric cars must keep near to power stations. The storage battery is too heavy. Steam cars won't do either, for they have a boiler and fire. Your car is self-contained—carries its own power plant—no fire, no boiler, no smoke, and no steam. You have the thing. Keep at it." With encouragement from the man whom Ford regarded as "the greatest inventive genius in the world" ringing in his ears, Ford returned home with the conviction that he should persevere. He told his wife, "You are not going to see much of me until I am through with this car."

We have only Ford's account of the meeting, and the purported details were set down on paper for the first time no fewer than thirty years later. The stagy dialogue rings false; nor did Ford immediately quit his day job at Edison Illuminating. It would take three more years before he felt ready to try to commercialize his automobile designs as a full-time entrepreneur. But he did meet Edison at the convention and did have a conversation that must have roughly resembled what he later recollected. The two had a second conversation, too: Ford recalled that Edison invited him to ride with him on the train back to New York City at the conclusion of the convention. Edison did not resume their conversation about the internal combustion engine but instead spoke of other topics, including his boyhood memories of Michigan.

There is no question that Henry Ford felt much encouraged. He would later regard Edison with worshipful regard and spend stupendous sums to honor the inventor. Whether Edison dispensed as large a dollop of encouragement as Ford perceived is open to doubt, however. Edison was reliably polite in such situations, but he virtually never praised the technical feats of others. Edison's subsequent actions suggest that he forgot the encounter; if he remembered it at all, he chose to pretend he did not. The second encounter came eleven years later, in 1907, when Ford, now the head of his own eponymous company, wrote

Edison with a mixture of familiarity and worshipfulness: "My Dear Mr. Edison," it began. "I am fitting up a den for my own private use at the factory and I thought I would like to have photographs of about three of the greatest inventors of this age to feast my eyes on in idle moments. Needless to say Mr. Edison is the first of the three and I would esteem it a great personal favor if you would send me a photograph of yourself."

Ford apparently believed that the life-changing impression left upon him by Edison eleven years earlier had been equally memorable to Edison. He may also have felt a comfortable familiarity because he had recently been contacted by Edison's son William, now twenty-nine years old, who was attempting to sell Ford Motor Company spark plugs of his own design (Will, who had briefly attended Yale's Sheffield Scientific School and was determined to succeed on his own, had not kept his father informed about his activities).

If Edison remembered the earlier encounter with Ford, his response to Ford's simple request for a photograph seems strange: Edison instructed his secretary not to respond. This was likely prompted by a spasm of competitiveness: Ford was one of many internal-combustion-engine-equipped car manufacturers that competed with the electric car equipped with Edison's newly developed alkaline battery. Or Edison's rebuff may have been the reaction of a famous person irritated by the presumptuous familiarity of an utter stranger whom he had no memory of ever meeting.

The episode is of interest because it occurred when Henry Ford was not yet a household name and was merely one of more than a hundred automobile manufacturers. The next year, he introduced the Model T, his fame swiftly reached the ethereal altitude of Edison's, and his business success far exceeded that of the older man's. This change in relative status made possible a friendship, not because Edison sought the company of the famous and successful—he did not seek the company of anyone—but because it removed the basis of Edison's fear that a business acquaintance sought to move close for ulterior reasons. As for celebrity, the two men now shared personal knowledge of the tribulations that came with fame.

Such was Edison's inherently solitary nature, however, that he would not likely have been willing to meet Ford in person again had it not been for the behind-the-scenes arrangements of William Bee, the sales manager at the Edison Storage Battery Company. In April 1911, Bee persuaded Edison to make amends for ignoring Ford's earlier request for a photograph and prepare one inscribed with a carefully measured compliment: "To Henry Ford. One of a group of men who have helped to make U.S.A. the most progressive nation in the World." Bee sent it off to Ford with a cover letter claiming that "Mr. Edison was only too glad to send you his photograph." At the same time, Bee sent through an intermediary a note inviting Ford to visit Edison at his laboratory. Ford accepted. That was the easy part for Bee. Persuading Edison to make himself available for Ford's visit required months of unsuccessful efforts. Finally, after Bee had arranged for Ford to pay his visit in January 1912, Edison reluctantly acquiesced: "Guess I will be here on the 9th."

Ford arrived in Orange eager to make a pitch to his hero: Would Edison be willing to design an electrical system—battery, generator, and starter—for the Model T? The car in its current incarnation had none. It was started with a hand crank, which was at best inconvenient to use, and when it kicked back, dangerous. Edison did not accept Ford's offer immediately but was sufficiently intrigued to mull the proposition over and return with a counterproposal later in 1912. Would Ford be interested in financing the development work on Edison's battery? His note to "Friend Ford" explained that he had self-financed his battery experiments with profits from other lines of business but these funds limited what he could do. Alternatively, "I could go to Wall St. and get more, but my experience over there is as sad as Chopin's Funeral March. I keep away."

No major business figure detested Wall Street as much as Thomas Edison—except Henry Ford. The two men had this in common. "Wall Street" was less a geographic place than a shorthand for grasping Jews. The two men had lots of things to say about Jews, Ford doing so publicly and Edison, privately. If Jews "are as wise as they claim to be," Ford wrote in his autobiography, "they will labor to make Jews American, instead of labouring to make America Jewish." Edison sent Ford clippings to add to his file on "The Jewish Question." "Please read this—it's very funny," Edison added as an annotation to the text of a speech delivered to a convention of the National Builder's Supply Association that he sent Ford. Edison helpfully highlighted with pencil the two paragraphs at the beginning, which were the speaker's opening jokes. As a self-identified Irishman, the speaker, one Herbert N. Casson, claimed to speak for all Irish, lamenting their willingness to fight someone else's war and then lose whatever it was they were supposed to have gained. "I have generally found that after the fight some Jew has got what we started out to get." The audience's laughter was transcribed along with the punch line.

The men's anti-Semitism shaped their business plans. Henry Ford would not permit "Wall Street" to get hold of his revered Edison. He stepped forward to offer Edison forgivable loans, at 5 percent annual interest, to finance the development work on the battery. The loans were secured by future royalties that Edison's laboratory would earn from batteries; Ford said Edison could expect sales to Ford Motor of $4 million a year. The package on offer had everything Edison could ever want: It paid homage to his expertise in electrical systems; it gave a new direction for his battery work, in case the electric car did not succeed commercially; and it provided complete autonomy, free of obligation to report to Wall Street financiers about his spending. Once staff members for Ford and Edison worked out legal and financial details, Edison signed off on the agreement in November 1912. The next month, the first slice of $150,000 arrived; the following March, another $100,000; and by the end of the year, Edison had borrowed a total of $700,000. More payments from Ford followed.

Edison did not abandon his previous ambitions to make a success of an electric car; he simply made Henry Ford his new partner. In January 1914, Ford announced that he planned within the year to begin manufacturing an electric car using a lightweight battery that Edison had been preparing for some time. Ford told reporters, "I think Mr. Edison is the greatest man in the world and I guess everyone does." Ford, who had also just announced the adoption of the "Five-Dollar Day," effectively doubling the wages of virtually all of his workers, was at this historical moment the single most influential businessperson in the country. The New York newspapers, however, had not realized it. When they reported on the plans for the Ford-Edison electric car, they mostly paid compliments to Edison. Ford was portrayed as the party in the transaction who was most in need ("Henry Ford Seeks Mr. Edison's Aid.").

Edison was not averse to the flattery, but more important, he responded to the opportunity to have a relationship with an equal, another technically inclined person who had been pushed into the strange land of the extremely famous. The two men brought their families together, too, intertwining personal and business ties. The Edisons visited the Fords at their home in Dearborn, Michigan; the Fords came down to Fort Myers, Florida, to share a winter vacation, discuss their mutual interest in gardening, and "motor" together in the Everglades area. Edison did not realize that the combination of the two families would increase a celebrity index exponentially greater than his alone, drawing reporters and curiosity seekers and unwanted attention to his remote winter hideaway. On the evening that the Fords arrived, two thousand townspeople came out to welcome them and ogle. Seeing reporters present, Edison is said to have complained, "There is only one Fort Myers, and now ninety million people are going to find out."

It was fitting that Fort Myers would play a role in the broadening personal relationship between Edison and Ford. The last time that Edison had let down his natural guard and spent vacation time with a business colleague as he did with Ford was when he and Ezra Gilliland had bought twin plots in Fort Myers thirty years earlier. Gilliland had introduced Edison to his future wife, but the two men were not equals in the shared realm of the phonograph business. When Edison thought that Gilliland had taken pecuniary advantage of him, the relationship had ended acrimoniously. Since then, Edison had deliberately kept acquaintances from coming closer. "Mr. Edison has few friends," Mina once observed. "Because of his work he has had to live a great deal by himself and in himself—shut out from the social contacts open to most men."

Now, in the company of Ford, someone much wealthier than he, Edison did not need to worry about behind-the-scenes machinations. He relaxed. Ford became his neighbor—just like Gilliland, though undoubtedly unaware of the earlier history—when Ford bought a plot of land for his winter vacation home adjoining Edison's.

Except for vacations, the two men did not have many opportunities to spend time in person with each other, and they did not, as a rule, correspond with each other. If they needed to communicate, they relied upon their secretaries to relay messages. One exception, and a revealing one, is a letter that Ford wrote Edison in March 1914, after returning home following his first visit to Fort Myers. He maintained a formal tone when addressing Edison, sixteen years his senior—"My dear Mr. Edison," he began. He and his wife wished to thank him for the enjoyable vacation they had had with the Edisons. No, that did not capture his feelings; this vacation was "in fact the most enjoyable one we have ever had." With the thank-you out of the way, he added a little bit of small talk, one manufacturer addressing another.

Then Ford arrived at the primary reason for writing: to make a request. During the recent vacation, the two men happened to talk about the harmful effects of cigarette smoking. Ford recalled Edison's remark that the damage it caused was incurable. Would Edison be kind enough to write a letter that explained the nature of the harm and why it was irreversible? With Edison's permission, Ford planned to use the letter in his antismoking campaign among workers. In asking Edison to serve as a quotable authority on the subject, Ford reveals his understanding of how celebrity—his, Edison's, anybody's—confers, in the eyes of the not-famous, expertise on all manner of subjects. Edison could speak about the deleterious effects of smoking not because of a background in respiratory disease or epidemiology, but because he was Edison. If Ford's fame alone could not persuade his employees to quit smoking, perhaps the combination with Edison's would be persuasive.

Edison sent off the requested letter in his best handwriting. He did not pause to first have it proofread, so Ford had his secretary, Ernest Liebold, write Edison's underling, William Bee, about the delicate matter of two misspelled words. "I know Mr. Edison would prefer to have it correct if given publicity," Liebold wrote, sending along a sheet that Edison could use to recopy the letter. Edison complied without complaint.

> The injurious agent in Cigarettes comes principally from the burning paper wrapper. The substance thereby formed is called "Acrolein." It has a violent action on the nerve centers, producing degeneration of the cells of the brain, which is quite rapid among boys. Unlike most narcotics this degeneration is permanent and uncontrollable. I employ no person who smokes cigarettes. Yours, Thomas A. Edison

Edison had not, in fact, excluded smokers from his employee rolls. After the letter had been drafted, he hurriedly had signs posted at his plants: "Cigarettes Not Tolerated. They Dull The Brain."

If Ford anticipated the firestorm of criticism from the tobacco interests that would surely follow, he did not warn Edison, who appears to have been completely unprepared. Edison was accustomed to having his own tobacco habits treated by the press as a subject of amusement, such as when he was vacationing in Florida and sent word to the laboratory in New Jersey that he needed a replenished supply of chewing tobacco from one of his employees, Red Kelly in Building 18, who "knows a good chew," to be sent "in a hurry." He did not have to answer questions from the press about his fondness of cigars. Reporters had listened respectfully when he criticized only one form of tobacco consumption, cigarette smoking, which happened to be the one form that he disliked. He explained, with the tone of a world-renowned expert addressing a lay audience, that poisonous cigarette papers dulled the mind, and that is why Mexicans, whom he had heard were heavy smokers, "as a race are not clear headed."

Then, with the arrival of the controversy when Ford published Edison's letter, the same press turned on Edison, treating his disquisitions about cigarettes derisively. A *New York Times* editorial, "An Inventor out of His Field," wondered aloud about his lack of scientific authority on this subject. If, as Edison claimed, cigarettes dulled the mind, so, too, did a good dinner and a good sleep. Edison's own habits were examined. Should not Edison consider the effects on the mind of "irregular meals and excessive hours of continuous work"?

Percival Hill, president of the American Tobacco Company, led his industry's counterattack with a devastatingly polite response to Edison's letter. Hill publicly dared Edison to repeat his charges while naming in particular any of the brands of American Tobacco. Should he do so, Hill promised to initiate legal proceedings to obtain damages. Whatever sums Hill recovered, he would donate to charity. Edison elected not to accept the challenge.

Following Hill, James Zobian, the advertising representative of Philip Morris & Company, published in the New York newspapers full-page open letters addressed to Edison that were reprinted and quoted at length elsewhere. Zobian had sent cigarette papers used by Philip Morris to an independent laboratory and now brandished the certificates attesting to the lack of "any poisonous ingredients therein." Granting that Edison had acquired his "prominence and fame" in an honest and deserving way, Zobian said, "When it comes to analytical chemistry, I believe Mr. Edison himself will admit that supremacy in that branch of science belongs to others!"

The last time Edison had been the subject of widespread criticism had been three years earlier, when he had casually announced that he planned to offer furniture made of concrete, providing a full line to complement the concrete cabinet for his phonograph that he had already made. Claiming that the surface could be stained to resemble any kind of wood desired, he said his concrete furniture would "make it possible for the laboring man to put furniture in his home more artistic and more durable than is now to be found in the most palatial residences in Paris."

At least the hoots that followed were brought upon Edison entirely by his own misconceived plans. Some commentators were not even certain that Edison was serious (he was). Cartoonists had no difficulty extracting humor from Edison's announcement (sample: Edison tells two moving men straining under a concrete sofa, "Don't be afraid of hurting it, boys, but look out for your feet").

The cartoons and jokes soon passed, and the controversy came and went without challenging Edison's authority as a technical expert. The cigarette flap, however, was hurtful because his technical expertise was directly questioned—his critics paid no attention to his claims that his extensive research on paper filaments for the lightbulb had acquainted him with the poisonous substances in cigarettes. And the criticism was harder to bear because the controversy had been incited by someone else, and Edison had been pulled in without anticipating what would follow. He would never repeat the mistake of publicly following Ford into new campaigns and controversy.

Once past the cigarettes episode, Edison derived nothing but benefits from his association with Henry Ford. Edison and his family members were the recipients of gifts personally selected by Ford. Some were expensive: Tom and Mina Edison received so many Ford cars that it is not possible to tally exactly how many. Other gifts showed great expenditure of that most scarce resource, Ford's attention. Edison would receive from him a birthday telegram; Mina, a birdhouse. The adult children were not neglected, either. In 1914, thirty-eight-year-old Tom Edison Jr., now living on a farm his father had bought for him in Burlington, New Jersey, and tinkering with carburetors, received from Henry Ford a Model T engine that he had requested for experimenting, followed by a new car. Twenty-four-year-old Charles Edison received one of Ford's prized rifles in a custom-built case. When Theodore Edison, the youngest of Edison's six children, turned sixteen in 1914, he found a new car waiting for him, sent by Ford.

On one occasion, in 1916, when Ford heard from his dealer in Fort Myers that Edison had just paid for a new Ford touring car to be readied for delivery the next day, Ford had the dealer present the car to Edison with Ford's compliments and a refund of the purchase price. (The dealer turned out to be quite vexed when he learned afterward that no one in Henry Ford's office had given thought to the commission he lost because of the gift; much correspondence went back and forth between Michigan and Florida about this single transaction.)

The gifts flowed almost totally in one direction, from Ford's family to Edison's. It was not in Edison's nature to come up with gift ideas, but he was responsive if a suggestion was placed in front of him. When Ford first visited Fort Myers, he noticed a steam engine on the property that Edison had decommissioned upon the arrival of a gas engine. When he returned to Michigan, he wrote Edison explaining that it had sentimental value to him. Could he purchase it for the price Edison had paid for his new engine? Edison instructed his secretary to ship it to Ford as a present.

It was business that engaged Edison more than personal matters, and he found a number of Edison products to sell to Ford Motor Company that had nothing to do with automotive electrical systems. Movies made with Edison equipment were to be used to train new hands on the Ford assembly line, at least according to Henry Ford in January 1914, speaking without having tried using the medium for this purpose. Edison dictating machines were installed in Ford shops and were utterly useless (they lacked sufficient volume to be audible). Cement made by the Edison Portland Cement Company would be the sole source in all construction at Ford Motor Company. Ford Motor's chief architect could not believe initially that Henry Ford would have agreed to an exclusive arrangement with a single supplier and had to be sternly instructed by Ford's personal secretary to follow Ford's wishes in the matter.

The evidence suggests that Henry Ford made all of these accommodations gladly. He was not doing business with Edison so much as he was indulging his idol, and there was no limit to Ford's generosity. In December 1914, when Edison's works were devastated by fire, Ford happened to be in New York and could rush over that night to offer comfort. Another $100,000 loan arrived the next week. Ford's willingness to assist Edison in whatever way he could was put to the most severe test two months after the fire when Edison was finalizing plans for the layout of his rebuilt factory and wanted to use the services of one of Ford's "Efficiency Engineers." Edison was not asking for a gift and kept the matter on a purely business footing. He wrote Ernest Liebold to ask if "Mr. Ford could loan me one of his Efficiency Engineers for a little while, and if so, what would be the cost per week." This simple request turned out to be more complicated than it first appeared.

It turned out that there was no such thing as a free-floating "Efficiency Engineer" at Ford Motor. Every department had specialists who knew only their one corner of operations. Ford did not know of anyone who would fit the description of the engineer Edison wanted. In a situation such as this, when complications arose, the titans used their minions to do the communicating. Ford's secretary wrote Edison's, explaining that it was Mr. Ford's suggestion to have two or three of Edison's best hands come to Detroit to look over the factory and learn directly from the various department managers who had contributed to the Ford plant's efficiency.

Edison would have none of this. Speaking through his secretary, who again addressed Ford's, he said he could not spare anyone at his end and reiterated his request: just send me one person for one week. Ford relayed that he was "at a loss to know who he should send." He did have one more suggestion, which was unintentionally comical: Edison should send one person to Detroit who would select the one person at Ford who would go to West Orange to assist. Never mind, Edison telegraphed back. He would "not need your efficiency men as I have got all information wanted from eight articles on Ford factory published in engineering magazine."

In October 1915, Edison and his wife were invited officially by the city of San Francisco to be present for the celebration of "Edison Day," which would coincide with the city's hosting of a world's fair, the Panama-Pacific International Exposition. He decided he could not go on a three-week-long trip and had his secretary write a lengthy letter explaining that his personal attention was needed at his factories. If the work was not completed, "a great many employees connected with the various industries would be thrown out of work."

The next week, however, Edison changed his mind and decided to go to San Francisco after all and ignore the specter of shuttered factories at home. He may have been persuaded to make the trip because of a personal appeal by Henry Ford. In any case, the Edisons and the Fords made plans together. When they arrived in San Francisco, press coverage was exhaustive. The conjunction of Edison and Ford, reclusive figures who had assumed larger-than-life dimensions, brought attention to their every move and casual utterance. The two men spent one day walking around the exposition together without their wives, though they were accompanied by a police officer who had been detailed to protect them (Edison had been threatened with death were he to make "any invention which would make war more terrible"). Curious members of the public were also in tow. At one point, a young man stepped up to Ford to introduce himself and ask for Ford's recipe for success. "Work" was Ford's not-so-helpful answer.

That terse exchange shows that the presence of these two celebrities was not to be mistaken for a statement of their availability for conversation with strangers. This was not the case at all. They could not avoid being surrounded by the crowd, however, close enough to have their own conversation overheard. "Great Scott, Ford, we were to meet our wives at one o'clock—here it is now two," Edison supposedly said to his companion. The two men "almost sprinted" to the teahouse, where Mina Edison had remained when her husband did not show; Clara Ford, not as forbearing, had returned to her hotel long before. "Noted Pair Keep Walking Eight Hours" ran the *San Francisco Chronicle*'s headline; a subheadline was "Wives Have Long Wait." The story offered a comforting universal moral to readers who were not themselves rich and famous: Husbands, even celebrity husbands, are forgetful by nature, and upon occasion neglect their good wives, proving Celebrities Are Just Like Us.

While in San Francisco, Edison and Ford also were feted at San Francisco's Commercial Club. The overflow crowd of attendees begged Ford to stand and say a few words, but he demurred. Edison laughed at Ford's discomfort, and was spared being asked himself only because he had long before established that he did not make speeches in public. From San Francisco, the Edisons and Fords traveled by private train to Santa Rosa, where they visited Luther Burbank, the country's best known horticulturalist, then headed south via train and automobile to San Diego.

Press coverage of their joint California trip served to make more well known Edison's association with Ford, and this brought some complications. Strangers wrote Edison trying to reach Ford through his intercession. Some of Edison's own associates and distant acquaintances made similar requests, assuming that they could count on Edison's introduction to gain entrée to Ford's office, in order to make a business pitch of one kind or another. Edison shunned all such requests.

Turning aside a request from a stranger was one thing; from a member of his own staff or own roster of musical talent, another. Edison had his secretary, William Meadowcroft, do his best in 1916 to mollify Alice Verlet, a singer who recorded for Edison's label and had sought a letter of introduction to Ford. Meadowcroft explained that Edison and Ford "preserve a strict neutrality in regard to each other's business affairs, and never give these letters of introduction" for which they were frequently asked. He also said that the intertwining of the business and personal lives was "of a very delicate nature," and the two were "exceedingly punctilious" in keeping the two domains separate. Edison's company had bought fifty automobiles from Ford's, paying the same price as "absolute strangers to Mr. Ford or his Company." Conversely, Ford had not received any discount when purchasing Edison phonographs or records.

Edison brushed aside countless requests like Verlet's. But a few years later, in 1919, he relented in one case involving a distant associate whom he had not personally met. The petitioner was one Lemuel Calvert Curlin, proprietor of Curlin's Drug Company, of Waxahachie, Texas, whose store sold Edison phonographs, in addition to chocolates, typewriters, silver and china, rings, lamps, and Kodak cameras. (Curlin was ecumenical about brands: he sold Victor Victrolas, too.) Curlin had written Ford Motor directly to apply for a Ford dealership and asked if

Edison would write a letter on his behalf, testifying to the soundness of his record. "I would not trouble a busy man like you," Curlin wrote Edison, "but for the fact that your organization knows my ability and Mr. Ford's organization does not." The previous year, Curlin's company had purchased $40,000 worth of Edison phonographs and records, even though the cotton crop was poor and the influenza epidemic had hit his territory hard, keeping prospective customers home. Curlin was respectful, without fawning. He had a track record with Edison, and asked for nothing more than a letter documenting it.

When it arrived, Curlin's letter caught the eye of Meadowcroft (who overlooked the Victrolas). "Mr. Edison," Meadowcroft wrote in a corner of the letter. "Shall you break your rule in this case?" Edison responded positively, directing that it be passed on to Ford's secretary. "Say I send it because I want to make myself solid with one of our hustling dealers." The choice of adjective, "hustling," brings to mind Edison's wish, expressed many years earlier, to hear the voice of Napoléon rather than that of Jesus Christ because "I like a hustler."

When Meadowcroft dispatched Curlin's letter to Ernest Liebold, his cover letter called attention to how "Mr. Edison rarely, if ever" wrote to Ford in a matter that concerned Ford's business affairs. Liebold received the request favorably and wrote Curlin immediately (though no deal was arranged before Curlin's sudden death in 1922). Liebold also wrote Meadowcroft with reassuring words, "We understand the many situations which arise as a result of the widely known friendship between Mr. Ford and Mr. Edison." He said Ford would be happy to consider whatever business-related requests Edison chose to send his way. Nevertheless, Edison continued to screen and deflect almost every request that asked him to open the door to Ford's office.

Family members, however, enjoyed special status automatically. Thomas Edison Jr. knew this and attempted repeatedly to strike business deals with Ford, writing Ford and Liebold directly. If he were not the son of Ford's friend but merely a correspondent with unending requests, he would not have received any response. But Ford and Liebold felt they could not ignore him, no matter what he asked for, so they humored him as best they could. They were also discreet; there is no evidence that they ever divulged to Edison their tribulations in dealing with this son.

In June 1914, shortly after receiving the news that he would receive a new car from Ford, Tom Jr. had the opportunity of meeting Ford for the first time, and thanking him in person, at the wedding of his half sister, Madeleine, at Glenmont. At that point, his car was being prepared at the factory for shipment. When it finally was shipped out, Liebold wrote Tom Jr. to expect it, and wrote him a second time about two weeks later to see if it had arrived in good condition. Tom Jr. had picked the new car up but failed to write Liebold back.

William Bee, who served as the principal liaison between the Edison interests and Ford Motor Company, got an earful from Liebold about Tom Jr.'s perplexing behavior. Tom Jr. had merely been slow in attending to the basic courtesies. On the same day that Liebold was unloading his complaints in a letter to Bee—and before Bee could pass those on to Tom Jr.—Tom Jr. sent a thank-you letter to Liebold, opening with an apology: "I have been so very enthusiastic over my new 'Ford Car' which arrived a day or two ago that apparently I have neglected everything." He said that his wife complained that he "simply cannot leave its side long enough to come in the house and eat."

Tom Jr.'s letter did not contain anything untoward, but it did not bring a gratifying end to the ministry of Henry Ford's gift of a new car to Thomas Edison's eldest son. A little complication remained to be resolved. Ford Motor Company provided the new car with the understanding that it would be exchanged for Tom Jr.'s old Ford. The company took possession, planning to recondition it and find uses for it as a demonstrator model. When Tom Jr. said he did not want to relinquish it, a game of tug-of-war began: Ford Motor Company, one of the largest corporations in the country, was pulling from one direction, and Tom Jr., seemingly ungrateful recipient of a new car, was pulling from the other. At stake was a banged-up car with more than sixty thousand miles on it.

Tom Jr. did make a good case for holding on to the older car, even if he risked appearing ungrateful. As he explained to Bee, the car had been given to him by his father and he held on to every gift his father had ever provided for sentimental reasons. Having two cars would allow him to continue his experiments in carburetion on one when the other was needed to go into town on errands. Bee served as his advocate, forwarding Tom Jr.'s letter to Liebold and adding an offer to buy back the older car that was now in the hands of Ford Motor Company. This offer appears to have embarrassed Liebold, who hastened to accommodate Tom Jr. He told Bee that he would gladly return the car to Tom Jr., once it had been fixed up in "first-class shape." Liebold would be glad to drive it out personally.

When Liebold agreed that Tom Jr. was "fully justified in asking to return" his old car, he said that he understood how highly prized it was as an object of sentimental value. He did not say anything about Tom Jr.'s work with carburetors, which Liebold knew from previous correspondence was work that Tom Jr. thought was destined to have great commercial value to Ford Motor Company. Though living on a peach farm, Tom Jr. was still pursuing his dream of becoming a world-renowned inventor—now, however, he was determined to make his mark in the automotive world. Liebold, as the principal gatekeeper guarding the inner sanctum of Ford's office, had to manage Tom Jr. with delicacy, being warm to the person, the son of Thomas Edison, but blocking the unproven inventor from interfering with Ford Motor Company's actual operations.

Managing Tom Jr. was made all the more difficult because of his behavior, which increasingly became erratic. In January 1915, he wrote to Henry Ford, appealing for donations in the form of spark plugs and other supplies that would help him perfect a "device," left unnamed, "which I hope might prove of mutual benefit to us both." At this point, before his mental decline had incapacitated him, Tom Jr. still understood, at least in the recesses of his consciousness, that Henry Ford was surrounded by layers of protection designed to shield him from requests such as this. "Mr. Ford dont [sic] think I am trying to take advantage of you, my dearest and best friend on Earth." He reassured Ford that he had Ford's interests at heart. Later in the year, he addressed Ford as "almost a Parent." He said he was overjoyed when he read that Ford had attended the Panama Pacific fair so that the masses could "see the one and only Mr. Ford." In the next sentence, he said, "At no time am I away from you because my thoughts keep me with you and your many gifts to me keep us companionship." In 1917, after visiting Ford in Detroit, Tom Jr. wrote Ford to thank him for the "infinite love you tendered me" and begged Ford for his photograph, whose place Tom Jr. had marked out in advance on the wall, next to his father's.

The work on his gadget, intended to save fuel and named the "Ecometer," was hampered by Tom Jr.'s progressively worsening illness. His wife, Beatrice, described to Liebold in 1919 her husband's increasingly severe headaches, culminating in a "collapse" that prevented him from getting out of bed. His Ecometer attached to the air inlet of the carburetor and, according to Tom Jr., increased fuel efficiency by 20 to 50 percent. Ford's engineers, however, were unable to duplicate these results. Both Tom Jr. and Beatrice attempted for years to persuade the company to purchase the Ecometer for factory installation in all Ford cars, but their lobbying efforts did not produce an order. The disappointment appears to have exacerbated Tom Jr.'s incapacitating depression.

Tom Jr. could have taken some solace from the fact that his father's plans to make his mark in the automotive field and win sales to Ford Motor Company were no more successful than his own. Edison worked on many facets simultaneously: a battery and related electrical equipment for a car equipped with an internal combustion engine, and, separately, a battery for an electric car. In late 1913, Edison excitedly notified Ford that he had successfully run in his laboratory a stock Ford engine, removed from a car chassis and equipped with his new electrical system, for 130 continuous hours. The next year, however, when Edison sent his batteries and equipment to Detroit for testing outside of his laboratory, they performed poorly. Liebold installed one of the Edison alkaline batteries in his own car and discovered that it was insufficient to power the car's lights, let alone a starter motor.

As the sales manager responsible for the Edison storage battery, William Bee did his best in April 1914 to convince Liebold and Ford to give Edison and his battery researchers more time. The performance of the batteries at this point was so embarrassing that Bee could do little but commiserate with Liebold, telling his own stories of how the batteries had let Bee down, too. Recently, he had put his car in a paint shop for a few hours and when he returned to retrieve it, "I couldn't start it to save my life." Another time, a company-owned Ford had broken down on Broadway and had had to be towed a couple of blocks before the engine would catch. Essentially conceding that the batteries were not close to being ready for commercial use, Bee said, "Everything has got to be in apple pie order" for the batteries to work at all.

Bee could confirm the fatal flaws of the current generation of batteries because he also had an excellent excuse: Edison had been too busy at work on phonograph records and had neglected work on them. The next month, Bee wrote Henry Ford with the happy news that Edison would devote more time to the battery project. "When Mr. Edison finds out that the present battery will not do the work," Bee said in another letter, "HE WILL MAKE A BATTERY WHICH WILL DO THE WORK."

Edison was unable, however, to deliver on the promise. When the newest versions of his batteries were sent to Ford in the summer of 1914, Henry Ford showed impatience with their deficiencies. Ford also complained that Bee was leaking confidential information to others. Bee avowed his innocence and reported that a starter motor he had installed in his own car powered by an Edison battery had never failed to start. The battery had also powered two headlights, two side lights, a taillight, a meter light, an odometer light, and a Klaxon horn, and the battery had never failed to maintain its charge. He wrote Liebold that these were "absolutely straight facts and my battery has not been tampered with."

Ford placed considerable trust in Liebold's opinions, and Liebold, by the end of 1914, had lost patience with Bee and the Edison alkaline battery. On a frosty December morning, he had given the battery one final chance to prove its reliability in cold weather. Liebold had had at his command factory mechanics to charge up the battery in his car and make sure that all the equipment was in proper adjustment. When Liebold came by the factory to pick up the car, he wrote Bee, "You can imagine my surprise to get nothing more than a groan out of the battery." When he finally got under way, the engine quit four or five times during the morning's drive, and he had to rely on the hand crank to restart it, as "there was no juice obtainable." At the end of the day, Liebold directed the factory mechanics to disassemble the car and return the Edison battery and starter to New Jersey.

Eventually, another company, Gray & Davis, would win the contract to supply Ford Motor with starters and generators for Ford cars. So that its equipment would work with Edison batteries, it invested in a refrigeration plant to simulate cold conditions and its staff tried to engineer an electrical system that could accommodate the battery's shortcomings. The experiments ended without success; the task of making the Edison battery work was declared "impossible." Ford dealers also registered their negative feelings about the Edison battery, telling Gray & Davis that if Ford equipped cars at the factory with Edison batteries, the dealers could not in good faith sell the cars to customers without first taking on the new expense of replacing the factory batteries.

Throughout the process of evaluating options, Henry Ford stood apart, maintaining an agnostic attitude until the test results were definitive. He did not intervene when Liebold, the company engineers, and the dealers all agreed that the Edison battery was woefully underpowered and unsuitable. By having Liebold serve as liaison between his company and Edison's, Henry Ford was able to protect his personal relationship with Edison. For his part, Edison also valued the personal relationship and did not ask Ford to reconsider when the company selected other suppliers and technology. By the time of the 1914 fire, Ford and his staff no longer regarded the Edison battery as a viable candidate for use in Fords. Edison did not share his disappointment with others and harbored no ill feelings toward Ford himself.

After Ford extended the disaster-relief loan of $100,000 immediately after the fire, he made the tenth and last loan to Edison in May 1916.

The total provided from 1912 to 1916 was $1.2 million. The first $900,000 had been issued as notes secured by Edison Storage Battery Company stock, but beginning with another slice in February 1914, the last $300,000 had been unsecured, suggesting that Henry Ford had no expectation of placing a future order with Edison's company, as there were no anticipated royalty payments that could serve as collateral. Edison did not give up hope entirely and continued to pursue a battery powerful enough to start an engine. But later that year, he did concede tacitly that sales to Ford Motor Company were not imminent when he began to pay interest and repay the principal. Having a personal friend as his company's banker was helpful when pinched finances forced him in 1917 to ask Ford not to cash a check he had sent for $50,000, and when he was ready to have that one cashed, to ask Ford at the same time to put $196,102.81 of new checks in his pocket for "a little while" until Edison had the funds to cover them. "The "little while" turned out to be sixteen months. There were other instances when Edison could not make regular payments, but he always returned to the schedule when he could. In 1925, Ford forgave whatever debt remained—the records are not clear about the amount—and the legal departments of the two companies were put to work on memos that clarified the tax implications.

Even when the fire placed Edison in his most dire financial straits, Ford did not show the slightest concern about the repayment of the loans. To Ford, Edison was an American hero—for inventing. Ford knew from the beginning that Edison would likely have trouble managing the business end of their relationship. When Ford described his friend as "the world's worst businessman," he had gone on to say that Edison "knows almost nothing of business." Business had brought the two men together originally, but when business partnerships failed, their personal ties were not weakened. The two actually got to spend more time together than before because they began to take a camping vacation together annually.

In the first year plans were made, 1916, Ford was unable to join Edison and the two others: Harvey Firestone, the tire manufacturer and a principal supplier to Ford, and John Burroughs, the naturalist. The group traveled by car through the Adirondack and Green Mountains and were equipped for comfortable camping by what Burroughs named their "Waldorf-Astoria on Wheels that followed us everywhere." Schedules could not be arranged for a joint vacation the next year, but in August 1918, Ford was finally able to join Edison, Firestone, and Burroughs for the first of three road trips traveling as a famous quartet, and three more trips as a trio following Burroughs's death in 1921.

From the beginning in 1918, the group drew attention. Setting out from Pittsburgh, the men spent ten days driving mountainous roads through West Virginia, Virginia, and North Carolina. A contemporary feature article would describe them as four grown men of varying ages—Burroughs was eighty-one; Edison, seventy-one; Ford, fifty-five; and Firestone, forty-nine—who briefly became boys again. These "boys," however, did not shed their collective wealth and celebrity and regain unself-conscious innocence. The four were part of a contingent of fourteen, including Firestone's son, Harvey Jr., three friends, a chef, and various assistants. The group rode in three cars and the camping equipment and commissary followed in three trucks. A photographer was always on hand to take still photos for distribution to the press and movies for newsreels.

A trip diary kept by the Firestones, senior and junior, shows how Ford and Edison had different traveling preferences, Ford being the restless, perpetually active one, and Edison, sedentary. When one of the vehicles broke down, which was almost a daily occurrence, Ford would set to work on repairs, which he often completed on the spot without need of new parts (on one occasion he secured a replacement bolt from a farm implement and its cooperative owner). Edison would take a mid-day nap, curled up under a tree, "dropping off to sleep like a baby," wrote Burroughs. Edison was the only member of the group who had brought newspapers and books along. He also packed batteries, wires, and lamps, providing light for reading at camp in the evening. If his attention was not required for something else, he would take up a newspaper.

The diary also shows that the ten-day trip was anything but a private one. Each little mountain town that they approached knew in advance of the group's approach and sent out a contingent of local notables in many cars to greet the approaching celebrities and their factotums. Each town presented new challenges to group members in how to manage crowds of fans seeking autographs, or the opportunity to say hello or ask that the esteemed visitors provide them with a speech. (In lieu of speaking, Edison would offer deep bows to a gathering.) When the campers reached the spot where the assistants had set up camp for the night, they were often followed by curious locals. Their arrival anywhere caused such predictable excitement that the only events worthy of noting became those rare instances when someone failed to recognize them or was inordinately shy.

The members reassembled for a similar expedition the next summer in 1919. Now the caravan had swollen to fifty cars and trucks transformed into moving billboards carrying placards "Buy Firestone Tires." The group's arrival in every town was made into an occasion of considerable commercial benefit to the local Ford dealer, who used the free publicity to push sales of new Fords. Newsreels about the campers, such as *Genius to Sleep Under the Stars,* pretended to capture candid views of the celebrities relaxing and were shown in movie theaters across the country. A diary entry in a trip scrapbook suggests how the images were obtained: "Members of the party accepted their fate and allowed the camera-man to direct their motions and activities for the next quarter of an hour."

In the late evening, after the cameramen and interlopers had left, the men sat around the campfire and listened while Ford and Edison lectured the group about the nefarious deeds of Jews. Burroughs wrote in his diary of how Ford "attributes all evil to the Jews or the Jewish capitalists—the Jews caused the war, the Jews caused the outbreak of thieving and robbery all over the country, the Jews caused the inefficiency of the navy of which Edison talked last night." Burroughs was the only voice present to counter the anti-Semitism. When Ford used Jay Gould as an example of how Jews controlled Wall Street, Burroughs, who had been a childhood playmate of Gould's, took pleasure in telling Ford that Gould's family was Presbyterian.

The camping vacation dispensed with the camping portion altogether in 1920, when the wives of the principals were invited for the first time and the group slept in hotels rather than tents. The next year, the collection of star power was boosted, for one night, by the participation of President Warren Harding, a friend of Firestone's. The president arrived with an entourage of six Secret Service officers and ten reporters.

Edison did not greet the president with warmth. Instead, he used the opportunity to make a show of his disdain of this "dude," as he called any man who failed to meet his standards of manliness. When the president offered cigars to the men in the camp, Edison declared, "I don't smoke, I chew." This was pure contrariness—everyone knew that Edison was a heavy smoker of cigars. Firestone, who observed the scene, tried to put the best face on it later when describing the encounter, interpreting what Edison said as a declaration that he "does not set up as a hail fellow." Harding, the smooth politician, did not miss a beat. He replied, "I think I can accommodate you" and pulled out a plug of chewing tobacco from his hip pocket, which Edison accepted. Edison later announced, "Harding is all right. Any man who chews tobacco is all right."

In 1924, the final year of the camping trips, the caravan stopped in Plymouth, Vermont, to visit Harding's successor, Calvin Coolidge, at his father's home. The participants enjoyed a joke that later circulated about the group's ride to the local factory for a tour.

> Something went wrong with the car and they stopped near a farmhouse. The farmer came over to the party and offered his help and at the same time started to lift the hood when Mr. Ford stopped him and said: "There's nothing the matter with that engine: I'm Henry Ford and I know all about engines." The farmer then suggested the trouble might be in the battery and Mr. Edison spoke up and said: "No, I'm Thomas A. Edison and I know

all about batteries. That one is all right." The farmer began to look incredulous but tried again by suggesting the tires needed air and offered to pump them up, but Mr. Firestone put in with, "No, I'm Harvey Firestone and I made those tires; they're just right." The farmer exploded at this with, "Well, Ford, Edison, and Firestone, eh? I reckon that little runt in the back seat's Calvin Coolidge?"

Henry Ford took a keen interest in how fully the press paid attention to the trips. In 1918, his first year with the group, he had his staff prepare a report that contained the full text of every newspaper story that had reported on the expedition. Later, he claimed in his memoirs that "the trips were good fun—except that they began to attract too much attention." This does not jibe with the contemporaneous evidence that Ford loved nothing as much as the attention the trips attracted. Charles Sorensen, Ford's longtime lieutenant, presented in his own memoirs a skeptical view of Ford's claim: "With squads of news writers and platoons of cameramen to report and film the posed nature studies of the four eminent campers, these well-equipped excursions . . . were as private and secluded as a Hollywood opening, and Ford appreciated the publicity."

Edison never commented on the trips, but his daughter Madeleine did, when reflecting back upon them from the vantage point of 1972, when she was in her eighties. She retrospectively dismissed them as a "publicity stunt" that had been staged by Firestone. Her father did not really care for them, but "he would let himself be taken in to these things." It is not likely that this was the case, however. In all other domains, her father did exactly as he pleased. We can assume that Edison went on the trips because he enjoyed them.

The most detailed vignette we have of Edison and Ford conversing together is from a later time, in 1929, when Edison was eighty-two. The scene is preserved in the autobiography of Edward Bernays, the master practitioner of modern public relations, who was working as a consultant to Ford and happened to be on hand one afternoon when Ford and Edison had lunch together. The difference between what Bernays expected to witness and what he actually saw was great.

> After our little walk we sat on the porch for lunch. I was delighted to be lunching with two of the great men of the time and looked forward to learning something from their words of wisdom. Mr. Ford cupped his hands (Edison was extremely hard of hearing) and said in a loud voice, "What makes you look so well, Tom?"
>
> Edison didn't hear the first time and Ford repeated the question. A look of understanding and warmth came into the old man's face and in a low voice he said, "My wife makes me take liver pills every day."
>
> "How many pills does she give you, Tom?"
>
> That, too, demanded a repeat. "Three a day, Henry."
>
> Throughout the luncheon the conversation revolved around this subject. So all I really learned at that luncheon was that Mrs. Edison's liver pills seemed to help the inventor.

CHAPTER TWELVE

LETTING GO

L IKE TOM SAWYER, Thomas Edison heard eulogies delivered
well in advance of his actual funeral—in Edison's case, up to
thirty years early. The Man Who Defeated Darkness. The Dean
of Inventors. The Man Who Struck the Magic Spark. The Greatest Single
Benefactor of the Race. The Archdeacon of the World. The Greatest
Citizen of the World. Flattering, yes, but such honors were those bestowed upon a has-been, a statue for a museum. In his fifties, Edison
was not ready—he would never be ready, even in his eighties—to step
off the stage, to leave the lab, to rest on the laurels that went back to
1877 and those magical five years that followed. He resented being
treated like a statue; admirers no longer seemed to listen to what he had
to say. When an eighth-grader wrote him in 1915 with a few questions,
asking for advice that would be useful to a student "wishing to take up
your work," Edison replied that he did not like "to give advice as no
one ever takes it."

Even as he said these words, he was being asked for advice from a
source that had never asked before: the federal government. Invited to
head up the new Naval Consulting Board, which would offer the military the perspective and guidance of the civilian scientific community,
Edison agreed to serve. When the United States entered World War I, he
increased his advice-giving activity, volunteering to devote all of his
time to applied research on behalf of the U.S. Navy. At the end of the
experience, he learned that nothing had changed: His advice was not

acted upon. "I produced forty-five different inventions for the Government during the war," Edison said afterward. "Every one of them was pigeon-holed."

Edison wanted to live in the present, not in the past. At the same time that his current research interests were slighted, he was showered with praise for having created in the past entire industries out of nothingness. One moving tribute he received was in the form of a letter of appreciation sent in 1921 by one Mrs. W. C. Lathrop, of Norton, Kansas. Lathrop was a college graduate, the wife of a surgeon, the mother of four children, and the sole housekeeper of a large home. While her electric washing machine chugged away happily, she realized that "it does seem as though I am entirely dependent on the fertile brain of one thousand miles away for every pleasure and labor saving device I have." The house was lighted with electricity, cooled with electric fans, and cleaned with an electric vacuum cleaner; her kitchen was equipped with a Westinghouse electric range and an electric dishwasher and an electric pressure cooker (handy on one occasion for an impromptu dinner with the visiting governor); the family's clothes were sewed and washed and ironed with electric appliances. For relaxation, she enjoyed the use of an electric massager and a Victrola, "forgetting I'm living in a tiny town of two thousand where nothing much ever happens." When her husband returned home exhausted at the end of his workday, she was "now rested and ready to serve the tired man." If he did not want to listen to music on the Victrola, she would take him to see "a masterpiece at the 'Movies.'" For all this, she said, "please accept the thanks, Mr. Edison, of one of the most truly appreciative woman [sic]."

As a testimonial to the conveniences provided by electrical appliances, this was a most gratifying letter. Lathrop's reliance on electricity was far ahead of many parts of the country—even ahead of Edison's household at Glenmont, which was still using a small army of human housekeepers and relying on a gas stove (an electric range was never installed). But the very fact that the only two brand names that Lathrop mentioned—Victrola and Westinghouse—were his competitors' says much about the Wizard's mismanagement of business opportunity. Edison's legacy was enhanced more by mistaken associations between his name and competitors' products than by the sales of his own.

Over time, however, Edison had become an accidental captain of industry in several lines. Aside from musical records and phonographs, these were in fields that the general public would not likely associate with the famous inventor. Each represented a story of Edison's ambition that had been thwarted elsewhere—the failed venture in ore processing that had led to cement production; the failed venture in automotive batteries that had developed into an industrial-battery business specializing in sales to ships and railroads. Or, in the case of the "Ediphone," the version of the phonograph sold for office dictation, it was a story of the inventor's stubborn refusal to relinquish his very first idea of what the phonograph was best suited for. In 1911, he set up a new umbrella company, Thomas A. Edison, Inc., which would soon encompass most of his existing businesses, including the phonograph, records, movie equipment (retained after he had left the movie-production business), batteries, and chemicals. This company's fate would determine the longevity of the Edison brand name in the marketplace.

Like any technology-based business, Thomas A. Edison, Inc., needed technical and managerial talent to direct its many separate business divisions. Edison had never been comfortable sharing control, however, and his tight grip on the rudder did not weaken as he grew older. Even at the entry level, new employees were selected for docility. Edison wrote to a correspondent in 1916 about a candidate who was recommended for his great promise as an inventor, "We have found it very undesirable to take into our employ young men whose talents run to invention." He stated flatly that he had no place for the candidate.

Long before this, in the 1880s, Edison had been unwilling to step aside for the manager who most clearly had shown precocious brilliance—Samuel Insull. Edison's businesses would have grown manyfold if they followed the growth of the companies that Insull went on to manage in his post-Edison career.

Insull's story is characterized by boldness of action that exceeded anything Edison had tried. When he had left Edison's side, he had been determined to find a chief executive position. In 1892, he passed up an offer to be a vice president in Henry Villard's North American Company in order to become president of Edison Chicago, a small electrical power utility that could pay him only half of what he had made in New York. He also had to move to Chicago, a place that seemed to a New Yorker like a "frontier town." Willing to take risks, he picked up for a bargain price a state-of-the-art engine and pair of generators from General Electric that had been on display at the 1893 world's fair. In only his second year on the job, he arranged to acquire his larger competitor, the Chicago Arc Light and Power Company. Branching farther out, he acquired coal mines and a steam railroad that provided vertical integration. Most innovative of all, he introduced new pricing schemes to encourage high-volume residential use spread over the entire day so that he could optimize the greatest volume of business for the least possible capital investment. With the acquisition of neighboring utilities, he created a six-thousand-square-mile regional network of power.

Insull was no less an innovator in the spending of his wealth. He gave generously to many charities and used his clout to press Chicago's wealthiest to join him, even if they did not share his color-blind enthusiasm for some causes, including the Chinese YMCA and the education of African doctors. He paid to send a young African American singer on a study tour of Africa and an African American Pullman conductor on a European trip. Tweaking his fellow plutocrats, he built a new opera house in Chicago that by design lacked boxes: All patrons would be seated shoulder to shoulder on the same plane.

Even as Insull became famous—officially so when his portrait was placed on the cover of *Time* magazine in 1926—he continued to make himself available to whoever wished to call him at home, and he insisted that his phone number remain publicly available. One caller asked, "Mr. Insull, I don't want to be rude, but some of us fellows got to talking, and we wondered, well . . . Are you Jewish?" (Insull answered, "Not as far as I know.")

Insull's generosity in philanthropy and willingness to speak personally to anyone stand out in sharp relief to the habits of Edison. When asked in 1911 to donate to a building drive for a YMCA in Port Huron, a boyhood home, Edison responded with a small pledge and provided an explanation of why he would not provide more: "I can use surplus money to greater advantage for all the people in conducting experiments."

Edison clung to the notion that whatever he worked on would benefit the world. The cult of celebrity had constructed for him the story that whatever he touched, ipso facto, would benefit humanity. Having heard it too many times to count, he had come to believe it was empirical fact, and not recognize it for what it was: a frothy fiction created to entertain readers. Without a philanthropic agenda of his own, he could only react to whatever proposals randomly came his way.

Most of the time, his reaction was negative, but he was unpredictable. He replied no to his own town, the City of Orange, which requested a subscription to its summer concert series. Yes, $100 to the Aviation Section of the Militia of the State of Ohio. No to the "colored section" of the Orange YMCA, explaining he had already given $100 to the non-"colored" Y. Yes, a phonograph and 150 records to the Essex County Jail in Newark to "bring to the inmates a little sunshine in their confinement." No, returning a ticket to a concert benefit during World War I for the New Jersey Soldiers' Relief Concert because "[i]nasmuch as I am paying full salary of 47 of my employees now at the front it seems to me that I am doing my share." Yes, $25 to a telegraph-skills tournament to show that he had not "changed a particle" and would "rather have the smallpox than a swelled head." No to Oberlin College because he was using all of his "spare cash to start the pouring of concrete houses for the labouring man."

In fact, Edison did not himself invest in the concrete houses. A New Jersey real estate investor poured fourteen rental homes in Montclair and Orange—claiming that they would stand for a thousand years without need of any repair—but that seems to be as far as the investing got. The only philanthropist who actually paid to have concrete houses poured was Mrs. Mirabeau L. Towns, the wife of a Brooklyn attorney, who paid for twenty thousand concrete homes—concrete *toy* homes, that is, that were distributed among the children of low-income families in New York. The molds were miniatures of those designed by Edison.

In the early twentieth century, husband-and-wife couples maintained separate spheres, including civic and philanthropic causes. Mr. and Mrs. Edison were not exceptions: Mina Edison's ideas about social improvement were hers alone. In the 1910s and 1920s, her favorite cause was "play and recreation," which she believed should be "woven through the warp of our whole existence."

Other social issues also drew her attention. She and fellow members of the local Woman's Club of Orange took on the alarming appearance of low-necked ball gowns, but their ability to enforce their own definition of what she called "a high tone of quiet respectability" was limited to the club's own balls. She also belonged to the Housewives League, which was incensed about the retail price of eggs. To make their point, the league rented a storefront and members personally sold eggs for less than local grocers. With Mina's participation, the affair drew the attention of the press, which described the unusual tableau of various classes mingling at the league's store: "Handsomely gowned women waited on poor Italian and negro housewives, who were eager to take advantage of the bargains in eggs. Other women opened the crates and did heavy lifting."

Mina did not have the imagination to address big problems, and Edison, who had the imagination, did not have the interest. The one philanthropic venture to which he attached his name was the Edison Scholarship, which was first awarded in 1929. It was conceived by one of Edison's staff members and was intended to encourage high school students to pursue technical studies in college. Each of the forty-eight states and the District of Columbia were to name a top scholarship designate, and these finalists would answer a questionnaire addressing moral fitness as well as general knowledge, with questions composed not just by Edison, but also by the other judges, who included Henry Ford and Charles Lindbergh. This elaborate nationwide selection apparatus would lead to the selection of a single winner who would receive a four-year scholarship to the Massachusetts Institute of Technology.

In his business and research projects, Edison became more timid as he became older. While in his thirties, he had had the energy to tackle a problem that had seemed to many to be insoluble: the "subdivision" of the electric light that would make indoor use technically and economically feasible. In his forties, he had continued to dream big and put his winnings from the electric light business into the mining business. It had ended disappointingly, but he cannot be criticized for timidity. In his fifties, he did make another sizable bet. However, for this venture, pursuing the improvement of the battery for an electric car, he had financing from Ford that insulated him from personal risk. He continued to steer clear of risk in his sixties and seventies.

Perhaps his timidity was a simple matter of the aging process, but Samuel Insull provides a counterexample. At the time of the market crash in 1929, Insull was himself seventy years old, but his age did not prevent him from personally attempting to save the country from the worsening depression. Insull was everywhere, financing new infrastructure projects, rescuing beleaguered textile and shipbuilding industries, saving the city of Chicago when it teetered on the edge of bankruptcy. Biographer Forrest McDonald writes that "it appeared as if he were attempting to carry the entire American economy on his shoulders."

Insull put everything he had into the battle against impersonal economic forces far more powerful than he. His personal fortune had increased from around $5 million in 1927 to $150 million in 1929. But his wealth resided entirely in shares of his holding company, the publicly traded Insull Utility Investments. By 1932, those shares were worthless, and he had fallen so far in debt that a banker described him as "too broke to be bankrupt."

Hundreds of thousands of investors in Insull Utility Investments had placed their faith in him and had ridden along as the stock plummeted to the ground. They then turned upon the man they had viewed as civic benefactor. The trajectory of his public career ended catastrophically. Insull was indicted for mail fraud, embezzlement, and violations of the Bankruptcy Act, enduring three trials in 1934 and 1935, and winning exoneration in all three. (The prosecution's case in one instance had not been helped when it introduced as supporting evidence Insull's tax returns, which showed that his annual salary was more than $500,000 a year before the collapse, but his charitable contributions had annually exceeded even that.) Insull died in 1938 in Paris, taking with him first-hand knowledge of Edison that only he possessed. He had told a State Department escort in 1934 that he had "hundreds of stories" from an earlier time before there were codes of ethics in business, but "I think that it is best to let them die with me. If I told them I would be accused of sullying Edison's memory and that I certainly have no desire to do."

Edison never had to pass through a mortifying ordeal such as Insull's trials. Nor did he ever feel a civic obligation to offer service to the community that was his longtime home, as Insull did in Chicago. Edison had always sought isolation to protect his work routines, first in Menlo Park, and then in West Orange, but this isolation left him unaware of what his neighbors thought of him and his factories. When environmental problems, including mercury poisoning, caused by his battery plant's use of industrial chemicals were called to his attention by a member of his staff, he was dismissive. The pollution, however, and the complaints, continued for years. One resident who lived across the street from the plant sought to protect his daughter's endangered health by demanding that the company either control its emissions or buy his house so he could move elsewhere, and if the company did neither, he promised he would personally kill Edison. The residents had no way of knowing that Edison's company had hired a shady fixer to pay the mayor and other local officials to turn their attention elsewhere (and we know this only because the fixer, Joseph McCoy, talked about his activities in his reminiscences as matter-of-factly as if his assigned post had been at a lab bench).

Edison was self-absorbed, isolated, and convinced that he, and only he, knew best how to manage his business affairs. For a founder like Edison, interested in retaining control above all else, the only possible successor would be pliable by temperament and a close relation by blood. For Mina Edison, keeping control of the business within the family was also a matter of the highest priority. Charles Edison, her next-to-youngest child, was an amiable and compliant young man perfectly fitted to the role. In 1914, at the age of twenty-four, Charles was named "first assistant" to his father.

As a child placed in the care of a French governess, his education had begun well before starting kindergarten. But he had been an indifferent student at the Hotchkiss School in Connecticut. By his own admission, he was not much interested in becoming an engineer when he went to Boston Tech (soon to be relocated to Cambridge and renamed the Massachusetts Institute of Technology). After three years of college, he could not muster the interest to finish his degree, especially when he had a more interesting opportunity dangled before him. He chanced to mention to a family friend his lack of interest in the specialized studies awaiting him in the fourth year at college. This friend happened to be the head of the Boston Edison Company and in a position to offer an unusual job to an undergraduate with no prior work experience: CEO-in-training, at full salary. Charles would rotate through the various departments and "see what makes a business tick." Even if his older half brother Tom had once lamented being the son of the famous inventor, Charles had no cause for similar complaint.

When Charles told his parents of his plan to abandon the remaining course work for his degree and spend the next year as a senior management apprentice in a real business, his father readily assented and his mother eventually came around. After his year at Boston Edison, he and a buddy set off on a cross-country trip that took them to Colorado and then to California, where they ran out of money and relied on their own ingenuity to get themselves back home. This brief experiment in self-reliance came to an end, of course, when he took his assigned position at his father's side at Thomas A. Edison, Inc.

Charles's older sister, Madeleine, would say years later that she hated being asked the question "What does it feel like to be Edison's daughter?" Looking back, she said, "It didn't feel like anything but having a nice father that I cared about." She did sometimes wonder if her friends were genuine friends of hers or "Thomas Edison's daughter's friends." Charles, however, had no reason to doubt the genuineness of one friendship he had struck up two years before he joined his father's business—with Henry and Clara Ford's only child, Edsel, who was three years younger than Charles. Both young men would very early take up positions of nominal power at their fathers' companies, and both would discover that their fathers would not be willing to step aside, even with the passing of years. Whether they anticipated how their futures would mirror each other's, they did sense that they already shared the experience of being children of famous fathers, just as their fathers were beginning a friendship that was partly based on the two men recognizing the similarity of their experiences as celebrities. Charles and Edsel also shared an impulse to defy their fathers in small ways. Both were cigarette smokers and conspiratorially savored the discovery that the other also had failed to follow his father's anticigarette strictures. "Dear Fellow Criminal," Charles began a letter to Edsel in 1914, reporting on the latest tests at the Edison lab of an electric light system for cars. He closed, "Sincerely yours in Crime."

In his first year at Thomas A. Edison, Inc., Charles was not given much to do. Even had he been inclined to begin to make changes immediately, he would not have been able to do so. His father made clear that he had final say over all company matters, small and large. The only place Charles had some autonomy was by stepping off the premises. He and two senior company officials decided to set up an experimental side business, selling Edison phonographs out of a retail shop in nearby East Orange. Each of the three put in $10,000 as passive investors. The plan was to hire a store manager and test new marketing techniques that once validated in practice could be adopted by Edison's nationwide network of phonograph dealers. The Edison Shop of East Orange would depart from standard retail practice by selling only phonographs. By renting space in an unlikely location, a low-income neighborhood devoid of other retail storefronts, the investors believed that their success in the face of unpromising circumstances would hasten the wide adoption of their new approach to selling phonographs in a specialty shop.

Edison gave his approval, with this proviso: "You fellows mustn't expect me to carry you." The terms would be the same as for other dealers, though if they should end up losing money in the venture, he said he might make them whole. The three partners vowed never to accept Edison's largesse. "It's a bet," said one. "If we lose we shan't welch; we'll pocket our losses and smile."

Of the three investors, Charles Edison was the one who showed the earliest understanding of the absurdity of filling a tony shop with classical music and live recitals to sell the most expensive phonographs as if it sat on Fifth Avenue, not in a dreary working-class suburb amid households struggling to stay solvent. In September 1914, after the store had been open one week, he playfully wrote Carolyn Hawkins, his girlfriend in Cambridge, that "the store is going fine and tomorrow we're going to figure up how little we are loosing [sic]." As a newly christened tradesman, he was happy to report that he did not "have to pretend to be a gentleman anymore." He did notice that the prospective customers who had responded to an invitation-only opening "were all to [sic] rich to buy this week although several have come in and sneered fashionably at us since." Charles offered to send pictures of the shop so Hawkins could sneer, too.

Without waiting, Edison boasted to a business colleague that Charles— proudly referred to as "that boy of mine"—was proving a great success at the phonograph shop. To his credit, Charles did not make any such claims for himself. The shop, ill-conceived from the start, produced sparse sales and ran up debts that it could not repay. After three years of operation, it owed Thomas A. Edison, Inc., more than $21,000, a situation that alarmed Charles more than his two partners. "This is awful," he wrote William Maxwell, one of the other investors. "What can we do?" Maxwell was not concerned and argued that the "experimental" nature of the store had "done a good deal of good" for the company. No one else could see the claimed benefits—Maxwell himself had complained to the hapless store manager that "it seems incredible that day after day should pass without the sale of a single instrument." None of the investors were willing to continue the dismal experiment; the shop closed.

The ignominious end of the Edison Shop did not noticeably harm Charles's nascent career as a business executive. In 1917, he was promoted from assistant to the founder to acting CEO. The rapid advance—he was still only twenty-seven—came not because Thomas Edison believed the time had arrived to permit a younger generation to step forward. Nor did it come because Charles had been carefully rotated through the various departments, as he had at Boston Edison, to gain a panoptic view of Thomas A. Edison, Inc. His father had continued to run the phonograph business unilaterally as always, and the executive education he provided Charles consisted primarily of posing trivia questions at home: *How many records were rejected at the plant today? What is the name of the Edison dealer in Dubuque?* Charles's promotion came only because the Naval Consulting Board needed Thomas Edison's presence full-time in Washington and at a Navy research laboratory. When the father departed, the son became the head of the company—temporarily.

Charles did not dare tamper with any of the core business functions. Instead, he busied himself in the one neglected corner in which his father had no interest: personnel matters. Thomas Edison paid little notice to his workers (except, of course, Red Kelley in Building 18, the one who knew "a good chew"), and paid no attention to what lives they inhabited when they stepped outside the gates of his plant. Charles did notice. Factory hours were 6:00 A.M. to 6:00 P.M.; in the winter, it was dark when workers went in and dark when they came out. Twenty-two saloons and bars lined the street that faced the main plant, and they opened at 5:00 A.M. for workers who had difficulty facing the grimness of the workday without anesthetic.

Work was dangerous as well as dull. While serving his brief apprenticeship at the company, Charles Edison had taken in a sight one day that would long stay with him. The laboratory, though owned by the man who as much as anyone made it possible for its lathes and other metal-working machines to be powered by electric motors, was still filled with the overhead line shafts, belts, and pulleys of the pre-Edison era. The sleeve of William Benedict, a maintenance worker who was attempting to put a belt on a pulley while the line shaft was still turning, was caught by the belt. Before the power could be shut off, he had been pulled up to the shaft, then battered against the ceiling as he was whirled around. The victim was carried out of the shop without any medically trained person attending to him. The company's accident report blamed the dead man for failing to abide by the company's rule to shut off power prior to changing a belt. When asked to suggest "a practical method" to prevent a repetition of this accident, the company did not say, "By investing in electric motors, which use the power that our company founder helped move out of the laboratory more than thirty years ago." Instead, it recommended for itself a simpler, less-expensive course of action: dismissing any employee who failed to follow the company's safety rules.

When Thomas Edison departed for Washington, Charles Edison got the chance to make changes at Thomas A. Edison, Inc., that made life for factory workers less harsh and dangerous. Charles shortened the workday to ten hours; put in a dispensary staffed with a nurse or doctor on duty; and subscribed to the state's workmen's compensation plan, even though other managers were convinced it would bankrupt the company.

He was young enough that when he began to search for ways to stanch employee absenteeism, he turned to his old prep school, Hotchkiss, for guidance on how to adapt the school's system of demerits to the Edison factory. The two settings did not seem to him to be all that different. He wrote the head of Hotchkiss, "The average mentality of a collection of workers is about on the same plane of immaturity as the High School undergraduate." From his personal experience, he knew the Hotchkiss system worked well. He still remembered "what healthy fear I stood of getting beyond the allotted number of cuts."

As he felt his way in the new position of "Operating Manager and Chief Executive," he was given the opportunity to tell the general public what it was like to find himself at the top of the organization's pyramid at the age of only twenty-seven. In an article published in *American* magazine, Charles described "My Experiences Working for Father." The principal purpose of his controversy-free account was to correct the impression that some readers may have had that his was an easy life. He described how, when he had walked into a notary office one day and made his identity known, the notary had laughed: "Well, I guess you don't have to worry much! It's pretty soft for you fellows that can work for your old man." Charles smiled politely, but told readers that working for his father was anything but easy because he did not receive special treatment. (It did not occur to him to mention his appointment as CEO.)

Within Thomas A. Edison, Inc., Charles was aware that he was regarded as green and inexperienced by older line managers and that he could not make major changes without stirring up criticism and resistance. He tried to disguise his reforms by putting them in the hands of the second in command. Mina, who insisted on detailed accounts of everything he did, was unhappy her "Charlsie" would not receive the credit he deserved. She told him, "I do want your hand at the helm without any doubt about it."

In March 1918, Charles Edison announced his intention to make one more change: While he and Carolyn Hawkins were vacationing with Mina in Fort Myers, the young couple decided to marry—immediately. Charles wired his father aboard the USS *Sachem*, which was stationed not far away, off Key West, to ask for his blessing. Edison bestowed his approval with characteristic absence of sentiment. "If you have decided it must be, then the sooner it is done the better," Edison wrote his son. He lightened this with an attempt at levity: "It can't be worse than life in front line trenches." He closed by saying that it would be impossible for him to attend the wedding.

When the war ended, so, too, did Edison's unhappy experience with the Navy, which had consistently ignored his suggestions. He returned to his own laboratory, where he was master of his domain. Charles was permitted to remain as the head of the business, but only nominally. His father had no interest in Charles's new Personnel Department and reduced its size, then eliminated it altogether, growling, "Hell, I'm doin'

the hirin' and firin' around here." Edison ordered dismissals throughout the executive ranks, over the protests of Charles, and then, beginning in 1920, when the postwar depression arrived, Edison fired plant
workers in large numbers. ("Merrily the axe swings," said Charles sardonically during one of his father's campaigns to reduce the workforce.) Employees were selected for severance by Edison personally.
A. E. Johnson, a longtime employee, described Edison's methodology:
"What he'd do, whenever he'd think that the overhead was getting too
much, you know, and they'd been hiring a lot of men that weren't
needed, he'd start on one of his firing campaigns. . . . If he saw you
coming down he'd stop you and say, 'Who are you, what do you do?'
You'd tell him, he'd ask a couple of questions . . . [and if he did not like
the answers] he'd say, 'You're fired.'" Johnson thought the process was
harmless because many of those "fired" would report the news to their
supervisor, who would then instruct them not to pay any attention to
what Edison had said. Still, between 1920 and 1922, Edison did succeed in drastically reducing employment in the company's manufacturing plants from ten thousand to three thousand.

While Charles Edison sat mutely as the figurehead chief executive, his
father put into place a "mental fitness" test that all college graduates
who applied for work at Thomas A. Edison, Inc., were required to pass.
Edison composed the test himself. It drew wide attention because of the
audacity of Edison's antimodern message: To him, the college degree
was a meaningless credential; the subjects studied in college had no rel-
evance to managerial decision making; and the prevailing ethos of the
college education—that an educated person learned where to look for
knowledge—was useless. All he cared about was what facts a management candidate could produce on command by answering 163 questions in ninety minutes. In its first two years of administration, only
about 4 percent of applicants passed. The average college man, he drily
commented, is "amazingly ignorant."

Thanks to an unsuccessful candidate who claimed to recall 141 questions (which, if true, should have earned him a passing mark in a special
category), newspapers published the test and the reading public had the

chance to see how it would do. A question sampler: What countries bound France? Where is Spitsbergen? Where do we get prunes from? Of what wood are kerosene barrels made? What states bound West Virginia? Where are condors to be found? What states produce phosphates? What is the weight of air in a room 20' x 30' x 10'? How is sulfuric acid made?

When the questions were revealed, editorial writers picked up their pens to condemn the examination from every angle. The *New York Times* pointed out that Edison could not grade "the human soul." Why was it important to know what copra was, it asked, unless one clerked in a grocery store? The *Chicago Tribune* sent a reporter to the University of Chicago to see how well current students would do on the test and, not surprisingly, they did not do well (no one, in fact, could handle that question on the bounding of West Virginia). When Albert Einstein arrived in Boston, he was confronted with what one paper called the "ever-present Edison questionnaire" and was asked, "What is the speed of sound?" He was not able to say, he replied calmly through his secretary, but pointed out that the answer was readily available in reference books. The headline in the *New York Times* gave readers this summary of the news story: "Einstein Sees Boston; Fails on Edison Test."

The test originally began without publicity, and Edison is likely to have devised it simply to cut off the annoying importuning by various managers and acquaintances to place their own sons, nephews, and grandsons into management positions in his company. That said, having placed Charles as company head, Edison was in no position to pretend that he proscribed nepotism.

Once the examination had come to the attention of the general public, however, and the pettiness of its content was roundly criticized, Edison defended his creation with justifications that were, by all appearances, conjured as he went along. He said that he needed the kind of manager who could make decisions without delay, without "waiting to find something out that he might have had right in his head." The inability of one of his managers to have memorized crucial data had, he claimed, cost the company as much as $5,000 (in a way that was left unspecified). The more that Edison's exam was criticized, the more obdurate he became. When newspapers published the correct answers in addition to the questions, rendering the exam useless, Edison was undaunted and drew up a second exam consisting of questions as picayune in nature as those in the first. Later, he said he was surprised to discover that he could continue to use the first exam because candidates did no better on it than on the second, which proved to him that "the average college man doesn't read newspapers."

Few businesspeople defended Edison's methodology. Nor was Edison's friendship with Henry Ford helpful in Edison's public campaign to defend the questionnaire. In a letter to the editor of the *New York Times,* a resident of West Orange asked Edison to explain his close relationship to "a well-known automobile manufacturer whose inability to answer the most elementary questions asked him in the courtroom about a year ago made him the laughing-stock of the entire English-speaking world." Ford had initiated a libel suit against the *Chicago Tribune* and testified at the trial that he did not read anything in the newspaper but headlines. Inadvertently contradicting the basic premise of the Edison questionnaire, Ford had said he was not concerned about his own lack of understanding a given topic because "I could find a man in five minutes who could tell me all about it."

Edison's youngest son, Theodore, was a sophomore at the Massachusetts Institute of Technology, and, unlike Charles, academically inclined with special strengths in mathematics and the sciences. He gamely sat in his dormitory room for a mock examination by a reporter who administered Edison's questionnaire. Theodore's impromptu calculation of the vibrations per second of a red ray of light was impressively accurate, but he did not know where La Paz was the capital, what states bounded Idaho, nor what two rivers converged near Pittsburgh. At the end of the exercise, his self-evaluation was that he had "failed" the test. The pretend exam would be all he would face, however. When he graduated two years later, his father said Theodore could have a position at the family company without having to endure the questionnaire. Theodore was in no hurry: He elected to stay at college for graduate work before joining his brother at the company.

As the phonograph business declined, the famed Edison name was attached to small kitchen appliances that the company resorted to selling in desperation. Theodore was put to work on electric coffeemakers, waffle irons, and toasters. His technical talents would have been a valuable addition to Thomas A. Edison, Inc., had his father been more receptive to his and brother Charles's suggestions for a fundamental change in strategic direction for the struggling company. The phonograph business faced a challenge in the 1920s unlike any that had come before: the advent of commercial radio stations and the wide availability of free music broadcasts and other entertainment. By the end of 1921, an estimated 1 million listeners had access to radios and listened to programs broadcast from the eastern seaboard. A single station in Roselle, New Jersey, which offered the voices of operatic stars among its musical programs, had a broadcast range of a thousand miles, covering New England and the mid-Atlantic states, and reaching as far west as Missouri. A contemporary newspaper account explained to readers not yet acquainted with the phenomenon that those who owned radio sets could enjoy entertainment that was "literally as free as the air."

Charles and Theodore Edison could see that if the company were positioned as being in the music business rather than just in the phonograph business, it could offer a combination phonograph-radio that would permit its product line to evolve with this new line of consumer technology. Their father need not feel slighted because the vacuum tube, the key component in the radio set, was a modern descendant of Edison's experimental work on the incandescent bulb.

Edison did feel slighted, however. Such, at least, was the opinion of Thomas Cowan, a former employee who was working for Westinghouse in 1921, conducting experiments in radio broadcasts with the aid of a phonograph that Edison was willing to loan him. Cowan had several conversations about radio with Edison, who became upset and recalled the loaner when he heard the Westinghouse broadcasts and was appalled at the poor quality of the sound. Edison appeared resentful that he had not personally developed the vacuum tube. He did not quash this impression when he hung a sign on his door: "I will not talk radio to anyone."

Theodore Edison held to a different explanation of his father's refusal to consider his and Charles's recommendation to enter the radio business. His father's hearing had deteriorated further. The only way he could hear music that was reproduced electrically was by wearing headphones with the volume set to an extremely high level, producing extreme distortion. It also produced sparks that darted out from the earphones, making the staff uneasy about accidentally electrocuting their employer. That experience convinced his father that radio could not reproduce music without distortion. Without Edison's personal approval, the company's preparations to enter the radio business were frozen.

Edison's sentimental attachment to the phonograph and his resistance to entering the radio business were on display side by side in 1922, on the occasion of the phonograph's forty-fifth birthday. "I have the phonograph close to perfection," Edison boasted, not for the first time. As for radio, his experience with it on submarines during his wartime research had shown him that the "mutilation of sounds" was a problem that was not amenable to solution. He had all the empirical data he needed, and once his opinion was set, he had no wish to reopen the matter. In 1924, he reiterated, "We would not for a moment think of combining a phonograph with a radio."

Until 1925, radio receivers were powered by batteries. When manufacturers introduced a new design that drew upon electrical current, sales climbed steeply. His sons continued to press him to reconsider and enter the radio business, but Edison remained unmoved: The "radio fad," as he called it, would soon pass.

Father and sons could see that their phonograph business was disappearing, and none of them showed much interest in the waffle irons and other kitchen appliances that had been introduced to carry on the Edison name in the form of the "Edicraft" line. The design of the small appliances was innovative—the Edicraft Automatic Toaster had springs that pushed the heating elements away from the toast rather than popping it into the air—but customers did not want to see novelty tricks performed by their toaster, nor did they wish to pay premium prices.

The business struggled. With Edison in his eighties and still working, he and his sons wanted to distance themselves from the humiliations of plying the electric toaster trade. They shared existential anxiety about defining Edison's legacy in the domain of business with a project that was as grand in scale as those in the past that had secured his reputation. Where should Thomas A. Edison, Inc., head during Edison's remaining time among the living? The two generations did not agree on the answer.

Edison elected to start an entirely new career in industrial botany, based at his winter home in Fort Myers. With the financial support of Henry Ford and Harvey Firestone, he established a new company, the Edison Botanic Research Company, whose mission was to discover a source of rubber that could be cultivated in the United States as a backup source in case war interrupted imports from Southeast Asia. Ford and Firestone provided Edison with $500,000 annually to pursue the project. The official history gives us an inspiring tale of the octogenarian testing seventeen thousand different varieties of domestic plants in the course of discovering that goldenrod would serve as an alternative source. This sanitized version acknowledges that his findings were never actually used; by the time of World War II, synthetic rubber had been invented. But the story still serves the purpose of showing Edison's desire for new challenges, even when his age was advanced and his health was failing; he suffered from diabetes and stomach problems that probably were caused by radiation exposure in his laboratory years earlier.

Edison's rubber research was not successful, and he apparently covered up the failure in order to keep his external funding intact. An employee of the Fort Myers laboratory claimed that the goldenrod mixture, which Edison showed Ford to be able to demonstrate that the research had achieved success, had surreptitiously been enriched with real rubber—from condoms purchased in bulk for this purpose. The same employee also observed Harvey Firestone tearfully explaining to Edison that the collapse of business due to the Depression meant that he could no longer continue his support of Edison's laboratory. After Firestone left, Edison was heard sneering, "He's a God damned lightweight." (Ford doubled his own contribution so that the funding continued undiminished.)

While their father was absorbed in the rubber project and spending more time in Fort Myers, Charles and Theodore took steps out of his view to try to ensure that the Edison name would have a place in the evolving music business. Late though the hour was, they set up a research group in Orange to make a phonograph with an electric pickup and moved ahead on plans to introduce a radio. With prototypes ready, they succeeded in extracting their father's grudging assent, but he predicted the experiment would result in a financial bath.

Edison's fears were realized, though it had been his intransigence that put the company at such a great disadvantage as a late entrant. Even when Charles and Theodore were free to act without stealth, they were dogged by problems obtaining a necessary license from General Electric, setting up an expensive production facility, and selecting a design that would be affordable to consumers. On 9 October 1929, Charles prepared a report for his father that showed a loss for the company of $1.3 million due to start-up costs for the radio, which, to put the best face on it, was no more than the average annual loss for the company in the previous five years. Still, the company had assets in the form of Liberty Bonds, and Charles remained hopeful that losses from the radio would not, as he put it, "sink the ship." He could not know that two weeks later the stock sell-off would begin with Black Thursday, on 24 October—followed by Black Monday and Black Tuesday—and business conditions would deteriorate apace.

A few days later, Thomas A. Edison, Inc., announced that it would cease producing records and refit the factory for the production of radios. The announcement was accompanied by mention of regret as the phonograph "was one of Mr. Edison's favorite inventions." If the company was going to succeed in home entertainment, everything would ride on the success of its new radios and radio-phonographs. These were sold not as tabletop sets but as stunningly beautiful pieces of furniture designed for the high end of the market, not the best positioning in depression conditions. Each model was encased in a wide console standing about four feet high, finished in walnut and hidden behind sliding doors. The sales literature seemed to be addressed less to the general public than to Edison himself, the sons boasting of the "engineering refinement" that provided volume levels ranging "from a whisper to a mighty crescendo and both without distortion!"

A year later, Charles and Theodore informed their father that there was no point in continuing a hopeless endeavor, and the radio production was shut down immediately. Charles wrote his father with bittersweet feelings about the end of the experiment: "Radio is the last of our products to carry the name Edison in the house. Altho [sic] we have lost a pile of money there is at least the solace of knowing that it was a good product worthy of the name, and that we have nothing to be ashamed of in the way it was sold." He thanked his father for being willing to pay the bills despite his personal misgivings. "We have had our battles and differences of opinion," Charles wrote, "but when all is said and done you will stand out for me as the 'world's best sport.'"

The sons could not undo decades of poor decisions that their father had made regarding the phonograph and the entertainment business. Edison had insisted on keeping control of the phonograph for too long, to the detriment of the business. But his reputation as the nation's super-inventor nonpareil, the man who had single-handedly brought into being multiple industries, was so unquestioned that he did not have to do anything more in order to collect compound interest denominated in fame. In 1923, Edison was credited with the creation of industries then worth $15.6 billion and employing 1.5 million people. Henry Ford's personal net worth was estimated at that point to be $2 billion, but the *New York Times* said that "the business community has found Edison eight times as valuable as Ford."

Polls that inquired about the Most Useful American or the Greatest American were a perennial source of entertainment during Edison's life-

time, and his name always ranked high. Perhaps the most unintentionally entertaining poll was that conducted in 1922 among the 750,000
youth group members of the Methodist Episcopal Church who were
asked to vote for the "greatest man in history." Edison was given top
place, edging out Theodore Roosevelt and Shakespeare. Henry Ford
gave Edison top place, too, and his vote would count more than anyone
else's because of the funds he cheerfully deployed to honor his designee
and friend. About a decade before Ford famously declared in 1922 that
"history is bunk," he had begun purchasing old agricultural imple-
ments, wagons, pre-Ford horseless carriages, and other artifacts of an
earlier age. He had no interest in history that was ancient and foreign
and intellectual—he had followed his "history is bunk" declaration
with the rhetorical question "What difference does it make how many
times the ancient Greeks flew their kites?"—but he was passionately interested in history that was near-recent, American, centered on technology, and tactile. He began plans to build a "historic village" in Dearborn
that would provide visitors with an appreciation of the nation's technical ingenuity. It emerged as Greenfield Village, and contained a full-
scale re-creation of Thomas Edison's Menlo Park laboratory complex
built as much as possible with materials salvaged from the original site.
Ford had seven railcars deliver soil from the New Jersey site, so authen-
ticity could be claimed even for the dirt.

For Edison's eighty-second birthday in February 1929, Ford made a gift
of $5 million to establish an endowment for his museums' collection of
Edisonia and to establish a technical school in Edison's name. Later that
year, he arranged to dedicate the opening of Greenfield Village with an
enormous celebration, Light's Golden Jubilee, honoring Edison on the
occasion of the fiftieth anniversary of the invention of incandescent
light. President Herbert Hoover, John D. Rockefeller Jr., J. P. Morgan,
Marie Curie, Orville Wright, and Will Rogers were among the five hundred invited guests who joined Ford and Edison for the festivities. After
the evening banquet, Edison, Ford, and Hoover walked to the unlit

Menlo Park laboratory to play a scripted melodrama fancifully recreating the first lighting of the electric light. The radio announcer solemnly intoned: "Mr. Edison has two wires in his hand; now he is reaching up to the old lamp, now he is making the connection. It lights! Light's Golden Jubilee has come to a triumphant climax!" Americans around the country who were listening to the live broadcast had dutifully followed the instruction to turn off their household lights until Edison had again provided the world with light, and then, upon cue, they turned on their lights again as car horns blared.

When the party returned to the banquet hall, Edison plopped on a davenport just inside the door. He appeared overwhelmed by emotion and told Mina, "I can't go in." She said, "You are the whole show, you know," and offered to get him a glass of milk. The milk provided what he needed. He got up, reentered the hall, and carried on. On this exceptional evening he did that rarest of things: He made a public speech. It offered thanks to President Hoover, the guests, and Henry Ford, about whom he said, "I can only say to you that in the fullest and richest meaning of the term, 'He is my friend.' Good night."

EPILOGUE

FTER THE LIGHT'S Golden Jubilee, Edison lived two more
years, working less, napping more. He summoned the energy in
January 1931 to sign off on one more patent application, for a
"Holder for Article to Be Electroplated." Its issuance brought his personal total to 1,093, the leader in the patent office by a wide margin.
Most of the patents were for minor variations on previous ones—more
than 400 concerned electric light and power and almost 200 were for
phonographs and recording—and Edison had no compunction about
claiming credit for work done by assistants. But under his name, he
compiled a record that seemed to be unassailable.

Health matters, naturally enough, became Edison's principal preoccupation at the end. He remained unshakably certain that he was an expert
on medical matters and had long before developed all-encompassing claims
for a milk-only diet. When Mina Edison's sister Jane had died suddenly in
1898, Edison wrote Mina expressing shock—and admonished that if
Jane had only been put on a milk diet, nature would have had the opportunity to "throw off the poisonous defective digestion and she would be
strong and hearty today." Over time, Edison had become more attached
to milk as an ever-reliable tonic, as he had shown on the evening of the
Golden Jubilee. In 1930, he explained he did just fine with nothing but
one glass of milk every two hours. He maintained that "80 percent of our
deaths are due to over-eating." This conviction arose from his insight that
"auto-intoxication," that is, the accumulation of diseases in the bowels,

was the cause of most deaths. The solution was "a matter of diet and lubrication." He was the same medical authority who years before had said that clothing that pinched was literally a killer: "Pressure ANYWHERE means that a certain part of your body is deprived of its natural flood. And starvation and death begin where the body is pressed and choked."

The theories did not protect him from kidney failure. In August 1931, he collapsed in his living room and spent ten days near death, while a battalion of newspaper reporters turned Glenmont's ten-car garage into a pressroom. He moved out of immediate danger, but his energy had disappeared and familiar routines were abandoned. By October, he was too weak to leave bed and remained "mentally drowsy," according to his doctor; he passed in and out of a coma and hovered on the edge of death for two weeks. Newspapers issued multiple bulletins each day reporting the slightest sign of improvement or decline. In the early morning of 18 October 1931, Thomas Alva Edison died at the age of eighty-four at home with his family at his bedside.

That day, the *New York Times* carried twenty-two stories about Edison's life and death. The blanket coverage was mirrored across all media outlets. For more than fifty years, Edison had promoted his own image and the notion that it was his hands alone that had performed miracles. That preparatory work made the eulogies he received upon death easy to write. His "genius" was credited in the *Times* with bestowing upon humanity the gifts of the electric light, the phonograph, the motion-picture camera, and "a thousand of other inventions," hyperbole that confused the patent count with separate wonders. The asterisk that should have been attached to each major invention was long gone and history became the simplest form of story: In the beginning, before Edison, there was only darkness. The governor of New Jersey suggested that everyone in the state turn off their lights at 7:00 P.M. on the day of the funeral "as a reminder of what life would have been like if the inventor of the incandescent light had never lived."

Edison was given credit not only for bestowing light upon benighted humanity, but also for making life worth living. When John Ott, seventy-five, a retired employee who had spent his entire working career with

Edison, was told of Edison's death, he took the news hard, even though it could not have been a surprise. Ott died within hours, and his death was attributed to "shock" because he was "so stunned by the news of the master's passing," according to fellow former employee Francis Jehl. Ott's wheelchair and crutches were placed reverently at the foot of "his master's" bier.

Whether Ott felt quite as bereft as press accounts described is an open question, however. When Mary Childs Nerney had interviewed him earlier for her biography *Thomas A. Edison: A Modern Olympian,* Ott had observed with evident sadness that his children had grown up without knowing their father because he worked late every night at Edison's side and never saw them. "Why did you do it?" Nerney had asked, and Ott replied, "We all hoped to get rich with him," but he ruefully observed that the only ones who succeeded in that ambition were those who had left Edison's employ.

Employees, former or current, who harbored any bitterness toward Edison made no appearance in the send-off, which resembled a state funeral. For two days, his bier was placed in the library of his laboratory and made available for employees and the general public to file past and pay a silent farewell. Declining the offer of the governor for a military presence, his oldest employees formed themselves into an ad hoc honor guard, standing with folded hands and bent heads at the foot and head of the coffin, relieving one another at fifteen-minute intervals. Ten thousand people filed past on the first day, and forty thousand the second.

Making New Jersey's plan to turn off all lights a national one, President Hoover asked the country's citizens to mark their sorrow at Edison's death by turning off all electric lights simultaneously across the country on the evening of Edison's funeral, at ten o'clock eastern time. He had considered shutting down generators to effect a perfectly synchronized tribute but realized that it might lead to deaths; even this thought was put in service of a tribute to Edison, for the country's life-and-death dependence upon electricity, he said, "is in itself a monument to Mr. Edison's genius."

Edison really had been privileged to hear his own eulogy in advance:

The one read at the Light's Golden Jubilee two years before was used again at his service. That night, the two radio networks, the National Broadcasting Company and the Columbia Broadcasting Company, jointly broadcast an eight-minute tribute that ended on the hour, when listeners were asked to turn out the lights. The White House did so and much of the nation followed, more or less together, some a minute before the hour, others on the hour. On Broadway, about 75 percent of the electrified signs were turned off briefly. Movie theaters went dark for a moment. Traffic lights blinked out. Everything seemed connected to Edison: the indoor lights, the traffic lights, the electric advertising, everyone connected via radio, which Edison now received credit for helping "to perfect." In the simple narrative that provided inspiration for posterity, one man had done it all.

His would be a hard act to follow, yet it was irresistible. All four of his sons chose to pursue careers in the invention business. The two eldest sons died not long after their father died. Thomas Edison Jr., after failing to make a living from his Ecometer, had ended up working for Thomas A. Edison, Inc., at the time of Edison's death. He died in 1935 at the age of fifty-nine. William, the only one of the four who did not work for the company, maintained a laboratory in his home basement, tinkering with radio equipment and hoping to find the money to market a one-tube radio set that he designed. He died in 1937 at the age of fifty-eight.

Charles and Theodore lived much longer but were not able to move away from the shadow of their father. Charles continued to direct the company, then was appointed secretary of the Navy and elected governor of New Jersey. He died in 1969 at the age of seventy-eight. Theodore left his brother's side and set up a small technical consulting company. He died in 1992 at the age of ninety-four. Even then, sixty years after his famous father had died, Theodore's life was defined by reference to the "Illustrious Father" mentioned prominently in the headline of his obituary.

Neither Charles nor Theodore accepted their father's belief that working in a technology-based business was itself a form of world betterment; both sons gave away substantial portions of their wealth. The enduring nature of an endowed foundation, such as the one that

Charles established, shows the shortcomings of Thomas Edison's neglect of the fundamentals of philanthropy. His scholarship program had run only two years, ending when he became too sick to attend to it.

At the time of his death in 1931, Edison's estate was estimated in the press to be valued at $12 million. As the culmination of a long lifetime in the business of invention, it is a sum that says much or little about Edison's career and acumen, depending upon one's vantage point. Measured against Edison's impecunious beginnings, it is a sizable figure, and larger than might have been guessed when he had appeared desperate for the research subsidies from Ford and Firestone for his rubber research. Still, the $12 million was not so large when Edison's loyal employees measured his wealth against the total capitalization of the industries that they credited the great man for conjuring into existence, modestly claiming little of the resulting wealth for himself. The size of the estate seems modest, too, when placed next to the Ford Foundation's endowment of $109 million and the $70 million estate for his family that Henry Ford left at the time of his death in 1947.

The $12 million figure for the Edison estate turned out to be inflated and subject to the crushing effects of the Depression. Time passed while the will was processed slowly by the courts. Four years later, when the executors gave the court the first accounting, the value of the estate was put at $2.9 million, and reduced by 50 percent to $1.5 million by the time the second accounting of the estate was filed two years later in 1937. Mina Edison was not affected by the disappearing inheritance. Edison had placed Glenmont, other real estate, and stocks and bonds in her name, providing for her financial security without placing her in the will. This arrangement spared her from being caught in cross fire between her stepchildren and children over the disposition of the estate. Four years after Edison's death, at the age of seventy, she remarried a seventy-three-year-old retired businessman whom she had known since childhood. She was widowed again five years later and died in 1947 at the age of eighty-two.

The Edison family name was not carried by succeeding generations. Unlike Henry Ford, however, whose male heirs have handed down the

Ford name through the present, when great-grandson William Clay Ford Jr. is the company's executive chairman, Thomas Edison's sons did not have children themselves. Only his daughter Madeleine Edison Sloane did so. The Edison family name, the symbolic repository of his fame, would not be passed on to a third generation.

Nor would the corporate name Thomas A. Edison, Inc., survive. In 1956, Charles Edison arranged for a merger with the larger McGraw Electric Company, based in Chicago. Just as in the nineteenth century Edison Electric had had to share the marquee, becoming Edison General Electric before "Edison" was dropped completely, this time the newly merged entity was renamed McGraw-Edison. The company sold fuses, home appliances, test instruments, and equipment for generating plants. Once again the value of the Edison name on the tag sank without the presence of the inventor himself to remind customers of his omniscient oversight. In 1985, McGraw-Edison was absorbed into Cooper Industries, an industrial conglomerate based in Houston.

Without an eponymous company selling new versions of Edison's inventions, his fame would be subject to the normal wear and tear from the passage of time. It is not a little surprising how durable it has proven to be. One measure is a poll of Chinese who were asked in 1998 to list the best-known Americans: Ahead of Mark Twain, number four, and Albert Einstein, number three, and even ahead of Michael Jordan, number two, was Thomas Alva Edison.

In the history of modern invention, Edison fortuitously lived at just the right time, close enough to the present to be associated with the origins of the modern entertainment business and also the basic electrical infrastructure needed for just about everything, yet not too late to be able to get away with claiming sole authorship of the inventions produced in close collaboration with a large but publicly invisible technical staff. Today, the proliferation of technical wonders and the anonymity of the worker bees in corporate labs who produced them prevent the emergence of any single individual engineer who could rival Edison. Shunpei Yamazaki, currently affiliated with Japan's Semiconductor Energy Laboratory, has a long way to go before his name is recognized as readily in

America as Edison's, but Yamazaki now has more than 1,560 patents issued in the United States. We rely upon the microprocessor, the personal computer, the cell phone, and the iPod without even a faint idea of who should be credited for bringing the accoutrements of modern life into existence. Edison, however, made sure that no one would be confused about whom to credit for the inventions that came out of his lab.

Edison's fame acquired an indestructible shine because he worked in technical areas that the public sensed were going to shape that historical moment. This was not the case in the earliest portion of his inventing career, when he was known only among telegraph-equipment specialists. But once he chanced upon the phonograph and, overnight, the press anointed him the Wizard of Menlo Park, he occupied a space different from everywhere else: He, and anyone working for him, were perceived as standing at the very outer edge of the present, where it abuts the future. When a young John Lawson sought a position at Edison's lab and wrote in 1879 that he was "willing to do anything, dirty work—become anything, almost a slave, only give me a chance," he spoke with a fervency familiar to applicants knocking today on the door of the hot tech company du jour. In the age of the computer, different companies at different times—for example, Apple in the early 1980s, Microsoft in the early 1990s, Google in the first decade of the twenty-first century—inherited the temporary aura that once hovered over Edison's Menlo Park laboratory, attracting young talents who applied in impossibly large numbers, all seeking a role in the creation of the zeitgeist (and, like John Ott, at the same time open to a chance to become wealthy). The lucky ones got inside (Lawson got a position and worked on electric light).

Menlo Park became *the* iconic site for American ingenuity, but it was a highly burnished image that floated free of the actual place. Edison did not stay in the actual Menlo Park for very long—only four years after the phonograph was invented in 1877, he moved to New York City to be close to the work on the electric light system and would never return. When he built the new, far larger laboratory complex in Orange, New Jersey, he still was seen by the public as a permanent resident of the imaginary Menlo

Park, the place where the invention factory seemed capable of mastering anything. It was an image that popular culture did not want to relinquish because it perfectly embodied the nation's idealized image of itself.

Edison's work was not merely his principal preoccupation; it was the organizing leitmotif of his entire waking existence. He also made it a defining characteristic of his public image. He made sure the press understood that no one worked longer hours than he did, no one needed less sleep than he did, no one was more passionately devoted to invention than he was. He was a prickly person who was used to getting his own way, insufferably opinionated and a carrier of the hateful prejudices of his day. Still, the reader who sees that Edison could neither enjoy his celebrity nor shed it may be inclined to view Edison more sympathetically. No different from most mortals, Edison was a creature of habit, and he stuck to the routines that seemed to have served him so well as a young inventor. After the phonograph and electric light, his inventive efforts across five decades produced one claim to a major success, movies—a claim contested by others—as well as minor hits in other fields and some major misses. For all his accomplishments, Edison failed to invent a way to free himself from unrealistic expectations produced by his own past.

For more than half a century, Edison enjoyed and endured fame. His two wives and six children would also have to contend with the complications that inevitably come when an individual is no longer able to keep private life separate from public, no longer able to keep strangers from presuming intimate ties. Edison did not spare much time to reflect aloud upon how celebrity had shaped the course of his life for good or for ill. He gave no indication whether over time he lost the ability to distinguish the exaggerated public image of the Wizard from the one that he saw in the mirror. One exception, when Edison actually referred at least indirectly to his own celebrity, occurred late in his life. One of his employees recalled walking past him one day as the inventor stepped briskly between buildings at the lab. He cheerfully greeted his employer: "Morning, Mr. Edison." Edison gave him a glance, raised his finger to show a major pronouncement would follow, and said, "The world's greatest inventor, world's greatest damn fool," then hurried on.

NOTES

The following abbreviations are used in the notes:

ENHS   Edison National Historic Site, West Orange, New Jersey

HFM & GVRC Henry Ford Museum and Greenfield Village Research Center, Dearborn, Michigan. All box references are for the Edison Papers, Accession #1630.

NYDG   *New York Daily Graphic*

NYH   *New York Herald*

NYS   *New York Sun*

NYT   *New York Times*

NYW   *New York World*

PTAE   *The Papers of Thomas Alva Edison* (Baltimore: Johns Hopkins University Press, 1989–)

Vol. 1: Reese V. Jenkins, Leonard S. Reich, Paul B. Israel, Toby Appel, Andrew J. Butrica, Robert A. Rosenberg, Keith A. Nier, Melodie Andrews, and Thomas E. Jeffrey, eds., *The Making of an Inventor, February 1847–June 1873*

Vol. 2: Robert A. Rosenberg, Paul B. Israel, Keith A. Nier, and Melodie Andrews, eds., *From Workshop to Laboratory, June 1873–March 1876*

Vol. 3: Robert A. Rosenberg, Paul B. Israel, Keith A. Nier, and Martha J. King, eds., *Menlo Park: The Early Years, April 1876–December 1877*

Vol. 4: Paul B. Israel, Keith A. Nier, and Louis Carlat, eds., *The Wizard of Menlo Park, 1876*

Vol. 5: Paul B. Israel, Louis Carlat, David Hochfelder, and Keith A. Nier, eds., *Research to Development at Menlo Park, January 1879–March 1881*

TAE   Thomas Alva Edison

PTAED   *The Papers of Thomas Alva Edison* (digital edition). The home page for the Digital Edition is http://edison.rutgers.edu. Individual documents may be retrieved using the form at http://edison.rutgers. edu/singldoc.htm.

TAEPM   *Thomas A. Edison Papers: A Selective Microfilm Edition*

The following works are cited by short title in more than one chapter:

Conot, *Streak of Luck:* Robert Conot, *A Streak of Luck* (New York: Seaview Books, 1979).

Dyer and Martin, *Edison:* Frank L. Dyer and Thomas C. Martin, with William Meadowcroft, *Edison: His Life and Inventions* (New York: Harper & Brothers, 1910, rev. ed. 1929).

Friedel and Israel, *Edison's Electric Light:* Robert Friedel and Paul Israel, *Edison's Electric Light: Biography of an Invention* (New Brunswick, N.J.: Rutgers University Press, 1986).

Israel, *Edison:* Paul Israel, *Edison: A Life of Invention* (New York: John Wiley & Sons, 1998).

Jehl, *Reminiscences:* Francis Jehl, *Reminiscences of Menlo Park* (Dearborn, Mich.: Edison Institute, 1939). 3v.

Josephson, *Edison:* Matthew Josephson, *Edison: A Biography* (New York: McGraw-Hill, 1959).

Nerney, *Edison:* Mary Childs Nerney, *Thomas A. Edison: A Modern Olympian* (New York: Harrison Smith and Robert Haas, 1934).

Tate, *Edison's Open Door:* Alfred O. Tate, *Edison's Open Door* (New York: E. F. Dutton, 1938).

INTRODUCTION

page 1: **stood five foot nine:** "The Phonograph, Etc.," *Daily Evening Traveler,* 23 May 1878, *PTAED,* SM029106a.

page 1: **first celebrities in American history:** Richard Schickel, *Intimate Strangers: The Culture of Celebrity* (Garden City, N.Y.: Doubleday, 1985). Schickel assumes that the phenomenon of celebrity did not begin until the early twentieth century. He excludes Edison from his survey.

page 2: **Other nineteenth-century figures:** Leo Braudy points out that "after the Civil War, no president until Theodore Roosevelt could compete in name and face recognition with men such as Barnum, Mark Twain, and Thomas A. Edison." Leo Braudy, *The Frenzy of Renown: Fame and Its History* (New York: Oxford University Press, 1986), 498.

page 2: **an envelope mailed:** Wilson Drug Company to TAE, 12 April 1911, ENHS. It was mailed on a bet—the envelope lacked a letter inside—and reached Edison nineteen days later.

page 3: **inspiring essayists to expect:** "Phonograph," *Brooklyn Eagle,* 26 February 1878, *PTAED,* MBSB10385X.

page 3: **one humorist suggested:** "Edisonia," *NYDG,* 9 May 1878, *PTAED,* MBSB10590X.

page 3: **the two previous generations:** *PTAE,* 1:3–6, 19n2; Josephson, *Edison,* 1–3.

page 4: **loss of hearing:** Edison attributed his hearing loss to an incident when he was working on the Grand Trunk Railroad. In his telling, many years later, he said he been standing below the door of a freight car with arms full with newspapers, unable to get himself up and in, when a conductor who was standing inside lifted him up—by his ears—to help him board. Edison said, "I felt something snap inside my head, and my deafness started from that time and has ever since progressed." Dyer and Martin, *Edison*, 37.

page 4: **he persuaded his mother:** TAE reminiscence, "Book No. 1," 11 September 1908, *PTAE*, 1:629. Unlike the carefully polished tales told of his childhood in hagiographies, the fragments of oral history that were transcribed in 1908 contain enough rough edges to possess verisimilitude.

page 4: **Edison expanded into newspaper publishing:** *PTAE*, 1:25–26. TAE reminiscence, "Book No. 1," *PTAE*, 1:629. The British traveler was Robert Stephenson, a civil engineer, who, with his father, George Stephenson, were one of the most famous pair of engineers in Victorian England. I could not confirm that the *Times* ever mentioned Edison's newspaper as Edison believed it had. The incident occurred years before Edison maintained scrapbooks of clippings, and I was unable to find any story resembling this in *Palmer's Index to the Times*.

page 5: **When a bottle of phosphorus:** *PTAE*, 1:8; Dyer and Martin, *Edison*, 37.

page 5: **Edison fell into the good graces:** TAE reminiscence, "Book No. 1," *PTAE*, 1:631. When MacKenzie got back in touch with Edison many years later, in 1877, he mentioned that his son Jimmy was now almost as tall as his father and had been working as assistant lineman on the railroad. James MacKenzie to TAE, 18 September 1877, *PTAED*, D7719ZBX. In his reply, Edison recalled that "Jimmy was only 2½ feet high when I used to plague him," and signed his note with atypical warmth as "Your old friend." TAE to James MacKenzie, 21 September 1877, *PTAED*, LB001291. MacKenzie became one of Edison's Menlo Park employees.

page 5: **role was anything but heroic:** TAE reminiscence, "Book No. 1," *PTAE*, 1:631. For a discussion of the claim that Edison's inattention in this incident resulted in the loss of lives, a claim for which there is no documentary evidence, see *PTAE*, 1:671–672.

page 6: **renewed acquaintance:** Ezra Gilliland was one friend whom Edison made when the two worked together in Adrian, Michigan. The two later roomed together, along with two actors, in Cincinnati. Gilliland helped Edison keep his skills sharp by sending plays over the wire; presumably, these sessions explain the recurring phrase in Edison's laboratory notebooks from the opening of *Richard III:* "Now is the winter of our discontent . . ." *PTAE*, 1:16, 1:22n45. The two men's careers led in different directions for a number of years, but Gilliland would later become a key business associate and very close personal friend of Edison's.

page 6: **In a rare surviving letter:** TAE [to family], Spring 1866 [conjectured], *PTAE*, 1:28.

page 7: **great prowess:** *PTAE,* 1:671. In Edison's own phrase, he was "a complete failure" as a sender.

page 7: **He had diligently investigated:** TAE reminiscence, "Book No. 1," *PTAE,* 1:637.

page 7: **In Cincinnati in 1867:** TAE reminiscence, "Book No. 1," *PTAE,* 1:637. Edison put batteries to another use when he found his apartment overrun with cockroaches. He pasted two strips of tinfoil across their path, attached wires to the strips and to a battery, and when the insect stepped across both strips, "there was a flash of light and the cockroach went into gas." TAE reminiscence, "Book No. 1," *PTAE,* 1:637–638.

page 7: **When he landed in Boston:** "The Napoleon of Science," *NYS,* 10 March 1878, *PTAED,* SB031032b.

page 8: **in exchange for half-interest:** The documentary record for Edison and his backers in 1868 is not complete, but the papers that are available suggest that the sums that Edison received were not large. One example: In July 1868, he signed a contract with E. Baker Welch, signing over a half-interest in the fire-alarm telegraph for $20. TAE and E. Baker Welch, 28 July 1868. National Archives. *PTAED,* W100CAC. Earlier that month, Edison had signed a contract that gave Baker a half-interest in a double transmitter for a down payment of only $5.50. Receipt for E. Baker Welch, 11 July 1868, *PTAE,* 1:70–71. When the full contract for this project was signed by the two men the next year, Edison referred to unspecified "various sums of money" that Baker had advanced to him, but the figure paid that day was still a modest $40. TAE, patent assignment to E. Baker Welch, 7 April 1869, *PTAED,* D6901A.

page 8: **Three individuals:** *PTAE,* 1:52.

page 8: **When Edison and his investor angel:** George Parsons Lathrop, "Talks with Edison," *Harper's New Monthly Magazine,* February 1890, 431–432.

page 9: **A fellow boarder:** W. E. Sharren to TAE, 31 July 1878, *PTAED,* D7802ZUB.

page 9: **could collect contributions:** *PTAE,* 1:52; "The undersigned promise . . . ," notebook entry, 1 December 1868, *PTAED,* D6801A.

page 9: **once got in trouble:** TAE reminiscence, "Book No. 1," *PTAE,* 1:638.

page 9: **He claimed that the deafness:** Thomas A. Edison as told to Edward Marshall, "My Deafness Helped You to Hear the Phonograph," *Hearst International/Cosmopolitan,* April 1925.

page 9: **better suited:** Ibid.

page 10: **One occasion:** Tate, *Edison's Open Door,* 164.

CHAPTER 1. ALMOST FAMOUS

page 14: **On the eve of founding:** TAE to Samuel and Nancy Edison, 30 October 1870, *PTAE,* 1:212. Edison offered to send money so his father could purchase "a good peice [*sic*] of property very cheap" that his father had mentioned in a prior letter.

page 14: **meeting the weekly payroll:** TAE to George Harrington, 22 July 1871 [conjectured], *PTAED*, D7103L. How pinched Edison really was is hard to say. Two days later, he sent his father $300 for an investment in a Port Huron liquor store that his father was interested in. TAE to Samuel Edison, 24 July 1871, HFM & GVRC, *PTAE*, 1:308–309.

page 14: **his hair turned white:** TAE to Frank Hanaford, 17 September 1869, *PTAED*, D6901H; TAE to Frank Hanaford, 26 January 1870 [conjectured], *PTAED*, D7001C.

page 14: **When he and partner William Unger:** Edison and Unger Summary Account, 1 January 1872, *PTAED*, D7212C.

page 14: **When R. G. Dun & Company:** R. G. Dun & Co. Credit Report, July 1872, Baker Library, Harvard, *PTAE*, 1:472.

page 15: **offered subscribers a private telegraph line:** News Reporting Telegraph Company, "An American Idea," advertising circular, October 1871 [conjectured], *PTAED*, SB178B1.

page 15: **daughter of a lawyer:** *PTAE*, 1:385n5.

page 15: **Among the young women:** J. B. McClure, *Edison and His Inventions* (Chicago: Rhodes & McClure, 1879), 67.

page 16: **a strikingly similar account:** "Thomas A. Edison: Inventor of Electric Light and Phonograph," *Christian Herald & Signs of Our Times*, 25 July 1888, *PTAED*, SC88058A. Here is the alternative account:

> She was seated, working; he was standing behind her quietly. "Mr. Edison," she said, swinging around suddenly, "I can always tell when you are behind me or near me."
>
> "How do you account for that?"
>
> "I don't know, I am sure," she answered, "but I seem to feel when you are near me."
>
> "Miss Stillwell," said Edison, "I've been thinking considerable of you of late, and if you are willing to have me, I'd like to marry you."
>
> "You astonish me," she protested, "I—I never—."
>
> "I know you never thought I would be your wooer," interrupted Mr. Edison, "but think over my proposal, Miss Stillwell, and talk it over with your mother."

It is possible that the *Christian Herald* account is derived wholly from McClure's, and does not provide independent corroboration. But it does have a few details that are not found in the version published earlier.

page 16: **a telegrapher friend:** McClure, *Edison and His Inventions*, 68. The story's credibility is not enhanced when we observe that Edison and friend have their encounter on an evening that was by appearances no different from any other, yet Edison's wedding was on Christmas Day, 1871.

page 16: **After the wedding and a weeklong honeymoon:** *PTAE*, 1:385n2.

page 16: **According to one source:** This is the recollection of Edward Ten Eyck Jr., who was passing along the impressions of others who were older than him—Mary Stillwell Edison died in 1884, when Eyck was five years old. David Trumbull Marshall, *Recollections of Edison* (Boston: Christopher, 1931), 108.

page 16: **She remembered:** Jehl, *Reminiscences*, 511. According to Jehl, Edison, for his part, was pleased that his wife, and her unmarried sister Alice, who also lived with them to provide Mary companionship during Edison's prolonged work hours, were "amusing themselves while he was interesting himself at the laboratory."

page 16: **financially comfortable:** *PTAE*, 1:301.

page 17: **had to sell his house:** *PTAE*, 2:312.

page 17: **placed the first working system:** The first regular operations of a duplex system in the United States began in March 1768, between New York and Boston. *PTAE*, 1:32n7.

page 17: **"any damned fool ought to know":** "The Napoleon of Science," *NYS*, 10 March 1878, *PTAED*, SB031032b.

page 17: **He later tried, but failed:** *PTAE*, 3:280–281.

page 18: **"should be in every family":** Edison & Murray, circular, n.d., *PTAE*, 2:208.

page 18: **It sold well enough:** *PTAE*, 2:207.

page 19: **"You captivate my whole heart":** Daniel Craig to TAE, 18 January 1871, *PTAED*, D7110B.

page 19: **The next month:** Daniel Craig to TAE, 13 February 1871, *PTAED*, D7110D.

page 19: **This was Edison's:** George Bliss to TAE, 25 September 1878, *PTAED*, D7822ZBD.

page 19: **pen had a sharp needle:** *PTAE*, 2:463. For a sample of the circular produced by the pen, see *PTAE*, 2:561.

page 19: **"There is more money":** TAE to Stephen Field, 13 September 1875, *PTAED*, LB001023.

page 19: **one year older:** When cross-examined in a civil case on 12 March 1896, Batchelor said he was fifty years old, so he was at least one year, and perhaps was two years, older than Edison. See his testimony in *American Graphophone v. U.S. Phonograph*, *PTAED*, QP001585.

page 19: **had come to the United States:** Israel, *Edison*, 86.

page 19: **"We have now":** Charles Batchelor to James Batchelor, 28 May 1877, *PTAED*, MBLB1125.

page 20: **Edison's ongoing work on automatic telegraphy:** TAE, notebook, PN-75-01-05, *PTAED*, A204; *PTAE*, 2:375. Freed from the financial worries that had weighed on her the year before, Mary Edison threw a masquerade party for her husband on February 11, 1875, the occasion of his twenty-eighth birthday. *PTAED*, SB178, scrapbook image 11.

page 20: **settled on land in Menlo Park:** The proximate reason for Edison's move to Menlo Park was a dispute he had with the municipality of Newark. Earlier, Edison had rented factory space from a Newark landlord on what Edison had been given to understand was a monthly basis. When

Edison gave notice in his third month, paid the rent he owed, and moved to another space in Newark, he was served with a notice that he still owed rent for nine more months on the original space. A city ordinance guaranteed landlords one year's rent, he learned belatedly. When he recalled the story years later, he said, "This seemed so unjust that I determined to get out of a place that permitted such injustice." He spent several Sundays investigating possible sites for a relocated lab, one of which, Menlo Park, was suggested by his bookkeeper, whose family happened to live about a mile away. See Dyer and Martin, *Edison,* 267.

page 20: **It consisted of:** "A Visit to Edison," *Philadelphia Weekly Times,* 29 April 1878, *PTAED,* SM029055f.

page 20: **No town hall:** Jehl, *Reminiscences,* 498.

page 20: **One saloon:** Dyer and Martin, *Edison,* 269.

page 20: **The town was too small:** E. C. Baker, *Sir William Preece: Victorian Engineer Extraordinary* (London: Hutchinson, 1976), 162.

page 21: **in New York City:** Ibid., 156.

page 21: **one could glimpse:** "Edison's Phonograph," *Newark Daily Advertiser,* 3 May 1878, *PTAED,* MBSB10574X.

page 21: **"an elongated schoolhouse":** "A Visit to Edison," *Philadelphia Weekly Times,* 29 April 1878, *PTAED,* SM029055f.

page 21: **"country shoe factory":** "The Phonograph Etc.," *Boston Daily Evening Traveler,* 23 May 1878, *PTAED,* SM029128b.

page 21: **At the rear:** Ibid.

page 21: **The first floor:** "An Hour with Edison," *Scientific American,* 13 July 1878, *PTAED,* SM009042a.

page 21: **A "spider web":** "That Wonderful Edison," *NYW,* 29 March 1878, *PTAED,* MBSB10463.

page 21: **The twelve or so:** Bernard S. Finn, "Working at Menlo Park," in *Working at Inventing: Thomas Edison and the Menlo Park Experience,* ed. William S. Pretzer (Baltimore: Johns Hopkins University Press, 2002), 34.

page 21: **a disheveled figure:** "A Marvelous Discovery," *NYS,* 22 February 1878, *PTAED,* MBSB10378.

page 22: **"the fire of genius":** Ibid.

page 22: **Thomas Alva Edison was already:** To his rivals in the telegraphy world, he was unflatteringly described as "gray as a badger and rapidly growing old." See "Echoes from 197," *Operator,* 15 June 1877, 9, quoted in *PTAE,* 3:289.

page 22: **in Preece's diary:** Baker, *Sir William Preece,* 162.

page 22: **It was likened:** "The Latest Newark Invention," reprint from *Daily Advertiser* [Newark, N.J.], n. d., *TAEPM,* 13:960.

page 22: **A sales manager:** P. Mullarkey to TAE, 17 September 1875, *PTAED,* D7504C. Mullarkey reported to Edison the next week, "One man yesterday wasted three hours of my time and then pronounced it 'quite a curiosity.' I am so tired from today's that I am hardly able to stand." P. Mullarkey to TAE, 23 September 1875, *PTAED,* D7504E.

page 22: **The fault:** Frederic Ireland to TAE, 26 October 1876, *PTAED,* D7608N. High-tech companies in the following century would also blame the victim, their customer. Edison's pen venture also anticipated the latter-day discovery by Hewlett-Packard that the right pricing strategy could yield boggling profits in the printer business. HP practically gives away ink-jet printers, in order to secure a highly profitable, perpetually renewing succession of ink-jet-cartridge purchases. In the case of the electric pen, Batchelor and Edison tried to experiment with prices, floating the idea in 1877 of slashing the price of a new pen and giving a bottle of ink away for free as a sales-promotion gimmick. Charles Batchelor to Robert Gilliland, 8 May 1877, *PTAED,* MBLB1113. George Bliss, the general manager of the Electric Pen & Duplicating Press Company, scolded them for not placing a high price on the ink. Bliss wielded his considerable sales and marketing experience like a cudgel over the inexperienced Edison and Batchelor: "The men who make the most money are those who put a first class price on their goods & stick to it." George Bliss to TAE, 23 May 1877, *PTAED,* D7711S. This was easy to say when no other products were on the market; a year later, though, with competitive products flooding in, Bliss had to abandon high prices and smug certainty. The newest competitive entrant "can be made for nothing and sold for less, so the parties claim. When will it end?" he lamented. George Bliss to TAE, 16 April 1878, *PTAED,* D7822W.

page 22: **American Novelty Company:** *PTAE,* 3:193n11.

page 23: **Batchelor's "Office Door Attachment":** Charles Batchelor, technical note, 18 November 1876, *PTAED,* MBN001059.

page 23: **An idea:** Charles Batchelor, technical note, 8 January 1877, *PTAED,* NE1695044.

page 23: **American Novelty Company:** The company was incorporated in November 1876 but had failed by June 1877, by which time it had been renamed the Electro-Chemical Manufacturing Company and stripped of the one business that actually had customers, that of duplicating ink. *PTAE,* 3:192n10, 289.

page 23: **It was while:** Robert V. Bruce, *Bell: Alexander Graham Bell and the Conquest of Solitude* (Boston: Little, Brown, 1973), 147.

page 23: **The more famous rendering:** Ibid., 181.

page 24: **Bell lacked the gifts:** "Sound and Electricity," *NYT,* 18 May 1877.

page 24: **former sales agent:** *PTAE,* 2:207.

page 24: **Johnson's excitability:** In January 1877, Johnson was the general manager of the American Novelty Company and, having heard rumors that Edison had been critical of Johnson's management of funds advanced to him, he had written Edison that he understood that "I am a burden to you" and offered to resign. Edward Johnson to TAE, 3 January [1877], *PTAED,* D7701A. The squall passed as quickly as it had come; two days later, the two corresponded as if it had never happened. Edward Johnson to TAE, 5 January 1877, *PTAED,* D7701B.

page 24: **his eagerness in April 1876:** Edward Johnson to TAE, 24 April 1876, *PTAED,* D7601F.

page 25: **"We should not be at all surprised":** "The Edison Telephone," *Woodbridge Independent,* 14 June 1877, *PTAED,* MBSB10192X.

page 25: **"Mr. Edison has been so often scoffed at":** "The Motograph," *Newark Daily Advertiser,* 2 May 1877, *PTAED,* MBSB10147X.

page 25: **competing musical telephone:** "Prof. Gray's Telephone Concert," *NYT,* 3 April 1877.

page 25: **Compared to Gray's:** "Prof. Edison's New Telephone," *NYT,* 17 July 1877.

page 25: **When Johnson saw the review:** Edward Johnson to TAE, 20 July 1877 [conjectured], *PTAED,* D7719V.

page 25: **he was happy:** Edward Johnson to TAE, 17 July 1877, *PTAED,* D7719T.

page 25: **he begged Edison.** Ibid.

page 25: **The *New York Daily Graphic:*** Ibid.

page 26: **On the day of the concert:** Edward Johnson to Josiah Reiff, 20 July 1877, *PTAED,* D7719U.

page 26: **now the *Times* was impressed:** "Prof. Edison's Telephone Concert," *NYT,* 19 July 1877.

page 26: **Johnson, fond of exaggeration:** Edward Johnson to TAE, 20 July 1877 [conjectured], *PTAED,* D7719V.

page 26: **The songs:** "Prof. Edison's Telephone Concert," *NYT,* 19 July 1877.

page 26: **Johnson knew:** Edward Johnson to Josiah Reiff, 20 July 1877, *PTAED,* D7719U.

page 26: **one Joseph Hipple:** Hipple's remarkable vision deserves to be reproduced in full:

> If I understand the telephone, and I think I do, because I have read all the newspapers I could get hold of, I don't see why in a big city like New York they shouldn't have music in every house, the same as water and gas. All they would have to do would be to have one room in the city and have the best musicians they could find there, and enough of them to give all parts and perhaps some good singers, too. Then have wires reaching to any man's house who wanted to pay for them. When he didn't want any music he needn't have any, because he could take the wire out of the machine. This would be cheap. It wouldn't cost half as much as a piano, and would be better music. A company could go into it; but they should have the best musicians. They should play all the time. I don't mean all day and all night but from about three o'clock in the afternoon, until bedtime, say nine o'clock. [T]hey could have relays. Of course we couldn't have such a thing here [Spruce Mills, Iowa]. Another might get up a room with dance-music in it for those that wanted to buy that kind and have wires, etc.

Joseph Hipple, "Music On Tap," letter to editor, *NYDG*, 26 March 1877, *PTAED*, MBSB10104X.

page 27: **telegraphy remained:** Laboratory notebook, 11 July 1877, *PTAED*, TI2186.

page 27: **He did have a vision:** Ibid.

page 27: **the practicality of the telephone:** *PTAE*, 3:441n1.

page 28: **New York Paper Barrel Company:** J. L. Thomson to TAE, 10 March 1877, *PTAED*, D7702G.

page 28: **A legacy of this work:** Charles Batchelor, Journal, October 1906, *PTAED*, MBJ007.

page 28: **A sketch and brief caption:** Laboratory notebook, 17 July 1877, *PTAED*, NV12016.

page 28: **A partial list:** Laboratory notebook, 20 July 1877, *PTAED*, NV12023.

page 29: **An employee described:** The account is that of Charles Clarke. Bernard S. Finn, "Working at Menlo Park," in *Working at Inventing*, 42–43.

page 29: **The day after:** The narrative that follows is based on Batchelor's testimony on 12 March 1896 in *American Graphophone v. U.S. Phonograph*, *PTAED*, QP001585 and a similar account, with a few additional details, in his journal, October 1906, *PTAED*, MBJ007. The only substantive detail in these accounts that is demonstrably in error is Batchelor's placing the date in November 1877, instead of the actual month, July 1877, a forgivable lapse after having listened to Edison for decades subsequent to the event tell reporters his own garbled and conflated chronology of the phonograph's invention.

page 30: **The entries for 18 July 1877:** Laboratory notebook, 18 July 1877, *PTAED*, TI2196.

page 30: **James Adams:** Adams, a former seaman and a failed salesperson who had tried to peddle the Inductorum, had started working at the laboratory as a night watchman and had worked his way into the ranks of the experimenters. Robert Conot characterizes him as a "hard-swearing, hard-drinking, tubercular man of considerable talent." Conot, *Streak of Luck*, 72.

page 30: **failed to appreciate:** When Edison got back in touch with William Preece in England in early August 1877, three months after Preece's visit to Menlo Park, Edison spoke excitedly of the speaking version of the telephone, able to articulate human speech, dog barks, cricket chirps—it is "now *absolutely perfect*," he claimed. TAE to William Preece, 2 August 1877, *PTAED*, Z005AB. His motive in writing Preece was to ask him to find an agency that would market his telephones in England ("I should feel greatly obliged"), so he put the very best face on the current state of his telephone equipment. Yet Edison did not deem his discovery two weeks' previous of how to record sound to be sufficiently important to mention.

page 30: **Batchelor's diary:** Charles Batchelor, Diary, 1877–78, *PTAED*, MBJ001.

page 31: **George Field:** George Field to TAE, 18 July 1877, *PTAED*, D7702ZAM. ENHS has no record that indicates Edison replied to Field.

page 31: **Edward Johnson told:** ENHS does not have a copy of the clipping, which apparently appeared on 14 August 1877 in the *Philadelphia Record*. In an interview with a reporter from the same paper the following year, the reporter claimed that the August 1877 brief had been the first public announcement of the phonograph. Edison requested a copy "for my scrapbook," and the reporter reprinted the item in its brief entirety. See "Edison 'At Home'," *Philadelphia Record*, 6 June 1878 [conjectured], *PTAED*, MBSB10648.

page 31: **By this time:** Laboratory notebook, 12 August 1877, *PTAED*, NS7703A. Side note: 12 August 1877 is the same date affixed erroneously (and, I believe, intentionally) to a sketch of a cylinder phonograph actually drawn much later and signed by Edison. See *PTAE*, 3:495n1.

page 31: **An unidentified staff member:** Untitled sheets with T. A. Edison letterhead on first page, n.d., *PTAED*, D7702ZEO.

page 32: **The sensitivity of Edison's carbon microphone:** TAE to William Orton, 27 July 1877, *PTAE*, 3:469.

page 32: **In September:** TAE to Franklin Badger, 17 September 1877, *PTAED*, LB001285.

page 32: **he wrote his father:** TAE to Samuel Edison, 21 October [1877], *PTAE*, 3:599–600.

page 32: **Edison seems to have been disappointed:** TAE to Benjamin Butler, 13 October 1877, *PTAED*, LB001306.

page 32: **Benjamin Butler:** *PTAE*, 3:324n6.

page 33: **could at least capture:** Ibid.

page 33: **Butler thought:** Benjamin Butler to TAE, 23 October 1877, *PTAED*, D7702ZCQ.

page 33: **He was infuriated by an article:** "Speech Automatically Transmitted in Shorthand by the Telegraph," *Scientific American*, 3 November 1877, 273. This brief article served to preview the longer article that appeared, with illustrations, in the next issue: "Graphic Phonetics," *Scientific American*, 14 November 1877, *PTAED*, MBSB10276X.

page 33: **With Edison's permission:** Edward Johnson, "Wonderful Invention: Speech Capable of Indefinite Repetition from Automatic Records," letter to the editor, *Scientific American*, 17 November 1877, *PTAED*, MBSB10274 (or identical copy: SM030022a). Although the cover date was 17 November 1877, the journal was available by 6 November 1877, the same date it was reprinted in the *New York Sun* (see the following citation). *PTAE*, 3:617n1.

page 34: **The *New York Sun*:** "Echoes from Dead Voices," *NYS*, 6 November 1877, *PTAED*, MBSB10269X.

page 34: **The *New York Times*:** It is striking how the disparagement of women seems to have been endlessly amusing to male writers, and presumably their male readers, in 1877. "Bottled sermons" would not displace the sermons delivered in person by clergy because "in no other way can a weekly opportunity be afforded to ladies for mutual bonnet inspections." "The Phonograph," *NYT,* 7 November 1877.

page 34: **To the** *English Mechanic:* "Edison's Phonograph," *English Mechanic,* 30 November 1877, *PTAED,* MBSB10290X.

page 34: **Edison had shifted his experimental focus:** Johnson most likely composed his undated letter on 6 November 1877. The Menlo Park notebooks show that on 1 November 1877 work continued on strips of wax paper (*PTAED,* QP001779), but on 5 November 1877 Edison proposed using a sheet of tinfoil to be placed on a grooved cylinder (*PTAED,* TI2348).

page 35: **When setting down:** Laboratory notebook, 5 November 1877, *PTAED,* TI2348.

page 35: **Edison had begun:** *PTAE,* 1:xliii. Edison wrote in a pocket notebook in October 1870 that "all new inventions I will here after keep a full record."

page 35: **On a page:** Laboratory notebook, 23 November 1877, *PTAED,* NV17018.

page 35: **conceptualized, then refined:** A sketch entered on 29 November 1877, just before Kruesi started building the first model, shows side and end views of the design of what would, in a few days, be realized as a working model. Laboratory notebook, 29 November 1877, *PTAED,* NS7703D.

page 35: **On 4 December 1877:** Charles Batchelor, Diary, 1877–1878, *PTAED,* MBJ001.

page 35: **Even the loquacious Johnson:** Edward Johnson to Uriah Painter, 7 December 1877, *PTAE,* 3:661.

page 36: **feeling quite well:** Over one hundred years later, Steve Jobs borrowed the same parlor trick when he pulled the first Macintosh computer out of a bag and had it introduce itself on stage in January 1984: "Hello, I am Macintosh. It sure is great to get out of that bag." See Steven Levy, *Insanely Great: The Life and Times of Macintosh, the Computer That Changed Everything* (New York: Viking, 1994), 182.

page 36: **Edison was given credit:** "The Talking Phonograph," *Scientific American,* 22 December 1877, *PTAED,* MBSB10300. In France, Leon Scott claimed that his phonautograph anticipated Edison's phonograph, which he criticized for not creating an intelligible visual record of human speech. See *PTAE,* 4:188n3.

page 37: **This was stop-the-presses news:** Edward Johnson to Uriah Painter, 8 December 1877, *PTAE,* 3:663–667. On the same day, Edison composed an unrelated letter to a famous figure whom he did not know, seeking recognition. "Dear Sir," wrote Edison to Charles Darwin, "several small green colored insects were caught by me this summer having come into my laboratory windows at night." The bugs gave off a strong smell that resembled naphthalene, and if Darwin was not already aware of such an insect, Edison offered to mail him some specimens the following summer.

It was signed "Thomas A. Edison, Telegraph Engineer." Darwin's son Francis politely declined the offer, explaining his father was already "at work on different subjects." TAE to Charles Darwin, 7 December 1877, Cambridge University Library, UK, *PTAE*, 3:657–658.

page 37: "I want to know you": Amos Cummings to TAE, 8 January 1878, *PTAED*, D7805C.

page 37: Edison welcomed: *PTAE*, 4:195.

page 38: The *New York World* referred: "Mr. Edison's Inventions," *NYW*, 12 January 1878, *PTAED*, MBSB10327.

page 38: This was especially galling: Alexander Graham Bell to Gardiner Hubbard, 18 March 1878, Library of Congress, Alexander Graham Bell Papers, *PTAE*, 4:185–186.

page 38: He recovered sufficiently: Alexander Graham Bell to Gardiner Hubbard, n.d., American Telephone and Telegraph Company, Corporate Research Archives, *PTAE*, 4:187n2.

CHAPTER 2. THE WIZARD OF MENLO PARK

page 39: "The Phonograph is creating": Edward Johnson to Uriah Painter, 4 January [1878], *PTAE*, 4:15–17.

page 39: In early January 1878: Edison's Toy Contract, 7 January 1878, *PTAED*, D7932ZBF08.

page 39: To pursue opportunities: Edison Speaking Phonograph Company, Memorandum of Agreement, 30 January 1878, *PTAED*, D7932ZBF01.

page 40: The investors feared: Charles Cheever to Gardiner Hubbard, 9 February 1878, *PTAE*, 4:68–69.

page 40: According to a psychological profile: "Thomas A. Edison," *Phrenological Journal* 66.2 (February 1878), *PTAED*, MBSB10352X.

page 40: Edison wrote one of his representatives: TAE to Theodore Puskas, 12 February 1878, *PTAED*, Z400AF.

page 40: When Edison finally wrote to Preece: TAE to William Preece, 11 February 1878, *PTAED*, Z005AL.

page 41: A clockwork mechanism also: TAE to Alfred Mayer, 11 February 1878, *PTAED*, X095AA.

page 41: Listening comprehension was influenced: Ibid.

page 41: If a speaker shouted: TAE to Henry Edmunds Jr., 12 February 1878, *PTAED*, X322AA.

page 41: He got the idea: *PTAE*, 4:89n1. The germ of the idea can be seen in his doodling a design for a steam telephone to be used in railroad signaling, which he had also called an "airophone." TAE, technical note, 17 January 1878, *PTAED*, NV14015.

page 41: Recitations, conversational remarks: Edward Johnson, prospectus, 18 February 1878, *PTAED*, D7838J1.

page 42: His show played: Edward Johnson to Uriah Painter, 27 January 1878, *PTAE*, 4:43–44.

page 42: **sent out a premature announcement:** TAE to Henry Edmunds Jr., 12 February 1878, *PTAED*, X322AA.

page 42: **To another friend:** TAE to Benjamin Butler, 12 February 1878, *PTAED*, X042AB.

page 43: **In the early 1870s:** Walter P. Phillips, *Sketches Old and New* (New York: J. H. Bunnell, 1897), 184–185. This usage of "bugs" occurs in a reminiscence, I grant. But even if it is used anachronistically here and was not used in 1872 or 1873, when Edison was working on the quadruplex, it was definitely used by Edison in November 1878, as we shall see in a later chapter. The *Oxford English Dictionary* cites Edison's mention of a "bug" in his phonograph as the first instance of the word's usage meaning "defect or fault in a machine plan," but this example comes from 1889, at least eleven years later than earlier instances of Edison's usage.

page 43: **For example, Alfred Mayer:** Alfred M. Mayer to TAE, 15 January 1878, *PTAED*, D7829C.

page 43: **In early February:** TAE to Clarence Blake, [9 February 1878], *PTAED*, X011AA; Charles Cheever to Gardiner Hubbard, 9 February 1878, *PTAED*, X012G1AF.

page 44: **Edison must have slapped:** Amos Cummings to TAE, 7 February 1878, *PTAED*, D7805F.

page 44: **Cummings was not to be denied:** Amos Cummings to TAE, 14 February 1878, *PTAED*, D7805L. In a postscript to his letter confirming the date of the interview, Cummings joked, "Hope electricity is not so much a fraud as 'newspapericity.'"

page 44: **the resulting story:** "A Marvelous Discovery," *NYS*, 22 February 1878, *PTAED*, MBSB10378. The discussion below is based on this article.

page 45: **"My wife Dearly Beloved":** Laboratory notebook, Newark Shops, 1 February 1872, *PTAED*, NE1676031A. Edison had made the same point again in another notebook entry: "My Wife Popsy Wopsy Can't Invent." 14 February 1872, *PTAED*, NE1678055, notebook p. 56.

page 45: **Mary would leave:** Jehl, *Reminiscences*, 499.

page 45: **Robert Heller:** *PTAE*, 4:35n3. A detailed account of the Hellers' performance is provided in "The Mystery of Second Sight," *NYS*, 7 February 1878, *PTAED*, MBSB10353, but the copy that was microfilmed is in poor shape and illegible in places.

page 45: **unsettled clergy:** Milbourne Christopher and Maurine Christopher, *The Illustrated History of Magic* (1973; reprint, Portsmouth, N.H.: Heinemann, 1996), 212.

page 46: **The evening's entertainment:** "That Wonderful Edison," *NYW*, 29 March 1878, *PTAED*, MBSB10463.

page 46: **"The one thing":** "The Magician of Science," *NYS*, 31 May 1878, *PTAED*, MBSB10632X.

page 46: **Having noticed sparks:** *PTAE*, 2:581.

page 47: **the etheric force could revolutionize telegraphy:** For a full discussion of Edison's "etheric force," see Israel, *Edison*, 111–115.

page 47: **scientists came to realize:** Ibid., 115.

page 50: **"I find I cannot get away":** TAE to Benjamin Butler, 25 March 1878, Library of Congress, Benjamin F. Butler Papers, *PTAED*, X042AC.

page 50: **His "telephonoscope":** "The Phonograph, Etc.," *Daily Evening Traveler*, 23 May 1878, *PTAED*, SM029106a.

page 50: **When letters came pouring in:** "He Is a Great Man Now," unlabeled clipping, 24 May 1878, *PTAED*, SM029099b.

page 50: **When Vanity Fair:** William S. Kimball & Co. to TAE, 25 March 1878, *PTAED*, D7802ZEO.

page 50: **"I am very sorry":** "Inventor Edison's Last," *NYW*, 21 March 1878, *PTAED*, SB031052a.

page 51: **In early March:** Gardiner Hubbard to Thomas Watson, 24 April 1878, American Telephone and Telegraph Company, Corporate Research Archives, *PTAED*, X012IAR; "Inventor Edison's Last." Hubbard's letter describes the Menlo Park lab as he saw it when he visited on 23 March 1878.

page 51: **Ladies and gentlemen:** "Edison, the Magician," *Cincinnati Commercial*, 1 April 1878, *PTAED*, SB031094a. The reporter described Edison as "an atheist in religion, and doesn't believe in guesswork about anything." This may well have been the last time Edison talked publicly about his atheism; subsequently, he sensed the unspoken parameters for those in the American public's eye, and atheism fell outside of them.

page 51: **Edison complained:** TAE to J. W. S. Arnold, in margin of J. W. S. Arnold to TAE, 20 March 1878, *PTAED*, D7802ZDX1.

page 52: **the advertising was too effective:** Charles Cheever to Gardiner Hubbard, 15 March 1878, *PTAED*, X012G1AO.

page 52: **Gardiner Hubbard:** Gardiner Hubbard to Uriah Painter, 2 April 1878, *PTAE*, 4:210–213.

page 52: **Cheever was more concerned:** Charles Cheever to Gardiner Hubbard, 20 March 1878, *PTAED*, X012G1AW.

page 53: **he doggedly insisted:** "Edison, the Magician."

page 53: **reported Edison's claim:** "The Inventor of the Age," *NYS*, 29 April 1878, *PTAED*, MBSB10561.

page 53: **a bright little three-year-old:** "Inventor Edison's Last," *NYW*, 21 March 1878, *PTAED*, SB031052a.

page 53: **the phonograph as a source of humor:** "Miseries of the Phonograph," *Washington Herald*, 1 April 1878, *PTAED*, SM029004b.

page 53: **The *New York Times* said:** "The Aerophone," *NYT*, 25 March 1878. The *Times* also ribbed Edison for his claimed discovery of the etheric force and the embarrassment that had followed: "He has been addicted to electricity for many years, and it is not very long ago that he became notorious for having discovered a new force that he has kept carefully concealed, either upon his person or elsewhere."

page 54: **One professor urged Edison:** "The Inventor of the Age," *NYS*, 29 April 1878, *PTAED*, MBSB10561.

page 54: **Croffut wrote of a lunch:** "A Food Creator," *NYDG*, 1 April 1878, *PTAED*, MBSB10470X.

page 54: **some listeners failed to hear:** "Radio Listeners in Panic, Taking War Drama as Fact," *NYT*, 31 October 1938.

page 54: **some readers, and some newspapers:** "They Bite," *NYDG*, 6 April 1878, *PTAED*, SB031084a.

page 55: **Edison was tickled:** TAE to William Croffut, 6 April 1878, *PTAE*, 4:223–224.

page 55: **another visiting reporter:** "Long-Range Chatting," *Philadelphia Times*, 3 April 1878, *PTAED*, MBSB10493X.

page 55: **Ten days after:** "The Wizard of Menlo Park," *NYDG*, 10 April 1878, *PTAED*, MBSB10500X.

page 55: **Croffut's previous attempt:** "The Papa of the Phonograph," *NYDG*, 2 April 1878, *PTAED*, MBSB10472.

page 55: **the Mania has broken out:** George Bliss to TAE, 13 April 1878, *PTAED*, D7805ZAL.

page 55: **Croffut had similar news:** William Croffut to TAE, 25 April 1878, *PTAED*, D7805ZAR.

page 55: **In a recent profile:** "Papa of the Phonograph."

page 56: **Six days after the publication:** TAE to Uriah Painter, 16 April 1878, *PTAE*, 4:234.

page 56: **Mrs. Andrew Coburn:** Mrs. Andrew W. Coburn to TAE, 13 May 1878, *PTAED*, D7802ZLG.

page 56: **A few weeks later:** Mrs. Andrew D. Coburn to TAE, 13 July 1878, *PTAED*, D7802ZSI.

page 56: **Then Mr. Coburn:** Andrew Coburn to Charles Batchelor, 25 July 1878, *PTAED*, D7802ZTQ.

page 56: **separately the surgeon wrote:** George Fowler to TAE, 1 September 1878, *PTAED*, D7802ZXQ.

page 56: **Mrs. Coburn followed:** Mrs. Andrew Coburn to TAE, 31 October 1878, *PTAED*, D7802ZZIM.

page 56: **Zenas Wilber:** *PTAE*, 4:225n3.

page 56: **He said he had to borrow:** Zenas Wilber to TAE, 31 March 1878, *PTAED*, D7802ZFN. Robert Conot provides interesting detail about Wilber, whom he says was an alcoholic, was chronically in need of money, and was the person whom Edison's associates had persuaded to execute a crude forgery in the Patent Office to protect the group's interest in the quadruplex. See Conot, *Streak of Luck*, 82–83.

page 56: **He had Batchelor send:** Charles Batchelor, diary entry, 6 April 1878, *PTAED*, MBJ001 for beginning of diary; this entry also found in *PTAE*, 4:225.

page 56: **He had accepted an invitation:** Conot, *Streak of Luck*, 109.

page 56: **Before the meeting:** "The Man Who Invents," *Washington Post and Union,* 19 April 1878, *PTAED,* MBSB10532.

page 57: **The phonograph demonstration:** "National Academy of Sciences," *Washington Star,* 19 April 1878, *PTAED,* SM005003.

page 57: **Edison was set free:** Conot, *Streak of Luck,* 82, 109.

page 57: **A command performance:** TAE reminiscence, "Book No. 2," 1908–1909 [conjectured], *PTAE,* 4:863. A contemporaneous account contains a direct quotation of Edison's that is opaque to a modern reader but appears to say that Hayes did not reveal his reaction. Recounting the next month his encounter at the White House, Edison said to a reporter: "I scanned [Hayes's] forehead very carefully, but the letters were not there." "The Magician of Science," *NYS,* 31 May 1878, *PTAED,* MBSB10632X.

page 58: **Edison, Batchelor, and the phonograph:** "Astonished Congressmen," *Baltimore Gazette,* 20 April 1878, *PTAED,* MBSB10538X.

page 58: **leaving Congress:** "Edisonia," *NYDG,* 9 May 1878, *PTAED,* MBSB10590X.

page 58: **Having been honored:** "The Inventor of the Age," *NYS,* 29 April 1878, *PTAED,* MBSB10561.

page 58: **Beneath Edison's unassuming appearance:** "A Visit to Edison," *Philadelphia Weekly Times,* 29 April 1878, *PTAED,* SM029055t.

CHAPTER 3. FLIGHT

page 59: **as a member of a class of "martyrs":** The author, who signed the letter only with "S.," heaped praise on Edison in terms that are notable for their excess: "Gods! how an Edison towers, head and shoulders above the 'professors' assembled at the Smithsonian last week! Stand aside, examiners of old fossils, delvers in the earth, dissectors of insects, book-learned bigots— day is dawning. . . . What has the Government done for the discoverer, the originator, the inventor? Messrs. Representatives, your constituents are asking these questions. The time must come when the king among men will be recognized." "The Man Who Towers," *Washington Post and Union,* 22 April 1878, *PTAED,* MBSB10544X.

page 60: **Typical was his remark:** TAE to Uriah Painter, 12 March 1878, *PTAE,* 4:171. Here "[money]" is substituted for the slang term Edison used in the quoted passage: "rhino."

page 60: **Gardiner Hubbard lamented:** Gardiner Hubbard to Thomas Watson, 24 April 1878, *PTAED,* X012IAP.

page 60: **Edison decided to renew:** "Edison's 'Ear Telescope,'" *NYS,* 8 June 1878, *PTAED,* SM029144a.

page 61: **Uriah Painter:** Uriah Painter to TAE, 29 April 1878, *PTAED,* D7802ZJF.

page 61: **Edward Johnson:** Edward Johnson to Uriah Painter, 15 March 1878, *PTAE,* 4:179.

page 61: **It would turn out:** *PTAE,* 4:253n5.

page 61: **Imagining fabulous profits:** Uriah Painter to TAE, 29 April 1878, *PTAED*, D7802ZJF. The portraits were taken not by Brady but by Levin Handy.

page 61: **no one at the Edison Speaking Phonograph Company:** *PTAE*, 4:251n2.

page 62: **a group of thirty businesspeople:** "Bores of Science," *Sentinel of Freedom and Weekly Advertiser,* 21 May 1878, *PTAED*, MBSB10609X.

page 62: **A Newark paper:** "A Call upon the Phonograph," *Newark Daily Advertiser,* 3 May 1878, *PTAED*, MBSB10574X.

page 62: **Another paper suggested:** "Bores of Science."

page 62: **Edison was cooperative:** Thomas A. Edison, "To the Editor of the Daily Graphic," *NYDG*, 16 May 1878, *PTAED*, SM029062a.

page 62: **What the letter did not disclose:** William Croffut to TAE, 10 May 1878, *PTAED*, D7805ZAW. That it was Croffut who proposed the letter is my hypothesis, based on context. The Edison-Croffut exchange makes little sense were we to assume the alternative scenario, that it was Edison who proposed to Croffut a letter of praise, and then asked Croffut to ghostwrite it for him.

page 63: **While giving Croffut a tour:** "Papa of the Phonograph."

page 63: **relationship of diet to national destiny:** "New York Letter," *Cincinnati Commercial,* 5 May 1878, *PTAED*, SM029047a.

page 64: **He told a visiting reporter:** Ibid.

page 64: **In May, he accepted:** "Magician of Science."

page 65: **Before Batchelor began:** "Mr. Edison in a Convent," *NYW,* 31 May 1878, *PTAED*, SM029120b.

page 65: **A few weeks later:** "An Evening with Edison," *NYT,* 4 June 1878.

page 65: **One journalist described Mary:** "Phonograph, Etc."

page 66: **Edward Johnson pretended to confide:** "Edison, the Magician."

page 66: **On another occasion:** "Edison's Trip and Inventions," *NYS,* 28 August 1878, *PTAED*, MBSB10858.

page 66: **The "telescopophon":** Edison said he hoped to have the miniature ear trumpet released before Christmas. "Ears for the Deaf," *NYDG,* 5 June 1878, *PTAED*, SM029128a.

page 67: **yet be so small:** "Edison 'at Home,'" *Philadelphia Record,* [6 June 1878?], *PTAED*, MBSB10648.

page 67: **Theodore Puskas:** "Edison's Phonograph in Paris," *NYDG,* 8 June 1878, *PTAED*, MBSB10664X.

page 67: **Puskas secured:** "Edison's Trip and Inventions." Edison was impressed that Puskas cleared the hall "every hour and begins a new exhibition, and if a man wants to stay he has to pay over again." The *New York Daily Graphic* (*PTAED*, MBSB10664X) said that the exhibition was held three times a day, not hourly. A brief mention in a Paris newspaper said shows ran "four or five times a day." See untitled article from the *Paris Advertiser,* 9 May 1878, *PTAED*, SM029060c. Puskas was perhaps too zealous in his pursuit of pecuniary gain: in the opinion of Andrew White, the honorary U.S. commissioner at the exposition, Puskas was so preoccupied with extracting profits from the commercial exhibition that he neglected an opportunity to put the phonograph before a key Paris Exposition committee that awarded prizes. *PTAE*, 4:408n.11.

page 67: **One of Edison's associates:** James Adams to Charles Batchelor, 5 July 1878, *PTAED*, D7802ZRK.

page 67: **Typical was this brief item:** "America Is Still Ahead," *NYDG*, 11 June 1878, *PTAED*, MBSB10667X. The *Daily Graphic* credited the item to the *Boston Post*. Another example from this same story, which had originally appeared in the *Buffalo Express:* "We shall have the great question regarding the hereafter settled beyond dispute directly, for have we not Mr. Edison?"

page 67: **they were harmless:** The phonograph was also the subject of good-natured teasing. Humorists said it was going to be a surrogate mother in the nursery; a cost-saving replacement of human chaplains in the Army; and a boon to tongue-tied lovers. See Mrs. Elizabeth S. Bladen, "Ladie's Department," *Philadelphia Times*, 7 June 1878, *PTAED*, SB031099a; "Army Chaplains vs. Phonographs," *NYT*, 2 June 1878.

page 67: **letters from strangers:** "Edison 'At Home.' "

page 68: **making plans to stay:** John Vincent to TAE, 25 February 1878, *PTAED*, D7829N. The prior correspondence that included Vincent's original invitation is missing; I assume that the participation of Edison's family was included in the arrangement, even though it was not made explicit here.

page 68: **"all the marvels of electricity":** John Vincent to TAE, 27 February 1878, *PTAED*, D7829N.

page 68: **Vincent pressed on:** John Vincent to TAE, 25 February 1878, *PTAED*, D7829N.

page 68: **Vincent was unmoved:** John Vincent to TAE, 27 February 1878, *PTAED*, D7829N.

page 68: **Croffut was also proving rather pushy:** William Croffut to TAE, 1 June 1878, *PTAED*, D7802ZNN, is Croffut's announcement of his plans. Given how close Menlo Park was situated to New York, his claim that he and his wife needed to stay overnight makes little sense. Edison's reply is not extant, but its tone can be guessed by the chagrin in Croffut's letter that followed: "Yours of yesterday is at hand. I don't know when I've felt so much like a fool as I do this minute. It didn't seem exactly so when I wrote you the other day, but now I feel like a self-invited guest. It isn't my way to impose myself upon friends, but I allowed my interest in you and my desire to gratify my wife's inclination to get the better of my discretion." William Croffut to TAE, 8 June 1878, *PTAED*, D7802ZOH.

page 68: **Painter urged Edison:** Uriah Painter to TAE, 12 June 1878, *PTAED*, D7802ZOU.

page 69: **a threat he had made:** J. W. S. Arnold to TAE, 20 March 1878, ENHS, in *PTAED*, D7802ZDX1.

page 69: **He abruptly accepted:** Edison apparently made the decision in early July. See his telegram to Professor Henry Draper, apparently sent in July 1878, *PTAED*, D7802ZUC.

page 69: **It was Barker's inspired idea:** George Barker to TAE, 12 July [1878], *PTAED*, D7802ZSG.

page 69: **The journal told readers:** "How to Build a Working Phonograph," *Scientific American*, 20 July 1878, *PTAED*.

page 70: **Batchelor's first reaction:** Charles Batchelor to TAE, 24 July 1878, *PTAED*, MBLB2003. If Edison responded, his letter or cable is not cataloged by *PTAED*.

page 70: **The manufacture, sale or use:** Office of Edison Speaking Phonograph Co., circular, 1 August 1878, *PTAED*, SB032127.

page 70: **Johnson also protested:** *PTAE*, 4:408n12.

page 70: **"Investigators have rights":** "The Rights of Investigators," *Scientific American*, 31 August 1878, *PTAED*, SB032035a.

page 71: **obtaining permission to ride:** TAE reminiscence, "First Batch," n.d., *PTAE*, 4:858.

page 71: **After the eclipse:** Ibid.

page 71: **When the two men:** TAE reminiscence, "Book No. 1," *PTAE*, 4:857.

page 72: **Edison did not fully appreciate:** Ibid., 4:856.

page 72: **he and his wife did not correspond:** I am mindful of the old adage "Absence of evidence is not evidence of absence," and know that, theoretically, the two could have corresponded and the letters subsequently lost or destroyed. Based on the documentary record, this seems most unlikely.

page 72: **Mrs. E's health is not:** Stockton Griffin to TAE, 5 August 1878, *PTAED*, D7802ZUQ.

page 73: **Barker formally presented Edison:** "Science at St. Louis," *New York Daily Herald*, 24 August 1878, *PTAED*, SB032055c.

page 73: **"The people":** "Edison's Trip and Inventions."

page 73: **His trip had been "bang-up":** "Tom Edison Back Again," *NYW*, 27 August 1878, *PTAED*, SB032075a.

page 73: **read a letter from an inventor:** "Tom Edison Back Again."

page 74: **He returned with lots of dazzling ideas:** "Four Hours with Edison," *NYS*, 29 August 1878.

page 75: **"Did you get":** "Tom Edison Back Again."

page 75: **It was also the very day:** Laboratory notebook, 27 August 1878, *PTAED*, NV16006.

CHAPTER 4. GETTING AHEAD

page 76: **In 1808, Humphry Davy:** Friedel and Israel, *Edison's Electric Light*, 7.

page 76: **An experimental installation:** Wolfgang Schivelbusch, *Disenchanted Night: The Industrialization of Light in the Nineteenth Century* (Berkeley: University of California Press, 1988), 55.

page 77: **Robert Louis Stevenson:** Quoted in Al Parsons, *Lightning in the Sun: A History of Florida Power Corporation, 1899–1974* (St. Petersburg, Fla.: Florida Power Corporation, 1974), 33.

page 77: **When an inventor:** Mel Gorman, "Charles F. Brush and the First Public Electric Street Lighting System in America," *Ohio Historical Quarterly,* April 1961, 133–134.

page 77: **The *New York Times* described:** "The Electric Light," *NYT,* 22 April 1878.

page 78: **J. W. Starr:** Friedel and Israel, *Edison's Electric Light,* 8. Friedel and Israel point out that Starr's inventions simply were not practical. Then again, I would add, neither were Edison's first attempts at designing a practical bulb.

page 78: **on his trip out west:** Ibid., 4.

page 79: **a curiously ghoulish thought:** "A Great Triumph," *New York Mall,* 10 September 1878, *PTAED,* SB032119a. The original article appeared in the *New York Sun.* The *Mall* reprinted it the same day, and it was the clipping from the *Mall* that Batchelor preserved in his scrapbook.

page 79: **Mr. Edison was enraptured:** Ibid. The excitement of the visitor brings to mind Apple's Steve Jobs's storied visit to Xerox's Palo Alto Research Center in 1979, when he glimpsed the first personal computer with software featuring Windows and guided by mice. Five years later, Apple introduced the Macintosh. In the view of Xerox PARC's later regretful director, George Pake, the significance of the visit was that it convinced Jobs that such a computer was "doable." Pake likened it to the Soviets' building of their first atomic bomb: "They developed it very quickly once they knew it was doable." See Douglas K. Smith and Robert C. Alexander, *Fumbling the Future: How Xerox Invented, then Ignored, the First Personal Computer* (New York: William Morrow, 1988), 242.

page 79: **"so simple":** "Edison's Electric Light," *NYS,* 20 October 1878, *PTAED,* MBSB20963.

page 80: **he recorded his excitement:** Laboratory pocket notebook, 1 January 1871, *PTAED,* NP002A1.

page 80: **set a far more ambitious goal:** William H. Bishop, "A Night with Edison," *Scribner's,* November 1878, 99.

page 80: **"I don't care":** "Mr. Edison's Use of Electricity," *New York Tribune,* 28 September 1878, *PTAED,* SB032142a.

page 81: **On the following Saturday:** "Edison's Newest Marvel," *NYS,* 16 September 1878, *PTAED,* SB032123a.

page 81: **He wrote Theodore Puskas:** TAE to Theodore Puskas, 22 September 1878, *PTAED,* D7802ZZBL.

page 81: **When Edison missed a meeting:** Stockton Griffin to Grosvenor Lowrey, 24 September 1878, *PTAED,* D7820K.

page 82: **When Lowrey tried again:** TAE to Grosvenor Lowrey, 26 September 1878, *PTAED,* D7820N.

page 82: **Drawing on his experience:** Friedel and Israel, *Edison's Electric Light*, 23.

page 82: **He had not yet succeeded:** Charles Bazerman, *The Languages of Edison's Light* (Cambridge, Mass: MIT Press, 1999), 161.

page 82: **He cabled George Gouraud:** TAE to George Gouraud, draft of cable, 8 October 1878, *PTAED*, D7821G.

page 82: **"panic in gas shares":** George Gouraud to TAE, cable, 7 October 1878, *PTAED*, D7821F.

page 82: **Gouraud wished:** George Gouraud to TAE, 16 October 1878, *PTAED*, D7802ZZFC.

page 83: **The British equivalent:** George Gouraud to TAE, 24 October 1878, *PTAED*, D7821U.

page 83: **When the *New York Herald* arrived:** "Edison's Electric Light," *NYH*, 12 October 1878, *PTAED*, MBSB20949.

page 83: **Running the sham demonstration:** "Edison's New Light," *NYDG*, 21 October 1878, *PTAED*, MBSB20960.

page 83: **reporter from a third newspaper:** "Edison's Electric Light," *NYH*, 12 October 1878, *PTAED*, MBSB20949.

page 83: **For another newspaper:** "Edison's Electric Light," *NYS*.

page 83: **The time sheets from his laboratory:** *PTAE*, 4:567n1.

page 84: **The exhibition model's best month:** *PTAE*, 4:572n1.

page 84: **netting Edison a commission:** Charles Bailey to TAE, 8 October 1878, *PTAED*, D7831C.

page 84: **The treasurer:** Charles Bailey to TAE, 8 October 1878, *PTAED*, D7831C.

page 84: **A couple of months later:** "Two Hours at Menlo Park," *NYDG*, 28 December 1878, *PTAED*, MBSB21091.

page 84: **William Vanderbilt and his friends:** TAE to Theodore Puskas, 5 October 1878, *PTAE*, 4:562.

page 84: **At the beginning of the nineteenth century:** Schivelbusch, *Disenchanted Night*, 51.

page 85: **It was also expensive:** Thomas J. Schlereth, *Victorian America: Transformations in Everyday Life* (New York: HarperPerennial, 1992), 114.

page 85: **The *New York Times*:** "Gas Stocks and Light," *NYT*, 27 October 1878.

page 85: **Edison credited the gas monopoly:** "Edison's Electric Light," *NYS*.

page 85: **The *Brooklyn Daily Eagle*:** "Revenge Is Sweet," *Brooklyn Daily Eagle*, 1 December 1878, *PTAED*, MBSB21072X.

page 85: **An "enormous abandonment":** "Gas Stocks and Light," *NYT*, 27 October 1878.

page 85: **The previous month:** Gorman, "Charles F. Brush," 135–136.

page 85: **William Sharon:** Charles M. Coleman, *P.G. & E. of California: The Centennial Story of Pacific Gas and Electric Company, 1852–1952* (New York: McGraw-Hill, 1952), 55.

page 85: **The gas-industry conventioneers:** "Gas Men in Council," *NYT*, 19 October 1878.

page 86: Speakers at the gas-industry convention: Ibid.

page 86: Edison had sent Charles Batchelor: "Edison's New Light," *NYDG.*

page 86: One independent observer: [Albert Salomon von Rothschild] to August Belmont, 25 October 1878, *PTAED,* D7821ZAW.

page 86: He blamed his reticence: Lemuel Serrell to TAE, 16 December 1878, *PTAED,* D7828ZFB. The phrase "than they are worth" was crossed out in the letter, but is restored here, as Serrell left it in perfectly legible form.

page 86: Not so easily put off: George Barker to TAE, 23 October 1878, *PTAED,* D7819ZAT.

page 87: had not yet signed: Barker wrote Edison on 23 October 1878, but Edison did not sign his agreement with the company until 15 November.

page 87: "Positively No Admittance": "Edison's New Light," *NYDG.*

page 87: Professor Barker would not be denied: George Barker to TAE, 23 October 1878, *PTAED,* D7819ZAT.

page 88: In the event: George Barker to TAE, 22 November 1878, *PTAED,* D7819ZCJ.

page 88: publicly covered for him: *PTAED,* 4:726n5.

page 88: privately indulged with Edison: George Barker to TAE, 22 November 1878, *PTAED,* D7819ZCJ.

page 88: The press was fascinated: "Edison's Electric Light," *NYS.*

page 88: Talking at such length: Edwin Fox to TAE, 20 October 1878, *PTAED,* D7805ZDW.

page 88: write two volumes of bestselling memoirs: Ulysses S. Grant, *Personal Memoirs of U.S. Grant* (New York: C. J. Webster, 1885–1886).

page 88: Days after he wrote this: Edwin Fox to TAE, 5 November 1878, *PTAED,* D7805ZEG.

page 89: A speed record in sycophancy: "Edison's Baby," *NYT,* 27 October 1878. The story suggested that the two hours of struggle over being dressed may have been masculine reaction to effeminate attire—"the daintiest muslin, with ruffles and furbelows, such as only a mother's fancy can imagine."

page 89: Without being privy: George Barker to TAE, 3 November 1878, *PTAED,* D7802ZZJD.

page 89: Edison had a different theory: "Two Hours at Menlo Park." The article does not mention that he was hurt by arc lights, but only arc lights could produce the intense light described here, and it is known from other sources that Edison rigged up arc lights for experimental purposes in the laboratory at this time. See Friedel and Israel, *Edison's Electric Light,* 48–49.

page 90: Now claims to have solved: R. G. Dun & Co. Credit Report, 10 December 1878, *PTAE,* 4:773.

page 90: When R. G. Dun wrote him: R. G. Dun & Co. to TAE, 4 February 1881, *PTAED,* D8123E.

page 90: He left negotiations: TAE to Grosvenor P. Lowrey, 3 October 1878, *PTAED,* LB003390.

page 90: **Lowrey, in turn:** Grosvenor P. Lowrey to Hamilton Twombly, 1 October 1878, *PTAED,* D7820ZAC. The lead investors in the Edison Electric Light Company included Twombly (whose father-in-law was William Vanderbilt), Tracy Edson, Norvin Green, and James Banker, associated with Western Union; Robert Cutting Jr., a law partner of Lowrey's; and Egisto Fabbri, representing the interests of Drexel, Morgan. The incorporation papers were filed on 16 October 1878 and are found in *PTAED,* QD012B0208.

page 90: **On 15 November:** Edison Electric Light Company and TAE, Agreement, 15 November 1878, *PTAED,* HM780053.

page 91: **A few days later:** Grosvenor Lowrey to TAE, 25 November 1878, *PTAED,* D7820ZCA.

page 91: **Lowrey again labored:** Grosvenor Lowrey to TAE, 10 December 1878, *PTAED,* D7821ZBR.

page 91: **In a matter of just a few weeks:** Grosvenor Lowrey to TAE, 23 December 1878, *PTAED,* D7820ZDI.

page 91: **In his telling:** "Invention by Accident," *NYW,* 17 November 1878, *PTAED,* MBSB21019X.

page 91: **"I have begun":** "Two Hours at Menlo Park."

page 92: **In January 1879:** Calvin Goddard to TAE, 22 January 1879, *PTAED,* D7920M.

page 92: **Not having heard:** William Croffut to TAE, 3 February 1879, *PTAED,* D7920W.

page 92: **note that Fox sent to Edison:** Edwin Fox to TAE, 26 January 1879, *PTAED,* D7920R.

page 93: **Francis Upton, a twenty-six-year-old physicist:** *PTAE,* 5:141n1.

page 93: **at Princeton:** Upton studied at Princeton's Green School of Science from 1875 to 1877, becoming the first student to receive an M.S. from Princeton. The university archives do not have information about his thesis, or whether one was submitted.

page 93: **in the Astor Library:** Francis Upton to Charles Farley, 29 December 1878, *PTAED,* MU005.

page 93: **In November 1878:** Francis Upton to Charles Farley, 22 November 1878, *PTAED,* MU002. Accepting the offer to move to Menlo Park meant Upton could not return to Germany to resume his postgraduate studies. Life in Germany would have been "extremely pleasant," he wrote his mother, but "there I would only learn how to spend money. Here I will learn how to earn it." Francis Upton to Lucy Upton, 7 November 1878, *PTAED,* MU001.

page 93: **Upon arrival in Menlo Park:** "Two Hours at Menlo Park." Edison referred in a latter to working with "6 experimental assistants." TAE to Theodore Puskas, 3 January 1879, *PTAED,* LB004079. Upton arrived on 13 or 14 December, and two weeks later was "learning how to sleep daytimes." Francis Upton to Charles Farley, 29 December 1878, *PTAED,* MU005.

page 93: **When a tornado:** "The Electric Light," *NYH,* 11 December 1878, *PTAED,* MBSB21048X.

page 93: **when Edison was coming to the realization:** Friedel and Israel, *Edison's Electric Light*, 51.

page 94: **Even when he decided:** Grosvenor Lowrey to TAE, 25 January 1879, *PTAED*, D7920Q.

page 94: **The investors did stand by the inventor:** Francis Upton to Elijah Upton, 23 February 1879, *PTAED*, MU007.

page 94: **At times:** Francis Upton to Elijah Upton, 2 March 1879, *PTAED*, MU008.

page 94: **A few weeks later:** Francis Upton to Elijah Upton, 23 March [1879], *PTAED*, MU009.

page 94: **In May:** Francis Upton to TAE, 19 May 1879, *PTAED*, D7919ZAP.

page 95: **Inexperience with the world:** Francis Upton to TAE, 19 May 1879, *PTAED*, D7919ZAQ. Upton sent his note with the correct figures on the same day as he had sent the first note to Edison.

page 95: **Edison made his offer:** Francis Upton to Elijah Upton, 15 June 1879, *PTAED*, MU017. In Silicon Valley in the 1990s, equity in the form of stock options became the most important component of compensation at technology-based start-up companies. For a good description of the "options culture," see Justin Fox, "The Next Best Thing to Free Money," *Fortune*, 7 July 1997, 70–84.

page 95: **In writing about his quandary:** Francis Upton to Elijah Upton, 22 June 1879, *PTAED*, MU018.

page 95: **Upton elected:** Francis Upton to Elijah Upton, 6 July 1879, *PTAED*, MU021.

page 95: **He immediately felt:** Francis Upton to Elijah Upton, 7 September 1879, *PTAED*, MU030.

page 95: **As time passed:** Francis Upton to Elijah Upton, 19 October 1879, *PTAED*, MU031.

page 96: **his laboratory colleague:** Jehl, *Reminiscences*, 351–356.

page 96: **Batchelor wrote:** Charles Batchelor, laboratory notebook, 22 October 1879, *PTAED*, N052105.

page 96: **He did tell the *New York Times*:** "Edison's Electric Light," *NYT*, 21 October 1879.

page 97: **"He is always sanguine":** Francis Upton to Elijah Upton, 2 November 1879, *PTAED*, MU033.

page 97: **"Continual trouble":** Francis Upton to Elijah Upton, 9 November 1879, *PTAED*, MU034.

page 97: **in mid-November:** Francis Upton to Elijah Upton, 22 November 1879, *PTAED*, MU036.

page 97: **Upton, however, did not have to wait:** Francis Upton to Elijah Upton, 30 November 1879, *PTAED*, MU037.

CHAPTER 5. STAGECRAFT

page 98: **Occasionally, on a Saturday night:** Jehl, *Reminiscences,* 503.

page 98: **one New York paper:** "Edison's Life," *NYH,* 10 January 1880, *PTAED,* MBSB21414X.

page 98: **French actress and singer:** On the occasion of the opening in December 2005 of an exhibition, Sarah Bernhardt: The Art of High Drama, at the Jewish Museum in New York, the *New York Times* art critic Edward Rothstein said contemporaneous accounts of Bernhardt's voice described it as being "almost animalistic." See "A Celebrity Extraordinaire Who Rivaled Eiffel Tower," *NYT,* 2 December 2005.

page 99: **Bernhardt's original plan:** Sarah Bernhardt, *My Double Life: The Memoirs of Sarah Bernhardt* (Albany: State University of New York, 1999), 261–264; Dyer and Martin, *Edison,* 737.

page 100: **By that time:** Francis Upton to Elijah Upton, 7 December 1879, *PTAED,* MU038. Lizzie Upton came up with the idea of decorating the lamps with ribbons and flowers. Francis Upton to Elijah Upton, 21 December 1879, *PTAED,* MU040.

page 100: **was given exclusive access:** Jehl, *Reminiscences,* 380. Fox knew he would be able to paint a much better "pen picture" if he could gain access to the laboratory and witness events for himself rather than rely upon someone else's account obtained through an interview. In a letter he had sent Edison a year earlier, he wrote, "A man may sit down and open out words by the hour descriptive, say, if you please of the beauty of some picturesque landscape, yet unless his eyes have feasted upon the glory he describes his words fall flat and aimless." Edwin Fox to TAE, 5 November 1878, *PTAED,* D7805ZEG.

page 101: **On Sunday:** "Edison's Light," *NYH,* 28 December 1879, *PTAED,* MBSB21395X.

page 101: **catching Edison by surprise:** Upton assumed that Fox had deliberately broken his agreement with Edison, selling out "at a good price." Francis Upton to Elijah Upton, 21 December 1879, *PTAED,* MU040; Jehl's later account told a different story: that the *Herald* had been given clearance by someone at the laboratory, but not by Edison. Jehl repeatedly refers to Edwin Fox as "Marshall Fox." Jehl, *Reminiscences,* 380–381.

page 101: **A *New York Herald* editorial:** "Edison's Eureka—the Electric Light at Last," *NYH,* 21 December 1879, *PTAED,* MBSB21378X.

page 101: **William Sawyer:** "Edison's Electric Light," *NYW,* 24 December 1879, *PTAED,* QD012G4172.

page 101: **He dared Edison:** William Sawyer, "Electrician Sawyer's Challenge to Electrician Edison," *NYS,* 22 December 1879, *PTAED,* CC014016.

page 101: **Edison returned the challenge:** "Edison's Horseshoe Light," *NYS,* 23 December 1879, *PTAED,* MBSB21390.

page 101: **the publicity:** "Edison's Electric Light."

page 102: **At that time, Edison bragged:** "Edison's Lamp Yet Burning," *NYS,* 24 December 1879, *PTAED,* MBSB21392X.

page 102: **He responded with a public promise:** "Edison's Horseshoe Light."
page 102: **On 26 December:** Egisto Fabbri to TAE, 26 December 1879, *PTAED*, D7920ZBO.
page 102: **He did not openly defy:** "Edison's Light," *NYH*, 28 December 1879, *PTAED*, MBSB21395X.
page 102: **The next night:** [article title omitted], *NYH*, 29 December 1879, cited in Jehl, *Reminiscences*, 411.
page 102: **more arrived the next night:** "Electricity and Gas," *NYH*, 30 December 1879, *PTAED*, MBSB21401X.
page 103: **Two and then four more:** "A Night with Edison," *NYH*, 31 December 1879, *PTAED*, MBSB21402b. Sarah Jordan was Mary Edison's stepsister.
page 103: **Edison Electric Light Company:** Grosvenor Lowrey to TAE, 13 November 1879, *PTAED*, D7920ZBI.
page 103: **Company stock:** Francis Upton to Elijah Upton, 28 December 1879, *PTAED*, MU041.
page 103: **The spike in prices:** "Edison and the Skeptics," *NYT*, 4 January 1880.
page 103: **On New Year's Eve:** "Edison's Great Work," *NYH*, 1 January 1880, *PTAED*, MBSB21405a.
page 104: **When he appeared:** "Crowding Edison," *NYH*, 2 January 1880, *PTAED*, MBSB21407a.
page 104: **lab assistants were convinced:** *PTAE*, 5:540.
page 104: **the printed condemnation:** "Crowding Edison."
page 104: **Their vigilance was needed:** TAE reminiscence, "Second Batch," n.d., *PTAE*, 5:1025–1026.
page 104: **the *New York Tribune*:** "A Malicious Visitor," *New York Tribune*, 2 January 1880, *PTAED*, MBSB21407b.
page 105: **What a happy man:** "The Great Edison Scare," *Journal of Gas Lighting*, 20 January 1880, *PTAED*, MBSB21440X. Reprinted from the *Saturday Review* published in England on 10 January 1880.
page 105: **The price of Edison Electric Light Company stock:** "Mr. Edison and His Critics," *NYS*, 24 January 1880, *PTAED*, MBSB21450X.
page 105: **At this moment Edison:** "The Coming Light," *Philadelphia Record*, 12 February 1880, *PTAED*, SM014034.
page 105: **Edward Johnson sighed:** Edward Johnson to Uriah Painter, 10 December 1880, *PTAE*, 5:492–493n5.
page 106: **Edison took what solace he could:** "The Coming Light."
page 106: **A professional snoop:** Jehl, *Reminiscences*, 700–703.
page 106: **The company directors were willing:** Ibid., 558–559, 562–563.
page 107: **"Be thou to me":** Grosvenor Lowrey to Kate Armour, n.d. [May 1880], HFM & GVRC, Box 10, Folder 34.
page 107: **Lowrey also told his beloved:** Grosvenor Lowrey to Kate Armour [written in Menlo Park, New Jersey], 30 April 1880, HFM & GVRC, Box 10, Folder 34.
page 107: **When Lowrey showed Edison:** Grosvenor Lowrey to Kate Armour, 14 March 1880, HFM & GVRC, Box 10, Folder 34.

page 107: **A man who did odd jobs:** David Trumbull Marshall, *Recollections of Edison* (Boston: Christopher, 1931), 26.

page 108: **he first sketched out:** "Edison at Home," *Denver Tribune,* 25 April 1880, *PTAED,* SM015018a.

page 108: **It was the picture:** Marshall, *Recollections of Edison,* 17–18.

page 109: **"The smell was terrific":** Dyer and Martin, *Edison,* 634–635.

page 109: **In early June:** Grosvenor Lowrey to Kate Armour, 5 June 1880, HFM & GVRC, Box 10, Folder 34.

page 109: **The first bamboo hunter:** Dyer and Martin, *Edison,* 636–637.

page 110: **Edison placed the blame:** TAE to Vesey Butler, 4 November 1880, *PTAED,* LB006521.

page 110: **another emissary, William Moore,** Dyer and Martin, *Edison,* 300–301. Before departing from San Francisco in October, Moore visited the *Columbia* and wrote back to Edison that half of the bulbs had burned out, leaving the captain rather desperate for replacements. William Moore to TAE, 17 October 1880, *PTAED,* D8020ZHY.

page 110: **John Branner:** Dyer and Martin, *Edison,* 301–302. Dyer and Martin misspell Branner's name as "Brauner." Many decades later, Branner served as president of Stanford University, from 1913 to 1915. Edison funded another bamboo hunter, Frank McGowan, who was sent to Brazil in September 1887 and returned a year and a half later with bamboo and incredible stories of his inland travels. See "Frank McGowan's Journey Through South American Wilds," *NYS,* 2 May 1889, *PTAED,* MBSB2457.

page 110: **Edison designated Menlo Park itself:** Francis Upton to Elijah Upton, 9 May 1880, *PTAED,* MU048.

page 110: **The work was well advanced:** Friedel and Israel, *Edison's Electric Light,* 179.

page 111: **In October, Edwin Fox:** Edwin Fox to TAE, 22 October 1880, *PTAED,* D8020ZHZ.

page 111: **As far as Edison was concerned:** "Electric Light," *NYH,* 18 November 1880.

page 111: **installed a working exhibition:** "Lights for a Great City," *NYT,* 21 December 1880.

page 111: **Edison must have been upset:** George Barker to TAE, 26 November 1880, *PTAED,* D8020ZJC.

page 111: **cartoons that turned:** Cartoon captioned "The Decadence of the Wizard of Menlo Park," General Electric Corporation, 1880, cited in David E. Nye, *The Invented Self: An Anti-Biography from Documents of Thomas A. Edison* (Odense, Denmark: Odense University Press, 1983), 116–117.

page 112: **The Brush Electric Light Company:** "The Electric Light," *New York Post,* 21 December 1880, *PTAED,* MBSB21560X; "Rival Electric Lights," *New York Star,* 21 December 1880, *PTAED,* MBSB21559X.

page 112: **The debut of Brush lighting:** "Lights for a Great City"; "Broadway Illuminated," *NYH,* 21 December 1880; "Electric Light," *New York Post.*

page 113: **Department of Public Works tried:** "Electric Light," *New York Post.*

page 113: **Edison's consent:** Lowrey had Edison handwrite the invitation, which was a very straightforward invitation to see "an exhibition of Electric Lighting," without reference to a special feast. Letterpress invitation to exhibition of lighting at Menlo Park, 18 December 1880, HFM & GVRC, Box 47, Folder 47–40,

page 114: **All were alight:** "The Aldermen Visit Edison," *NYT*, 21 December 1880.

page 114: **Two years before:** Jehl, *Reminiscences,* 690–693.

page 114: **one reporter described Edison:** "Rival Electric Lights."

page 115: **"That's the last":** "The Wizard of Menlo Park," *NYH*, 21 December 1880.

page 115: **It fell to Lowrey:** Jehl, *Reminiscences,* 781–782.

page 115: **Edison did not know:** "The Aldermen Visit Edison."

page 116: **The guests then followed:** "Aldermen at Menlo Park," *New York Truth,* 21 December 1880, *PTAED,* MBSB21557X.

page 116: **the aldermen would not back down:** "Lightning over Snow," *NYH*, 20 January 1881, *PTAED,* MBSB21573.

page 116: **Brush Electric had not had to pay:** "The Aldermen and the Electric Light," *NYH*, 21 January 1881, *PTAED,* MBSB21571X.

page 116: **He also made noises:** Charles Bazerman, *The Languages of Edison's Light* (Cambridge, Mass: MIT Press, 1999), 226.

page 116: **His representatives:** Friedel and Israel, *Edison's Electric Light,* 207.

page 116: **In the meantime:** Ibid., 192–193.

page 117: **on Fifth Avenue:** Jehl, *Reminiscences,* 924.

page 117: **With the installation of a gas-powered power plant:** Edward Johnson to Uriah Painter, 9 February 1881, *PTAE,* 5:983–984.

page 117: **In early February 1881:** Ibid.

page 117: **At the end of the month:** Jehl, *Reminiscences,* 926.

page 117: **make himself available:** Samuel Insull, *The Memoirs of Samuel Insull: An Autobiography,* ed. Larry Plachno (Polo, Ill.: Transportation Trails, 1992), 32.

page 118: **he would do wicked impressions:** Jehl, *Reminiscences,* 996.

page 118: **In its first year:** Dyer and Martin, *Edison,* 361.

page 118: **The Menlo Park laboratory:** Jehl, *Reminiscences,* 862.

CHAPTER 6. IMMERSION

page 119: **Only "the very rich":** James D. McCabe, *New York by Sunlight and Gaslight* (Philadelphia: Douglass Bros.; repr. by Greenwich House, 1882; 1984 repr.), 62–63.

page 119: **Edison had drawn up blueprints:** Commerford Martin, *Forty Years of Edison Service, 1882–1922* (New York: New York Edison Press, 1922), 34.

page 119: **When the directors:** TAE to George Gouraud, 7 March 1881, *PTAED,* LB008024. This letter book copy is exceedingly difficult to read. A typeset and annotated copy is provided in *PTAE,* 5:996–997.

page 119: **Etna Iron Works:** Roach's property was located on Goerck Street, a street that later disappeared in the course of urban renewal.

page 120: **The two partners decided:** Jehl, *Reminiscences,* 744.

page 120: **One reporter marveled:** "The Doom of Gas," *St. Louis Post-Dispatch,* 1 May 1882, *PTAED,* MBSB52192.

page 121: **The family doctor:** Leslie D. Ward to TAE, 18 January 1882, *PTAED,* D8214C.

page 121: **Often he napped on the premises:** Dyer and Martin, *Edison,* 400.

page 121: **He insisted on custom building:** Friedel and Israel, *Edison's Electric Light,* 173.

page 121: **Edison had originally planned:** Dyer and Martin, *Edison,* 385.

page 121: **H. O. Thompson, the city's commissioner of public works:** Ibid., 393.

page 122: **They read in the newspaper:** "Killed by an Electric Shock," *NYT,* 11 August 1881, reprinted from the *Buffalo Commercial Advertiser,* 8 August 1881.

page 122: **In England:** Untitled article in *Morning Advertiser,* 10 January 1882, *PTAED,* MBSB51975.

page 122: **a German proposed building:** "A Chair for Criminals," *NYT,* 28 July 1881.

page 122: **Edison's company:** "Underground Wires," *Bulletin of the Edison Electric Light Company,* no. 4 (24 February 1882), 9.

page 122: **fibrillation follows:** Today, defibrillators apply a jolt of electric current to the chest to restart the heart's regular beating pattern, but it is direct current that supplies the corrective shock.

page 123: **When the Pearl Street station:** Jehl, *Reminiscences,* 1059–1061.

page 123: **The police officers present:** Dyer and Martin, *Edison,* 408–409.

page 123: **the newspapers had received word:** Jehl, *Reminiscences,* 1059–1061.

page 123: **The president of Edison Electric:** "Horses Shocked," *NYT,* 25 August 1882.

page 123: **Edison was privately telling Charles Clarke:** Jehl, *Reminiscences,* 1059–1061. Faulty Edison Electric lines beneath the street knocked horses down in an incident a few years later. Here, too, "people who saw the affair thought it was very funny." See "Horses Thrown Down," *NYT,* 2 June 1889. The problem of street-level electrical shocks is not merely a curiosity of that early era. On 16 January 2004, a young woman, Jodie Lane, was electrocuted while walking her dogs in the East Village. The dogs stepped on a metal plate that was electrified by stray current; they survived, but Lane did not. Regrettably, Major Eaton's inclination to deny, deny, deny lives on in his latter-day successors in New York City. Consolidated Edison was less than forthcoming about the origins of the accident, and reporters uncovered 539 complaints of electrical jolts delivered by the streets of New York in the five years preceding Lane's death, only a small portion of which had been reported to the city authorities. "Con Ed's Shocking Plea for Mercy," *New York Daily News,* 13 March 2004. Lane's family reached a $7.2 million settlement with Con Ed, which included $1 million that funded a scholarship in the victim's name at Columbia University. "Utility Will Pay $7.2 Million in Electrocution," *NYT*, 24 November 2004.

page 124: **The** *Bulletin:* "Danger from Gas," *Bulletin of the Edison Electric Light Company,* no. 6 (27 March 1882), *PTAED*, CB006:4–5; "Danger from Gas," *Bulletin of the Edison Electric Light Company*, no. 7 (17 April 1882): 9–10.

page 124: **the simple physical fact:** "Light Ahead," *Los Angeles Times*, 12 February 1882.

page 124: **The gas industry:** Untitled article, *Morning Advertiser*, 10 January 1882, *PTAED*, MBSB51975.

page 124: **An electric corset:** "A New Use of Electricity," *NYT*, 12 January 1882.

page 124: **The prospective advantages:** Owen Gill to TAE, 27 January 1881, *PTAED*, D8120X.

page 125: **Such installations:** TAE to Owen Gill, 29 January 1881, *PTAED*, LB006874.

page 125: **One New York company:** "Hinds, Ketcham & Co., New York," *Edison Electric Light Company Bulletin* (24 February 1882), *PTAED*, CB004:2.

page 125: **The Blue Mountain House:** Dyer and Martin, *Edison*, 446.

page 125: **Brush was selling:** "The Electric Light," *New York Post*, 1 December 1881, *PTAED*, MBSB41778.

page 126: **In the three months:** "Edison's Electric Light," *NYT*, 1 March 1881.

page 126: **The laying of the mains:** "The Electric Light," *New York Post*.

page 126: **a new possibility had appeared:** Peter Tocco, "The Night They Turned the Lights on in Wabash," *Indiana Magazine of History* 95 (December 1999): 352.

page 127: **In San Jose:** Charles M. Coleman, *P.G. & E. of California: The Centennial Story of Pacific Gas and Electric Company, 1852–1952* (New York: McGraw-Hill, 1952), 72–74. The public subscription raised $3,456, but construction costs turned out to be more than expected and the tower was sold in 1882 to the San Jose Brush Electric Company. See "The Day the Tower Fell," *San Jose Mercury News*, 18 September 1884.

page 127: **Wild fowl crashed:** "The Famous Old Electric Tower," *San Jose Mercury News*, 14 March 1965.

page 127: **In Detroit:** Raymond Miller, *Kilowatts at Work: A History of the Detroit Edison Company* (Detroit: Wayne State University Press, 1984), 33.

page 127: **A British observer:** "The Tower System of Lighting Towns," *Electrical Engineer*, February 1885, 129.

page 127: **Wabash, the pioneer:** Tocco, "The Night They Turned the Lights on in Wabash," 352.

page 127: **shall search the roads:** "Light Ahead," *Los Angeles Times*, 12 February 1882.

page 127: **When a history of Detroit:** George B. Catlin, *The Story of Detroit* (Detroit: Detroit News, 1923), 608.

page 128: **The only way Edison Electric:** E. A. Mills, "The Development of Electric Sign Lighting," *Transactions of the Illuminating Engineering Society* 15:6 (30 August 1920): 370–371.

page 128: **Edison was able to test:** Friedel and Israel, *Edison's Electric Light,* 217–218.

page 128: **Edison deployed:** Dyer and Martin, *Edison,* 385–386.

page 128: **He also learned:** "The Electric Light in Houses," *Harper's Weekly,* 24 June 1882, 394.

page 129: **In May 1882:** "The Doom of Gas," *St. Louis Post-Dispatch,* 1 May 1882, *PTAED,* MBSB52192.

page 129: **Edison also boasted:** Ibid.

page 129: **William Vanderbilt was the first:** Dyer and Martin, *Edison,* 373–374.

page 130: **The unhappy ending:** "Doom of Gas."

page 130: **J. P. Morgan wanted Edison:** Herbert L. Satterlee, *J. Pierpoint Morgan: An Intimate Portrait* (New York: Macmillan, 1939), 207–208. The engineer's technical expertise was needed to make repairs. Problems began on the very first day of operation, when a defective aperture threw off a shower of sparks. See Sherburne Eaton to TAE, 8 June 1882, *PTAED,* D8226S.

page 131: **The generating plant:** Satterlee, *J. Pierpoint Morgan,* 208.

page 131: **Morgan prized:** Ibid., 212–215.

page 132: **In Appleton, Wisconsin:** Forrest McDonald, *Let There Be Light: The Electric Utility Industry in Wisconsin, 1881–1955* (Madison, Wis.: American History Research Center, 1957), 35–36.

page 132: **It could have been ready:** Ibid., 15.

page 133: **not all portions:** "Edison's Illuminators," *NYH,* 5 September 1882, *PTAED,* SM016006b.

page 133: **On the afternoon of 4 September 1882:** Friedel and Israel, *Edison's Electric Light,* 222. The *Herald* places Edison in the Pearl Street workshop, not in Morgan's office, when the power was turned on. "Edison's Illuminators," *NYH,* 5 September 1882, *PTAED,* SM016006b.

page 133: **It received the most complete coverage:** "Edison's Electric Light," *NYT,* 5 September 1882.

page 133: **The official beginning:** "Edison's Illuminators."

page 134: **It had taken four long years:** Charles Bazerman, *The Languages of Edison's Light* (Cambridge, Mass: MIT Press, 1999), 233–234.

page 134: **At the time of the first announcement:** "Edison's Newest Marvel," *NYS,* 16 September 1878, *PTAED,* SB032123a.

page 134: **After a few weeks:** "Edison's Electric Light," *NYS,* 20 October 1878, *PTAED,* MBSB20963.

page 135: **Characteristically, Edison announced:** "Edison's Electric Light," *NYH,* 3 December 1878, *PTAED,* MBSB21047; Friedel and Israel, *Edison's Electric Light,* 64.

page 135: **The only shortcoming:** Harold Passer, *The Electrical Manufacturers, 1875–1900* (Cambridge, Mass.: Harvard University Press, 1953), 183.

page 135: **Edison Electric did not charge:** Dyer and Martin, *Edison,* 409.

page 135: **Short circuits:** Jehl, *Reminiscences,* 1083–1084. Short circuits beneath New York's streets produced sights more unusual than this. Almost twenty years later, a short circuit in an electric trolley sent up through the trolley's street-level slot a sheet of flame four feet tall that traveled up the street. Fortunately, there were no injuries. "Electric Display at Bridge," *NYT,* 4 October 1902.

page 135: **Some customers seemed:** T. A. Edison, "Introduction," in Edison Construction Department, "Questions for Central Stations Engineers," 1883, *PTAED,* CD001: image 42.

page 135: **One such customer:** Dyer and Martin, *Edison,* 437.

page 136: **J. P. Morgan:** Martin, *Forty Years of Edison Service,* 61–62; Dyer and Martin, *Edison,* 410–411.

page 137: **The initial data:** Martin, *Forty Years of Edison Service,* 66–67.

page 137: **He had said the previous year:** "Doom of Gas."

page 137: **Two months after Edison Electric:** "Edison and His Light" clipping from unidentified publication [but likely a Port Huron, Michigan, newspaper], 13 March 1883, *PTAED,* D8320D1.

page 137: **After a year:** Martin, *Forty Years of Edison Service,* 66–67.

page 137: **To Edison's credit:** Jehl, *Reminiscences,* 936.

page 138: **The second district:** Passer, *Electrical Manufacturers,* 120.

page 138: **the nation's first hydropower plant:** McDonald, *Let There Be Light,* 35–37.

page 138: **The only line of products:** Forrest McDonald, *Insull* (Chicago: University of Chicago Press, 1962), 29–30.

page 139: **he was invited to Boston:** Jehl, *Reminiscences,* 997–998.

CHAPTER 7. STARTING ANEW

page 143: **She was plagued:** Paul Israel corrects a mistake perpetuated by previous biographers who assumed Edison was referring to his ailing wife when he telegraphed Samuel Insull in April 1884: "Send trained man nurse who is not afraid of person out of mind. Send as soon as possible." TAE to Samuel Insull, telegram, 7 April 1884, *PTAED,* D8414F. Israel says the nurse was needed not for Mary but for her father, who died two days later. Israel, *Edison,* 232. We do have fragmentary evidence, however, that at that same time Mary was unwell, too, such as her complaint that "I am so awfully sick I am afraid. . . . My head is nearly splitting and my throat is very sore." Mary Edison to Samuel Insull, 30 April 1884, *PTAED,* D8414I.

page 143: **what her doctor termed:** Robert Lozier to John Tomlinson, 9 August 1884, *PTAED,* D841401.

page 143: **His daughter Marion:** Marion Edison Oser reminiscences, quoted in Israel, *Edison,* 230. Israel suggests that Edison "felt a sense of guilt for the long, hard hours he had worked at the expense of his family."

page 143: **Mary's mother, Margaret:** Conot, *Streak of Luck,* 22; Madeleine Sloane, Oral History, 1 December 1972, ENHS, Interview #1, 18.

page 144: newspapers and magazines: Wyn Wachhorst, *Thomas Alva Edison: An American Myth* (Cambridge, Mass.: MIT Press, 1981), 44–45.

page 144: A book about prominent New Yorkers: Stephen Fiske, *Off-Hand Portraits of Prominent New Yorkers* (New York: Geo. R. Lockwood & Son, 1884), 108.

page 144: With Edison's blessing: Jehl, *Reminiscences,* 1000.

page 144: marched down Madison Avenue: "Electrical Stunts in 1884," *Edison Monthly,* October 1925, 237–238.

page 144: the "Edison Darkey": "The Edison Exhibit at the Philadelphia Electrical Exhibition," *Scientific American,* 18 October 1884, 246.

page 144: One report said: "Electrical Stunts in 1884."

page 144: Longtime Edison associate William Hammer: Electrical Diablerie, n.d., Smithsonian/National Museum of American History, William J. Hammer Collection. The pamphlet credits two primary sources: *NYW,* 3 January 1885, and *Newark Daily Advertising and Journal,* 3 January 1885. The Smithsonian has placed the full text of the pamphlet online; see http://americanhistory.si.edu/archives/d8069d.htm.

page 145: Edison wrote privately: Dagobert D. Runes, ed., *The Diary and Sundry Observations of Thomas Alva Edison* (1948; reprint, New York: Greenwood Press, 1968), 29.

page 145: Reading a headline: "John Roach Embarrassed," *NYT,* 19 July 1885.

page 145: Just a year before: TAE to John Roach, 25 June 1884, *PTAED,* LBCD7013.

page 145: William Croffut, the reporter: W. A. Croffut, "Edison's Latest Invention," *Omaha Bee,* 20 June 1885, *PTAED,* SB017010a.

page 146: a director of the company: "Overhead Wires," *Philadelphia Press,* 31 May 1885, *PTAED,* SB017083b and SB017014a.

page 146: let go of the captain's chair: In the summer and fall of 1884, Edison's twenty-two-year-old assistant Samuel Insull had conducted a brilliant and successful proxy fight that bested J. P. Morgan and secured his employer's control of the board. Forrest McDonald, *Insull* (Chicago: University of Chicago Press, 1962), 31–32.

page 146: he asked his old friend: Israel, *Edison,* 234.

page 146: the two men founded: Ibid., 237.

page 146: William Croffut obligingly offered: "The Wizard Edison," *Chicago Tribune,* 30 April 1885, *PTAED,* SM062040. This wireless technology is more interesting today perhaps than it would have been then. The technology relied upon the principle of induction, so cannot be said to be a direct antecedent of today's cell phones or wireless broadband. But it does offer an early instance of the quest to employ electricity to communicate while on the move.

page 147: Edison directed Samuel Insull: TAE to Samuel Insull, n.d. [early May 1885], *PTAED,* D8503ZEX.

page 147: In his note of thanks: William Croffut to Samuel Insull, 15 May 1885, *PTAED,* D8541M.

page 147: **Edison had sent the shares:** TAE to Samuel Insull, n.d. [early May 1885], *PTAED*, D8503ZEX.

page 147: **Insull soon concluded:** Samuel Insull to TAE, 29 March 1886, *PTAED*, LB021464.

page 148: **Edison met:** *New Orleans Picayune*, 8 February 1886, *PTAED*, SB017124d. The clipping is untitled.

page 148: **Edison invited Insull:** TAE to Samuel Insull, 27 June 1885, *PTAED*, D8503ZBD. Edison failed to make his verb agree with the plural subject; he also omitted "of" after "lots."

page 149: **entertainment of the group:** Edison refers at one point to the guests sitting around a table while making individual entries. Sharing must have begun before the ink was dry; Edison declared another's efforts "very witty." Runes, *Diary*, 20.

page 149: **The first entry:** Ibid., 3.

page 149: **a later entry:** Ibid., 22.

page 149: **Edison reported:** Ibid., 6–7, 8.

page 149: **he submitted out of fear:** Ibid., 14. On p. 29 he again refers to the shirts: "Donned a boiled and starched emblem of respectability."

page 149: **a book by Hawthorne:** Ibid., 4.

page 149: **two suicides:** Ibid., 10.

page 149: **his description of a clerk:** Ibid., 31–32.

page 149: **Edison's trip into town:** Ibid., 17.

page 149: **When Marion showed her father:** Ibid., 6–7.

page 150: **Edison thinks Marion's jealousy:** Ibid., 22.

page 150: **Edison had noticed:** Ibid., 16.

page 150: **A contemporary newspaper:** *New Orleans Picayune*, 8 February 1886.

page 150: **The first meeting:** The two men could not have gotten to know each other very well, or Miller would not have had so much to tell his daughter two years later, after a stay with Edison that afforded "a better opportunity to get acquainted with him." Lewis Miller to Mina Miller Edison, 26 April 1887, *PTAED*, FH001AAA.

page 150: **traveled farther upstate:** Israel, *Edison*, 247.

page 150: **Looking back on the trip:** "Autobiographical," in Runes, *Diary*, 54–55.

page 150: **story from family lore:** Lillian P. Warren, interview transcript, 2 July 1973, ENHS, 3. Warren was the niece of Lillian Gilliland, Ezra T. Gilliland's wife.

page 151: **Edison said that Miller tapped back:** "Autobiographical," in Runes, *Diary*, 54–55.

page 151: **Edison formally wrote:** TAE to Lewis Miller, 30 September 1885, *PTAED*, B037AA. Paul Israel points out the possibility that Insull helped with the letter. Insull was a skilled writer and Edison was not. Insull's role would explain how the letter was polished to a high gloss. Israel, *Edison*, 247.

page 151: **Reporters were present:** "Mr. Edison's Wedding," *NYT*, 25 February

1886. Edison was accompanied by his closest colleagues, including Insull, Edward Johnson, Charles Batchelor, and Sigmund Bergmann.

page 151: **train trip south:** "Edison to Invent a Cotton-Picker," *NYW,* 27 February 1886, *PTAED,* SB017119c.

page 152: **each entry dated:** For an example, see the entry about incandescent bulbs for 18 March 1886 in *PTAED,* N314003.

page 152: **she commuted daily:** Norman Speiden, transcript of ENHS tour, 8 January 1971, ENHS, 24.

page 152: **after almost forty years:** Martha Coman and Hugh Weir, "The Most Difficult Husband in America," *Collier's,* 18 July 1925.

page 152: **She weighed the advantages:** Ibid.

page 152: **planned suburban community:** Samuel Swift, "Llewellyn Park: The First American Suburban Community," *House and Garden,* June 1903, 327. Llewellyn Haskell, the community's founder, belonged to a religious group self-named the Perfectionists. For an early contemporaneous account of the community's founding, see "Llewellyn Park," *NYT,* 23 April 1865.

page 152: **Henry Pedder:** "Mr. Pedder's Luxurious Habits," *NYT,* 19 July 1884. Pedder was a longtime employee of the Arnold, Constable & Company department store ("Everything from Cradle to Grave"). He was a clerk, not a principal, but by dint of his seniority, he was privy to all the financial details of the business. The New York newspapers savored the story, but did not explain why no one at Arnold, Constable had wondered before then how a clerk earning $30,000 a year had managed to pay cash for a home that cost at least $200,000.

page 152: **The real estate agent:** Edward P. Hamilton & Co. to TAE, 12 January 1886, *PTAED,* D8603L.

page 153: **So eager was the department store:** W. A. Croffut, Interview with TAE, *New York Mail and Express,* 8 October 1887, cited in Nerney, *Edison,* 277. The price of $125,000 is the amount listed in the county records. See Kristin S. Herron, *The House at Glenmont: Historic Furnishings Report I* (West Orange, N.J.: National Park Service, Edison National Historic Site, 1998), 14n16.

page 153: **exhibition space:** In the 1990s, Bill Gates, uneasy about the expense of his own budget-busting family home, wanted the public to know that its Tomorrowland furnishings would help Microsoft show company guests the way to the future. Bill Gates, Nathan Myhrvold, and Peter Rinearson, *The Road Ahead: Completely Revised and Up to Date* (New York: Penguin, 1996), 249–258.

page 153: **Chandeliers had gas burners:** Charles Edison, Oral History, 14 April 1953, ENHS.

page 153: **Speaking tubes:** Theodore M. Edison, Oral History, 26 July 1970, ENHS.

page 153: **He wrote in his diary:** Runes, *Diary,* 8.

page 154: **The three-story main building:** TAE to James Hood Wright, August 1887 [conjectured], *PTAED*, NA011005.

page 155: **When his fund-raising efforts petered out:** Andre Millard, *Edison and the Business of Invention* (Baltimore: Johns Hopkins University Press, 1990), 46, 54–55.

page 155: **About this time she directed:** Herron, *House at Glenmont*, 18, 19. The list of household staff members is based on a note written in September 1892, which also included mention of a nurse, a position that was likely added after the birth of Madeleine.

page 155: **Earlier, in 1887:** Lewis Miller to Mina Miller Edison, 26 April 1887, *PTAED*, FH001AAA,

page 155: **After spending about $180,000:** TAE to Henry Villard, 19 January 1888, *PTAED*, D8805AAI.

page 156: **When Edison subsequently revised:** Israel, *Edison*, 269.

page 156: **In 1884:** Fiske, *Off-Hand Portraits*, 113.

page 156: **After reviewing the legal issues:** TAE to Edward H. Johnson [conjectured], 22 November 1887, *PTAED*, D8750AAK.

page 156: **The Graphophone Company, for its part:** Tate, *Edison's Open Door*, 135–136, 139.

page 157: **Company officials tried:** George Gouraud to TAE, 2 July 1887, *PTAED*, D8751AAA.

page 157: **He fired off a tart note:** TAE to George Gouraud, 21 July 1887, *PTAED*, D8751AAB.

page 157: **Gouraud congratulated Edison:** George Gouraud to TAE, 1 August 1887, *PTAED*, D8751AAC,

page 157: **Alfred Tate, a senior manager:** Tate, *Edison's Open Door*, 136.

page 157: **Edison spoke dismissively:** Ibid., 138.

page 157: **A story made the rounds:** *Proceedings of the First Annual Convention of Local Phonograph Companies* (Nashville, Tenn.: Country Music Foundation Press, 1890 [reprint 1974]), 110–112. A business magazine, *Manufacturer and Builder,* attempted to sort out the conflicting claims of the two sides. After reviewing the relevant patents, it declared unequivocally that it was indeed Tainter, not Edison, who deserved the credit for the principal improvement, which was successfully using wax as the recording medium. "The Graphophone," *Manufacturer and Builder,* August 1888, 177.

page 158: **Tate described the scene:** Tate, *Edison's Open Door*, 155. The two men referred to in the quoted passage were Thomas Dolan and Thomas Cochrane.

page 159: **The Edison phonographs that were produced:** Ezra Gilliland to TAE, 16 December 1887, *PTAED*, D8750AAU.

page 159: **When the press heard:** "Edison Was Out $250,000," *New York News,* 18 January 1889, *PTAED*, SB019002E. The actual amount would have been half that reported, or $125,000.

page 159: **Edison was shocked:** Tate, *Edison's Open Door*, 172.

page 160: **Even though Edison announced:** "Perfected Phonograph," *Manufacturer and Builder,* June 1888, 128.

page 160: **he continued to tinker:** Alfred Tate to Frank McGowan, 2 July 1888, *PTAED,* D8818AOH.

page 160: **Edison privately told Batchelor:** TAE to Charles Batchelor, 7 May 1889, *PTAED,* LB029325.

page 160: **The governor of Wyoming:** *Proceedings of the First Annual Convention of Local Phonograph Companies,* 73.

page 160: **A distributor in New York:** Ibid., 191–192.

page 161: **The *Atlantic Monthly:*** Philip G. Hubert Jr., "The New Talking-Machines," *Atlantic Monthly,* February 1889, 258.

page 161: **Edison, however, was exasperated:** TAE to Charles Batchelor, 7 May 1889, *PTAED,* LB029325.

page 161: **"I was the 'dog'":** Tate, *Edison's Open Door,* 161. The same image would reappear in the contemporary software industry, when employees at Microsoft, for example, would "eat our own dog food," using the pre-release version of their software for their own regular work, not just in artificial tests.

page 161: **He noticed that acids:** Ibid., 161–162.

page 161: **Eight thousand Edison machines:** Ibid., 247–248.

page 161: **Quality problems:** *Proceedings of the First Annual Convention of Local Phonograph Companies,* 36, 39.

page 162: **At the first convention:** Ibid., 195.

page 162: **did not give the business issues as much attention:** Millard, *Edison and the Business of Invention,* 81.

page 162: **Tate speculated:** Tate, *Edison's Open Door,* 302.

page 162: **talking doll:** "Dolls That Really Talk," *New York Evening Sun,* 22 November 1888, *PTAED,* SC88130a.

page 162: **In the spring of 1890:** "Edison's Phonographic Doll," *Scientific American,* 26 April 1890, 263.

page 163: **He and toy distributors:** "A Boom That Collapsed," *Philadelphia Times,* 2 January 1891, *PTAED,* SC91001A.

page 163: **On a parallel track:** Tate, *Edison's Open Door,* 247–248.

page 163: **Edison had declared publicly:** "Wizard Edison at Home," *NYW,* 17 November 1889, *PTAED,* MBSB62500.

CHAPTER 8. BATTLE LOST

page 165: **Edison had earned a reputation:** Josephson, *Edison,* 428. Josephson does not provide a source for the quotation and suggests that he himself relied on a secondary source when he wrote, "Ford . . . was reported to have said of Edison . . ."

page 165: **attributed to Henry Ford:** The full quotation is the following: "Edison is easily the world's greatest scientist. I am not sure that he is not also the world's worst business man. He knows almost nothing of business."

Henry Ford, in collaboration with Samuel Crowther, *My Life and Work* (Garden City, N.Y.: Doubleday, Page, 1922), 235.

page 165: **He spoke well:** Forrest McDonald, *Insull* (Chicago: University of Chicago Press, 1962), 35–36.

page 166: **Technically gifted individuals:** Tesla came up with many ingenious electrical devices, including a brilliant design for an electric motor; Sprague designed, and then commercialized, electric streetcars.

page 166: **the cocky lad:** Samuel Insull, *The Memoirs of Samuel Insull: An Autobiography*, ed. Larry Plachno (Polo, Ill.: Transportation Trails, 1992), 25, 31.

page 166: **One evening:** Ibid., 38–39.

page 167: **The financial reports:** Edison Electric Illuminating Company, Monthly Reports, 1886, HFM & GVRC, Box 16, Folders 16–2, 16–3, 16–6, 16–7.

page 167: **One wag wrote:** William D. MacQuesten, "The Edison United Manufacturing Co.," typescript, 1886, *PTAED*, D8629E.

page 167: **the two hunched over the books:** Insull, *Memoirs*, 43–45.

page 168: **It seems I had:** Dyer and Martin, *Edison*, 381–382.

page 168: **they were pleased to discover:** Ibid., 382. On another occasion, Edison described what must have been the same incident with slightly different details—one week, rather than two weeks, passed—and drew the following lesson: "That's the way to settle difficulties—give the people no chance to talk." See "Edison Compares the Swiss People to the Japanese," *NYW*, 26 August 1911.

page 168: **no more demands:** Edison took pleasure in circumventing the power of organized labor. A few years before this incident, when lightbulb production had depended upon the esoteric skills that only members of the Glass Blowers Trade Guild possessed, Edison had protested when the guild demanded that he reinstate the son of a local guild official, who had been fired for sleeping on the job. Edison had to give in, but he set out to obtain revenge: He put some of his lab workers to work on a secret project to develop machinery for lightbulb production that could be operated by unskilled hands. The project succeeded, and Edison no longer had to deal with the Glass Blowers Trade Guild. See Paul Kasakove, untitled reminiscences, typescript, n.d., ENHS, 12.

page 169: **The Machine Works was so cramped:** Dyer and Martin, *Edison*, 381.

page 169: **a piece of property:** "Driven Away by Strikes," *NYT*, 24 June 1886.

page 169: **The new position:** Insull, *Memoirs*, 48–49.

page 169: **he reorganized the office:** Samuel Insull to TAE, 5 November 1887, *PTAED*, D8736AEL.

page 169: **After his first year:** Insull, *Memoirs*, 51.

page 170: **he berated Alfred Tate:** Samuel Insull to A. O. Tate, 4 June 1887, *PTAED*, D8736ACI.

page 170: **When he noticed:** Samuel Insull to A. O. Tate, 2 September 1887, *PTAED*, D8719ABE.

page 170: **In his second year:** Samuel Insull to A. O. Tate, 5 July 1888, *PTAED*, D8835ADJ.

page 170: **"The large and rapid calls":** Samuel Insull to A. O. Tate, 7 January 1888, *PTAED*, D8835AAI.

page 170: **furious at new charges:** Samuel Insull to A. O. Tate, 5 July 1888, *PTAED*, D8835ADJ.

page 171: **Under Insull's management:** Insull, *Memoirs*, 49.

page 171: **Looking back:** Quoted in McDonald, *Insull*, 27–28.

page 171: **A frustrated sales agent:** W. J. Jenks to John H. Vail, 12 November 1887, *PTAED*, D8732ABP.

page 171: **Edison's longtime lieutenant:** Edward Johnson to TAE, 9 December 1887, *PTAED*, D8732ABU.

page 171: **"If our patents":** TAE to George Bliss, n.d., handwritten on back of Bliss to TAE, 12 May 1888, *PTAED*, D8805ACU.

page 172: **A sample story:** "Killed By an Electric Shock," *NYT*, 7 October 1887.

page 172: **When a manager:** "Killed By an Electric Shock," *NYT*, 6 December 1887.

page 172: **In another incident:** "Struck Dead in a Second," *NYT*, 21 January 1887.

page 172: **In April 1888:** "Death Courses Overhead," *NYW*, 17 April 1888.

page 173: **An alert person:** "Street Perils," *NYW*, 16 April 1888.

page 173: **The lethal potential of electricity:** The report also recommended that after execution and postmortem the body be buried in the prison cemetery, closing off the opportunity for the deceased's friends to obtain the body and indulge in "the most drunken and beastly orgies" that traditionally followed hangings. *Report of the Commission to Investigate and Report the Most Humane and Practical Method of Carrying into Effect the Sentence of Death in Capital Cases* (Albany, N.Y.: Troy Press, 1888), 88–90.

page 173: **Edison personally favored:** TAE to A. P. Southwick, 19 December 1887, *PTAED*, LB026116.

page 173: **One associate suggested:** Eugene Lewis to Sherburne Eaton, 1 June 1889, *PTAED*, D8933ABD.

page 174: **The *New York Times:*** Untitled editorial, *NYT*, 11 July 1889.

page 174: **In Edison's view:** TAE to Edward Johnson, "Notes on Distribution of Alternating Current," 1886, *PTAED*, ME004.

page 175: **no competition stood in its way:** In New Orleans, where Westinghouse, in combination with Brush, dramatically undercut Edison's prices, Edison's field manager told his supervisor that "they are robbing our business pretty badly, and are able to run away into districts that we at present cannot touch." Edison's direct-current system remained restricted to a tightly circumscribed area around the generating plant, a fact that Westinghouse's agents happily pointed out to customers. Edison's New Orleans manager pleaded with the home office to pay attention and to "fight them with their own weapons," that is, with alternating current. "If we don't wake up pretty soon to this fact, we shall suffer in the future for our negligence." W. S. Andrews to John Vail, 12 May 1887, *PTAED*, D8732AAR.

page 175: **In June 1888:** George Westinghouse Jr. to TAE, 7 June 1888, *PTAED*, D8828ABV.

page 175: **Edison turned down:** TAE to George Westinghouse Jr., 12 June 1888, *PTAED*, LB026270.

page 175: **He would later say:** TAE to E. D. Adams, 2 February 1889, quoted in Harold Passer, *The Electrical Manufacturers, 1875–1900* (Cambridge, Mass.: Harvard University Press, 1953), 174.

page 175: **Stray dogs were used:** Mark Essig, *Edison and the Electric Chair: A Story of Light and Death* (New York: Walker, 2003), 143.

page 176: **Edison told the *Brooklyn Citizen*:** "Edison's New Ideas," *Brooklyn Citizen*, 4 November 1888, *PTAED*, SM038071d.

page 176: **Edison's bounty offer:** Essig, *Edison and the Electric Chair*, 143.

page 176: **The very day:** TAE to Henry Bergh, 13 July 1888, *PTAED*, LB026273.

page 176: **Henry Bergh:** Henry Bergh to TAE, 14 July 1888, *PTAED*, D8828ACI.

page 176: **It had been his letter:** TAE to A. P. Southwick, 19 December 1887, *PTAED*, LB026116.

page 176: **had persuaded one member:** Essig, *Edison and the Electric Chair*, 118.

page 177: **a new attorney who volunteered:** Ibid., 173.

page 177: **What would happen:** "Edison Says It Will Kill," *NYS*, [24 July 1889], *PTAED*, MBSB62484A; *Kemmler v. Durston* hearing, 23 July 1889, *PTAED*, QE003A0623.

page 177: **George Westinghouse stepped forward:** George Westinghouse, "No Special Danger," letter to the editor, *NYT*, 13 December 1888; Harold P. Brown, "The Comparative Danger to Life of the Alternating and Continuous Electrical Currents," 1889, *PTAED*, QE003A1016A. Brown reproduced Westinghouse's widely circulated letter in order to rebut it, point by point.

page 178: **On 11 October 1889:** "Met Death in the Wires," *NYT*, 12 October 1889.

page 178: **among the witnesses:** One of the witnesses, Charles Thompson, who was a superintendent of the Brooklyn American District Telegraph Company, collapsed with "apoplexy" the next day and was in critical condition. The *New York Times* said he had been in excellent condition and "had witnessed the frightful death of Feeks, and the sight made him very ill." "Excited by Feeks's Death," *NYT*, 13 October 1889.

page 179: **the fatal current could not be traced:** A coroner's jury that was convened heard testimony from representatives of many companies, each pointing the finger of blame at someone else. "How Feeks Met His Death," *NYT*, 22 October 1889.

page 179: **Edison did not add his support:** "Death in the Wires," *Wilmington News,* 14 October 1889, *PTAED,* SC89179B.

page 179: **In October 1889, he urged:** "Edison's Remedy," *New York Evening Sun,* 14 October 1889, *PTAED,* SC89182A.

page 179: **When George Westinghouse read:** Sherburne Eaton to TAE, 7 October 1889, *PTAED,* D8954ADC.

page 179: **Westinghouse decided to speak:** "Mr. Westinghouse Talks," *NYT,* 24 October 1889.

page 180: **"If all things involving":** Ibid.

page 180: **seized an opportunity:** TAE, "Dangers of Electric Lighting," *North American Review,* November 1889, 628. Edison put the disquieting image of nitroglycerin to work once again: "If a nitro-glycerin factory were being operated in the city of New York and the people desired to remove the danger, no one would suggest putting it underground."

page 180: **sixty-four people were killed:** George Westinghouse, "A Reply to Mr. Edison," *North American Review,* December 1889, 661.

page 181: **Don't underestimate the power:** Ibid., 657.

page 181: **Westinghouse also dredged up:** Ibid., 655.

page 181: **Those customers who had a choice:** Ibid., 664.

page 181: **As historian Mark Essig:** Essig, *Edison and the Electric Chair,* 290. Essig mentions a medical-journal article from the early twentieth century to illustrate his point that Edison's fears about electric shocks for a long while appeared to have been borne out: "A Case of Death from the Electric Current While Handling the Telephone."

page 182: **In his official biography:** Dyer and Martin, *Edison,* 382.

page 182: **the value of the shares:** Insull, *Memoirs,* 53.

page 182: **an opportunity to cash out:** "Mr. Edison Is Satisfied," *NYT,* 21 February 1892.

page 182: **He wrote Villard afterward:** TAE to Henry Villard, 8 February 1890, *PTAED,* LB037198.

page 182: **Iron-ore mining:** "An Iron Mine Reopened," *NYT,* 2 December 1889.

page 182: **Insull wrote a colleague:** Samuel Insull to Alfred Tate, 30 July 1889, *PTAED,* LB031451, 6.

page 183: **"my usefulness":** "Mr. Edison's Reply to Thomson-Houston Memoranda of March 23rd, 1889," 1 April 1889, *PTAED,* HM89AAI, 6.

page 183: **Edison had assumed that his laboratory:** TAE to Henry Villard, 8 February 1890, *PTAED,* LB037198.

page 184: **Insull, not bothering to hide his anger:** Samuel Insull to Thomas Alva Edison, 16 July 1890, *PTAED,* D9033AAN.

page 184: **Edison did not like:** Alfred Tate to Samuel Insull, 18 July 1890, *PTAED,* LB042394.

page 184: **Only the warden:** "Far Worse Than Hanging," *NYT,* 7 August 1890.

page 185: **One of the first individuals:** Westinghouse is not mentioned by name. The telegram was sent "to the electric-light company which has been carrying on all the opposition to electrical executions, because it was its dynamos that were being used." "Far Worse Than Hanging."

page 185: **When asked for his reaction:** "Westinghouse Is Satisfied," *NYT,* 7 August 1890.

page 185: **Shibuya Jugiro:** Many contemporaneous and secondary English-language sources mistook Shibuya's personal name, Jugiro, for his surname.

page 185: **the electric chair got another chance:** Essig, *Edison and the Electric Chair,* 258–259, 263, 285.

page 186: **Edison's claim:** "As Revolting as Hanging," *NYW,* 24 June 1888.

page 186: **the sales leader:** In 1891, the last year before the merger, Edison General Electric had annual sales of $10.9 million; Thomson-Houston, $10.3 million; and Westinghouse, $5 million. The difference in cost structures among the three companies can be readily seen by comparing payroll costs. Edison General Electric had 6,000 employees; Thomson-Houston, 4,000; and Westinghouse, 1,300. Passer, *Electrical Manufacturers,* 150.

page 186: **historian Forrest McDonald:** McDonald, *Insull,* 46.

page 186: **Samuel Insull appreciated:** Insull, *Memoirs,* 56.

page 187: **When the press asked him:** "Mr. Edison Is Satisfied."

page 187: **"I have always regretted":** Tate, *Edison's Open Door,* 261.

page 187: **Edison could say:** "Mr. Edison Is Satisfied."

page 187: **Years later, Insull said:** Insull, *Memoirs,* 56.

page 188: **When Edison's own children:** Madeleine Sloane, Oral History, 1 December 1972, ENHS, Interview #1, 31; Matthew Josephson quotes correspondence he had with Charles Edison on the same point. See Josephson, *Edison,* 365n.

page 188: **narrowly escaped bankruptcy:** J. P. Morgan led a syndicate of bankers that supplied the cash that got the company through the worst of the crisis. Passer, *Electrical Manufacturers,* 328.

CHAPTER 9. FUN

page 189: **"I'm going to do something":** Tate, *Edison's Open Door,* 278. Tate's account is a reconstruction written many years later, and it does not provide reliable information about when it took place. The author said this conversation took place several months after the Edison General Electric merger with Thomson-Houston, but at that point Edison was already well along in building his ore-processing plant at the Ogden mine. It must have taken place earlier, perhaps shortly after the consolidation that resulted in the formation of Edison General Electric.

page 189: **a laboratory notebook recorded:** Charles Mott, Journal, 25 March 1880, *PTAED,* N053:17.

page 190: **bought the Ogden iron mine:** "An Iron Mine Reopened," *NYT,* 2 December 1889.

page 190: **it was cheaper:** Charles Edison, Oral History, 14 April 1953, ENHS.

page 190: **a five-ton chunk:** "The Edison Concentrating Works," *Iron Age,* 28 October 1897.

page 191: **In the winter:** Charles Edison, Oral History, 14 April 1953, ENHS.

page 191: **In the summer:** TAE to Mina Edison, 9 August 1895, *PTAED*, B037AAY.

page 191: **Ambient dust:** TAE to Mina Edison, 11 August 1895, *PTAED*, B037AAZ.

page 191: **It lasted five years:** Dyer and Martin, *Edison*, 501.

page 192: **"Darling Sweetest":** TAE to Mina Edison, 12 August 1895, *PTAED*, B037ABA. Edison wrote "cuteist" in the original, but love letters should be spared the academic apparatus of "*sic*" superimposed.

page 192: **"Last night I felt blue":** TAE to Mina Edison, 11 August 1895, *PTAED*, B037AAZ.

page 192: **He humored her:** TAE to Mina Edison, 9 August 1895, *PTAED*, B037AAY.

page 192: **He teased her:** TAE to Mina Edison, 12 August 1895, *PTAED*, B037ABA.

page 192: **He praised her:** TAE to Mina Edison, 15 August 1895, *PTAED*, B037ABB.

page 192: **He lectured her:** TAE to Mina Edison, 16 August 1895, *PTAED*, B037ABC.

page 192: **He teased her:** TAE to Mina Edison, 18 August 1895, *PTAED*, B037ABD.

page 192: **He advised her:** TAE to Mina Edison, 15 August 1895, *PTAED*, B037ABB.

page 192: **His chief assistant:** TAE to Mina Edison, 21 August 1895, *PTAED*, B037ABE.

page 193: **Edison wrote a colleague:** TAE to Richard Bowker, 6 August 1897, *PTAED*, LM245410.

page 193: **he was proud:** TAE to Mina Edison, n.d. [summer 1896 conjectured], *PTAED*, B037ABM.

page 193: **In 1902, at a time when General Electric shares:** Dyer and Martin, *Edison*, 504–505.

page 194: **As late as 1892:** Tate, *Edison's Open Door*, 253.

page 194: **By the next year:** TAE to Edison United Phonograph Company, 16 June 1893, *TAEPM*, 134:740.

page 194: **Public health authorities worried:** Untitled, *Chicago News*, 31 July 1890, *PTAED*, SC90041D.

page 195: **Phonograph dealers who invested:** The general manager of the Chicago Central Phonograph Company declared that he felt the 50 percent royalty was unjust, and that his company would not give it up "if we can possibly help it, and I believe we can." *Proceedings of the First Annual Convention of Local Phonograph Companies* (Nashville, Tenn.: Country Music Foundation Press, 1890 [reprint 1974]), 181–182.

page 195: **A San Francisco distributor:** Ibid., 163–164.

page 195: **prurient storytelling:** Charles Musser, *The Emergence of Cinema: The American Screen to 1907* (Berkeley: University of California Press, 1990), 61.

page 195: "Kinetoscope Moving View": TAE, patent caveat, filed 8 October 1888, *PTAED*, PT031AAA1.

page 195: The first version: W. K. L. Dickson and Antonia Dickson, *History of the Kinetograph, Kinetoscope, and Kinetophotograph* (privately printed, 1895) [facsimile edition, Museum of Modern Art, New York, 2000], 8.

page 196: **It was Dickson who would advance:** Historians of early cinema have given much attention to apportioning credit for the development of the technology we would recognize today. In these appraisals, Dickson receives the bulk of the credit that the general public has mistakenly bestowed upon Edison. Gordon Hendricks's *The Edison Motion Picture Myth* (Berkeley: University of California Press, 1961) is particularly critical of Edison's ethical lapses, listing in detail numerous examples of Edison laboratory records that were altered in order to give a false impression that Edison's contributions were greater, and took place earlier, than was in fact the case.

page 196: **designed an ingenious camera:** Israel, *Edison*, 294; Hendricks, *Edison Motion Picture Myth*, 52; Terry Ramsaye, *A Million and One Nights: A History of the Motion Picture Through 1925* (New York: Simon & Schuster, 1926), 145.

page 196: **While Edison was in Paris:** Dickson and Dickson, *History of the Kinetograph*, 19.

page 197: **Another month went by:** Hendricks, *Edison Motion Picture Myth*, 82.

page 197: **a console made of wood:** Tate, *Edison's Open Door*, 283.

page 197: ***Blacksmith Scene:*** Charles Musser, *Thomas A. Edison and His Kinetographic Motion Pictures* (New Brunswick, N.J.: Rutgers University Press, 1995), 14–15.

page 197: **When he filed:** Ramsaye, *Million and One Nights*, 76. Historian Charles Musser suggests that Edison knew that his patent claims were so dependent upon the prior work of Europeans that they would never survive challenge overseas. Musser, *Emergence of Cinema*, 71–72.

page 197: **When Edison visited Chicago:** "Wizard Edison's Vision," *NYT*, 13 May 1891.

page 197: **would provide one visitor:** Katherine M. Rogers, *L. Frank Baum, Creator of Oz* (New York: St. Martin's Press, 2002), 46.

page 198: **the Wizard of Oz:** Frank Morgan, the actor who played the Wizard in the 1939 film adaptation of Baum's book, bears considerable physical resemblance to Edison.

page 198: **burden proved too much to bear:** Charles Musser, *Before the Nickelodeon: Edwin S. Porter and the Edison Manufacturing Company* (Berkeley: University of California Press, 1991), 38.

page 198: **Tate had proceeded:** Tate, *Edison's Open Door*, 284–285.

page 198: **Before closing in October:** Norm Bolotin and Christine Laing, *The World's Columbian Exposition: The Chicago World's Fair of 1893* (Urbana: University of Illinois Press, 2002), 20.

page 198: **machines were not completed:** Tate, *Edison's Open Door*, 284–285.

page 198: **too late for the fair:** Expectations were so high that a number of writers who have written about the 1893 fair have erroneously assumed that the kinetoscopes had been delivered as promised. See, for example, Erik Larson, *The Devil in the White City* (New York: Crown, 2003), 247; and Robert Sklar, *Movie-Made America: A Social History of the American Movies* (New York: Random House, 1975), 13.

page 198: **In February 1894:** TAE to Eadweard Muybridge, 21 February 1894 [conjectured], *PTAED*, D9425AAF.

page 199: **"The wizard Edison's idea":** "Fun in a Phonograph," *New York Morning Advertiser,* 8 April 1894, *PTAED*, SC94013a.

page 199: **an Albany newspaper:** "Some of Edison's Latest," *Albany Telegram,* 7 January 1894, *PTAED*, SC94001A.

page 199: **Edison, however, continued:** Thomas A. Edison, "Introduction to 'Edison's Invention of the Kineto-Phonograph,'" *Century,* June 1894, 206.

page 200: **The bodybuilder had agreed:** "Sandow at the Edison Laboratory," *Orange Chronicle,* 10 March 1894. The very short film *Sandow,* like *Blacksmith Scene* (mentioned above), is now available on DVD. Kino International and the Film and Media department of the Museum of Modern Art, with the Library of Congress, released in 2005 *Edison: The Invention of the Movies,* a beautifully produced set of four DVDs containing 140 Edison Company films produced between 1891 and 1918.

page 200: **It does not, however, include:** "Sandow at the Edison Laboratory."

page 201: **a group of young entrepreneurs:** Ramsaye, *A Million and One Nights,* 106–107.

page 201: **Rector, who had a background:** Ibid., 108; Tilden Co. and Enoch Rector to Edison Manufacturing Company, 30 July 1894, *PTAED,* D9427AAH.

page 202: **On 15 June 1894:** "Jack Cushing's Waterloo," *NYW,* 16 June 1894.

page 202: **Edison took great personal interest:** Ibid.; "Fight for Edison," *New York Journal,* 16 June 1894, *PTAED,* SC94009C.

page 203: **The plan went well:** "Jack Cushing's Waterloo."

page 203: **When the Kinetoscope Exhibiting Company:** Ramsaye, *Million and One Nights,* 109–110.

page 203: **the Latham brothers moved quickly:** Ibid., 110.

page 203: **Corbett, on his part:** Musser, *Emergence of Cinema,* 84.

page 204: **Gentleman Jack:** Gentleman Jim, the 1942 movie adaptation of his autobiography, starred Errol Flynn.

page 204: **On the day of Corbett's fight:** "Knocked Out by Corbett," *NYS,* 8 September 1894.

page 204: **One account said:** "Before the Wizard," *Los Angeles Times,* 8 September 1894.

page 204: **A bit later:** "Knocked Out by Corbett."

page 204: **when a local judge heard:** "Pugilist Corbett May Be Indicted," *NYT,* 9 September 1894.

page 204: **Mina told the authorities:** "Inventor Edison and the Grand Jury," *NYT,* 14 September 1894.

page 205: **As pleased as they were:** Ramsaye, *Million and One Nights,* 110–112.

page 205: **others urged Edison:** Ramsaye, *Million and One Nights,* 119.

page 206: **"there will be a use":** Edison's prediction brings to mind the prediction invariably attributed to IBM chairman Thomas J. Watson, circa 1943: "I think there is a world market for maybe five computers." The Watson quotation turns out to be difficult to verify. Biographer Kevin Maney did his best and concluded, "No evidence exists that Watson made the remark about five computers." See Kevin Maney, *The Maverick and His Machine: Thomas Watson, Sr., and the Making of IBM* (Hoboken, N.J.: John Wiley & Sons, 2003), 355.

page 206: **without his boss's approval:** Ramsaye, *A Million and One Nights,* 118–119, 121, 126.

page 206: **The projected images:** "Magic Lantern Kinetoscope," *NYS,* 22 April 1895.

page 207: **Professor Latham wrote a letter:** "Latham's Pantopticon," *NYS,* 23 April 1895.

page 207: **A few weeks later:** Ramsaye, *Million and One Nights,* 134–136.

page 207: **a broadside printed for the occasion:** "Latham's Eidoloscope," broadside, reproduced in Musser, *Emergence of Cinema,* 98.

page 207: **"Edison Not in It!":** Ramsaye, *Million and One Nights,* 135. The source for the headline is the *Chicago Inter-Ocean,* 11 June 1895.

page 207: **Not only in the United States:** Musser, *Emergence of Cinema,* 91.

page 208: **In September 1895:** Ibid., 103–104.

page 208: **Edison personally handwrote:** TAE to Ingersoll-Sergeant Drill Co., 3 October 1895, *PTAED,* LM229175.

page 208: **In one letter he tells her:** TAE to Mina Edison, n.d. [1896 conjectured], *PTAED,* B037ABN. In a subsequent letter to Mina, Edison asked if she had figured out the "Coming Woman" joke. If she hadn't, he joked that when he returned home "I will bring diagrams and explanatory notes." TAE to Mina Edison, n.d. [1896 conjectured], *PTAED,* B037ABO.

page 208: **While Raff & Gammon:** Ramsaye, *Million and One Nights,* 218–219.

page 209: **Their plan also required:** Raff & Gammon to Thomas Armat, 5 March 1896, quoted in ibid., 224–225.

page 209: **when it made its debut:** "Edison's Vitascope Cheered," *NYT,* 24 April 1896; "Edison's Latest Invention," *NYT,* 26 April 1896.

page 209: **The inaugural film program offered:** "At the Playhouses," *Los Angeles Times,* 7 July 1896.

page 210: **At another site:** "Edison Vitascope," *Los Angeles Times,* 25 July 1896.

page 210: **In the first week:** "A Mysterious Invention," *Los Angeles Times,* 12 July 1896.

CHAPTER 10. KINGLY PRIVILEGE

page 211: **Edison Chemical Company:** "Suit by Inventor Edison," *Wilmington Evening*, 21 January 1903, *TAEPM*, 221:241.

page 212: **I probably never will:** TAE Jr. to Mina Edison, 15 May 1897, *PTAED*, FC001AAK.

page 212: **Later that year:** TAE Jr. to Mina Edison, 12 November 1897, *PTAED*, FC001ABC.

page 212: **Within a few days:** "Edison, Jr., Wizard," *NYH*, 5 December 1897, *PTAED*, SC97058A.

page 213: **He soon landed:** "The Electrical Exhibition," *NYT*, 24 April 1898.

page 213: **A small accident:** "Accident in the Garden," *NYT*, 24 May 1898; "Electrical Inventors' Risks," *NYT*, 3 July 1898.

page 213: **So it was he:** "Cooking by Electricity," *NYT*, 22 May 1898.

page 213: **Fortuitously, investors appeared:** Israel, *Edison*, 390.

page 214: **Edison Sr. was outraged:** William Edison to TAE Jr., [Dec] 1898, *TAEPM*, 227:591.

page 214: **Tom Jr. wrote his father:** TAE Jr. to TAE, 19 Dec 1898, *TAEPM*, 227:586–90.

page 214: **gold-digging strumpet:** Israel, *Edison*, 390.

page 214: **His brother Will:** William Edison to Mina Edison, 25 May 1899, *TAEPM*, 221:749.

page 214: **He had come up with:** "Young Edison's Fame Is Now International," *NYT*, 1 June 1903.

page 214: **the Edison Chemical Company:** "Suit by Inventor Edison," *Wilmington Evening*, 21 January 1903, *TAEPM*, 221:241.

page 215: **he wrote his father:** TAE Jr., to TAE, 29 December 1902. Tom Jr. claimed to be in a desperate situation exacerbated by poor health. He told his father that "I am confined to my bed and have been for several weeks past with the prospect of remaining there for sometime to come." He was fully aware that his business dealings with strangers eager to exploit his name would end unhappily—"I know of no business deal that I have ever made that [sic] I was not taken advantage of." But he believed he had no choice because the contracts "are of course the only means by which I derive a living." *TAEPM*, 187:756.

page 215: **In the father's retrospective account:** "Wizard Edison Menaces with Prison the Men Who Used His Son's Name," *New York American*, 8 October 1904, *TAEPM*, 221:283.

page 215: **A press account:** "Suit by Inventor Edison."

page 215: **The future would bear this out:** H. F. Miller to Mrs. Martha H. Kirk, 8 March 1911, ENHS.

page 215: **"incapable of making":** "Barred by Fraud Order," *NYT*, 5 October 1904. Tom Jr. was persuaded to falsely attest in a separate affidavit that he was not the Vitalizer's inventor. See "Suit by Inventor Edison."

page 216: **Contending that selling:** "Barred by Fraud Order"; "That Edison

Company," *NYT*, 6 October 1904; "Edison Jr. Mail Held for Fraud," *NYH*, 6 October 1904, *TAEPM*, 221:282.

page 216: **He told the** *New York American:* "Wizard Edison Menaces with Prison the Men Who Used His Son's Name."

page 216: **In 1900:** "Edison Will Make Automobiles the Poor Man's Vehicle," *Elmira Telegram*, 22 June 1902, *TAEPM*, 221:217.

page 216: **prototype electric car:** "Edison's Most Important Discovery," *Harper's Weekly*, 21 December 1901, 1302.

page 216: **By 1902:** "Chauffeur Gave Edison a Scare," *NYW*, 30 June 1902, *TAEPM*, 221:219.

page 217: **he was excited to see:** TAE to George B. Dresher, 18 May 1910, ENHS, Letterbook, vol. 82.

page 217: **Prospective customers were told:** "Mr. Edison's Perpetual Hobby," advertisement, n.d. [1910?], ENHS, Primary Printed—Edison Companies Box 24, National Phonograph Company—Advertisements. The fact that its trademarked name, "phonograph," had entered the language and the dictionary was also offered as proof of its uniqueness.

page 217: **In at least one instance:** "Thos A. Edison" [composed by George Silzer of Harger & Blish] to George Sturgis, 10 February 1915, ENHS, TAE Inc. Phonograph Division, Maxwell files, Box 1, Correspondence, February 1915.

page 218: **Edison's staff was so aghast:** William Maxwell to George C. Silzer, 17 February 1915, ENHS, TAE Inc. Phonograph Division, Maxwell files, Box 1, Correspondence, February 1915.

page 218: **one man, writing from Marcus:** George Hooper to TAE, 17 February 1915. ENHS, TAE Inc. Phonograph Division, Maxwell files, Box 1, Correspondence, February 1915.

page 218: **William Maxwell:** William Maxwell to George C. Silzer, 25 February 1915, ENHS, TAE Inc. Phonograph Division, Maxwell files, Box 1, Correspondence, February 1915.

page 218: **The dealer replied:** George Silzer to William Maxwell, 5 March 1915, ENHS, TAE Inc. Phonograph Division, Maxwell files, Box 1, Correspondence, February 1915.

page 218: **An entire block:** Paul Kasakove, untitled reminiscences, n.d., ENHS, 15.

page 218: **By 1907:** "Something About Our Concrete Buildings," *Edison Phonograph Monthly*, July 1907, 3. Concrete also permitted Edison to thumb his nose at the bricklayer's union, which had threatened to blacklist him when he earlier had used his own nonunion staff to quickly throw up a small brick out-building. See Kasakove, untitled reminiscences, 15.

page 218: **A pithy rubric:** "Made in America in 1888—Made Perfect in 1914," advertisement in *Detroit Times*, 12 January 1915, ENHS, TAE Inc. Phonograph Division, Maxwell files, Box 1, Correspondence, 1914.

page 218: **"When the King of England":** Advertisement, *Edison Phonograph Monthly*, December 1906, 15.

page 219: **In 1908:** Edison phonograph advertisement, *Cosmopolitan,* June 1908.

page 219: **Another advertisement promised:** "Never overlook the value of an Edison Phonograph as an ice breaker . . . ," advertisement, April 1907, ENHS, Primary Printed—Edison Companies Box 24. National Phonograph Company—Advertisements.

page 219: **Victrola:** Andre Millard, *America on Record: A History of Recorded Sound* (Cambridge: Cambridge University Press, 1995), 130, 131.

page 219: **cost about seven cents:** Ibid., 49.

page 220: **insisted that his discs be twice the thickness:** Andre Millard, *Edison and the Business of Invention* (Baltimore: Johns Hopkins University Press, 1990), 301.

page 220: **An adapter permitted:** TAE to G. M. Gregg, 18 February 1914, ENHS; William H. Meadowcroft to D. J. Walker, 5 May 1914, ENHS.

page 220: **"these miserable dance":** TAE to A. G. Spencer, 23 November 1915, ENHS.

page 220: **Jazz was for:** Hugh R. Fraser, "The Old Man," unpublished manuscript, 1954, ENHS, 463.

page 220: **He also dismissed:** TAE to Thomas Graf, 20 November 1911, ENHS.

page 220: **Sergei Rachmaninoff:** Emily Thompson, "Machines, Music, and the Quest for Fidelity: Marketing the Edison Phonograph in America, 1877–1925," *Musical Quarterly* 79:1 (Spring 1995): 169n90. Paul Kasakove's recollection is slightly different. He remembers Edison's summary dismissal of Rachmaninoff as "He thumps!": Kasakove, untitled reminiscences, 35.

page 220: **In 1911, Edison wrote:** TAE to Thomas Graf, 20 November 1911, ENHS.

page 221: **Edison approached music:** "Edison Analyzes Music, Finds Lack of Originality," *NYW,* 12 February 1911.

page 221: **His daughter Madeleine:** Madeleine Sloane, Oral History, 1 December 1972, ENHS, Interview #1, 11.

page 221: **He spent a year and a half:** TAE to Ledger Smith, 25 June 1915, ENHS.

page 221: **He did his best:** Norman Speiden, transcript of ENHS tour, 8 January 1971, ENHS, 9.

page 221: **A little item:** "Thomas A. Edison Says He Hears Through His Teeth," *Schenectady Union-Star,* 6 November 1913.

page 222: **she came into the sitting room:** Madeleine Sloane, Oral History, 1 December 1972, ENHS, Interview #1, 14.

page 222: **recalled the disillusionment:** A. E. Johnson and K. Ehricke, Oral History, 29 March 1971, ENHS, 19–20.

page 222: **Workers spread word daily:** Nerney, *Edison,* 251.

page 222: **He was exasperated:** TAE to Marcella Goodspeed, 9 June 1911, ENHS.

page 222: **And it was those customers:** TAE to Thomas Graf, 20 November 1911, ENHS.

page 222: **By the time Edison's factory:** Kasakove, untitled reminiscences, 18.

page 222: **On rare occasions:** TAE to Alfred W. Doerx, 28 June 1913, ENHS.

page 223: **Victor signed Enrico Caruso:** "Talking Machine Companies Pay $1,000,000 for Voices of Artists," *Music Trades,* 17 August 1912.

page 223: **The others whom Victor signed:** John Harvith and Susan Edwards Harvith, eds., *Edison, Musicians and the Phonograph: A Century in Retrospect* (New York: Greenwood Press, 1987), 16.

page 223: **One exception:** "Sarah Bernhardt Secured for Our Records," *Edison Phonograph Monthly,* February 1910, 3. The Cylinder Preservation and Digitization Project at the University of California, Santa Barbara, has made available online more than six thousand cylinders whose music has been digitized, including a few of Bernhardt's. See http://cylinders.library.ucsb.edu.

page 224: **she did endorsements:** "A Celebrity Extraordinaire Who Rivaled Eiffel Tower," *NYT,* 2 December 2005.

page 224: **Edison hated the negotiations:** TAE to A. Kobb, 1 May 1914, ENHS.

page 224: **Stravinsky had written:** Fraser, "Old Man," 469–470. On another occasion, Edison was highly pleased by the phrasing of a correspondent, who referred to "the music of bank-notes." See William H. Meadowcroft to Frederick A. Whiting, 18 May 1917, ENHS.

page 224: **"I believe if you record":** TAE draft for F. L. Dyer letter of 26 December 1911, 20 December 1911, ENHS, cited in Harvith and Harvith, *Edison, Musicians and the Phonograph,* 5.

page 224: **Over time, Edison did add:** Ibid., 16.

page 224: **The first record to sell:** Roderic Peters, Oral History, 23 March 1973, ENHS, 6. Dalhart's name is rendered incorrectly in the transcript. "The Prisoner's Song" was first recorded acoustically in 1924.

page 225: **In 1912, the chairwoman:** Sadie American to TAE, 25 April 1912, ENHS, TAE Inc. Phonograph Division, Dyer folders, unmarked folder #1.

page 225: **The Topeka agency:** A. S. Thomas to Harger & Blish, 26 January 1915, EHNS, TAE Inc. Phonograph Division, Maxwell files, Box 1, Correspondence, January 1915.

page 225: **It fell to Edison's salespeople:** Thomas A. Edison, Inc., Edison Retail Salesman's Manual, June 1916, ENHS, Primary Printed—Edison Companies, Box 41, Phonograph Division (TAE Inc.), Dealer's Material—Sales Manuals [second folder of two with identical label], 19–20.

page 225: **"I am sure":** TAE to Santa Fe Watch Company, 16 April 1913, ENHS.

page 226: **The company immediately responded:** Thomas J. Schlereth, *Victorian America: Transformations in Everyday Life* (New York: HarperPerennial, 1991), 193.

page 226: **When a man leaves home:** Advertisement for the National Phonograph Company, *Edison Phonograph Monthly,* February 1907, 22.

page 227: **If one complained:** TAE to Harger & Blish, 8 February 1915, ENHS, TAE Inc. Phonograph Division, Maxwell files, Box 1, Correspondence, February 1915.

page 227: **A typical letter:** TAE to Santa Fe Watch Company, 30 November 1914, ENHS.

page 228: **all-concrete houses:** "Concrete Dwellings," *Insurance Press,* 30 October 1907, *TAEPM,* 221:414.

page 228: **film's frames were tiny:** *Edison Home Kinetoscope,* brochure, 15 April 1912, ENHS, Primary Printed—Edison Companies, TAE Inc. (Motion Pictures), Box 23, Folder: Kinetoscope-Apparatus Catalogs, 1912–1924.

page 228: **"suppose, instead of the dull":** "Edison and the New Education," *Harper's Weekly,* 4 November 1911, 8. The melding of education and entertainment, here championed by Edison, was brilliantly condemned in Neil Postman's polemic, *Amusing Ourselves to Death: Public Discourse in the Age of Show Business* (New York: Viking Press, 1985).

page 228: **He compiled a list:** Allen L. Benson, "Edison's Substitute for School Books," *World To-Day,* March 1912.

page 229: **His marketing pitch:** "Edison and the New Education."

page 229: **A year after the release:** Thomas A. Edison, Inc., Sales Department Bulletin No. 31, 16 December 1912, ENHS, Primary Printed—Edison Companies, Box 24, Motion Pictures, TAE Inc. Home Kinetoscope Dealer's Forms and Bulletins, 1912–1914. Seven years later, Edison proposed that the federal government assume the responsibility of producing educational films and offering them to schools for modest rental fees. See "Edison on Educationals," *NYT,* 9 February 1919.

page 229: **When a business colleague:** TAE to W. C. Anderson, 26 August 1912, HFM & GVRC, Box 2, Folder 2–27.

page 229: **The next month:** "Time Card in Edison's Laboratory," *Norwalk [Ohio] Reflection,* 5 October 1912.

page 229: **Edison had told reporters:** Israel, *Edison,* 422.

page 230: **warn off anyone:** Not every offender was pursued with equal fervor. After handling the problems with the businesses that rented the name of Thomas Edison Jr., the legal team found another problem: an Edison Employment Bureau in New York City. The owner claimed the Edison name by virtue of his brother-in-law, who possessed that surname, and expressed the hope that Edison "is not so much of an egotist as to think we named the Bureau to trade on his name." Edison directed his attorneys to drop the matter. Howard Hayes to TAE, 12 October 1903, *TAEPM,* 226:40.

page 230: **In the early evening:** "Edison Sees His Vast Plant Burn," *NYT,* 10 December 1914; "The Edison Plant Fire-Swept," *Edison Phonograph Monthly,* January 1915, 4–6; "Mrs. Edison Saved Husband's Records," *NYT,* 11 December 1914.

page 231: **The facilities for phonograph:** "Mrs. Edison Saved Husband's Records."

page 231: **A private letter:** W. G. Bee to Henry Ford, 10 December 1914, HFM & GVRC, Box 4, Folder 4–5. After the fire, Edison refused to publicly acknowledge any deficiencies in concrete. He argued that "temperatures were far in excess of those in the ordinary fire" and that the damage to his structures had been exaggerated by the brick manufacturers, who had published a pamphlet titled *The Edison Fire*. See Edison's letter to the editor: "Edison's Concrete," *NYT*, 30 April 1915.

page 231: **skipping over two thousand gallons:** W. G. Bee to E. G. Liebold, 17 December 1914, HFM & GVRC, Box 4, Folder 4–5.

page 231: **They also discovered:** William Maxwell to Southern California Music Company, 14 December 1914, ENHS, TAE Inc. Phonograph Division, Maxwell files, Box 1, Correspondence, 1914.

page 231: **would receive a kind offer:** W. G. Bee to E. G. Liebold, 11 December 1914, HFM & GVRC, Box 4, Folder 4–5.

page 231: **He cracked jokes:** W. G. Bee to Henry Ford, 10 December 1914, HFM & GVRC, Box 4, Folder 4–5.

page 231: **"Although I am":** "Edison Sees His Vast Plant Burn."

page 232: **The striking absence:** "Abnormality Like His a Blessing," *NYT*, 12 December 1914.

page 232: **"It's like the old days":** Edison made a similar statement the day after the fire: "It prevents a man from being afflicted with ennui." "Some Answers Which Mr. Edison Made to Telegrams and Letters Received the Day After the Fire," *Edison Phonograph Monthly*, January 1915, 6.

page 232: **"I never intend to retire":** "Edison Sails for Europe on First Trip in 22 Years, to Catch Up with Worries," *Evening World*, 2 August 1911.

CHAPTER 11. FRIEND FORD

page 233: **lopsided arithmetic:** A classic *Saturday Night Live* sketch playfully pretended that a celebrity musician knew as much about every one of his fans as they knew about him. As Paul Simon was standing in line outside a movie theater, a woman approached him.

> Woman: Paul Simon! Hi! Oh, I'm sure you don't remember, but I saw you in your concert at Central Park.
> Paul Simon: [pauses to think] You were sitting on a plaid blanket . . . under the elm tree.
> Woman: Yes, yes!
> Paul Simon: You've changed your hair since then. I like it very much.
> Woman: Thank you. Thank you!
> Paul Simon: And thank *you* for yelling, "More!"

Other strangers approach Simon, each bringing out a feat of memory more amazing than the last and each portraying the celebrity as intimately acquainted with the quotidian details of the stranger's life. Simon even remembered the man who had bought one of his records in a Seattle record store: "Oh, yes, you had a problem with the second side, there was a scratch on the second cut . . . ." The sketch concluded with Simon's memory failing him upon the arrival of Art Garfunkel, his collaborator for eleven years. Simon: "And your name is?" The show originally aired 22 November 1986. The transcript is posted to a Web site, Saturday Night Live Transcripts. See http://snltranscripts.jt.org/86/86ememory.phtml.

page 233: **At dinner on the first day:** Henry Ford, in collaboration with Samuel Crowther, *Edison as I Know Him* (New York: Cosmopolitan Book Corporation, 1930), 1–5, 11.

page 234: **The stagy dialogue:** Ford's first published account of the encounter was in his autobiography, published in 1922. There the account was brief. It was only with the publication of *Edison as I Know Him* eight years later that he filled out details and added the dialogue.

page 234: **Edison did not resume:** The second conversation between Edison and Ford adds verisimilitude to Ford's account of the first precisely because it does not follow his earlier inspirational theme.

page 235: **"My Dear Mr. Edison":** Henry Ford to TAE, 18 February 1907, *TAEPM,* 191:71.

page 235: **had recently been contacted:** Extant correspondence does not make clear if Will Edison had contacted Ford by February 1907. Later that year, he told his father about his spark plug when he asked him for a loan, and Edison turned him down. See William Edison to TAE, 13 November 1907, *TAEPM,* 191: 383–385. Will wrote that he had shown the prototype of his plug to Ford and other manufacturers and had received "nothing but praise and not one word against it." He also said that "Ford alone will take 16,000," but no order materialized. Three years earlier, Will headed the W. L. Edison Automobile Station and Laboratory, which manufactured spark plugs, plug testers, and spark coils. The manufacturing business apparently had to be supplemented because he also offered services such as brokerage services and car inspections for prospective purchasers of used cars. See William Edison to John Randolph, 12 February 1904, *TAEPM,* 189:190.

page 235: **spasm of competitiveness:** This is the theory suggested by an earlier Edison biographer, Robert Conot. See Conot, *Streak of Luck,* 382.

page 236: **In April 1911:** W. G. Bee to Henry Ford, 6 April 1911, HFM & GVRC, Box 2, Folder 2–18,

page 236: **At the same time:** W. G. Bee to W. C. Anderson, 6 April 1911, HFM & GVRC, Box 2, Folder 2–18.

page 236: **Ford accepted:** Henry Ford to TAE, 27 June 1911, cited in Conot, *Streak of Luck,* 382.

page 236: **Finally, after Bee had arranged:** TAE reply in margin of William Anderson to TAE, 29 December 1911, cited in Conot, *Streak of Luck,* 382.

page 236: **Would Ford be interested:** TAE to Henry Ford, 29 October 1912, HFM & GVRC, Box 2, Folder 2–28.

page 236: **If Jews "are as wise":** Henry Ford, in collaboration with Samuel Crowther, *My Life and Work* (Garden City, N.Y.: Doubleday, Page, 1922), 251.

page 237: **"Please read this"**: TAE to Henry Ford, [November 1916], HFM & GVRC, Box 2, Folder 2–43.

page 237: **Edison could expect sales**: Agreement between Ford and Edison, 29 November 1912, HFM & GVRC, Folder 159 A, Box 4, cited in Conot, *Streak of Luck*, 382.

page 237: **the first slice**: Stephen Mambert to Henry Ford, 23 January 1918, HFM & GVRC, Box 16, Folder 52.

page 237: **he simply made Henry Ford**: "Edison Batteries for New Ford Cars," *NYT*, 11 January 1914.

page 238: **The New York newspapers**: "Henry Ford Seeks Mr. Edison's Aid," *NYH*, 10 January 1914.

page 238: **mutual interest in gardening**: Martha Coman and Hugh Weir, "The Most Difficult Husband in America," *Collier's*, 18 July 1925.

page 238: **Edison is said to have complained**: Henry Ford and the Florida Everglades, typescript, n.d., HFM & GVRC, Vertical File: Edison/Ford Everglades.

page 238: **"Mr. Edison has few friends"**: "Why Edison Chooses to Be Deaf," *Literary Digest*, 8 August 1925. Mina Edison also noted that Edison's friendship with Ford had meant much to him.

page 239: **Ford became his neighbor**: The adjoining parcel of land owned by Gilliland had gone through several changes of ownership and eventually had been purchased by Edison in 1906 and absorbed into his property. In 1916, Ford purchased another plot, so did not occupy the exact spot as Gilliland had. Personal correspondence with Bonnie Newburg, Curatorial Department, Edison & Ford Winter Estates, 9 December 2005.

page 239: **One exception**: Henry Ford to TAE, 31 March 1914, HFM & GVRC, Box 2, Folder 2–42.

page 239: **He did not pause**: E. G. Liebold to W. G. Bee, 17 April 1914, HFM & GVRC, Box 2, Folder 2–37.

page 240: **Edison complied**: Ibid.

page 240: **The injurious agent in Cigarettes**: TAE to Friend Ford, 26 April 1914, HFM & GVRC, Box 2, Folder 2–37.

page 240: **hurriedly had signs posted**: "Edison Bans Cigarettes," *NYT*, 11 May 1914. Edison's managers would vainly attempt to enforce the ban for years. A. C. Frost, the manager of the company's insurance department, expressed concern that lax enforcement created a fire hazard and possibly risked the loss of fire insurance coverage. He told line managers that "in order to enforce this rule it may be necessary to make an example of one or two employees." See A. C. Frost, memorandum, 6 July 1920, ENHS, Stephen Mambert, Incoming Correspondence—1920—Edison Companies, Mambert, S. B.

page 240: **Edison was accustomed**: "Edison Wants a Good Chew," *NYT*, 6 April 1914.

page 240: **He did not have to**: "Edison Bans Cigarettes."

page 240: **A *New York Times* editorial:** "An Inventor out of His Field," *NYT,* 12 May 1914.

page 241: **Percival Hill:** "T. A. Edison Begins to Wince," *New York Commercial,* 18 May 1914.

page 241: **James Zobian:** "It Was Mr. Edison's Mistake," *Pittsburgh Leader,* 9 July 1914.

page 241: **furniture made of concrete:** "Joy for Newlyweds Promised by Edison," *Boston Evening American,* 10 December 1911.

page 241: **Some commentators were not even certain:** Untitled, *Albany Evening Journal,* 14 December 1911; "Concrete Furniture? No!" *Kansas City Times,* 16 December 1911.

page 241: **Cartoonists had no difficulty:** "A Concrete Example of the Triumph of Mind over Matter," cartoon, *Minneapolis Journal,* 9 December 1911. Also see "Mr. Edison's Concrete Furniture," *Topeka Daily Capital,* n.d. Another humorous treatment is found in "Will Concrete Furniture Be Used? Never," *Davenport Times,* 21 December 1911. All clippings at ENHS, Newspaper Clippings, January–December 1911.

page 242: **Edison would receive:** Henry Ford to TAE, telegram, 11 February 1914, HFM & GVRC, Box 2, Folder 2–34.

page 242: **Mina, a birdhouse:** W. G. Bee to E. G. Liebold, 25 April 1914, HFM & GVRC, Box 4, Folder 4–3.

page 242: **a Model T engine:** E. G. Liebold to TAE Jr, 19 February 1914; TAE Jr. to W. G. Bee, 4 June 1914; E. G. Liebold to TAE Jr., 11 June 1914. All three letters in HFM & GVRC, Box 8, Folder 8–17.

page 242: **followed by a new car:** W. G. Bee to E. G. Liebold, 1 July 1914, HFM & GVRC, Box 4, Folder 4–4.

page 242: **Charles Edison received:** E. G. Liebold to Charles Edison, 10 December 1914, HFM & GVRC, Box 4, Folder 4–6.

page 242: **Theodore Edison:** W. G. Bee to Henry Ford, 30 November 1914, HFM & GVRC, Box 4, Folder 4–5; "Ford Gives Auto to Young Edison," *NYT,* 26 December 1914. The Edisons were not the only recipients of Ford's generosity. Later, between 1921 and 1942, Ford gave away what one scholar estimated to be about 200 cars, 23 trucks, and 15 tractors, whose recipients included John D. Rockefeller and Randolph A. Hearst. See Reynold M. Wik, *Henry Ford and Grass-Roots America* (Ann Arbor: University of Michigan Press, 1971), 217. In 1920, the four members of the Edison family who lived at Glenmont—Tom, Mina, Charles, and Theodore—had nine cars: four Fords; two Detroit Electrics; a Cadillac; a Simplex; and a Locomobile limousine. See A. C. Frost to R. W. Kellow, 16 June 1920, ENHS, Stephen Mambert, Incoming Correspondence—1920— Edison Companies, Mambert, S. B.

page 242: **On one occasion:** J. W. Hill to Henry Ford, 1 April 1916, HFM & GVRC, Box 2, Folder 2–49.

page 243: **When Ford first visited:** W. G. Bee to TAE, 1 April 1914, HFM & GVRC, Box 2, Folder 2–41.

page 243: **Movies made with Edison equipment:** "Edison Batteries for New Ford Cars," *NYT*, 11 January 1914.

page 243: **Edison dictating machines:** E. G. Liebold to W. G. Bee, 20 January 1914, HFM & GVRC, Box 4, Folder 4–2.

page 243: **Cement made by the Edison Portland Cement Company:** Walter S. Mallory to John Graham, 1 August 1914, HFM & GVRC, Box 4, Folder 4–4.

page 243: **Ford Motor's chief architect:** E. G. Liebold to W. G. Bee, 10 August 1914, HFM & GVRC, Box 4, Folder 4–4.

page 243: **Ford happened to be in New York:** W. G. Bee to E. G. Liebold, 11 December 1914, HFM & GVRC, Box 4, Folder 4–5.

page 243: **Another $100,000 loan:** Stephen Mambert to Henry Ford, 23 January 1918, HFM & GVRC, Box 16, Folder 52.

page 243: **when Edison was finalizing plans:** TAE to E. G. Liebold, 23 February 1915, HFM & GVRC, Box 4, Folder 4–6.

page 244: **It turned out that there was no such thing:** E. G. Liebold to W. H. Meadowcroft, 25 February 1915, HFM & GVRC, Box 4, Folder 4-6.

page 244: **Edison would have none:** W. H. Meadowcroft to E. G. Liebold, 27 February 1915, HFM & GVRC, Box 4, Folder 4-6.

page 244: **he was "at a loss":** E. G. Liebold to W. H. Meadowcroft, 1 March 1915, HFM & GVRC, Box 4, Folder 4-6.

page 244: **Never mind:** TAE to E. G. Liebold, telegram, 18 March 1915, HFM & GVRC, Box 4, Folder 4-6. This was not the end of the tale. Ford then offered the services of one of his senior executives who was in New York, who did call Edison and pay a visit. See E. G. Liebold to W. H. Meadowcroft, 18 March 1915, HFM & GVRC, Box 4, Folder 4-6.

page 244: **In October 1915:** W. H. Meadowcroft to T. Commerford Martin, 5 October 1915, ENHS.

page 245: **accompanied by a police officer:** "Edison's Life Threatened," *NYT*, 27 October 1915. The year before, Edison publicly had disavowed any plans to work on weapons: "Making things which kill men is against my fibre." See "Edison Won't Invent Man-Killing Devices," *NYT*, 26 October 1914.

page 245: **could not avoid being surrounded:** "Noted Pair Keep Walking Eight Hours," *San Francisco Chronicle*, 20 October 1915.

page 245: **Edison and Ford also were feted:** "Edison Laughs at Plight of Friend Ford," *San Francisco Chronicle*, 21 October 1915.

page 246: **Edison had his secretary:** W. H. Meadowcroft to Alice Verlet, 22 March 1916, ENHS.

page 247: **"I would not trouble":** L. C. Curlin to TAE, 8 March 1919, and TAE marginal note in HFM & GVRC, Box 5, Folder 5-4.

page 247: **When Meadowcroft dispatched:** W. H. Meadowcroft to E. G. Liebold, 20 March 1919, HFM & GVRC, Box 5, Folder 5-4.

page 247: **Liebold received the request favorably:** E. G. Liebold to W. H. Meadowcroft, 24 March 1919, HFM & GVRC, Box 5, Folder 5-4.

page 247: **no deal was arranged:** Telephone interview with Jack Curlin, Lemuel Calvert Curlin's grandson, 22 June 2006.

page 248: **In June 1914:** TAE Jr. to E. G. Liebold, 3 July 1914, HFM & GVRC, Box 8, Folder 17. For Madeleine Edison's wedding, see "Bridal Party Dines on Eagle Rock," *NYT,* 16 June 1914 and "Madeleine Edison a Bride," *NYT,* 18 June 1914. Madeleine's new husband, John Sloane, apparently wasted no time trying to use his marital tie to Edison to advance his own business interests as an airplane manufacturer. He arranged a deal to sell planes to the Russian government to be financed by Japan's Mitsui Company and personally secured by funds he expected to obtain from his father-in-law. "Sloane found himself unable to get the financial aid he expected from his relatives," the *New York Times* later reported, when the deal unraveled and Sloane sued Mitsui. See "Edison's Son-in-Law Sues," *NYT,* 1 May 1917.

page 248: **When it finally was shipped:** E. G. Liebold to W. G. Bee, 3 July 1914, HFM & GVRC, Box 4, Folder 4-4.

page 248: **sent a thank-you letter:** TAE Jr. to E. G. Liebold, 3 July 1914, HFM & GVRC, Box 8, Folder 17.

page 248: **The company took possession:** E. G. Liebold to Ford Motor Company, Long Island City, 11 June 1914, HFM & GVRC, Box 8, Folder 8-17.

page 248: **Tom Jr. did make a good case:** TAE Jr. to Billy [W. G. Bee], 7 July 1914, HFM & GVRC, Box 4, Folder 4-4.

page 249: **Bee served as his advocate:** W. G. Bee to E. G. Liebold, 1 July 1914, HFM & GVRC, Box 4, Folder 4-4.

page 249: **appears to have embarrassed Liebold:** E. G. Liebold to W. G. Bee, 11 July 1914, HFM & GVRC, Box 4, Folder 4-4.

page 249: **When Liebold agreed:** Ibid.

page 249: **In January 1915, he wrote:** TAE Jr. to Henry Ford, 15 January 1915, HFM & GVRC, Box 8, Folder 16.

page 249: **Later in the year, he addressed:** TAE Jr. to Henry Ford, 14 November 1915, HFM & GVRC, Box 8, Folder 16.

page 250: **In 1917, after visiting Detroit:** TAE Jr. to Henry Ford, 16 February 1917, HFM & GVRC, Box 8, Folder 16. For other thank-you notes in this time frame, see TAE Jr. to Henry Ford, 10 June 1917, and TAE Jr. to Henry Ford, 7 July 1917, HFM & GVRC, Box 8, Folder 16.

page 250: **The work on his gadget:** Beatrice Edison to E. G. Liebold, 6 October 1919, HFM & GVRC, Box 8, Folder 17.

page 250: **His Ecometer attached:** *The Ecometer,* pamphlet, n.d. [May 1921 conjectured], HFM & GVRC, Box 8, Folder 8-17.

page 250: **Ford's engineers:** Tom Jr. told Liebold that he was not discouraged by the test results because the tests at Ford must not have been conducted according to his instructions. He also said that "my head does bother me more than any living being knows and all I can say is that these dreadful pains are indeed one great big handicap to me." TAE Jr. to E. G. Liebold, 7 May 1921; TAE Jr., and Beatrice Edison to E. G. Liebold, 8 June 1921;

E. J. Farkas to E. G. Liebold, 28 July 1921, HFM & GVRC, Box 8, Folder 8-17. Junior's company went into receivership in 1924. See "Receiver Gets Inventions," *NYT*, 22 June 1924.

page 250: **In late 1913:** W. G. Bee to E. G. Liebold, telegram, 20 November 1913, HFM & GVRC, Box 4, Folder 4-1.

page 250: **Liebold installed:** E. G. Liebold to W. G. Bee, 10 April 1914, HFM & GVRC, Box 4, Folder 4-3.

page 251: **As the sales manager:** W. G. Bee to E. G. Liebold, 16 April 1914, HFM & GVRC, Box 4, Folder 4-3.

page 251: **Edison would devote more time:** W. G. Bee to Henry Ford, 7 May 1914, HFM & GVRC, Box 4, Folder 4-3.

page 251: **"When Mr. Edison finds out":** W. G. Bee to E. G. Liebold, 27 July 1914, HFM & GVRC, Box 4, Folder 4-4. Capitalization in the original letter.

page 251: **Ford showed impatience:** W. G. Bee to E. G. Liebold, 23 July 1914, HFM & GVRC, Box 4, Folder 4-4.

page 251: **Ford also complained:** E. G. Liebold to W. G. Bee, 21 July 1914, HFM & GVRC, Box 4, Folder 4-4.

page 251: **Bee avowed his innocence:** W. G. Bee to E. G. Liebold, 23 July 1914, HFM & GVRC, Box 4, Folder 4-4.

page 251: **Liebold, by the end of 1914:** E. G. Liebold to W. G. Bee, 28 December 1914, HFM & GVRC, Box 4, Folder 4-6.

page 252: **another company, Gray & Davis:** E. G. Liebold to W. G. Bee, 21 July 1914, HFM & GVRC, Box 4, Folder 4-4.

page 252: **Ford dealers also registered:** E. G. Liebold to W. G. Bee, 25 July 1914, HFM & GVRC, Box 4, Folder 4-4.

page 252: **Throughout the process:** Ibid.

page 252: **After Ford extended:** Stephen B. Mambert to Henry Ford, 27 December 1919, HFM & GVRC, Box 2, Folder 2-60.

page 253: **Edison did not give up:** W. H. Meadowcroft to E. G. Liebold, 13 October 1919, HFM & GVRC, Box 5, Folder 5-4.

page 253: **But later that year:** Stephen Mambert to Henry Ford, 23 January 1918, HFM & GVRC, Box 16, Folder 52.

page 253: **Having a personal friend:** TAE to E. G. Liebold, 31 December 1917, HFM & GVRC, Box 2, Folder 2-57.

page 253: **The "little while":** Stephen Mambert to Henry Ford, 7 March 1919, HFM & GVRC, Box 16, Folder 52. For more payments that were not deposited immediately, see also Stephen Mambert to Henry Ford, 12 May 1919, HFM & GVRC, Box 16, Folder 52.

page 253: **There were other instances:** Stephen B. Mambert to Henry Ford, 20 March 1918; Stephen B. Mambert to E. G. Liebold, 25 December 1922; TAE to Henry Ford, 16 July 1924, all at HFM & GVRC, Box 16, Folder 52.

page 253: **In 1925, Ford forgave:** E. G. Liebold to Charles Edison, 25 November 1925, HFM & GVRC, Box 6, Folder 6-1.

page 253: **"the world's worst businessman":** Ford, *My Life and Work*, 235.

page 253: **a camping vacation together:** Firestone had accompanied the Edisons and the Fords in California in 1915. At the end of the California trip, Edison had suggested that the group plan to camp together the next year. Samuel Crowther, "My Vacations with Ford and Edison," *System,* May 1926, 643–645. Business and pleasure were intertwined not only for Edison and Ford but also for Firestone and Ford. In the middle of the series of trips, Firestone solidified his business ties with Ford, signing an agreement to supply 65 percent of the tires used by the Ford Motor Company. Dorothy Boyle Huyck, "Over Hill and Dale with Henry Ford and Famous Friends," *Smithsonian,* June 1978, 92.

page 254: **The group traveled by car:** John Burroughs to TAE and Harvey Firestone, 11 December 1916, HFM & GVRC, Vertical File—Ford, Henry—Camping.

page 254: **Schedules could not be arranged:** For mention of camping plans that were not realized that year, see H. S. Firestone to TAE, telegram, 17 August 1917, HFM & GVRC, Box 2, Folder 2-56.

page 254: **A contemporary feature article:** Mary B. Mullett, "Four Big Men Become Boys Again," *American Magazine,* February 1919. Firestone said Edison would also frequently be found in the car reading. Samuel Crowther, "Was There Another Vacation Like This?" *System,* June 1926, 793.

page 254: **A trip diary:** Harvey S. Firestone Jr. notes, followed by Harvey S. Firestone Sr., notes, typescript copy at HFM & GVRC, Vertical File—Ford, Henry—Camping; original held in Vierce Library, University of Akron, Firestone Collection.

page 254: **Edison would take a midday nap:** John Burroughs to TAE and Harvey Firestone, 11 December 1916, HFM & GVRC, Vertical File—Ford, Henry—Camping.

page 254: **take up a newspaper:** During President Harding's stay in camp, the president's friend Bishop W. F. Anderson delivered a sermon. While the president listened attentively, Edison "picked up a newspaper and buried himself in it." "Harding in Camp with Noted Party; Chops Fire Wood," *NYT,* 24 July 1921.

page 255: **the caravan had swollen:** Josephson, *Edison,* 466.

page 255: **Newsreels about the campers:** David L. Lewis, *The Public Image of Henry Ford* (Detroit: Wayne State University Press, 1976), 223.

page 255: **A diary entry:** Our Happy Days of 1919 and 1920, scrapbook, n.d. [1921?], HFM & GVRC, Vertical File—Henry Ford—Camping, 12.

page 255: **Burroughs wrote in his diary:** Edward Renehan, *John Burroughs: An American Naturalist* (Post Mills, Vt.: Chelsea Green, 1992), 276; Neil Baldwin, *Henry Ford and the Jews* (New York: Public Affairs, 2001), 88–89. Five years before the 1919 trip, Burroughs had spoken out and called for a new trial in Georgia in the case of Leo Frank, the Jewish defendant hastily convicted of rape and murder (and the next year abducted from the state prison farm and lynched). Burroughs also said that his position was shared by Edison and Ford as well, though they did not speak to the press themselves. See "Favors New Frank Trial," *NYT*, 1 April 1914.

page 256: **The president arrived:** Karl G. Pearson to W. D. Hines, 23 November 1931, cover letter and accompanying memo "Camping Trip Stories," original in Vierce Library, University of Akron Firestone Collection; copy held in HFM & GVRC, Vertical Files: Henry Ford—Camping.

page 256: **When the president offered:** Samuel Crowther, "What Vacations Have Taught Me About Business," *System*, July 1926, 106; "Edison Prizes Chewing Tobacco from Harding," *NYT*, 12 August 1922.

page 256: **Something went wrong:** Nelson Durand to TAE, 20 July 1925, HFM & GVRC, Box 3, Folder 5.

page 257: **Henry Ford took:** Lewis, *Public Image of Henry Ford*, 223.

page 257: **he claimed in his memoirs:** Ford, *My Life and Work*, 240.

page 257: **Charles Sorensen:** Charles Sorensen, *My Forty Years with Ford* (New York: Norton, 1956), 18.

page 257: **his daughter Madeleine:** Madeleine Sloane, Oral History, 1 December 1972, ENHS, Interview #1, 28.

page 258: **After our little walk:** Edward L. Bernays, *Biography of an Idea: Memoirs of Public Relations Counsel Edward L. Bernays* (New York: Simon & Schuster, 1965), 451.

CHAPTER 12. LETTING GO

page 259: **The Man Who Defeated Darkness:** The honorific titles listed here were heard at a single luncheon honoring Edison on the occasion of his seventy-seventh birthday. "Edison Honored by Movie Leaders," *NYT*, 16 February 1924.

page 259: **When an eighth-grader:** William Meadowcroft to Earle Shopen, 13 December 1915, ENHS.

page 259: **At the end of the experience:** "Edison at 76, Talks of Tut-Ankh-Amen, also Ruhr and Girls," *NYT*, 13 February 1923; "Navy Ignored 45 Inventions, Edison Relates on Birthday," *NYW*, 13 February 1923.

page 260: **One moving tribute:** W. C. Lathrop to TAE, 6 March 1921, ENHS. A copy of the letter is available online at the Library of Congress's American Memory Web site: http://memory.loc.gov/learn/lessons/99/edison/images/mrs2.gif. I am indebted to Leonard DeGraaf, the archivist at ENHS, for bringing the letter to my attention.

page 260: **a most gratifying letter:** For another first-person testimonial that credits wives' adoption of electrical appliances to increased availability to attend to the needs of husbands, see Anne Walker, "Three of Us and—Electricity," *Woman's Home Companion*, December 1919. Walker, speaking for herself and two friends, writes, "We three wives have less time for shopping, 'tea-ing,' and afternoon bridge, but we have lots more fun evenings with our husbands—motor trips, sextet dinners, theatre parties in town, and jolly games of cards."

page 261: **Edison wrote to a correspondent:** TAE to J. E. Franklin, 12 December 1916, ENHS.

page 262: **When he had left Edison's side:** Samuel Insull, *The Memoirs of Samuel Insull: An Autobiography,* ed. Larry Plachno (Polo, Ill.: Transportation Trails, 1992), 59, 62, 66, 76.

page 262: **new pricing schemes:** Insull, *Memoirs,* 73–74.

page 262: **acquisition of neighboring utilities:** Harold L. Platt, *The Electric City: Energy and the Growth of the Chicago Area, 1880–1930* (Chicago: University of Chicago Press, 1991), 253.

page 262: **the spending of his wealth:** Forrest McDonald, *Insull* (Chicago: University of Chicago Press, 1962), 240–241, 245. The new building was completed in the fall of 1929 and its first production staged ten days after the market crash, an entirely different fiscal era from the one in which it was conceived.

page 262: **placed on the cover of *Time:*** Cover, *Time,* 29 November 1926.

page 262: **continued to make himself available:** McDonald, *Insull,* 238–239.

page 263: **When asked in 1911:** TAE to *Port Huron Times-Herald,* 1 April 1911, ENHS.

page 263: **to his own town:** H. F. Miller to L. B. Markwith, 2 May 1911, ENHS.

page 263: **Aviation Section:** TAE to Alan R. Hawley, 27 January 1916, ENHS.

page 263: **"colored section":** H. F. Miller to Chairman, Colored Branch Committee, YMCA, 8 May 1912, ENHS.

page 263: **Essex County Jail:** H. F. Miller to Samuel Golcher, 31 December 1913, ENHS.

page 263: **New Jersey Soldiers' Relief Concert:** TAE to Mrs. I. M. Irwin, 18 July 1916, ENHS.

page 263: **telegraph-skills tournament:** Walter P. Phillips, *Sketches Old and New* (New York: J. H. Bunnell, 1897), 181.

page 263: **No to Oberlin:** H. T. Miller to Chas. W. Williams, 9 June 1910, ENHS, Letterbook, vol. 83.

page 263: **Edison did not himself invest:** Edison poured two experimental buildings—a two-story gardener's cottage and a garage—on the grounds of Glenmont and hired the New York firm of Mann & MacNeille to draw up plans that Edison made available royalty free to any builder willing to sell the completed house to "working men" at a price that capped the builder's profits at 10 percent. Michael Peterson, "Thomas Edison's Concrete Houses," *Invention and Technology* 11 (Winter 1996): 54, 55.

page 263: **A New Jersey real estate investor:** "Popularity of Concrete," *New York Tribune,* 11 June 1911. At the same time that the only investor in his concrete-home designs was using them as rental properties, Edison continued to believe that he had developed a solution to working-class discontent because the concrete home could be purchased by even a day laborer. Edison said, "Social discontent will die out when the working man owns his own home." See "Night Simply to Be Abolished," *Democrat (Madison, WI),* 27 July 1911.

page 263: **The only philanthropist:** "Cement Houses as Toys," *Morristown Jerseyman,* 6 January 1911.

page 264: **Mina Edison's ideas:** Mrs. Thomas A. Edison, "Leisure and Contentment," *Playground and Recreation* 23 (January 1930): 607.

page 264: **She and fellow members:** "Mrs. Thos. A. Edison Makes Fight Against Low Neck Ball Gowns," *New York Evening World,* 8 February 1916; "Women Divided in Attack on Low Neck Gowns That Stirs the Nation," *Superior (Wis.) Telegram,* 2 February 1916.

page 264: **"Handsomely gowned women waited on":** "Society Women Sell Eggs; Open Store in Orange, NJ, and War On Grocers," *Cumberland [MD] Times,* 20 November 1913.

page 264: **The one philanthropic venture:** "Boy, 16, Bishop's Son, Is Winner of First Edison Scholarship," *NYT,* 3 August 1929.

page 265: **At the time of the market crash:** McDonald, *Insull,* 284.

page 265: **His personal fortune:** Ibid., 277.

page 266: **The prosecution's case:** Ibid., 331–332.

page 266: **He had told a State Department escort:** Ibid., 44–45n38.

page 266: **When environmental problems:** William H. Hand, Oral History, 15 March 1973, ENHS, 13. Hand described how residents in the vicinity of Edison's plant in Silver Lake would appear with dead animals, claiming the deaths had been caused by pollution, and sought compensation. In one instance, an angry crowd set fire to the laboratory on the property, destroying it. See Hand, 24.

page 266: **One resident who lived across the street:** Joseph F. McCoy, Notes, 31 March 1937, ENHS, Biographical Collection: Edison Associates, Contemporaries, and Employees, Box 3, 18–19.

page 267: **placed in the care of a French governess:** Charles Edison, Oral History, 14 April 1953, ENHS.

page 267: **Charles's older sister, Madeleine:** Madeleine Sloane, Oral History, 13 March 1973, ENHS, Interview #2, 65.

page 268: **She did sometimes wonder:** Madeleine Sloane, Oral History, 1 December 1972, ENHS, Interview #1, 24.

page 268: **"Dear Fellow Criminal":** Charles Edison to Edsel Edison, 6 June 1914, HFM & GVRC, Box 8, Folder 8–15. A few months later, Charles sent Edsel a box of Philip Morris cigarettes with a card that read, "Wishing you many happy returns of the habit." Walter Holland to Charles Edison, 8 November 1914, ENHS, Charles Edison Fund Collection, Charles Edison Papers, Box 1, Correspondence 1912–1956.

page 268: **Each of the three:** William Maxwell, Edison Retail Sales Laboratory, 1915, ENHS, Primary Printed—Edison Companies, Box 50, Thomas A. Edison, Inc., Publications, 1.

page 268: **The Edison Shop of East Orange:** WM [William Maxwell] to Robert Bolan, 22 October 1915, ENHS, TAE Inc. Records, Charles Edison's Letterbooks, Box 4, 1915–1919.

page 269: **Edison gave his approval:** William Maxwell, Edison Retail Sales

Laboratory, 1915, ENHS, Primary Printed—Edison Companies, Box 50, Thomas A. Edison, Inc., Publications, 1.

page 269: **In September 1914:** Charles Edison to Carolyn Hawkins, 29 September 1914, ENHS, Charles Edison Fund Collection, Charles Edison Papers, Box 1, Correspondence 1912–1956.

page 269: **Without waiting, Edison boasted:** TAE to George C. Silzer, 30 November 1914, ENHS.

page 269: **After three years of operation:** Charles Edison to William Maxwell, 28 June 1917, ENHS, TAE Inc. Records, Charles Edison's Letterbooks, Box 4, 1915–1919. Charles had been unable to generate original ideas for saving the shop. He clutched with desperation to the unpromising ideas of others, suggesting phonograph recitals in nearby factories, catered "Porch Parties," demonstrations staffed by Boy Scouts—and a "Concert Automobile." Charles Edison to Godfrey, 21 June 1916, ENHS, TAE Inc. Records, Charles Edison's Letterbooks, Box 4, 1915–1919. The "Concert Automobile" actually existed: a department store in Birmingham, Alabama, had installed a large Edison phonograph in an electric car that was dispatched around the city, providing mobile demonstrations. See William Maxwell to Godfrey, 26 May 1916, ENHS, TAE Inc. Records, Charles Edison's Letterbooks, Box 4, 1915–1919. The staff at Edison's lab had tried to connect a phonograph to a car horn but the experiment had not produced satisfactory results. William Meadowcroft turned down a request for payment to a correspondent who suggested the idea in 1913, well after it had already been tried at the lab. William Meadowcroft to A. W. Smith, 22 November 1913, ENHS.

page 269: **Maxwell was not concerned:** William Maxwell to Charles Edison, 29 June 1917, ENHS, TAE Inc. Records, Charles Edison's Letterbooks, Box 4, 1915–1919.

page 269: **Maxwell himself had complained:** Maxwell to Godfrey, 14 June 1916, ENHS, TAE Inc. Records, Charles Edison's Letterbooks, Box 4, 1915–1919.

page 270: **Charles did notice:** Charles Edison, Oral History, 14 April 1953, ENHS, 162.

page 270: **had taken in a sight:** Ibid., 135, 162, 164, 166.

page 271: **The company's accident report:** Accident report, 16 June 1914, ENHS.

page 271: **When Thomas Edison departed for Washington:** Charles Edison suffered from severe hearing loss, which kept him out of active military service during the war. He had an opportunity to tell Newton D. Baker, the secretary of war, that he felt he should be in uniform, but Baker had said no, Charles's father had been "drafted" and Charles could serve his country best simply by "trying to operate the business," which had some contracts with the War Department. Charles Edison, Oral History, 14 April 1953, ENHS, 147.

page 271: **Charles shortened the workday:** Ibid., 166–168.

page 271: **He was young enough:** Charles Edison to Huber G. Buehler, 3 February 1919, ENHS, TAE Inc. Records, Charles Edison's Letterbooks, Box 4, 1915–1919.

page 271: **As he felt his way:** "My Experiences Working for Father," *American Magazine,* August 1918, 33–35.

page 272: **aware that he was regarded:** Mina Edison to Charles Edison, 23 November 1917, ENHS, Charles Edison Fund Collection, Charles Edison Papers, Box 1, Correspondence 1912–1956.

page 272: **While he and Carolyn Hawkins:** "Mrs. Charles Edison Talks of Navies, Peace, Hobbies, and a Novel Honeymoon," *NYT,* 19 February 1939.

page 272: **Edison bestowed his approval:** TAE to Charles Edison, [ca. 25 March 1918], ENHS, Charles Edison Fund Collection, Charles Edison Papers, Box 2, Correspondence 1957—Memorial Book, Correspondence: No Date.

page 272: **His father had no interest:** Josephson, *Edison,* 454–455.

page 273: **Edison ordered dismissals:** Israel, *Edison,* 454.

page 273: **"Merrily the axe swings":** Charles Edison to TAE, 12 July 1926, ENHS, cited in Andre Millard, *Edison and the Business of Invention* (Baltimore: Johns Hopkins University Press, 1990), 294.

page 273: **"What he'd do":** A. E. Johnson and K. Ehricke, Oral History, 29 March 1971, ENHS, 19. One worker, Roderic Peters, was dismissed by Edison soon after being hired, but he simply returned to his desk the next day and carried on with his work as if nothing had happened. Edison gave him critical looks, and after a couple of days, said to him, "I thought I let you go." Peters merely smiled and said nothing. Edison let the matter drop and Peters ended up working for him for four more years. See Roderic Peters, Oral History, 23 March 1973, ENHS, 3.

page 273: **drastically reducing employment:** Israel, *Edison,* 455. The workforce was reduced most dramatically in the complex at Orange, dropping from eight thousand workers during the war to about one thousand by August 1921. See "Edison Club Peters Out," *NYT,* 6 August 1921.

page 273: **All he cared about:** "Edison Condemns the Primary School," *NYT,* 7 May 1921.

page 273: **Thanks to an unsuccessful candidate:** "Edison Questions Stir Up a Storm," *NYT,* 11 May 1921. The 141 questions were exceeded by a list of 150 recalled by another unsuccessful candidate. See "Edison's Questions Still Puzzle City," *NYT,* 12 May 1912.

page 274: **The *New York Times* pointed out:** "Grade XYZ," *NYT,* 8 May 1921. Another editorial praised the irreverence of the young woman who refused to respond to Edison's exam questions seriously. Pig iron, she said, was so named because "it is unrefined." See "Her Answer Proved Intelligence," *NYT,* 12 May 1912. This was followed by "Mr. Edison's Mistake Is Revealed," *NYT,* 14 May 1921, which observed that Edison did not understand what a college education was designed to accomplish.

page 274: The *Chicago Tribune:* "Can't Answer Edison," *NYT,* 11 May 1921.

page 274: **When Albert Einstein:** "Einstein Sees Boston; Fails on Edison Test," *NYT,* 18 May 1921.

page 274: **the annoying importuning:** Paul Kasakove, untitled reminiscences, n.d., ENHS. Kasakove, a Cornell graduate who had majored in chemistry, tells a story about his first meeting with Edison as an applicant who had replied to a help-wanted advertisement. Kasakove was accompanied by the personnel manager and the plant superintendent, both of whom were terrified of Edison. When the trio arrived at the door of Edison's laboratory, the two managers fought over which one of them would get to stay behind and which one would accompany Kasakove and face the wrath of Edison should he judge the applicant to be unsuitable.

page 274: **he needed the kind of manager:** "Edison Answers Some of His Critics," *NYT,* 23 October 1921.

page 275: **When newspapers published:** "Here Is Edison's 4-Column Sheaf of Knowledge," *NYT,* 12 May 1921.

page 275: **Edison was undaunted:** "Edison Dashes Off New Questionnaire," *NYT,* 14 May 1921.

page 275: **he was surprised to discover:** "Edison at 76, Talks of Tut-Ankh-Amen, Also Ruhr and Girls."

page 275: **Few businesspeople:** "Mr. Edison's Questions; What Other Business Men Think of College Educations As They Affect the Workaday World," *NYT,* 15 May 1921; "Controversy Rages over Edison Test," *NYT,* 15 May 1921; "More Slams at Edison," *NYT,* 22 May 1921. Edison did draw some supportive letters to the editor, which were summarized in "Edison Is Upheld by Many Writers," *NYT,* 19 May 1921.

page 275: **In a letter to the editor:** "Comments on Edison List," *NYT,* 13 May 1921.

page 275: **Ford had initiated:** "Seldom Reads Below Headlines, Ford Admits," *NYT,* 19 July 1919; "Odd Definitions Given by Ford in Libel Suit," *NYT,* 17 July 1919. One of the strange definitions that Ford gave was that for an "idealist": "one who helps to make profits."

page 275: **He gamely sat:** "Edison's Son Fails in His Father's Test," *NYT,* 16 May 1921.

page 275: **When he graduated:** "Edison to Hire Son Without Usual Test," *NYT,* 12 June 1923.

page 276: **Theodore was in no hurry:** "Son Rejects Edison Job," *NYT,* 22 June 1923.

page 276: **Theodore was put to work:** Millard, *Edison and the Business of Invention,* 310.

page 276: **By the end of 1921:** "Broadcasting Broadway by Radio," *NYT,* 1 January 1922.

page 276: **Edison did feel slighted:** Erik Barnouw, *A Tower in Babel: A History of Broadcasting in the United States* (New York: Oxford University Press, 1966–1970), 84.

page 277: **held to a different explanation:** Theodore M. Edison, Oral History, 7 May 1970, ENHS, Transcript of tapes #45–46.

page 277: **Edison's sentimental attachment:** "Edison Still Busy on the Phonograph," *NYT*, 19 July 1922.

page 277: **he had no wish to reopen:** "Edison Calls Radio a Failure for Music: Thinks Phonograph Will Regain Its Own," *NYT*, 23 September 1926. Underlining the usefulness of radio for purposes other than musical programs, Edison did tune in to a radio broadcast of the Dempsey-Tunney fight in 1926, which he was too deaf to hear. He had to rely upon family members to summarize what had transpired at the end of each round. "Radio Satisfactory on Bout, Edison Says," *NYT*, 25 September 1926. Defending the quality of musical broadcasts, the nascent radio industry offered expert testimony to rebut Edison's claims. See "Broadcasters Disagree with Electrical Wizard," *NYT*, 3 October 1926.

page 277: **"We would not for a moment":** TAE to Frank Coombs, 5 May 1924, HFM & GVRC, Box 3, Folder 3-1.

page 277: **When manufacturers introduced:** Ronald C. Tobey, *Technology As Freedom: The New Deal and the Electrical Modernization of the American Home* (Berkeley: University of California Press, 1996), 22–23.

page 277: **The "radio fad":** "Edison Calls Radio a Failure for Music: Thinks Phonograph Will Regain Its Own." A few months later, Edison was willing to grant that radio might not disappear, but he had a new criticism: listeners' aesthetic sense would be damaged. "Undistorted music in time will sound strange to those brought up on radio music," he predicted, "and they will not like the real thing." "Thomas A. Edison Sees a Menace for Music in the Radio," *Musician*, January 1927, 12.

page 277: **Edicraft Automatic Toaster:** Products of Thomas A. Edison Industries, 1929, ENHS, Primary Printed—Edison Companies, Box 51, Thomas A. Edison, Inc. (McGraw-Edison), 56.

page 278: **customers did not want to see:** Walter K. Porzer Associates, Inc., report, August 1931, ENHS, Primary Printed—Edison Companies, Box 2, Edicraft Division (TAE, Inc.), Sales and Marketing Evaluation Book, 25.

page 278: **pay premium prices:** Edward Cary, Oral History, 6 June 1973, ENHS, 15.

page 278: **Ford and Firestone provided:** William H. Hand, Oral History, 15 March 1973, ENHS, 32.

page 278: **The official history:** Norman Speiden, transcript of ENHS tour, 8 January 1971, ENHS, 27–28.

page 278: **radiation exposure:** Israel, *Edison*, 422.

page 278: **employee of the Fort Myers laboratory:** William H. Hand, Oral History, 15 March 1973, ENHS, 34–37.

page 279: **they set up a research group:** Theodore M. Edison, Oral History, 7 May 1970, ENHS, Transcript of tapes #45–46.

page 279: **On 9 October 1929:** Charles Edison to TAE, 9 October, 1929, ENHS, Edison Family Papers, Series II, Edison, Charles—Charles Edison to TAE.

page 279: **Thomas A. Edison, Inc., announced:** "Drops Records for Radio," *NYT*, 8 November 1929.

page 280: **The sales literature:** "Edison Radio with Light-O-Matic Tuning," typescript, n.d., ENHS, Primary Printed—Edison Companies, Box 49, Folder: Catalogue of Products.

page 280: **A year later, Charles and Theodore:** Charles Edison to TAE, 16 October 1930, *PTAED*, B037ACM. By 1930, the business slump forced the company to lay off staff, including Frank Schell, who was credited for originating the Edison scholarship contest. Charles Edison also lost his private secretary. See "Edison Industries Cut Staff; Scholarship Idea Man Goes," *NYT*, 27 September 1930.

page 280: **In 1923, Edison was credited:** "Value of Edison's Genius Is Put at Fifteen Billions," *NYT*, 24 June 1923. The casual methodology behind these deceptively crisp numbers is suggested with a comparison: four years earlier, Edison was credited with creating industries worth only $1 billion. See "Edison, 72, Denies He Is Growing Old," *NYT*, 11 February 1919.

page 281: **conducted in 1922:** "Edison Greatest Man, Epworth League Votes," *NYT*, 25 November 1922. The story did not mention a fact that may have influenced some of the voters in the church's poll: Mina Edison was a member of the Methodist Episcopal Church. Earlier in the year, on the occasion of Edison's seventy-fifth birthday, reporters asked Edison, "Who is the greatest man in the world?" He had said he spent his time in the laboratory and had not met many candidates for the title, but allowed that he had once met and "liked" Theodore Roosevelt. See "Edison at 75 Still a Two-Shift Man," *NYT*, 12 February 1922.

page 281: **Ford famously declared:** "History Is Bunk, Says Henry Ford," *NYT*, 29 October 1921.

page 281: **He began plans to build:** "The Museum Is Born: A Brief History," The Henry Ford, http://www.thehenryford.org/museum/henryford.asp. What had been named The Henry Ford Museum and Greenfield Village has shortened its name to simply "The Henry Ford."

page 281: **seven railcars:** "Edison Young Again As He Relives Past in Old Laboratory," *NYT*, 21 October 1929.

page 281: **President Herbert Hoover:** "Light's Gold Jubilee Honors Thomas Edison and Dedicates a Museum," The Henry Ford, http://www.thehenryford.org/exhibits/pic/2004/october.asp.

page 282: **When the party returned:** "Edison Tries to Flee Dinner; Returns When Wife Insists," *NYT*, 22 October 1929.

page 282: **He made a public speech:** "Edison Accepts Honor As Paid to His Life Purpose, Advancing Human Understanding and Happiness," *NYT*, 22 October 1929. The Henry Ford provides online the recording made of Edison's speech at the Light's Golden Jubilee; see http://www.thehenryford.org/exhibits/pic/2004/jubilee/Edison_Speech.mp3.

EPILOGUE

page 283: **personal total to 1,093:** For lists of Edison's patents, grouped chronologically and by subject, see the Edison Papers's Web site: http://edison.rutgers.edu/patents.htm. Edison's reluctance to share credit with others is suggested by the following: For almost his entire career, beginning with work at his shop in Newark, he depended on the assistance—and inventiveness—of others. Yet among his 1,093 patents, in apparently only 20 instances did he share credit with a joint inventor. See the listing at About .com: http://inventors.about.com/library/inventors/bledisonpatents.htm.

page 283: **When Mina Edison's sister:** TAE to Mina Edison, 1 December 1898, *PTAED*, B037ABU.

page 283: **he explained he did just fine:** "Edison Assails Underthinking and Overeating," *Herald Tribune*, 24 December 1930.

page 283: **This conviction arose:** Allen L. Benson, "Edison Sees the 200-Year-Old Man," *Dearborn Independent*, 14 March 1925.

page 284: **He was the same medical authority:** "'You Don't Feel Pinched Anywhere, Do You?' Asked Mr. Edison," *Boston American*, 12 June 1916.

page 284: **In August 1931, he collapsed:** "World Followed News of His Illness," *NYT*, 18 October 1931.

page 284: **"mentally drowsy":** "Edison Has Good Day, but Vitality Ebbs," *NYT*, 5 October 1931.

page 284: **In the early morning:** "Thomas Edison Dies in Coma at 84; Family with Him As the End Comes," *NYT*, 18 October 1931.

page 284: **"genius" was credited:** Ibid.

page 284: **The governor of New Jersey:** "10,000 Mourners Pass Edison's Bier in Day; Nation Plans Tribute at Burial Tomorrow," *NYT*, 20 October 1931.

page 285: **was told of Edison's death:** Jehl, *Reminiscences*, 318–319. Sources differ on the reason Ott had been confined to a wheelchair. Either he had suffered a stroke ("Retired Edison Aide Dies," *NYT*, 20 October 1931) or had fallen down an empty elevator shaft at Bergmann's shop (Nerney, *Edison*, 299).

page 285: **When Mary Childs Nerney:** Nerney, *Edison*, 64–65.

page 285: **Declining the offer:** "10,000 Mourners Pass Edison's Bier in Day."

page 285: **forty thousand the second:** "Nation to Be Dark One Minute Tonight After Edison Burial," *NYT*, 21 October 1931.

page 285: **President Hoover asked:** Ibid.

page 285: **Edison really had been privileged to hear:** "Edison Is Buried on 52nd Anniversary of Electric Light," *NYT*, 22 October 1931.

page 286: **That night, the two radio networks:** "Lights of City Dimmed in Homage to Edison; the Nation Joins in the Brief Silent Tribute," *NYT*, 22 October 1931.

page 286: **Thomas Edison Jr.:** "T. A. Edison Jr. Dies; Son of Inventor, 59," *NYT*, 26 August 1936.

page 286: **maintained a laboratory:** "Older Son to Sue to Void Edison Will," *NYT*, 31 October 1931.

page 286: **died in 1937:** "William Leslie Edison," biography prepared for memorial service, n.d., HFM & GVRC, Box 8, Folder 37.

page 286: **died in 1969:** "Charles Edison, 78, Ex-Governor of Jersey and U.S. Aide, Is Dead," *NYT*, 1 August 1969.

page 286: **died in 1992:** "Theodore M. Edison; An Illustrious Father Guided Inventor, 94," *NYT*, 26 November 1992.

page 286: **reference to the "Illustrious Father":** Ibid.

page 286: **both sons gave away:** Charles Edison established the Charles Edison Fund when he was fifty-eight, to which he donated the bulk of his estate. See Charles Edison Fund, http://www.charlesedisonfund.org/edison.html. Theodore Edison donated half of his inheritance to the employees of Thomas A. Edison Industries. Josephson, *Edison*, 469n. Theodore also was a major supporter of efforts in the 1950s to preserve an endangered stand of bald cypress trees in southwest Florida. See "Theodore M. Edison; An Illustrious Father Guided Inventor, 94."

page 287: **His scholarship program:** Four years after Edison's death, the Thomas Alva Edison Foundation, formed to "perpetuate the name of the inventor," was incorporated in an attempt to raise funds for an endowment that would provide permanent support of a resuscitated scholarship program in Edison's name. "Edison's Aid Carried On," *NYT*, 24 June 1935. The fund-raisers apparently did not succeed, however. When the very first scholarship had been awarded in 1929, New York mayor Jimmy Walker had offered a grand oration: "When we are dead, when our children and grandchildren are no more, his name will remain as one of the greatest in the country. The present fine scholarship contest is the sort of thing one would almost expect from a Thomas A. Edison." See "Boy, 16, Bishop's Son, Is Winner of First Edison Scholarship," *NYT*, 3 August 1929.

page 287: **valued at $12 million:** "Edison Left 2 Sons Bulk of $12,000,000," *NYT*, 30 October 1931.

page 287: **Ford Foundation's endowment:** "Ford Foundation Owns $108,913,234," *NYT*, 22 April 1947.

page 287: **$70 million estate:** "Ford Tax Indicates $70,000,000 Estate," *NYT*, 29 October 1948.

page 287: **Four years later:** "Edison's Estate Is Valued at $2,871,758," *NYT*, 27 June 1935.

page 287: **reduced by 50 percent:** "Edison Estate $1,500,432," *NYT*, 21 April 1937.

page 287: **This arrangement spared her:** Mina's stepson William Edison threatened publicly to sue his younger half brothers, Charles and Theodore, but was persuaded to drop the idea. "Older Son to Sue to Void Edison Will"; "Edison Sons Avoid Fight over Estate," *NYT*, 26 February 1932.

page 287: **Four years after Edison's death:** "Widow of Edison to Be Wed Today," *NYT*, 30 October 1935.

page 287: **She was widowed again:** "Mrs. Edison Dead; Inventor's Widow," *NYT,* 25 August 1947. The obituary noted that she had "stirred up a minor squabble" in a radio speech given in 1930 when she urged women "to return to home-making and pay less attention to business." She had made similar remarks in preceding years, but "times had changed" and she drew many "replies" that clearly took a dissenting view.

page 288: **Charles Edison arranged:** "Edison-McGraw Merger Forms Electrical Giant," *NYT,* 3 January 1957.

page 288: **McGraw-Edison was absorbed:** "Cooper Industries Inc. Purchase," *Wall Street Journal,* 4 June 1985.

page 288: **poll of Chinese:** "In Beijing Students' Worldview, Jordan Rules," *NYT,* 16 June 1998. The results of the survey should not be generalized: the survey population was only one thousand respondents.

page 288: **Shunpei Yamazaki:** Yamazaki's first patent was filed in 1980, so he passed Edison at a pace that exceeded Edison's by far. Another prolific inventor, Donald E. Weder, has accumulated more than thirteen hundred without becoming a celebrity. The U.S. Patent and Trademark Office provides online access to its patent database at http://www.uspto.gov/patft/index.html.

page 289: **When a young John Lawson:** John Lawson to TAE, 6 January 1879, *PTAED,* D7913B.

page 290: **One of his employees:** A. E. Johnson and K. Ehricke, Oral History, 29 March 1971, ENHS, 20.

ACKNOWLEDGMENTS

THE EDITORS OF the Thomas A. Edison Papers Project deserve sanctification. They have brought talent, expertise, and patience to a vast project that is not yet complete: making the corpus of documents that Edison collected during his long life easily accessible to scholars, students, and the general public. The principal repository of Edison's papers, the Edison National Historic Site, in West Orange, New Jersey, contains an estimated 5 million documents—a rough guess because a complete inventory even now has yet to be completed. Thanks to the Edison Papers Project, however, many tools are available for excavating nuggets from any portion of the collection.

The first five volumes of the projected fifteen-volume set of *The Papers of Thomas A. Edison* have appeared, and they are modern wonders. I am grateful for the prodigious work that was poured into preparing the introductions, timelines, bibliographies, headnotes, and endnotes, which make them a model of contemporary scholarship.

I also was most fortunate to be able to gain access to nearly 180,000 Edison documents while sitting at home—the Project's easily searchable Web site came online shortly before I began my research. What a boon!

I would like to singly thank Paul Israel, the current director of the Edison Papers Project; former director Robert Rosenberg; and staff editors Theresa Collins and Brian Shipley, all of whom provided assistance to me in the course of research.

Not all of the Edison papers are yet available online. I would like to thank Leonard DeGraaf, Doug Tarr, and other staff members at the Edison National Historical Site for their help when I paid my visits to the archives at a busy time, during the year before the site was closed for renovation, as well as when I requested assistance with follow-up requests. I also was assisted by the staff of the Benson Ford Research Center at the Henry Ford, the new umbrella name encompassing the Henry Ford Museum and Greenfield Village, in Dearborn, Michigan.

The College of Business of San Jose State University gave generous, recurring gifts in the form of reduced teaching assignments, as well as financial support for a full year's leave. During the book's seven-year gestation, San Jose State administrators and faculty colleagues displayed imperturbable patience, at least in my presence, for which I am most appreciative.

The scholarly resources of Stanford University contributed much to the project. I am grateful for visiting scholar appointments over two years arranged by James Sheehan, chair of the department of history, and Tim Lenoir, director of the Program in History and Philosophy of Science. At Stanford's Archive of Recorded Sound, Richard Koprowski and Aurora Perez provided cheerful help.

Madeleine Sloane and David Sloane met with me and generously shared memories of their paternal grandmother, Madeleine Sloane, née Edison, and family lore.

My interlibrary loan requests were voluminous and must have created grievously lopsided accounts between borrowing and lending libraries. But Mary Munill, at Stanford, and Kara Fox and Shirley Miguel, at San Jose State, were unstinting in their work on my behalf.

Bonnie Newburg, of the Edison & Ford Winter Estates, and Ruth Ann Nyblod, of the United States Patent and Trademark Office, provided swift help with my queries. Jack Curlin supplied information about his grandfather that tied up a loose end. Martin Sheehan-Stross helped with library research.

The manuscript was much improved by the unsparing critiques supplied by Gail Hershatter and Pamela Basey, who flagged inconsistencies and forced me to look anew at the most basic assumptions embedded in the first draft.

As always, my agent, Elizabeth Kaplan, knew what I needed at any given point—a matter of intuition, as I often did not know myself until her assistance appeared.

At Crown, Emily Loose was extremely knowledgeable about Edison and this period of history; her enthusiasm for the project fired my own. Her successor, Luke Dempsey, has unusually sharp ears as well as eyes and gave the manuscript a gloriously old-fashioned close reading. I am grateful to both.

Jim Gullickson made countless corrections in the course of careful copy-editing. Lindsey Moore kept us all on schedule.

This work is dedicated to my most important collaborator, Ellen Stross. Her editorial suggestions made the book immeasurably better— and considerably shorter.

INDEX